POLITICS AND THE APPOINTMENT OF JUSTICES OF THE PEACE 1675–1720

by

LIONEL K.J. GLASSEY

OXFORD UNIVERSITY PRESS
1979

Oxford University Press, Walton Street, Oxford OX2 6DP

OXFORD LONDON GLASGOW
NEW YORK TORONTO MELBOURNE WELLINGTON
KUALA LUMPUR SINGAPORE JAKARTA HONG KONG TOKYO
DELHI BOMBAY CALCUTTA MADRAS KARACHI
NAIROBI DAR ES SALAAM CAPE TOWN

Published in the United States by
Oxford University Press, New York

British Library Cataloguing in Publication Data

Glassey, Lionel K J
    Politics and the appointment of justices of the
    peace, 1675–1720. — (Oxford historical monographs).
    1. Justices of the peace — England — Appointment,
    qualifications, tenure, etc. — History — 17th
    century   2. Justices of the peace — England —
    Appointment, qualifications, tenure, etc. — History
    — 18th century
    I. Title   II. Series
    347'.42'016   KD7309   79-40421
    ISBN 0 19 821875 3

Set by Hope Services, Abingdon
and printed in Great Britain by
Billing & Sons Ltd., Guildford and Worcester

To
my mother

PREFACE

I am grateful to the Rector and Fellows of Lincoln College, Oxford, for electing me to a Senior Scholarship in 1968-9, and to the University of Glasgow for a grant which facilitated my research in London in 1970. The late Duke of Marlborough, the late Duke of Portland, the Marquess of Bath, the Earl of Crawford and Balcarres, Lord Monson, Lady Salmond, and Mr E. W. A. Sanford kindly granted permission for me to examine family papers in their possession, and the Keeper of Manuscripts and Records at the National Library of Wales allowed me to have photocopies made of manuscripts in his care. The Editor of the *Bulletin of the Institute of Historical Research* has permitted me to repeat in the first chapter some points I made in an article written jointly with Dr Norma Landau, which appeared in that journal in 1972.

I owe a great deal to the suggestions and advice of many scholars at different times. In particular I am grateful to Dr John Beckett, Dr Elizabeth Carmichael, Dr David Cox, Dr Alan Downie, Mrs Christine Duffy, Dr Michael Duffy, Professor Geoffrey Holmes, Dr Henry Horwitz, the Revd. Geraint Jones, Dr Norma Landau, Professor John B. Owen, Miss Beth Rainey, and Dame Lucy Sutherland; to Mr Robert Latham, whose seminar at the Institute of Historical Research I attended with much profit in 1967-9; and to the invariably helpful members of staff in the libraries and record offices in which I worked. I am glad, too, to acknowledge the willingness of Dr Brian Dietz, Dr Alan Smith, and Mr Donald Henry, my colleagues at the University of Glasgow, to share their knowledge of the ways in which justices of the peace were appointed in periods before 1675 and after 1720. Miss Patricia Ferguson typed the final version of the book with meticulous professional skill, and with cheerful and unselfish forbearance.

My debt to Dr Anne Whiteman is greater than I can well express. She supervised the Oxford University D.Phil. thesis

on which this book is based, and then and subsequently she
has guided my work with the greatest patience, kindness, and
wisdom.

The University of Glasgow   LIONEL K. J. GLASSEY
May 1978

CONTENTS

ABBREVIATIONS

Add. MSS.	Additional Manuscripts (British Library)
B.I.H.R.	*Bulletin of the Institute of Historical Research*
B.L.	British Library
Bodl.	Bodleian Library, Oxford
Cal. S.P. Dom.	*Calendar of State Papers Domestic*
Cal. Treas. Books	*Calendar of Treasury Books*
C.J.	*Journals of the House of Commons*
C.U.L.	Cambridge University Library
Devon R.O.	Devonshire Record Office, Exeter
Harl. MSS.	Harleian MSS. (British Library)
Herts. R.O.	Hertfordshire Record Office, Hertford
H.L.Q.	*Huntington Library Quarterly*
H.L.R.O.	House of Lords Record Office
H.M.C.	Historical Manuscripts Commission
J.R.L.	John Rylands Library, Manchester
Lancs. R.O.	Lancashire Record Office, Preston
Leics. R.O.	Leicestershire Record Office, Leicester
Lincs. A.O.	Lincolnshire Archives Office, Lincoln
L.J.	*Journals of the House of Lords*
N.L.W.	National Library of Wales
N.S.	New Series
N.U.L.	Nottingham University Library
P.R.O.	Public Record Office
Rawl.	Rawlinson MSS. (Bodleian Library)
Shrops. R.O.	Shropshire Record Office, Shrewsbury
Som. R.O.	Somerset Record Office, Taunton
Surrey R.O.	Surrey Record Office, Kingston-upon-Thames
Trans. Roy. Hist. Soc.	*Transactions of the Royal Historical Society*
V.C.H.	*Victoria County History*
Wilts. R.O.	Wiltshire Record Office, Trowbridge

NOTE ON REFERENCES AND DATES

Two bodies of manuscript material used extensively in this study, the State Papers Domestic in the Public Record Office and the Portland Loan in the British Library, have been printed, in the *Calendar of State Papers Domestic* and in the *Reports on the MSS. of the Duke of Portland* published by the Historical Manuscripts Commission respectively. I have referred in the footnotes to the printed versions unless the manuscript adds further relevant information or unless some point of significance is lost in modernized grammar.

Quotations are as in the original, except that I have extended abbreviations and, in some cases, clarified the sense by modifying the punctuation.

Dates are in Old Style, except for a handful of instances where to avoid ambiguity I have given both Old and New Style. The year is taken to begin on 1 January. Unluckily, these are more than conventional reminders of standard practices in studies of British History in the early modern period. The Lord Chancellor's fiats to renew a commission of the peace generally followed the practice of the Crown Office in Chancery of beginning the year on 25 March, but a nineteenth-century archivist has marked them with the year to which they relate, and he assumed that the year began on 1 January. In cases where his errors lead to confusion, I have referred to the year in the form: 24 March 1707/8.

1

INTRODUCTION

I

The starting-point for much of what follows was the series of Ford Lectures delivered by Professor J. H. Plumb at Oxford in Michaelmas Term 1965 under the title *The Growth of Political Stability in England, 1675–1725*. In the first of his lectures, Professor Plumb observed that the English country gentry in the seventeenth century enjoyed formidable social and political power in their capacity as justices of the peace. The central government had tried, and failed, to discipline them in the years before 1660. 'To bring the independent country gentry into some ordered relationship with government, or to diminish their role in it, became an absolute necessity if stability was ever to be achieved.'[1] In later lectures Professor Plumb emphasized in more detail the central importance of the manipulation, by successive governments, of the local office-holding of the gentry. During the Exclusion Crisis, the Privy Council investigated the lists of justices of the peace to strengthen the Court party's hand against its Whig opponents.[2] 'Out they went', said Professor Plumb of the Anglican justices of the peace and deputy lieutenants in the time of James II, 'in purge after purge. . . .' Basing his argument on evidence from Yorkshire, Professor Plumb remarked that '. . . the total alienation of the majority of the aristocracy, gentry and commonalty lost him [James] the slightest hope of mass support, so that when the Revolution came, he was rejected by the nation. . . .'[3] Again, 'after the election of 1715 . . . the purges not only of the justices of the peace and the deputy lieutenants but also of tax-collectors and minor office-holders became much more extensive . . .

---

[1] The quotation is from the Ford Lectures in their published version. J. H. Plumb, *The Growth of Political Stability in England, 1675–1725* (London, 1967), p. 22.

[2] Ibid., p. 54.   [3] Ibid., pp. 60–1.

the Whigs were able to get rid of sixty-eight J.P.s in Middlesex, mostly loyal Tories . . .'.[1]

These remarks were very challenging. The importance of local affairs during the Exclusion Crisis, the Revolution of 1688, and the Hanoverian Succession had been discussed before, but rarely with such emphasis and vigour. Certain questions, however, remained. When the Privy Council investigated the names of the justices of the peace in 1679, did it follow up its inquiries with action? When the Anglican Tories in Yorkshire gave way to distress and despair at the changes in their magistracy in 1687 and 1688, were the gentry in other counties similarly afflicted? Was Middlesex typical, or unusual, in 1715? These questions can be merged into a broad historical problem. Would it be possible to construct a comprehensive picture of the changes in the county magistracy, during the period covering the transition from the politics of Court and Country in the 1670s, through the years of Whig and Tory party rivalry in the 1690s and 1700s, to the establishment of political stability in the 1720s? And if so, would this picture confirm Professor Plumb's implied hypothesis that sweeping regulation of the county benches over the whole nation crucially affected the attitude of the country gentry to great issues in national affairs?

This book is an attempt to go some way to solving this problem by examining the political background to, and the political element in, the choice of the gentlemen who were to act as justices of the peace in the counties of England and Wales. Regrettably, perhaps, there is little material in what follows to interest those historians primarily concerned with the numerous aspects of government and administration in which the justices of the peace were involved, such as the relief of the poor and the regulation of the local economy. The emphasis is on politics, and on national rather than local politics, throughout.

II

A commission of the peace was a document directed to specified gentlemen who were to act as justices of the peace within the boundaries of a geographical area. The most extensive of

[1] Plumb, *The Growth of Political Stability*, pp. 165, 169.

these areas were the counties of England, Wales, and (after 1707) Scotland. New commissions to change the names of the justices were issued at irregular intervals for each of these areas independently. In every commission, the duties and powers of a justice of the peace were defined. Certain of these powers could only be exercised in the presence of one or more justices specially qualified by legal knowledge; the names of justices so qualified were repeated in a separate clause, and they are generally described as 'justices of the quorum'. The last clause of the commission, introduced by the phrase *assignavimus denique*, named the *custos rotulorum*, who was the keeper of legal records within the area. The form of the commission was standardized in 1590. It was anglicized, temporarily between 1649 and 1660, permanently after 1733; otherwise it remained unchanged until the late nineteenth century.[1]

The counties were not the only areas to receive commissions of the peace. During the period from 1675 to 1720, similar commissions were issued to the liberties of Cawood, Ely, Peterborough, Ripon, St. Albans, St. Peter's York, Southwell, the Tower, and Westminster; and to the boroughs of Bedford, Buckingham, Cambridge, Haverfordwest, Oxford, St. Albans (the borough as distinct from the liberty) and Southwark.[2] The commissions of the peace for all of these liberties and boroughs, and for all except one of the counties, were granted by the Lord Chancellor under the great seal.[3] The odd county out was Lancashire, the commission for which was granted by the Chancellor of the Duchy under the seal of the County Palatine. In boroughs other than those named, the justices of the peace were nominated in the charter by their offices, although separate commissions might

---

[1] The form of a commission of the peace as it was between 1675 and 1720 is conveniently printed in G. W. Prothero, *Select Statutes and other Constitutional Documents illustrative of the reigns of Elizabeth and James I* (4th edn., Oxford, 1913), pp. 147-9.

[2] P.R.O., Records of Chancery, Crown Office Docquet Books, C. 231/7, C. 231/8, C. 231/9, *passim*; S. and B. Webb, *English Local Government*, i, *The Parish and the County* (reprinted edn., London, 1963), pp. 310-18, 320n.

[3] To avoid confusion I have in this chapter used the term 'Lord Chancellor' to mean 'the holder of the great seal'. In the context of the commissions of the peace, the powers of a Lord Keeper or of Commissioners of the Great Seal were the same as those of a Lord Chancellor.

be issued under the great seal for special purposes. To keep
this study within reasonable bounds, attention has principally
been concentrated on the commissions of the peace for the
counties of England and Wales, except that two of the liberties — Peterborough and Ely — have been regarded as similar
enough in size and character to the counties to be treated as
such.[1] If the three 'parts' of Lincolnshire, the three ridings of
Yorkshire, and Peterborough and Ely are included, then fifty-
seven English and Welsh counties received commissions of the
peace. Lancashire makes a fifty-eighth.

It is in the names included in the commissions of the
peace, the justices to whom the commission was directed,
that interest lies. A number of names in each commission are,
however, of little significance. The entire Privy Council, the
Attorney General, and the Solicitor General normally headed
the lists, but they were put in as a courtesy rather than for
any practical reason.[2] The assize judges for the circuit in
which the county concerned was situated were also included.
The commissions might contain, as a matter of course, office-
holders and dignitaries of a local kind: for instance, the bishop
of the see in most counties; the vice-chancellors of the universities in Oxfordshire and Cambridgeshire; various County
Palatine or Duchy officials in Lancashire, Cheshire, Durham,
and Cornwall; and naval officials from Plymouth, Portsmouth,
and Chatham in Devonshire, Hampshire, and Kent respectively.[3] Such 'courtesy' justices are naturally of less interest
than the local, resident gentlemen who were named in the
county commissions because they were expected to act as
justices of the peace; it is with the selection and character of
these gentlemen that this book is chiefly concerned.

The responsibility for the choice of local names had been
confusingly obscured by early statutes. In 1414 it was provided that justices were to be appointed by the advice of the

---

[1] For Lancashire, see Chapter 10; for the Scottish counties after 1707, see
Elizabeth K. Carmichael, 'The Scottish Commission of the Peace, 1707–1760'
(Glasgow University Ph.D. thesis, 1977).

[2] The holders of the great offices of state were the only Privy Councillors normally included in Peterborough, Ely, and some of the Welsh counties.

[3] When calculating the number of justices in commission for a particular
county, or the extent of the changes made at any one time, the Privy Councillors,
law officers, and judges have been ignored; but the justices included on account
of local office have been counted among the local names.

Chancellor and the Council.[1] This rule had been overlaid by subsequent statements. When a property qualification of £20 a year in land or tenements was established in 1439, the Chancellor was given discretionary powers to appoint un-qualified men if necessary.[2] This discretionary power of the Chancellor seemed to be confirmed by a statute of 1535 establishing justices of the peace in the Welsh counties by commissions under the great seal, but an act of 1542 qualified the Chancellor's responsibility by giving the President of the Council of Wales and the Welsh equivalents of the assize judges advisory powers.[3] Notwithstanding these contradictions, the constitutional position had become fairly clear by the early sixteenth century. The formal authority by which justices of the peace were appointed was the king's prerogative. The commission of the peace was an instrument under the great seal from the king to certain of his subjects who were to perform the duties of a justice of the peace. The practical responsibility for recommendation, selection and inclusion in the commission of the peace lay with the Lord Chancellor who held the seal.[4] The Council occasionally exercised its advisory powers, but it did not do so as a matter of routine, nor is it easy to see how it could have enforced its will on a reluctant Chancellor. The Chancellor's conduct of the business of selection was largely his own affair, but from time to time a Chancellor was criticized in Parliament for mismanaging it.

It was easy enough for the Chancellor to make and unmake justices of the peace. A new commission superseded the old one. New justices were appointed by including their names in the list engrossed in the new commission. The names of persons who were to cease to be justices for any reason were left out of the new list. The Chancellor, in conducting the practical procedure of appointment, thus enjoyed a considerable measure of patronage. It is a commonplace that justices of the peace in the counties were drawn from the class of property-owning gentry; while this assertion is not comprehensively

[1] 2 Henry V stat. 2 c. 1.   [2] 18 Henry VI c. 11.
[3] 27 Henry VIII c. 5; 34 & 35 Henry VIII c. 26, section 21.
[4] W. Lambarde, *Eirenarcha, or the Offices of the Justices of Peace* (edn. of 1592), Chapter 5: 'By whose authority, and by what means, Justices of the Peace be appointed; and of what sorts they be.'

true, the existence of a property qualification by the statute of 1439 suggests that the intention of the law was that only men of property should be entrusted with the extensive powers of magistracy. The place of the landed gentry in the political nation from the sixteenth to the nineteenth century hardly needs to be emphasized. Consequently the Chancellor's responsibility for appointing justices of the peace was patronage of a peculiarly valuable kind for the central government to have, in that it extended to the gentry all over the country, and in that it touched them at a sensitive point — their power and status within their local communities.

Furthermore, this patronage was not confined to appointment. The tenure of a justice of the peace was, and still is (in effect) *durante bene placito regis*, rather than *quamdiu se bene gesserit*. Before 1675 it had not been especially unusual for justices to be dismissed for reasons other than death or their own desire. In the reign of Queen Elizabeth there had been substantial alterations in the commissions of the peace on a national scale on at least seven occasions.[1] In the early Stuart period, inactive justices were not infrequently removed, and in 1626 seventeen former members of Parliament who would be likely to oppose a projected forced loan were omitted severally from ten county commissions.[2] There were sweeping changes in the county magistracy in the aftermath of the Civil Wars, notably in 1650, 1652, 1653, and 1660.[3]

In the early eighteenth century, many took the view that such political dismissals had become, if anything, more common. Lord Chancellor Cowper observed in 1715:

. . . But so late as in my own memory of business, very few if any were displaced without cause assignd & provd, because it was justly thought to be an injurious disgrace on any Gent[leman] in his country to be turned out . . . unless for some known or evident reason, & I have

---

[1] A. Hassell Smith, *County and Court: Government and Politics in Norfolk, 1558-1603* (Oxford, 1974), pp. 80-6.

[2] S. R. Gardiner, *History of England 1603-42* (cabinet edn., London, 1884), vi. 125-6, quoting B.L., Harl. MSS. 286, f. 297 (Gardiner missed two names in the manuscript). A recent study argues that in the early seventeenth century political dismissals were rare, and that in such cases restoration was rapid. J. H. Gleason, *The Justices of the Peace in England, 1558 to 1640* (Oxford, 1969), pp. 63-6, 72-82.

[3] D. Underdown, *Pride's Purge* (Oxford, 1971), pp. 300, 311, 340-1; J. Hurstfield, 'County Government, c. 1530-c. 1660', *V.C.H. Wiltshire*, v (1957), 109.

been present at several formal Hearings of accusations & defences in order to determin, whither the person accusd should be turnd out of the Comm[ission] or not.

But as the two partys grew more & more set & violent against one another, this commendable tenderness, I may say Justice, began by degrees to be laid aside. . . .[1]

Party conflict thus tended to diminish scruples; the period of the Revolution of 1688 and the Hanoverian Succession was one in which the boundary between political opposition and treason was ill-defined. It was not difficult to phrase a recommendation that a justice be dismissed in such a way that the Chancellor would feel justified in acting upon it.

The Chancellor's powers of dismissing justices therefore supplemented his powers of appointing. It was, indeed, the reaction to dismissal that indicates most clearly the value of a place on the commission of the peace and the importance of the Chancellor's patronage. Cowper, when Chancellor, received an insulting Latin letter from a justice whom he had put out.[2] Ex-Lord Treasurer Oxford wrote of several gentlemen put out of the commission that they had been unjustly marked out by a 'brand of infamy'.[3] A justice who was dismissed in the 1690s for disaffection to the government brought an action for damages against the person who had blackened his character, and won the case in the Exchequer court, though the decision was subsequently reversed.[4] 'It must be allowed', wrote one of Cowper's correspondents, 'that the honour of being in, is not so great as the disgrace of being turn'd out of the Commission.'[5]

---

[1] Herts. R.O., Cowper (Panshanger) MSS. D/EP F152: paper endorsed 'About the disposal of the Commissions for Justices of the Peace', to be translated into French for George I, no date but, from internal evidence, on or shortly before 16 July 1715. This memorandum is printed at Lord Campbell, *Lives of the Chancellors* (London, 1846), iv. 373–6; although Lord Campbell aimed at an accurate transcript, there are a number of errors, including the omission of a negative. It is therefore preferable to use the original. Henceforward I have cited the manuscript as 'Memorandum for George I'.

[2] Herts. R.O., Cowper (Panshanger) MSS. D/EP F152: letter endorsed 'This Latin letter I received by the Penny P[ost] . . . to thank me for removing the Anonymous author from the Commission of the Peace', 16 Dec. 1719. The 'anonymous author's' gratitude was, of course, ironical.

[3] N.U.L., Pw2 Hy 929: Oxford to Foley, 21 Dec. 1721.

[4] H.M.C., *House of Lords MSS.*, N.S. i. 397: Case of Duvall *v.* Price.

[5] Herts. R.O., Cowper (Panshanger) MSS. D/EP F55: Dr William Lloyd to Cowper, 25 July 1709.

The Chancellor's exercise of his powers of patronage was not a simple matter. It was naturally impossible to expect him to assess the merits of gentlemen in every county in England and Wales. The method of selection was dictated, to a considerable extent, by the administrative procedures by which commissions of the peace were passed under the great seal. Much of the routine work was done by a Secretary for Commissions, who was not a royal official but an employee of the Chancellor.[1] The normal course was that lists of names to be added to or subtracted from the names already in the commission were drawn up outside the Chancellor's view by one or more of a variety of sources, both in the locality and at the centre. These lists were sent to the Chancellor's office, where the Secretary of Commissions would check the credentials of persons recommended and report to the Chancellor. When the changes to be made were settled, the Secretary wrote an instruction from the Chancellor to the Clerk of the Crown in Chancery 'or his deputy' to draw up a new commission of the peace for the county concerned, putting specified names in or leaving other names out, or commonly both. When justices were to be left out, those who had died were generally, though not always, so described. Sometimes the instruction was simply a list of every name to be put into the new commission. The instructions are called fiats, from the order *Fiat Commissio* at the bottom. Once complete, the Secretary submitted the fiat to the Chancellor for signature. It was then taken to the Crown Office in Chancery, and the new commission was engrossed. After sealing, the commission was ready for delivery to the county; a record of the sealing, with a summary of the changes made according to the fiat, was entered in the Crown Office docquet book. At

---

[1] It is not certain, though it is highly probable, that every Lord Chancellor of the period 1675–1720 employed such a Secretary. Francis Bacon did in 1618; so too did every Chancellor after 1689. J. Spedding, *Letters and Life of Francis Bacon* (London, 1862–74), vi. 336; *Cal. S. P. Dom., 1698*, p. 285 (for Lord Somers); P.R.O., State Papers Domestic, Queen Anne, S.P. 34/4, ff. 191–2: certificate of Thomas Edwards, 17 Aug. 1704 (for Sir Nathan Wright); B.L., Stowe MSS. 416, ff. 27–9 (for Lords Cowper, Harcourt, and Macclesfield). For a summary of the Secretary's duties, which extended to commissions of *oyer and terminer*, gaol delivery, sewers, and charitable uses as well as commissions of the peace, see *Parl. Papers 1814–15*, xi, Report of Lords Commissioners . . . as to the Court of Chancery (1740), 69.

an earlier period the commissions of the peace had also been enrolled on the dorse of the Patent Rolls, but this practice had ceased by 1675.[1] The system, so described, sounds straightforward, but it was not, in practice, a smooth administrative procedure. There were obstacles in the path of . Chancellor who wanted to operate it as an instrument of local patronage.

One such obstacle was the fact that the Chancellor had to work through two different offices. The head of the Crown Office, the Clerk of the Crown in Chancery, was appointed for life, and might be on bad terms with the Chancellor. George Wright, appointed in 1701, was the son of Sir Nathan Wright, Lord Keeper from 1700 to 1705, and he remained Clerk of the Crown until 1725; Sir Nathan's successor, Cowper, went so far on one occasion as to call him 'the brute' whose 'malice' was responsible for an embarrassing error in a commission of the peace.[2] When such errors occurred they were usually blamed on the Crown Office. Moreover, delays in issuing commissions might be caused by the Clerk of the Crown's insistence on his fees.[3] There is even a case of a Clerk of the Crown putting an unsuitable person into a commission of the peace without the Chancellor's knowledge for sordid motives.[4] In the other office, that of the Secretary of Commissions, there was a break in continuity at each change of Chancellor caused by the appointment of a new Secretary. The new man was required to prepare himself for what was a difficult and complicated job.[5] The methods of successive

[1] This account is based on T. G. Barnes and A. Hassell Smith, 'Justices of the Peace from 1558 to 1688 — A Revised List of Sources', *B.I.H.R.* xxxii (1959), 222-32; *Minutes of Evidence taken by the Royal Commission on the Selection of Justices of the Peace*, 1910, Cd. 5358, Appendix I handed in by the Clerk of the Crown; and P.R.O., Justice of the Peace Fiats, C. 234/1-99, arranged in bundles by county. For most counties a complete series begins with the first commission issued by Cowper after his appointment as Lord Keeper on 11 Oct. 1705; there are several scattered fiats of an earlier date.

[2] H.M.C., Fifteenth Report, Appendix IV, *Portland MSS.* iv. 555-6.

[3] *Cal. S. P. Dom., 1680-1*, p. 395; *Cal. S. P. Dom., 1696*, p. 392.

[4] Bodl. MS. North c. 5, ff. 44-5: Sir William Spring to [Sir Matthew Hale?], 18 Oct. 1675.

[5] *Letters by several eminent persons deceased, including the Correspondence of John Hughes, Esq., and several of his friends* . . . (London, 1772), i. 116-17. Hughes, who earned a biography in Johnson's *Lives of the Poets*, was Cowper's Secretary of Commissions from October 1717; he was the only Secretary during the period who was continued in office by an incoming Chancellor.

Secretaries tended to differ slightly in detail. One good example lies in the method of dating the fiats and, subsequently, the commissions which they authorized. The Secretary usually wrote the date at the bottom of the fiat when he drew it up. The Chancellor's signature might be added days or weeks later. The commission, like all instruments under the great seal, bore a *teste* date, which was also the date entered in the Crown Office docquet book. Of the twenty-two surviving fiats signed by Somers, Chancellor from 1693 to 1700, every one bears an earlier date than that adopted in the Crown Office as the *teste* date, the time-lag varying from as little as one day to as much as seventy days. Under later Chancellors, however, it was exceptional for the *teste* date on the commission to differ from the date on the fiat at all. In the cases when it did, there was usually a note on the back of the fiat to the effect that it had been 'received' (in the Crown Office) at a later date tʰ an that on the fiat, and that this later date had been adop ᵗₑd as the *teste* date. The meaning of this change can only be conjectured; it is improbable that after 1700 it became common practice for fiats to be drawn up, signed, and sent to the Crown Office on the same day. There are rare examples of fiats in which a space was apparently left for the date for the Chancellor to fill up when he signed it. Probably there is no great significance in the different methods of dating. Nevertheless, they illustrate how the Secretary's office was subject to changes in character, whereas the Crown Office was a permanent office of routine business. This point suggests two conclusions. In the first place, it was difficult for a newly appointed Chancellor to make large-scale alterations in the commissions of the peace quickly; he had to wait for his Secretary to learn his job. Secondly, the Chancellor depended more than he might have liked on the willing co-operation of the Crown Office where the commissions were manufactured.

Another problem which hampered the free exercise of the Chancellor's powers of patronage was that of knowing who was in the existing commissions of the peace. It was not easy for either the Secretary of Commissions or the Crown Office to keep an up-to-date record of who the justices of the peace for a given county actually were. Until 1688, and probably for some years afterwards, the names were kept in entry books in the Crown Office.[1] *Libri pacis*, or copies of these entry books, were drawn up from time to time, at a fee of £3, for anyone who asked for them.[2] Entry books are, however, a clumsy method of recording long lists of names subject to frequent changes, because they rapidly become a confusing muddle of blotted crossings-out and untidy insertions. There is some evidence that the fiats themselves were used in the Crown Office either as a supplementary record, or as the working registers themselves, from about 1700. This would explain why fiats began to be kept at all, and why they were kept in bundles by county. Those fiats which were in the form of a complete list of names to be inserted in a county commission were often corrected in accordance with later fiats over a period of several years, and endorsed with a string of notes of *teste* dates. This system did not much improve on the entry book procedure; the corrections on the fiats, often in several different hands, still made it difficult to ascertain who was in commission and who was not. It is not unusual to find marginal notes on the fiats by the clerk who engrossed the commission to the effect that gentlemen he was ordered to put in, were in already; or that gentlemen he was ordered to put out were not in at all.[3] The use of the fiats as registers was made more complicated, too, by the occasional practice of incorporating changes for more than one county on the same fiat, which could only be kept in one of the bundles of fiats. The accidental loss of a single fiat would lead to disorganization. Moreover, the demands by Parliament to inspect the fiats signed by Somers (in 1700) and Wright (in 1705) must have dislocated the system.[4] This was, however, a Crown Office problem; the Secretary continued to rely on unwieldy entry books.[5] The central government's

---

[1] Barnes and Smith, op. cit., pp. 229–30.

[2] B.L., Add. MSS. 17748, ff. 2, 5, 9, 12.

[3] There is an example of both types of confusion in the same fiat at P.R.O., C. 234/14, Hampshire: 19 June 1716.

[4] *C.J.* xiii. 264; *L.J.* xvii. 483, 659. Of the five surviving fiats signed by Wright, three show that by 1704 the fiats were being used as working registers. P.R.O., C. 234/31, Rutland: 7 July 1704; C. 234/78, Anglesey: 5 Apr. 1705; C. 234/89, Pembrokeshire: 5 Aug. 1704.

[5] P.R.O., C. 231/9, pp. 217, 314, 445: entries of *libri pacis* for the Chancellor's Secretary.

difficulty in knowing who was in the commissions is reflected in the appearance of the document that reached the county. Names were commonly erased or inserted or both. Sometimes a name which did not appear at all in the main list turned up in the quorum list. Christian names would be left blank if neither the Secretary nor the Crown Office knew what it was; a gentleman variously spelled Cok and Coke was in the Leicestershire commission for eight years without a Christian name.[1] Misnomers were common, often being corrected by a special order in the next fiat; for instance, it appears that in the Buckinghamshire commission of the peace for 1718, two names had been inserted twice, two gentlemen recently promoted to baron and baronet had been included among the esquires as before as well as under their new names, and the list of Privy Councillors was out of date.[2] Mis-spellings were also frequent. One fiat for Cheshire ordered that no fewer than seventeen mis-spelt names be corrected.[3] Such ambiguities might be worse than a nuisance; in one case a parliamentary candidate took advantage of the omission of a distinguishing place-name to have sworn in as a justice for the liberty of St. Albans a friend brought up from London who was not the gentleman intended to be named.[4] Furthermore, the procedure for removing dead justices from the commissions was imperfect. The *custos rotulorum*, or the clerk of the peace, occasionally forwarded the names of justices who had died to the Secretary, who would either tie the list to the fiat, or copy the names onto the fiat and mark them 'dead'.[5] Alternatively it might be the Crown Office that heard of the deaths of justices, and their names would be crossed out of the entry books; in such cases the Secretary might not know of the removal. But *custodes* and clerks of the peace were not always conscientious, and the system was such that dead justices might remain in commission for years.

---

[1] Leics. R.O., QS 1/2–8: commissions of the peace dated between 1689 and 1697.

[2] P.R.O., C. 234/3, Buckinghamshire: 28 Feb. 1717/18.

[3] P.R.O., C. 234/5, Cheshire: 22 Mar. 1716/17.

[4] Herts. R.O., Cowper (Panshanger) MSS. D/EP F153: William Hale to Cowper, 18 Jan. 1714/15.

[5] There are good examples of both types of procedure in P.R.O., C. 234/9, Devonshire: 14 Feb. 1710/11 and 27 Dec. 1714.

The most formidable obstacle to the use of the commissions of the peace by the Chancellor as an instrument of
patronage was his reliance on local recommendation. By the
early nineteenth century, the principle that the lord-lieutenant,
acting in his capacity as *custos rotulorum*, made all recommendations, had become an established convention not lightly
broken.[1] This convention dates from the second half of the
eighteenth century. During the period from 1675 to 1720 the
Chancellor received and acted upon suggestions from a great
variety of local sources in addition to the *custos rotulorum*.
There is at least one example in these years of the submission
of the names of persons proposed to be put in or out from a
lord-lieutenant who was not also the *custos*,[2] a magnate who
was neither lord-lieutenant nor *custos*, the bishop of the diocese, the bench at quarter sessions, a single prominent justice
or group of justices, one of the members of Parliament for
the county, and even the gentleman proposed himself. Sometimes these local sources went straight to the Chancellor.
Sometimes they worked through sympathetic friends in the
government; for instance, Sir Joseph Williamson passed on
names recommended by his north country friends from
Queen's College, Oxford, when Secretary of State in the
1670s.[3] The central government also supervised the composition of the commissions. The Chancellor might receive
instructions from the Privy Council, one of the Secretaries of
State in the name of the Crown, any other member of the
government, Parliament, the Treasury, the Lords Justices
governing in King William's absences in the 1690s, the Cabinet,
or 'Lords of the Committee', in Queen Anne's reign, and even

[1] *Hansard*, 1st Ser., 1819–20, xli. 810–14; 2nd Ser., 1828, xviii. 162, 253–4;
3rd Ser., 1838, xliii. 1268–82. Lord Halsbury, Chancellor at various intervals
1885–1905, stated roundly in 1910 that he had accepted the nominations of
lords-lieutenant as a matter of course, and that he had further referred any other
recommendations to the lords-lieutenant. *Minutes of Evidence taken by the Royal
Commission on the Selection of Justices of the Peace*, 1910, Cd. 5358, p. 54,
questions 1124–6.

[2] The view that the offices of lord-lieutenant and *custos* were 'nearly always'
combined after the Revolution of 1688 — for which, see S. and B. Webb, *The
Parish and the County*, p. 285 — is erroneous. It was exceptional for the lord-
lieutenant of a Welsh county also to be the *custos*, at least until after 1720. The
number of English counties of which the lord-lieutenant was not also the *custos*
was twelve in 1691, ten at the end of Queen Anne's reign, and seven in 1722.

[3] *Cal. S. P. Dom., 1675–6*, pp. 547–8.

sometimes the Crown in a personal letter.[1] Another important source, neither precisely local nor central in character, were the assize judges on their return from the circuits.[2] Faced with this variety of sources, the Chancellor had to take many of the names offered as candidates for the commission of the peace on trust; to have checked the reliability of every recommendation would have involved his Secretary of Commissions in an impossible volume of correspondence.

It might seem that the local patronage exercised by a Chancellor was therefore of a mechanical kind, and that his role was confined to fixing the great seal on the commissions. This would be an over-simplification. The powers of the Chancellor were, admittedly, limited by the administrative routine by which commissions of the peace were issued, but the character of the Chancellor gave a general direction to the character of the commissions. He would naturally accept official nominations from the Council or the Secretary of State. However, the local recommendations might be judged by the character of the person making the recommendation. There was, for instance, little hope for the candidates of a Whig magnate during the 'Tory Reaction' at the end of Charles II's reign, or for the nominees of a Jacobite after the Hanoverian Succession. A Chancellor would not normally disregard the selections of *custodes rotulorum*, but he might subject the suggestions even of a *custos* to scrutiny with the help of local contacts thought to be more reliable.[3] Most Chancellors of the period from 1675 to 1720 were active in politics, in alliance with other politicians who could supply the blanks in their local knowledge. Some, like Guilford (Lord Keeper from 1682 to 1585) had ridden several circuits as a common-law judge, and knew the gentry well in at least some of the counties. Others, like Somers, Cowper, and Harcourt, had been members of Parliament, and had built up

[1] For an example of royal recommendation, see H.M.C., *Finch MSS.* ii. 42. There is an earlier illustration of the exercise of personal influence by the Crown in the passage from Hawarde's *Reportes del Cases in Camera Stellata* quoted in Gleason, *The Justices of the Peace in England, 1558–1640*, p. 63.

[2] J. S. Cockburn, *A History of English Assizes, 1558–1714* (Cambridge, 1972), pp. 157–63, 260.

[3] For an example, see P.R.O., State Papers Domestic, George I, S.P. 35/22, ff. 143–4: Coningsby, *custos* of Radnorshire, to Lord Chancellor, 16 June 1720 (copy); ff. 145–6: Lord Chancellor to Coningsby, 28 July 1720 (copy).

from their days in the Commons a network of local inform-
ants. The problems of utilizing tenure of the great seal as a
means of local patronage were certainly formidable, but they
were not, in practice, insoluble.

III

During the period from 1675 to 1720, some significant
changes in the character and composition of the commissions
of the peace took place. The most dramatic of these changes
was an increase in the number of local gentlemen named in
the lists in every county, in many cases to substantially more
than double the 1675 figure by 1720. There were short-term
fluctuations within this trend. The numbers in the commission for several counties actually fell slightly between 1680
and 1685, and again between 1714 and 1720: for example, in
the earlier period the number of justices in Herefordshire fell
by 25 per cent from 56 to 42; in the later period the number
of justices in Kent fell by 11 per cent from 201 to 178.[1] But
in no case did a temporary fall in numbers affect the over-all
rise. The figures for five counties selected more or less at random illustrate this point well:

	1675*	1685†	1702‡	1720§
Cheshire	44	38	54	90
Hampshire	59	84	104	168
Northamptonshire	47	61	80	94
Oxfordshire	36	51	107	96
Westmorland	23	23	28	29

*H.L.R.O., Main Papers, H.L., 9 Nov. 1680, corrected back to 1675 from
P.R.O., C. 231/7 and C. 231/8. This method is not wholly sound since the docquet
books are unreliable, but the figures are unlikely to be seriously misleading.
  †P.R.O., C. 193/12/5.   ‡B.L., Harl. MSS. 7512.
  §P.R.O., C. 234/5, /14, /27, /30, /39.

The spectacular increase of 183 per cent in Hampshire was
exceptional, but the much more modest increase of 26 per

[1] These judgements are based on: for 1680–5, a comparison of H.L.R.O.,
Main Papers, H.L., 9 Nov. 1680, and P.R.O., C. 193/12/5; and for 1714–20, the
fiats in P.R.O., C. 234. For the earlier period, see also G. C. F. Forster, *The East
Riding Justices of the Peace in the Seventeenth Century* (East Yorkshire Local
History Publications, xxx, 1973), pp. 20–1.

cent in Westmorland probably represents the smallest percentage rise of any county.[1]

The great expansion of numbers in most counties came in
the years immediately following the Revolution of 1688, and
again in the summer of 1700, when in a regulation involving
every county in England and Wales the Privy Council ordered
the inclusion of a total of 919 gentlemen and the omission of
only seventy-two; an average addition of fifteen justices per
county.[2] There is, however, one curious exception to the rule
that the numbers of names increased after 1688. A statute of
1542 had provided that there should only be eight justices in
each Welsh county besides the Privy Councillors. This rule
was presumably evaded by a *non obstante* clause in the commissions. One of the provisions of the Bill of Rights of 1689
was that no dispensation of or to any statute by a *non obstante* clause should be allowed.[3] Consequently there were
only eight justices in each Welsh county in the years after the
Revolution.[4] The extraordinary inconvenience caused by the
rule is shown by a letter from Radnorshire complaining that
of the seven justices in that county, one was 'as it were superannuated', another 'soe fatt that he can hardly Ride 3 miles
to the sessions & when he is there does only sleepe . . . we
want one of the Quorum to keep the sessions & therefore
we force him to come . . .'.[5] The 1542 act was repealed in
1693, when the numbers in the Welsh commissions rose
abruptly to, or beyond, the pre-1688 level.[6]

A variety of reasons might be suggested for the rise in
numbers in William's reign. The political factor was probably
the most important; successive governments were anxious to
buy support for the Revolution Settlement with local office,
without alienating opponents of that settlement by local
disgrace. Probably, too, the administrative exigencies of the
wars of 1689–97 and 1702–13 required more local agents. A

---

[1] There had been a similar expansion in Elizabeth's reign, but the numbers
seem to have been relatively stable in the first half of the seventeenth century.
Gleason, *The Justices of the Peace in England, 1558–1640*, pp. 48–50.

[2] P.R.O., Privy Council Register, P.C. 2/78, pp. 63ff.

[3] 34 & 35 Henry VIII, c. 26; 1 William & Mary, sess. 2, c. 2.

[4] Leics. R.O., Finch MSS. Law Papers 15: lists of justices put in for Anglesey,
Caernarvonshire, and Merionethshire in 1689.

[5] B.L., Loan 29/184, f. 380: John Waltham to Robert Harley, 12 Dec. 1690.

[6] 5 William & Mary, c. 4.

social explanation presents certain problems, however. The old property qualification of £20 a year from land had clearly become obsolete long before the 1690s. None the less, it is a generally accepted view that the late seventeenth and early eighteenth century saw the consolidation of large estates and the diminution of the estates of the smaller squires and lesser gentry.[1] This does not necessarily mean that gentlemen of old-established families, which had traditionally supplied their county's commission of the peace with names, fell below the social or economic standard that was required for a place in the commission; although, naturally, this did happen from time to time. All the same, the sharp rise in the number of justices does suggest two possibilities. One is that the commissions of the peace came to include, by 1720, persons of relatively lower economic standing than would have been acceptable in 1675. There is plenty of evidence that contemporaries thought that this was so, although there is, equally, evidence that some thought that too many justices were of low calibre before 1688.[2] The other is that persons whose wealth was not principally associated with land — that is, clergymen, prosperous tradesmen, lawyers, doctors, retired army and navy officers — began to claim places in the county commissions in greater numbers. It seems likely that both these hypotheses are true, but this is clearly a problem that requires detailed case studies to resolve.

Another general point about the commission of the peace from 1675 to 1720 is that there was, during this period, a marked decline in the frequency with which commissions were issued by the Chancellor, with the turning point coming in the years 1689 and 1690.[3] Between 1675 and 1689 the

[1] H. J. Habakkuk, 'English Landownership, 1680–1740', *Econ. Hist. Rev.*, 2nd Ser. x (1939–40), 4; G. E. Mingay, *English Landed Society in the Eighteenth Century* (London, 1963), p. 50.

[2] For the later period, see the preamble to the Justices of the Peace (Better Qualifications) Bill of 1711: 'Whereas it has been found by experience that the constituting persons of mean estates to be Justices of the Peace is highly prejudicial to the public welfare. . . .' H.M.C., *House of Lords MSS.*, N.S. ix. 154. For the earlier period, see A. Grey, *Debates of the House of Commons, 1667–1694* (London, 1769), viii. 187–8, 190: speeches of Hampden and Sir William Jones.

[3] The following calculations are based on P.R.O., C. 231/7, C. 231/8, C. 231/9. Lancashire, the commission for which county was issued separately, has been excluded; thus the total number of counties is fifty-seven.

lowest total of commissions issued in a single year had been 78, in 1686, and the average per year was 111·26. In 1690 the total was 74. Between 1690 and 1720 the total rose above 75 in only three years, in 1700, 1702, and 1714; and in 1702 and 1714 the commission for each county was renewed automatically on the demise of the Crown. The decline in frequency emerges clearly from a table of five-year averages:

1676–80	115·1 commissions per year on average
1681–5	100·0	,,	,,	,,	,,	,,
1686–90	106·2	,,	,,	,,	,,	,,
1691–5	50·8	,,	,,	,,	,,	,,
1696–1700	56·6	,,	,,	,,	,,	,,
1701–5	66·8	,,	,,	,,	,,	,,
1706–10	38·6	,,	,,	,,	,,	,,
1711–15	54·2	,,	,,	,,	,,	,,
1716–20	32·0	,,	,,	,,	,,	,,

These figures show that in the 1670s a county expected to receive a new commission more frequently than in the 1710s. Between the beginning of 1675 and the end of 1684, there were sixty-eight Middlesex commissions; on average, one every seven weeks. Admittedly, Middlesex consistently received more commissions than other counties; but a number of counties reached the average of a commission every twenty weeks. For the comparable period of ten years from 1711 to 1720, Middlesex received eighteen commissions, and the rate of frequency of issue dropped correspondingly for other counties.

The reason for this change was probably pressure of business in the Crown Office. A commission of the peace was a lengthy document, which presumably could not be drawn up quickly. The increase in the number of names in each commission aggravated this problem. To take one fairly typical example: in Northamptonshire, the total number of names, including Privy Councillors and judges, rose from about 100 in 1675 to about 165 in 1720; all of the extra names would also have to be added in the quorum list. In effect, the commission was about 130 names longer. Another point is that from 1692 the Irish Parliament, whose bills were approved under the great seal of England, began to meet comparatively regularly. These bills were engrossed in the Crown Office, and references to them take up a great volume of space in the docquet books.[1] Whatever the reason, the change was of some importance. Commissions to add or subtract single names, or to change the names of Privy Councillors or assize judges only, became much more rare. Furthermore, new commissions tended to embody recommendations from several sources rather than from a single source; it was no longer practicable to embody each recommendation as it was made in a new commission.

Two modifications of the procedure of the issue of commissions of the peace, introduced at the end of the period from 1675 to 1720, were probably connected with this decline in the frequency of issue. The first of these was a practice instituted by Lord Chancellor Macclesfield of sending to the Crown Office, not fiats for the renewal of a commission to add names, but 'instructions' for names to be added to the 'last' commission. Such an instruction was issued on 27 February 1719 to add three names to the 'last' commission for Wiltshire. The 'last' commission bore the *teste* date 12 December 1718. It is now in the Wiltshire Record Office, and the three names are neatly inserted above the line.[2] The transaction was not recorded in the docquet book. This procedure became fairly standard in the course of the eighteenth century. The Gloucestershire commission was not renewed for over forty years between 1767 and 1809, but numerous names were added and subtracted by means of 'instructions'.[3] The second modification of existing practice was the revival of an old method of removing a justice who had not died, not by a new commission in which his name was left out, but by a writ of *supersedeas*. Only one such *supersedeas* was directed to a justice during the period from 1675 to 1720. This was John Rotherham, who was put out of the Middlesex and Westminster commissions in July 1719. In the course of the eighteenth century such writs were issued more frequently. Blackstone referred to them as one

[1] W. E. H. Lecky, *A History of Ireland in the Eighteenth Century* (cabinet edn., London, 1916), i. 194; P.R.O., C. 231/8, pp. 295ff.

[2] P.R.O., C. 234/40, Wiltshire: 27 Feb. 1718/19; Wilts. R.O., A 1/1/5.

[3] E. Moir, *Local Government in Gloucestershire, 1775–1800* (Bristol and Gloucestershire Archaeological Society, Records Section, viii, 1969), p. 76, n. 25; P.R.O., C. 234/13, Gloucestershire.

of the ways in which a living justice could be dismissed.[1] A
supersedeas was generally associated with some misdemeanour
by the justice concerned; John Rotherham had sent the Rus-
sian minister an insulting message, and had committed one of
his servants to prison.[2]

Finally, it is worth pointing out that the distinction between
justices of the quorum and other justices was not entirely
defunct even by 1720. The assertion that '. . . by 1689 . . . the
[quorum] clause had become a mere form, as the practice was
to name, in each commission, all the justices as of the quorum'
is incorrect.[3] The number of justices not in the quorum in the
first post-Revolution commissions was quite high. In Leicestershire, for example, 8 out of 42 were not in the quorum in March
1689; by 1690, when the number of justices had risen to 62, 11
were not of the quorum.[4] In Devonshire, the figures in July
1689 were 19 out of 84.[5] This substantial proportion had not
diminished much by 1702 in either county: in Leicestershire,
9 justices out of 78, in Devonshire, 16 out of 119, were not
of the quorum. Nor were these counties unusual; in Norfolk,
as many as 30 out of 117 were not of the quorum in 1702,
and counties where all the justices except one or two were in
the quorum, like Oxfordshire and Denbighshire, were the exception rather than the rule.[6] During Anne's reign the proportion of non-quorum justices did drop. Lord Chancellor Harcourt, who held the great seal from 1710 to 1714, never added
a justice who was not to be in the quorum. In the nineteenth
century, it was thought that it had been customary for a long
time to omit one justice from the quorum as a matter of form.[7]

---

[1] W. Blackstone, *Commentaries on the Laws of England* (Oxford, 1765–9), i.
341. Blackstone distinguishes between a *supersedeas* to a single justice, and a
supersedeas to a complete commission. There was one example of the second type
of *supersedeas* during the period 1675–1720; in March 1685 the commission of
the peace for the liberty of St. Albans was annulled, and the liberty was (temporarily) united with Hertfordshire. P.R.O., C. 231/8, p. 120.

[2] P.R.O., S.P. 44/281, p. 107: Delafaye (Secretary of the Lords Justices) to
Lord Chancellor, 2 July 1719; C. 231/9, p. 474.

[3] S. and B. Webb, *The Parish and the County*, p. 303.

[4] Leics. R.O., QS 1/2, QS 1/4: commissions of the peace, 25 Mar. 1689, 8
Sept. 1690.

[5] Devon R. O., Q/JC: commission of the peace, 11 July 1689.

[6] B.L., Harl. MSS. 7512.

[7] F. W. Maitland, *Justice and Police* (London, 1885), p. 81 and note 2; see also
Blackstone, *Commentaries on the Laws of England*, i. 340.

This had not become standard practice even by 1720, although
it had become rare for more than three or four gentlemen not
to be in the quorum even in the biggest commissions. It was
still possible as late as 1715 for gentlemen who had been in
the quorum to be removed from it.[1] Earlier, a place in the
quorum was a minor distinction to be prized, and it could be
a weapon in county politics. The Earl of Carlisle had Sir John
Ballantyne included in the Cumberland quorum in 1676, and
a neighbour noted sarcastically that '. . . this much exalts
him'.[2] One of the members of Parliament for Thetford from
1708 to 1710 was in the commission, but not in the quorum,
for Norfolk, but he was placed in it before the 1710 election.[3]
Admittedly, the quorum had become rather irrelevant in
practical terms, and it bore no relation to legal learning. All
the same, its lapse into disuse should not be predated; indeed,
its revival as a serious distinction between two kinds of justice
has been twice suggested in the twentieth century.[4]

IV

A gentleman did not become qualified to act as a justice of
the peace simply by insertion in the commission. He was
obliged to take the oaths of allegiance and supremacy. After
1673 he had to declare that he did not believe in transub-
stantiation, and he required a certificate that he had taken
the sacraments according to the usages of the Church of
England. After 1701 he had to take an oath abjuring the
Pretender. In addition he took a special oath of office.[5]
This oath was administered on the authority of a writ of
dedimus potestatem from Chancery; these writs normally
accompanied a new commission into the county. They could
also be obtained through the office of the Secretary of

[1] P.R.O., C. 234/14, Hampshire: 5 Oct. 1714, 5 Aug. 1715; a comparison of
these lists shows that four justices were put out of the quorum. C. 234/34, Staffordshire: 22 Feb. 1714/15; three justices were put out of the quorum.
[2] *Cal. S.P. Dom., 1675–6*, pp. 573.
[3] Thomas de Grey. P.R.O., C. 234/26, Norfolk: 16 Mar. 1709/10.
[4] *Minutes of Evidence taken by the Royal Commission on the Selection of
Justices of the Peace*, 1910, Cd. 5358, pp. 26–8, questions 428–9, 465–75;
Minutes of Evidence taken before the Royal Commission on Justices of the Peace,
Supplements i–ii (London, 1946), para. 22.
[5] The oath of office is conveniently printed in Prothero, *Select Statutes and
other Constitutional Documents*, pp. 149–50.

Commissions.[1] Very occasionally a special *dedimus* was issued, probably when it was thought to be urgently necessary for a new justice to qualify himself.[2]

Not everyone named in the commission chose to act. There were a number of reasons for this reluctance. It was, in the first place, quite expensive to qualify; fees of upwards of £4 were payable. The Secretary of Commissions received £1. 5s. 0d., the Clerk of the Crown £1. 7s. 8d.; the clerk of the peace and his deputies would receive variable fees. Payment for the certificate of taking the sacraments, for the crier, and for other incidentals, added to the expenses.[3] Justices developed scruples over the purchase of a judicial office.[4] Sometimes, strangely for persons supposed to have £20 a year from land, they appeared not to be able to afford the fees. Edmund Bohun, for example, who published moral reflections on the duties of justices as well as his charges to the Suffolk grand jury, was highly incensed on his first appearance in the commission of the peace to find that he had to part with £4.[5] The House of Commons investigated the grievance of the fees in 1710; in the following year an assize judge reported from Cornwall that quite large numbers of justices refused to qualify because of the price of the *dedimus*.[6] Some justices found it not only expensive to qualify, but also expensive to act. A justice of the peace under the rank of baronet received four shillings for each day's attendance at quarter sessions, a sum which by 1675 had in most counties been commuted into a payment received

[1] A *dedimus* sent out in this way was entered in a special register. Those for 1675–1701, and 1713–20, do not survive, but the register covering the years 1701–13 is at P.R.O., C. 193/43.

[2] Special writs of *dedimus* were common in the 1660s, but the only examples thereafter are in 1680–1 (seventeen counties) and 1709 (three counties). P.R.O., C. 231/8, pp. 30, 31, 36, 40, 41, 45; C. 231/9, p. 196. See also Barnes and Smith, 'Justices of the Peace from 1558 to 1688 — A Revised List of Sources', pp. 226–7.

[3] An exact breakdown of the cost of becoming a justice would be impossible; the fees paid varied in different areas at different times. In 1684 the sum for a Westmorland justice was £4. By 1743 a Wiltshire justice paid £5. 5s. 6d. The fees were rather more for peers, rather less for justices not in the quorum. *Parl. Papers 1814–15*, xi. 27, 36, 69, 92–3; H.M.C., Twelfth Report, Appendix VII, *Le Fleming MSS.*, p. 401; S. and B. Webb, *The Parish and the County*, p. 303, n. 3.

[4] *Cal. S.P. Dom., 1682*, p. 145.

[5] Bodl. MS. Tanner 290, f. 143: Edmund Bohun to Sancroft, 20 Nov. 1674.

[6] *C.J.* xvi. 376, 380; H.M.C., *Portland MSS.* v. 72.

by the sheriff and used by him to provide a dinner for the justices. A justice also received a number of inconsiderable perquisites, such as a portion of forfeited 'Egyptian' property; the most considerable of these, a fee for enrolling deeds of sale of land, seems to have lapsed anyway after the Restoration.[1] However, it was common to speak of the justices as 'unpaid', and the office was sometimes described as unprofitable and burdensome, though it was usual to reserve the case of the Middlesex justices, who, it seems, were able to profit from the office.[2] Another substantial reason for reluctance to act was that the duties of a magistrate were troublesome, and even, on occasion, dangerous. The justice might be threatened with violence from rioters.[3] It was not uncommon for justices to be exposed to the insults, frequently obscene, of malefactors. In 1668, for example, a Cambridgeshire magistrate fell foul of a dissenter who 'would obey noe law that man sett forth, nor car'd a Turd for any Justice', and who threatened to kill the constable.[4] Lord Lovelace, on being presented with a warrant from a justice of the peace in 1687 or 1688, was reported to have announced that he would 'wipe his breech' with it.[5] Brooke Boothby and 'Justice' Trott of Derbyshire were manhandled at Boothby's own house in 1716 by soldiers celebrating the King's birthday, when Quarter Master Butler used exactly the same language as his Cambridgeshire counterpart of nearly fifty years before.[6] Also, a justice of the peace might incur severe legal penalties for an innocent error. One Middlesex justice claimed to have been fined £500 and imprisoned for a year for binding as apprentices two youths who had really been kidnapped.[7] Some justices, too, were unwilling to associate themselves on the bench with political

[1] C. A. Beard, *The Office of Justice of the Peace in England* (New York, 1904), pp. 150-1; J. C. Cox, *Three Centuries of Derbyshire Annals* (London, 1890), ii. 261-2.

[2] *Memoirs of the Life of Charles Montagu, late Earl of Halifax* (appended to the 2nd edn. of his *Poetical Works*, London, 1716), p. 228.

[3] H.M.C., Fifteenth Report, Appendix IV, *Portland MSS.* iv. 335.

[4] Bodl. MS. Rawl. D. 1136, p. 27: diary of Sir Thomas Sclater, 26 July 1668.

[5] B.L., Add. MSS. 34515, ff. 51-3: newsletter, 27 Feb. 1688.

[6] P.R.O., S.P. 35/6, ff. 136-52: examinations relating to a quarrel at the house of Brooke Boothby, 24 Nov. 1716.

[7] *Cal. Treas. Books*, viii. 671.

enemies.[1] Others, like John Evelyn, simply did not choose to take the trouble.[2] Cowper thought that vanity was responsible for some justices' inactivity; they affected to be 'titular' justices like the Privy Councillors, '. . . to enjoy the credit & title in their county without giving themselves the trouble of doing the Duty . . .'.[3]

The problem of justices who did not act was not new. It had been particularly severe at the end of Elizabeth's reign, in the 1630s, and again in 1665.[4] It is difficult to estimate what proportion of justices did not act at any given time. The judgement that only about 700 or 800 justices out of a total of 2,500 to 3,000 — 32 per cent at the most favourable estimate — acted at all during the period from 1650 to 1700, is pure hypothesis, though it does echo Cowper's verdict that not one in three of those he put in condescended to act.[5] The number of inactive justices would naturally vary from county to county, and from year to year. There are distinctions between justices who acted only when called upon to do so and never went to sessions, justices who were inactive through ill-health or non-residence, and justices who did not even take out the necessary *dedimus*.

What is certain is that, in the vast majority of cases, the gentlemen who were named in the commissions of the peace valued the distinction, whether they chose to exercise the powers it gave them or not. To be included in the commission of the peace gave them an opportunity to associate themselves with county administration and to figure among the leaders of county society. The principal attraction of the office for the justice who did choose to act was possibly the extent of his local power, which defies precise definition.[6]

[1] Bodl. MS. Carte 109, ff. 67–8: Westmorland justice to Wharton, 29 Apr. 1704.

[2] *The Diary of John Evelyn*, ed. E. S. de Beer (Oxford, 1955), iii. 433–4.

[3] Herts. R.O., Cowper (Panshanger) MSS. D/EP F152: Memorandum for George I.

[4] *Acts of the Privy Council*, N.S. xxviii. 388–9; T. G. Barnes, *Somerset 1625–1640* (Oxford, 1961), pp. 303–6; H.M.C., *Various Collections*, ii. 379–80.

[5] S. and B. Webb, *The Parish and the County*, p. 321; Herts. R.O., Cowper (Panshanger) MSS. D/EP F152: Memorandum for George I.

[6] It would be impossible, even if it were desirable for the purposes of this study, to describe fully the powers of a justice of the peace. In the sketch which follows, I have relied on editorial introductions to quarter sessions records for the period 1675–1720, especially *Minutes of Proceedings in Quarter Sessions*

Out of quarter sessions, a single justice, acting in his own house, could issue warrants against suspected persons, conduct preliminary inquiries into criminal cases, and investigate minor misdemeanours like drunkenness and swearing. He could punish, by summary conviction, such petty offenders as players of unlawful games and wandering vagrants. The single justice could take, from more serious offenders, recognizances, or sureties for good behaviour, until the next sessions; or he could commit them to gaol. This exercise of criminal jurisdiction was derived from the function of the justice as a keeper of the peace, as outlined in the commission, although many of the offences of which he had cognizance had been created by statute. The single justice outside sessions also had various administrative functions. He could, for instance, supervise the routine (but not the extra-ordinary) repair of roads; he could sign the certificates of travelling soldiers and sailors; and he could administer certain oaths. His supervisory authority over the numerous county, hundred, and parish officials extended to presenting them at sessions for negligence, appointing them if the proper appointing body defaulted, and in some cases examining their accounts.

Two justices acting together had further powers, especially if one was of the quorum. Those which involved most work were probably the provision of maintenance for paupers and illegitimate children and the grant of licences to keep alehouses. Two justices also had a wide jurisdiction over matters as various as the preservation of game, the manufacture of cloth, Roman Catholic recusancy, and the relations of masters and servants. The powers of more than one justice might be exercised in a private, unannounced meeting. However, in the course of the seventeenth century, such meetings tended to become advertised and formal, and the justices who attended them began to be identified, unofficially, with the particular 'division' of the county in which the meetings were held. Such meetings were described variously as 'petty sessions' and 'special sessions'. Petty sessions were regular meetings of

held for . . . Kesteven . . . 1674–1695, ed. S. A. Peyton (Lincoln Record Society, xxv, 1931), pp. xxv–xxxvi, lxiii–cxxv; on the numerous contemporary handbooks for justices; and on S. and B. Webb, *The Parish and the County*, Book II, Chapters III and IV.

justices in a division, attended by subordinate officials; principally designed to provide a more continuous execution of the poor law than could be achieved in quarter sessions, they were a convenient forum for the conduct of other business as well.[1] Special sessions were largely administrative in character, and were institutionalized by statute in 1691 and 1729 as the appropriate occasions for highway supervision and alehouse licensing respectively. After 1729 they were often referred to as 'Brewster Sessions'.[2]

It was, however, in quarter sessions that the collective jurisdiction of the justices was most extensive. Quarter sessions were held four times a year, although the manner of holding them varied from county to county. In some counties the court was always held at the county town. In others, the court was peripatetic. It might be held on a circuit of four towns in the county through the year, or it might at each sessions begin at one centre and be adjourned to several others in a regular sequence, the same circuit being repeated at the next quarter sessions.[3] But the powers of quarter sessions were the same, whether it met at the county town or not, by adjournment or otherwise. The criminals committed by the justices out of sessions were tried by a jury impanelled by the sheriff; serious felonies were, however, usually sent to assizes. The orders made by justices out of sessions were confirmed, and appeals against them heard. The grand jury of the county, made up of substantial freeholders, presented county grievances which were dealt with by the justices. Hundred juries and hundred constables were also supposed to present criminals and nuisances within their jurisdiction, and at the beginning of the period 1675–1720 they occasionally did so, but the practice of returning the presentment *omne bene* seems to have been almost universal by George I's reign. The administrative powers of the justices at quarter sessions included the assessment of wages and prices by fixing maximum rates, and they also fixed the costs of land carriage. This was normally done at Easter

---

[1] Barnes, *Somerset 1625–1640*, pp. 81–5. The main stage in the development of petty sessions in Somerset is there described as the publication of the Book of Orders in 1631.

[2] 3 & 4 William & Mary, c. 12; 2 George II, c. 28; S. and B. Webb, *The Parish and the County*, pp. 396–7.

[3] S. and B. Webb, op. cit., pp. 425–31.

sessions each year. They assessed county rates for different purposes; some traditional and customary, like the Marshalsea rate for the relief of prisoners for debt, some for special purposes, like the repair of the county gaol or of county bridges presented to be in decay. The justices administered the finances of the gaol and of the house of correction. They investigated misdemeanours by other royal officials within the county: the sheriff, the coroners, and the clerk of the market. They examined the accounts of the militia. In short, they exercised either direct or supervisory authority over virtually every aspect of local government.

It had been the practice since the sixteenth century for a senior justice to deliver the charge to the grand jury at the beginning of quarter sessions. This was principally an enumeration of the jury's functions, but it might be preceded by a lecture in law and political philosophy, a moral homily, or a discussion of matters of national interest; or a combination of all these.[1] Sometimes the justice acted under direction from the centre — in response to a proclamation, for instance — in drawing attention to particular offences which were to be treated with more severity.[2] The justice who delivered the charge probably acted as the unofficial chairman of the court. When the names of justices who attended sessions were entered in the rolls, the order of the names usually followed that in the commission of the peace, but it is common to find one name out of order at the head of the list. It is reasonable to suppose that this was the 'chairman'. However, the chairmanship of sessions was not a recognized office, as it became later in the eighteenth century. There is some evidence of dislike of permanent chairmen.[3] The chair was often taken with expressions of modest reluctance.[4] Nevertheless, the justice who

---

[1] J. S. Morrill, *The Cheshire Grand Jury 1625–1659* (Leicester, 1976), pp. 22-4; *Charges to the Grand Jury at Quarter Sessions, 1660–1677, by Sir Peter Leicester*, ed. E. M. Halcrow (Chetham Soc., 3rd Ser. v, 1953), pp. xxx–xxxv.

[2] Queen Anne's distaste for vice and profaneness was reflected in a number of charges delivered after her accession. Especially interesting, because not prepared for subsequent publication, is Simon Harcourt's charge at Buckinghamshire sessions in July 1704. B.L., Harl. MSS. 5137, f. 251.

[3] S. and B. Webb, *The Parish and the County*, pp. 434-5.

[4] The charge delivered by a Surrey justice in 1701 or 1702 begins '. . . there seems to be some kind of necessity of a charge to be given you & these gentlemen,

regularly received an invitation to deliver the charge was a respected figure among his colleagues, and he possessed a powerful means of influencing opinion. The phrase used to describe the position in Norfolk in the 1680s expresses this well; there the presiding justice was said to 'have the cushion'.[1]

The justices at quarter sessions were assisted by a small bureaucracy. The principal servant of the county was the clerk of the peace, who was appointed by the *custos rotulorum*.[2] As clerk to the *custos*, he kept the records of the court; as clerk of quarter sessions, he conducted its voluminous paperwork; as unofficial secretary to the justices he received communications addressed to them, both from subordinate officers within the county and from the organs of central government. The clerk of the peace in Somerset was already employing a fairly large staff as early as the 1630s.[3] The fees taken varied from county to county; the office of clerk of the peace was quite lucrative, and was often held by a member of a family of justice rank. The counties would also employ inferior officials: a gaoler, and a keeper of the house of correction, especially. The appointment of other officers proceeded rather haphazardly. In some cases, the various county rates were handled by justices nominated for the purpose; sometimes, treasurers for particular funds were appointed who were not justices. It was, however, unusual, though not unknown, for a county to employ a salaried treasurer responsible for all the county rates before 1739, when the justices were authorized to consolidate their various sources of income into a single fund by statute. County surveyors, who inspected roads and bridges, seem to have been appointed and paid by quarter sessions rather earlier in many counties, but the appointments were generally temporary and the experiment might be abandoned on the

whose commands I dare not disobey, have imposed this task upon me . . .'. Bodl. MS. Rawl. D. 1041, ff. 72-86.

[1] Bodl. MS. Tanner 259: Sir John Holland's Letter Book, ff. 1-2, 18, 19.

[2] Until 1689, the clerk's tenure ceased with the demise of the appointing *custos*. Thereafter, under 1 William & Mary c. 21, he held the place 'during behaviour'. There is, however, a late case of an incoming *custos* dismissing his predecessor's clerk of the peace in Cox, *Three Centuries of Derbyshire Annals*, i. 28.

[3] T. G. Barnes, *The Clerk of the Peace in Caroline Somerset* (Leicester, 1961), pp. 8-9.

grounds of expense.[1] The expansion of the county bureaucracy, and its professionalization, proceeded at different
speeds in different counties, and many counties were still
backward in this respect in the early nineteenth century.
What remained true in every county was that the justices of
the peace at quarter sessions retained control of the appointment, the salaries, and the performance of duties of all their
officials except the clerk of the peace, and even the clerk of
the peace was in a real sense the servant of quarter sessions.

Since quarter sessions was an occasion when members of
leading county families met to transact county business, it
naturally became an opportunity to transact other kinds of
business as well. Quarter sessions was from time to time a
forum for the choice of Parliamentary candidates.[2] After
elections, members of Parliament found attendance at sessions
a useful means of keeping in touch with county opinion.[3]
Indeed, after the election of 1702, the first meeting of the
new Parliament was postponed so that members who were
justices could attend sessions to be sworn; the consideration
that weighed with the ministers in granting the request was
that the members' appearance at sessions would be 'of good
use in the country'.[4] Petitions from quarter sessions, signed by
the grand jury as well as the justices, were thought to be
peculiarly influential as representing the considered opinion
of a county. The best-known example of such a petition was
that presented from Kent quarter sessions held at Maidstone
on 29 April 1701, urging Parliament to grant supplies to
enable William III to assist his allies. This was voted to be
scandalous, the leading justices in the county were imprisoned,
and the 'Kentish Petition' became a *cause célèbre* in national
politics. Quarter sessions were also an opportunity for pug-
nacious gentlemen to conduct quarrels, sometimes personal,
sometimes political. The Norfolk justices were in two camps

[1] S. and B. Webb, *The Parish and the County*, pp. 515–16.
[2] H.M.C., Fourteenth Report, Appendix IV, *Kenyon MSS.*, pp. 110–11;
H.M.C., *Downshire MSS.* i. 562; G. S. Holmes, *British Politics in the Age of Anne*
(London, 1967), p. 316.
[3] J. H. Plumb, *Sir Robert Walpole, The Making of a Statesman* (London,
1956), pp. 46–7.
[4] B.L., Add. MSS. 29588, f. 123: Sir C. Musgrave to Nottingham, 8 Aug. 1702;
ff. 171–2, Hedges to Nottingham, 2 Sept. 1702; *Cal. S.P. Dom., 1702–3*, pp.
235–6.

in 1682. In the following year, business at Northumberland sessions was transacted by 'clamour and voting', not by reasoned argument.[1] When two political opponents sat together on the Buckinghamshire bench in 1699, the Tory Lord Cheyne objected to the Whig Lord Wharton's place on the chairman's right hand, and at the conclusion of business they retired to duel.[2] The importance of quarter sessions in the social life of a county is underlined by the curious frequency of disputes over where sessions should be held; these could be very bitter, and required judicious compromise solutions, usually from the assize judge.[3]

Admittedly, while quarter sessions had a fundamental place in county government, the court was not all-powerful. Cases could be removed to higher courts by writs of *certiorari*. The administration of quarter sessions was limited by the inefficiency of inferior officers such as the hundred and parish constables. The conduct of the justices was to some extent supervised by higher authorities: the assize judges, the Privy Council, the Secretary of State. Furthermore, the commission of the peace was not the only means of acquiring local power and prestige. The land tax acts regularly included the names of men who were not justices among the commissioners. Lords-lieutenant occasionally gave deputy-lieutenancies in the militia to non-justices. Commissions of sewers and of charitable uses, also issued under the great seal, conferred certain powers not shared by the justices, although the justices supervised the work of the commissioners of sewers and indeed took over their functions if a commission of sewers lapsed.[4] The justice was not at the summit of county society; a place in the assize commission of *oyer and terminer*, in association with the judges, represented a further step reserved for a few senior justices of the peace. It was at assizes, not at quarter sessions, that Sir Roger de Coverley 'kept up his credit in the country' by adding some remarks to those of the judge.[5]

---

[1] *Cal. S.P. Dom., 1682*, p. 55; *Cal. S.P. Dom., 1683*, p. 72.
[2] B.L., Add. MSS. 40774, ff. 104–5: Vernon to William III, 18 July 1699.
[3] See for instance R. North, *Lives of the Norths* (London, 1826), i. 291–3.
[4] 13 Elizabeth I, c. 9.
[5] *The Spectator*, ed. D. F. Bond (Oxford, 1965), No. 122, i. 499.

Notwithstanding the reluctance of some justices to act, the limitations on the power of sessions, and the possibility of acquiring status by other means, a place in the commission of the peace was highly valued. Some justices, wrote Edmund Bohun at the end of the seventeenth century, 'look to nothing but the Credit, Honour and Reputation they shall gain by it, and if they can gain the Title of Right Worshipful, and have their neighbours stand bare-headed to them, they have their Designs'.[1] Bohun disapproved of gentlemen who enjoyed the prestige of a place on the bench without condescending to share the responsibilities, but for many justices the local power conferred by the office was a major attraction. It is not an exaggeration to ascribe to the justice of the peace, as historians frequently do, a crucial place in government and society, from the sixteenth to the nineteenth century.[2] There are few cases of gentlemen refusing the honour if it was offered to them, even if they did not intend to act. 'Through the ambition of many', as one contemporary law student succinctly put it, 'it is accounted a credit to be burthened with that authoritie.'[3]

[1] E. Bohun, *The Justice of the Peace, his Calling and Qualifications* (London, 1693), p. 135.
[2] F. W. Maitland, 'The Shallows and Silences of Real Life', in *Collected Papers of F. W. Maitland*, ed. H. A. L. Fisher (Cambridge, 1911), i. 468-9.
[3] B.L., Lansdowne MSS. 569, f. 30.

2

THE COMMISSION OF THE PEACE AND
THE ORIGINS OF PARTY, 1675-85

I

Charles II's leading minister in the mid-1670s was Sir Thomas
Osborne, created Lord Treasurer in 1673 and Earl of Danby
in 1674. Danby's objectives in politics were straightforward.
The early years of the decade had seen the collapse of the
King's policies in the spheres of finance, foreign policy, and
religion, more or less simultaneously in 1673. Danby sought
to rebuild the royal finances, to restore the confidence of the
Anglican Church, and to consolidate the independence of the
Crown in policy formulation. To achieve these aims, he set
himself to organize the political patronage available to the
ministers of the Crown in a more systematic way than his
predecessors had done, with a view to building a stable Court
party in both Houses of Parliament.[1]

The great seal was in the hands of Heneage, Lord Finch,
appointed Lord Keeper in 1673 and elevated to Lord Chancellor in December 1675. Finch's place in legal history is that
of the greatest lawyer of the Restoration period. Better
known to lawyers by his later title of Earl of Nottingham, he
was a judge of the highest distinction who developed many of
the modern principles of Chancery jurisdiction.[2] He was, like
Danby, a royalist and a firm Anglican. The two were close
political allies, and there is some evidence to suggest that
Danby in particular wanted to make use of local patronage
to create a grass-roots Court party in the localities which

---

[1] A. Browning, *Thomas Osborne, Earl of Danby and Duke of Leeds, 1632-1712*
(Glasgow, 1944-51), i. 167-73, 191-2, 273-5; K. Feiling, *A History of the Tory
Party, 1640-1714* (reprinted edn., Oxford, 1963), pp. 154-7; C. D. Chandaman,
The English Public Revenue, 1660-1688 (Oxford, 1975), pp. 231-47.
[2] Campbell, *Lives of the Chancellors*, iii. 392-425; E. Foss, *The Judges of
England, with Sketches of their Lives* (London, 1848-64), vii. 93-7; W. S. Holds-
worth, *A History of English Law* (reprinted edn., London, 1966), vi. 539-48.

would give a stable base to the Court party in Parliamentary politics.[1]

During the period from the establishment of Danby's regime in the summer of 1674 to his fall in March 1679, the commission of the peace was never manipulated in a simultaneous regulation, directed by the central government and involving all the counties together. Commissions of the peace were certainly sealed frequently, and the number of commissions renewed tended to be higher in February and March, and again in July (the months before assizes) than in other months of the year; but this was the normal pattern.[2] It seems that Finch treated the county benches as independent units. He does not seem to have regarded the magistracy of England and Wales as a collective whole.

This is not to say that the commissions for individual counties were not regulated from time to time. In twenty-six out of the fifty-seven English and Welsh counties (not counting Lancashire), gentlemen still living were put out of the commission of the peace between 1675 and March 1679.[3] In at least three of these counties the bench was apparently remodelled from the centre. The Middlesex bench was purged in 1676 for political reasons. Sir John Robinson, the Lieutenant of the Tower, wrote to the Secretary of State, Sir Joseph Williamson, that several Middlesex justices, especially all 'Sir Robert Peyton's gang', should go. 'It is', wrote Robinson, 'of great concern to his Majesty [and] the good government of the city and the adjacent parts that nobody be in Commission either military or civil but such as are faithful and love and affect the government. . . .'[4] Sir Robert Peyton was a wealthy and influential figure in the City. He had entered the circle of Country party M.P.s and financiers around Danby's enemy, Anthony Ashley Cooper, Earl of Shaftesbury, whose pamphlets urging a new Parliament had recently led Danby into an attempt to suppress the London coffee houses where

[1] Browning, *Danby*, ii. 66.   [2] P.R.O., C. 231/7.

[3] This figure is reached by combining the entries in the Crown Office docquet books with a list, compiled by Finch in late 1678 and annotated in law-French by his son Daniel Finch, of justices put out since 1674. P.R.O., C. 231/7, C. 231/8; H.M.C., *Finch MSS*. ii. 43–6.

[4] P.R.O., State Papers Domestic, Charles II, S.P. 29/379, f. 209: Robinson to Williamson, 6 Mar. 1676.

seditious literature was circulated.[1] Peyton had already been put out in February 1676 by the King's order; several more Middlesex gentlemen were dismissed in commissions sealed in March, April, and May.[2]

Norfolk was another county where a regulation with political overtones took place. The lord-lieutenant, Lord Townshend, had been replaced by the Earl of Yarmouth in March 1676 as part of Danby's campaign to consolidate the Court party in readiness for the parliamentary session of February 1677.[3] Townshend, disgruntled, joined forces with the ex-Cromwellian M.P. for the county, Sir John Hobart, and an anti-Court interest began to gather strength. In June 1676 Hobart, Sir Robert Kemp (the other M.P. for Norfolk, elected in a hard-fought by-election in May 1675), and Sir John Holland (M.P. for Aldborough) were left out of the Norfolk commission. The request that these three be dismissed came from the old Cavalier gentry of Norfolk, who asked Yarmouth for a complete sweep of all supporters of the Earl of Shaftesbury.[4] It is probable, though evidence is lacking, that a similar situation developed in Kent. In that county, four prominent gentlemen, of whom two were baronets and one was a Knight of the Bath, were put out by the King's order in March 1678.[5] Two of them, Sir Vere Fane and Sir John Tufton, were M.P.s.

If similar regulations involving leading local figures took place elsewhere, evidence has not survived; and three counties is a small proportion of the whole. In a number of other counties, however, justices were dismissed on the recommendation of local magnates, possibly but not certainly for political or quasi-political reasons. Finch seems to have accepted such recommendations without question when they came from reliable Courtiers. Thus, the Earl of Bath had four gentlemen dismissed in Devonshire in 1675, the Earl of

[1] K. H. D. Haley, *The First Earl of Shaftesbury* (Oxford, 1968), pp. 403–5.
[2] P.R.O., C. 231/7, pp. 508–12; H.M.C., *Finch MSS*. ii. 44.
[3] Browning, *Danby*, i. 196 and note 6; J. R. Jones, 'The First Whig Party in Norfolk', *Durham University Journal*, N.S. xv (1953), 14–15; H. A. Wyndham, *A Family History, 1410–1688; The Wyndhams of Norfolk and Somerset* (London, 1939), pp. 284–7.
[4] P.R.O., C. 231/7, p. 514; H.M.C., Sixth Report, Appendix, *Ingilby MSS*., p. 374.
[5] H.M.C., *Finch MSS*. ii. 44; P.R.O., C. 231/7, p. 542.

Lindsey one in Kesteven in 1676, and the Marquess of
Worcester a total of twelve in Breconshire, Glamorgan, and
Monmouthshire between 1674 and 1677.[1] However, when
the less reliable Lord Newport wanted to have one Daniel
Wycherley put out in Shropshire, Wycherley put up a spirited
case before the Privy Council before Finch decided that there
was some substance in the allegations against him.[2]

In many of the counties where living justices were put out,
the reasons were negligence, misdemeanour, or occasionally
opposition to government policy in an administrative matter.
For example, two North Riding justices and two Nottinghamshire justices were dismissed for disregarding the assize judges'
rule that hearth duty was payable on smiths' forges.[3] Cases
of individual discipline were common in Middlesex; three
justices were put out together in that county for 'abetting an
offender and going off the bench'.[4] More serious were cases
of religious disaffection. These were not common, but Catholic gentlemen were put out in Monmouthshire and the North
Riding, at least one notorious Protestant Dissenter (William
Trenchard in Wiltshire) lost his place in the commission, and
justices were dismissed in Essex, Hertfordshire, and Surrey
for not taking the oaths.[5]

There was nothing new about such regulation of the bench.
Justices had always been liable to dismissal for misdemeanour,
for religious disaffection, or for incurring the dislike of a
local magnate. There was nothing new, either, about cases in
which the composition of a county's commission of the peace
became an issue in local politics after a quarrel over purely
local issues. This happened in Westmorland in the 1670s over
the problem of where quarter sessions should be held. The
justices in the vicinity of Kendal insisted that sessions should
be held permanently in that town, instead of alternating
between Kendal and Appleby. The factious spirit engendered
by the dispute led to a tug-of-war over nominations to the

[1] H.M.C., *Finch MSS.* ii. 43-5.
[2] Ibid., p. 45; P.R.O., P.C. 2/64, pp. 317, 344, 392, 397; C. 231/7, p. 494.
[3] H.M.C., *Finch MSS.* ii. 45-6; P.R.O., P.C. 2/66, p. 78; *Memoirs of Sir John
Reresby*, ed. A. Browning (Glasgow, 1936), p. 125.
[4] H.M.C., *Finch MSS.* ii. 44.
[5] Ibid., pp. 43-6; for Trenchard, see D. R. Lacey, *Dissent and Parliamentary
Politics in England, 1661-1689* (New Brunswick, 1969), p. 452.

county bench between the Musgraves on one side and the
Howards, Fletchers, and Flemings on the other.[1] Neither side
was successful in displacing rivals, but in a similar situation in
Montgomeryshire, when three justices set up a 'splinter'
quarter sessions in defiance of the official writ, the *custos
rotulorum* (Lord Herbert of Cherbury) secured the omission
of at least one of the rebels.[2]

On the whole, it seems a reasonable assumption that, with
a few exceptions, the political influence on the county magistracy exercised by the Court was so exercised by accepting
nominations from Court party supporters that well-disposed
gentlemen should be added, rather than by removing opponents. Thus, for example, a Suffolk justice sought in 1677
to balance his enemies by the addition of his friends, rather
than by exercising his influence with the Bishop of Norwich
to disgrace those he disliked.[3] The commission of the peace
in the majority of counties (though not in Middlesex, Norfolk, or Kent) therefore can be said to have remained fairly
stable during the Danby regime. The changes made in Warwickshire have been described as 'routine'.[4] Dead justices
were omitted, and replacements of suitable standing were
found. The Court did not remove some gentlemen who had
sat on the bench during the Interregnum. Even so, Warwickshire counts as one of the counties for which a living justice
was removed.[5] Cheshire, which received one commission in
April 1675 adding one gentleman, and then nothing for
four years, or Anglesey, which did not receive a commission
at all between July 1670 and April 1680, were perhaps extreme examples of stability. However, counties as large and

---

[1] The course of the quarrel can be followed in H.M.C., Twelfth Report, Appendix VII, *Le Fleming MSS.*, pp. 115ff.; P.R.O., S.P. 29/378, f. 20: Sir P. Musgrave
to Williamson, 3 Jan. 1676; S.P. 29/379, f. 22: Fleming to Williamson, 10 Feb.
1676; ff. 99–100: Sir P. Musgrave to Sir C. Musgrave, 24 Feb. 1676; S.P. 29/381,
f. 150: Sir P. Musgrave to Williamson, 11 May 1676; S.P. 29/385, f. 180: Sir C.
Musgrave to Williamson, 18 Sept. 1676.

[2] P.R.O., P.C. 2/65, p. 216; H.M.C., *Finch MSS.* ii. 44.

[3] *Diary and Autobiography of Edmund Bohun*, ed. S. Wilton Rix (Beccles,
1853), p. 37.

[4] *Warwickshire Quarter Sessions Records, Easter, 1674 to Easter, 1682*, ed.
S. C. Ratcliffe and H. C. Johnson (Warwick County Records, vii, 1946), p. xxi.

[5] William Palmer, whose omission was ordered in 1677, although there is
some doubt as to whether he was in fact put out. H.M.C., *Finch MSS.* ii. 46; *Cal.
Treas. Books*, v. 479; *Warwickshire Quarter Sessions Records, 1674–82*, p. xxi.

as electorally important as (for example) Buckinghamshire, Dorset, Somerset, Sussex, and the West Riding did not receive commissions putting justices out. As far as can be judged, gentlemen were simply added in ones and twos. Thus, in spite of the exceptional cases of Middlesex and Norfolk, it is hard to escape the conclusion that the years of Danby's regime were among the more tranquil in the seventeenth century as far as the commission of the peace was concerned.

It is something of a paradox, therefore, that in early 1678 the House of Commons made the commission of the peace into one of the major issues in politics. It expressed concern over what it conceived to be, at best, neglect in examining the credentials of those put into the commissions of the peace, and, at worst, the manipulation of the commissions in the interests of Catholicism. The Court, it was argued, was trying to prevent the execution of the laws against recusants. A committee appointed by the Commons to inquire into the growth of Catholicism in South Wales reported that four justices of the peace and the coroner in Monmouthshire were all Catholics, and that the presentment and conviction of recusants at quarter sessions had been obstructed. The two principal witnesses before the committee, John Arnold and Henry Probert, claimed to have been turned out of the Monmouthshire commission because of their Protestant zeal, and there was a strong hint that the Catholic heir to the throne, the Duke of York, had recommended their disgrace. The committee also received information that one William Fenwick had been put into the Northumberland commission, although the M.P.s for that county had represented to Finch that he was a suspected Catholic; they had unsuccessfully recommended a suitable replacement.[1] The Commons voted to raise the matter at a conference with the Lords on the growth of Popery, and ordered the chairman of their committee to ask the Chancellor why the two Monmouthshire justices had been turned out.[2] Finch's reception of the deputation from the Commons is variously described. One M.P. later alleged

[1] *C.J.* ix. 466–70: 29 Apr. 1678; *Herbert Correspondence*, ed. W. J. Smith (Board of Celtic Studies, University of Wales History and Law Series, xxi, 1963), 197, 220.

[2] *C.J.* ix. 470–1; *Poems and Letters of Andrew Marvell*, ed. H. M. Margoliouth (2nd edn., Oxford, 1952), ii. 221–2.

that the Chancellor refused to answer the members.[1] The chairman told the Commons a year later that the deputation had decided that, since Arnold in particular had been put out at the instance of the Duke of York, it was not worth complaining to Finch, but he also said that Finch had promised to put one of the Catholic justices out of the Monmouthshire commission.[2]

There was very little substance in the case against Finch, at any rate in those counties on which the Commons concentrated. The Court's defence over the controversial Monmouthshire commission was fairly strong. One of the Catholic justices named by Arnold had, in fact, been put out as early as 1676, as soon as Finch had learned about his recusancy from the Bishop of Llandaff. Arnold and Probert may possibly have offended the Duke of York, but the Marquess of Worcester had also represented that they had committed misdemeanours, admittedly unspecified, in their office.[3] The complaints of Arnold in particular seem to have originated in a vendetta against Worcester as much as in zeal against Popery.[4] Furthermore, Finch acted promptly on receiving the views of the Commons. One of the Catholic justices in South Wales, Henry Milborne, was put out for three counties in May 1678, and William Fenwick was dismissed without delay from the Northumberland bench.[5]

Although the Country party campaign has a flavour of shadow-boxing, it is easy to see why the complaints over the magistracy were inflated. The opposition politicians in the Cavalier Long Parliament were eager to mount an attack on Danby's ally Finch as part of their campaign against the Court. The country gentlemen in the Commons feared nothing more than government intrusion into the closed world of county society. The successes of the Country party in 1678 — the addresses remonstrating against evil counsellors and the defeat of a motion for an increase of £300,000 in the King's annual revenue — can be attributed, at least in part, to the judicious handling of back-bench opinion on the subject of Catholic influence in the choice of justices of the peace.[6]

[1] Grey, *Debates*, vi. 181.   [2] Ibid. vii. 166–7.   [3] H.M.C., *Finch MSS*. ii. 44.
[4] J. P. Kenyon, *The Popish Plot* (London, 1972), p. 213; J. Miller, *Popery and Politics in England, 1660–1688* (Cambridge, 1973), p. 61.
[5] Ibid., pp. 43, 45; P.R.O., C. 231/7, pp. 543, 544.
[6] Grey, *Debates*, vi. 134, 281; *Cal. S.P. Dom., Charles II, Addenda*, p. 474.

II

In the late summer and early autumn of 1678, all minor
issues became submerged in the national panic of the 'Popish
Plot': the general belief, based on the disclosures of the
informer Titus Oates and others, that there existed a Catholic
conspiracy to assassinate the King and extirpate Protestant-
ism. During the Cavalier Parliament's last session in the last
three months of 1678, the opposition kept the subject of the
magistracy alive, to convince the country gentry of the
iniquity of the Court while Oates made sensational accusations and the former ambassador to France exposed the
King's receipt of French subsidies in Parliament. The Commons ordered the Clerk of the Crown to submit a list of
justices on 8 November; a similar order was later given to the
Chancellor of the Duchy of Lancaster; and the House further
requested a list of justices who had been dismissed within
the last seven years.[1] Finch prepared to meet criticism with
the help of his son Daniel, who was an M.P.[2] The prorogation
on 30 December forestalled an attack on Finch as well as an
attack on Danby.

The Court party was now hard pressed. The Cavalier Parliament was dissolved on 24 January 1679, and elections were
held in February. Danby, who was threatened with impeachment, reshuffled the ministry by sacrificing Williamson and
bringing in the Earl of Sunderland as Secretary of State. An
approach was made to the Duke of York to change his
religion; James rejected the suggestion completely.[3] The
survival of Danby depended on the elections. However, the
Court was not in a position to exert much influence on them.[4]
Finch was not able to assist the return of Court party supporters by changing the commissions of the peace. In the
first place, there was not enough time between the decision
to dissolve, which was a sudden one, and the elections themselves. In the second place, there was probably little that
Finch could do to help. It would have been unusual for the

---

[1] *C.J.* ix. 535, 539, 540.

[2] The frequently quoted list at H.M.C., *Finch MSS.* ii. 43–6, was almost certainly drawn up for this purpose.

[3] Browning, *Danby*, i. 313–14.

[4] J. R. Jones, *The First Whigs* (London, 1961), pp. 36–41.

Court's candidates and their supporters not to have been in
the appropriate commissions anyway, and to have ejected
Country party candidates immediately before the elections
would have done more harm than good. Only fifteen commissions of the peace were sealed in January and February, and
the changes that were made seem to have been routine; no
living justices were put out, according to the docquet books.[1]
The Court was thus not able to exert its powers of patronage.
If anything, it was seeking to mollify the opposition.

Even so, Finch was not prepared to give way completely to
the demands of the Country party. In January, the King in
Council gave orders for justices 'disaffected to the government
and the true Protestant religion' to be removed and replaced
by 'persons, who may be likely to act with more vigour and
good affection'.[2] Finch, to whom the order was addressed,
was to act if he received complaints. But no machinery for a
systematic regulation was set up, and the only tangible result
of this order was that an obscure justice in the liberty of
Southwark was dismissed for discharging a person suspected
of complicity in the murder of Sir Edmund Berry Godfrey,
the Middlesex justice whose death had first aroused public
interest in the Plot.[3] When Parliament met, the King promised
that, in future, only sincere Protestants would be chosen as
justices of the peace.[4] This, like the Council order in January,
was only a gesture, and it failed to appease the opposition. A
debate on the case of John Nalson, in commission for Ely,
illustrated the way in which the Court's handling of the commission of the peace could be made the subject of attacks on
the old ministers; Nalson had published a pamphlet attacking
some of the opposition M.P.s, and they recommended his omission from the Ely magistracy. During the debate, the Country
party spokesmen Titus, Powle, and Williams all criticized recent
appointments to the bench, and Shaftesbury's secretary moved
an address for the removal of all Popishly affected justices.[5]

---

[1] The docquet book entries for these months are at the end of P.R.O.,
C. 231/7, and the beginning of C. 231/8.
[2] P.R.O., P.C. 2/67, p. 64; H.M.C., Thirteenth Report, Appendix VI, *Fitzherbert MSS.*, p. 12.
[3] P.R.O., P.C. 2/67, p. 76.   [4] *C.J.* ix. 607: 30 Apr. 1679.
[5] Grey, *Debates*, vii. 166–7; *C.J.* ix. 608; [E. Bohun], *The Second Part of an
Address to the Freemen and Freeholders of the Nation* (1682), p. 26.

Finch's position was now growing more difficult. Two circumstances combined to bring the commission of the peace more into central politics in the spring of 1679. In the first place, Danby's failure to secure the election of his candidate as Speaker revealed that he had lost control of the Commons, and he fell in March. In April the King remodelled the Privy Council, admitting to it many of the opposition leaders, especially Shaftesbury who became Lord President. Charles's motives in this change were tactical; he was partly trying to gain time, and partly trying to divide the opposition leaders from the Country party rank and file, since the latter distrusted politicians in office impartially.[1] Although the King's attitude to his new Councillors was equivocal, they were in a position to exert influence on the Chancellor to remodel the commissions of the peace in the interests of their friends and supporters. In the second place, the emergence of divisive issues on a national scale sharpened the quarrels dividing local communities.[2] One such issue was Exclusion: that is, the policy advocated by Shaftesbury's Country party, shortly to be called the Whig party, of excluding Charles's Catholic brother James, the Duke of York, from the succession to the throne. An Exclusion bill was progressing through the Parliament elected in February 1679 before the King prorogued it on 27 May. A secondary issue, stimulated by the Popish Plot, directly affected the magistracy. This was the desirability of compelling the agents of government to enforce the recusancy laws. The admission to the Council of those committed both to Exclusion and to the enforcement of anti-Catholic legislation suggested that changes in the composition of the county benches were in prospect. This was what contemporaries expected.[3] This, indeed, was what Shaftesbury and his friends tried to do in the spring of 1679.

In May a 'regulation of justices' was proposed in Council, and the Clerk of the Crown was ordered to send in lists of justices as fast as they could be copied, '. . . his Majesty's

---

[1] *The Works of Sir William Temple* (Edinburgh, 1754), i. 413-17; *Memoirs of Thomas, Earl of Ailesbury*, ed. W. E. Buckley (Roxburghe Club, London, 1890), i. 34-5; Jones, *The First Whigs*, pp. 61-3; J. P. Kenyon, *Robert Spencer, Earl of Sunderland, 1641-1702* (London, 1958), pp. 25-6.

[2] Jones, 'The First Whig Party in Norfolk', pp. 13, 15.

[3] H.M.C., *Ormonde MSS.*, N.S. iv. 505; v. 58.

Service requiring a more than ordinary diligence in this matter'.[1] Shaftesbury suggested that two or three magnates be appointed for each county, to consult about the commission of the peace for that county with the Chancellor, the lord-lieutenant, the bishop of the diocese, the *custos rotulorum*, and the judges; this method was adopted.[2] The names of these magnates indicate the Whiggish nature of the proposed regulation. For instance, Bedfordshire was assigned to Lord Russell and Lord Cavendish; Cheshire was to be regulated by the Duke of Monmouth and the Earls of Shaftesbury and Bridgwater; the Duke of Monmouth had Staffordshire to himself; Sussex was to be managed by the Earls of Essex and Shaftesbury, and Lord Holles. Although, in some counties, peers who could not have been sympathetic to a regulation in the Whig interest were named, they were, with a very few exceptions, accompanied by committed Country party politicians. Thus, for instance, although the Marquess of Worcester was named for Gloucestershire, he was to be joined by Henry Powle and Sir Henry Capel. A partisan takeover of local power was in prospect. The Country party wanted to build up a stable interest in the countryside by rewarding their friends with, and depriving their enemies of, local office. The adoption of such Country measures in office would also quiet the suspicion of the Commons, that the leadership of the Country party had been corrupted by the Court.

Eager as the Whigs were to instal their supporters in local office and to disgrace their opponents, the King's hostility defeated them. Roger North described what happened as follows:

. . . the Rolls of the Justices were ordered to be laid before the Council, in order to be reformed. And (as some present related) it was pleasant to see with how much Wit and good Humour, the King ordered Affairs, to disappoint these Reformers. He would not suffer the Roll that was begun with, to be out of his Own Hand, but pretended to mark the Alterations upon it himself. Then, as many of the Council moved for Alterations upon the Account of good or bad Men (Terms of Art,

[1] P.R.O., P.C. 2/68, pp. 30, 42.
[2] B.L., Add. MSS. 15643, Minute Book of the Council's Committee of Intelligence, 1679–81, f. 2; P.R.O., P.C. 2/68, pp. 47–8: 21 May 1679; B.L., Loan 29/236, ff. 407, 409: the Privy Council orders sent to the Duke of Newcastle, lord-lieutenant of Northumberland and Nottinghamshire, apparently enclosing lists of justices for comment.

which, for Brevity, they used to signify such as the Party liked, or would have put out, or not) if the King was content a Man should out, he made a Mark at his Name; but if he would not part with him, he found some jocular Reason to let him stand; as that he was a good Cocker, understood Hunting, kept a good House, had good Chines of Beef, kept good Fox Hounds, or some such indifferent Matter, which it was ridiculous to contradict or dispute upon. And, in this Manner, he frustrated all their Intent, as to Removes, and, by crossing and puzzling the Work, made a plain Demonstration to his factious Counsellors, that they should not have their Will of him in what they intended, *viz.* to dash the best Friends he had, all over England, in the Face with such Affronts. In short, finding they could not prevail, they let the Business drop; and I do not know that any one Roll was, in this Manner, thoroughly perused. . . .[1]

The King and the inner circle of ministers thus disregarded the reports of the Whig magnates, and events moved too quickly for the attack on the commissions of the peace to be renewed. The dissolution of the first Exclusion Parliament and the elections in the summer of 1679 absorbed the energies of the regulators. A rising in Scotland, the political complications consequent upon the King's illness in August, and their own enmities, diverted the attention of the Council. The brief Whig ascendancy was not however entirely without effect. Some changes in the Whig interest were made in May — that is, before the organized Privy Council regulation. Sir John Hobart, Sir Robert Kemp, and Sir John Holland, the three Norfolk justices disgraced in 1676, were restored; so too were Sir Vere Fane and Sir John Tufton in Kent. Among anti-Court M.P.s who were placed on the bench in their home counties were John Speke in Somerset, Sir John Darell in Kent, and John Ashburnham in Sussex.[2] Again in Somerset, the royalist Edward Phelips was rumoured to have been put out, to the consternation of the Bishop of Bath and Wells. Already, however, the Whig regulation was misfiring. Whether or not it had been intended to leave Phelips out, his name, spelt Phillipps, is in the Somerset commission sealed in May.[3]

---

[1] Roger North, *Examen, or an Enquiry into the Credit and Veracity of a Pretended Complete History* . . . (London, 1740), pp. 77–8. See also the same author's *Lives of the Norths*, ii. 59–60. Roger North's brother, then Lord Chief Justice, was a Privy Councillor at this time.

[2] P.R.O., C. 231/8, pp. 6–8.

[3] Longleat MSS., Coventry Papers vii, f. 152: Bishop of Bath and Wells to Coventry, 9 June 1679; Som. R.O., Q/JC 83: commission of the peace, 3 May 1679.

The Council regulation itself, in the summer of 1679, was a failure. Commissions of the peace were sealed for twenty-seven counties between June and October 1679. In fifteen of these, according to the docquet book, the assize judges only were altered. In none of the twelve remaining counties[1] were the regulators exclusively Whig, and the alterations were unspectacular except in Kent, where seven gentlemen were added in July following the inclusion of Fane, Tufton, Darell, and four others in May. Indeed, if anything, they show a tendency to favour the Court. In Norfolk, for example, Hobart, Kemp, and Holland, restored in May, were left out again in June after the King had written to Finch that 'ther is no objection against it but in disobligeing those sorte of people who will never be obliged, and any countenance I give them is only used against myselfe and government'.[2] Two loyal Courtiers with interests in Worcestershire, Lord Windsor and Henry Coventry (one of the Secretaries of State) were actually conspiring in June to leave out the Whig knight of the shire, Thomas Foley, and also Edward Lechmere, the son of an active rebel of Cromwell's time.[3]

The Whig takeover of local power thus broke down. Finch sealed only three commissions of the peace in August 1679, and none at all in September. Meanwhile, the Whigs were losing ground. Parliament was dissolved on 12 July; elections, held in August and September, produced a House of Commons even more intransigent than the last had been, but this Parliament was immediately prorogued, and it remained prorogued by successive adjournments for twelve months until October 1680. The Duke of Monmouth, the prótegé of the Whigs as Charles's illegitimate son and an alternative Protestant heir, was dismissed as Commander-in-Chief of the army and exiled in Holland; while James, who had been banished to Brussels in March, returned to stiffen the resolution of the Court in September. In October, the Earl of

[1] Caernarvonshire, Cardiganshire, Flintshire, Gloucestershire (two), Kent, Kesteven, Norfolk, Northamptonshire, Oxfordshire, Radnorshire, Warwickshire, and Wiltshire. P.R.O., C. 231/8, pp. 8–15.

[2] H.M.C., *Finch MSS.* ii. 42, where the letter is wrongly conjectured to be dated 1678; P.R.O., C. 231/8, p. 12.

[3] Longleat MSS., Coventry Papers vi, f. 76: Windsor to Coventry, 16 June 1679.

Radnor replaced Shaftesbury as Lord President. The Earl of
Essex resigned as head of the Treasury Commission in November. Laurence Hyde and Sidney Godolphin, the new heads of
the Treasury, and Sunderland, Coventry's partner as one of
the two Secretaries of State, were thought to be the most
influential ministers. The remaining Whigs resigned from the
Privy Council in January 1680.[1]

III

A commission of the peace for Warwickshire sealed in November 1679, in which Sir Richard Newdigate and Thomas
Marriot were put out at the instance of the Earl of Denbigh
and Lord Brooke for standing against two Court candidates
in the August election for knights of the shire, was a fore-
taste of a comprehensive remodelling of the bench conducted
by the reconstituted ministry.[2] Unlike that planned in the
spring, this was to be a Court regulation, fully backed by the
King. A committee consisting of the Chancellor, the Lord
President, and the two Secretaries of State was appointed in
early December to review the lists of justices.[3] There was no
clumsy farming out of counties to individual magnates. The
experience of the Whig regulators led an observer well versed
in the workings of the Council, Sir Robert Southwell, to suggest pessimistically in a letter to the Duke of Ormonde that
the work of this committee would be 'tedious, if not difficult
and thankless'.[4] However, this time the review proceeded
rapidly. The committee worked on local recommendations
invited and collated by the Secretaries of State. A little evidence survives to illustrate the procedure. For example,
Henry Coventry wrote to the Earl of Longford that his list
would be shown to the King — presumably Longford's list
was for Surrey, where he had stood for election as knight of
the shire against two Country party candidates the previous
February. Coventry said that he was unable to comment on
the 'good and bad marks on so many men', not knowing the
county. He did not think that any one list would be accepted

---

[1] Jones, *The First Whigs*, pp. 87-92; Kenyon, *Sunderland*, pp. 29-34; Haley,
Shaftesbury, pp. 547-51, 556.
[2] *Warwickshire Quarter Sessions Records, 1674-82*, p. xxii.
[3] P.R.O., P.C. 2/68, p. 309.   [4] H.M.C., *Ormonde MSS.* N.S., iv. 566.

entire, but that the committee would consolidate the several lists received for each county and present the results to the King for final correction.[1] The Earl of Conway, whose main interests were in Warwickshire, was informed in January that the Earl of Denbigh had represented Colonel Archer, a colleague of the already disgraced Newdigate and Marriot in Warwickshire elections, as a man not fit to be in commission, and that if he wanted to recommend anybody himself he had better do it quickly. Conway was able to use his influence to keep another justice in the commission.[2] News of this activity at the centre had spread into the localities by Christmas. When the Archbishop of York had successfully recommended some 'strange' alterations in a commission of the peace for the liberty of Ripon sealed in November, the Dean of Ripon wrote on 26 December that he hoped that 'the alterations which the public intelligence tells us are to be made in other commissions' would not prove similar.[3]

The King, Finch, and Radnor reviewed the provisional lists compiled by the Secretaries of State in a series of meetings in the first six weeks of 1680; by 16 February they had perfected the lists for all the counties.[4] By the end of March every county in England except Cheshire had received a new commission; Cheshire and the Welsh counties followed in April.[5] In forty-six of the fifty-seven English and Welsh counties, at least one local justice was left out.[6]

Another regulation took place almost immediately. The judges, who had recently returned from the Lent assizes, were directed to return the names of justices who were not sworn or who had not acted. Three days later, on 17 April 1680, the Council ordered the inclusion and omission of justices in a total of thirty counties.[7] On 13 April Sunderland

[1] B.L., Add. MSS. 25125, Henry Coventry's Letter Book, f. 81: Coventry to Longford, 23 Dec. 1679.
[2] *Cal. S.P. Dom., 1679–80*, pp. 378, 393.
[3] H.M.C., *Various Collections*, ii. 167.
[4] H.M.C., *Ormonde MSS.*, N.S. iv. 574; v. 269, 270, 276.
[5] P.R.O., C. 231/8, pp. 19ff.
[6] The exceptions were Anglesey, Cardiganshire, Carmarthenshire, Cumberland, Huntingdonshire, Lindsey, Merionethshire, Radnorshire, Rutland, Staffordshire, and Westmorland.
[7] H.M.C., *Ormonde MSS.*, N.S. v. 301–2; P.R.O., P.C. 2/68, pp. 475, 480, 482–4.

had written to the Earl of Rutland, lord-lieutenant of Leicestershire, sending a list of justices for that county, which was
one of those involved in the regulation; this suggests that the
Secretaries again prepared draft lists with the help of local
office-holders for submission to the King, Finch, and Radnor.[1]
The warrants were issued within a week, and the commissions
embodying these changes were sealed by June or July.[2] The
committee continued through the summer to make regulations in the commissions for single counties. The Wiltshire
commission, for instance, acquired no fewer than fifteen new
names in July.[3]

There were naturally rumblings of discontent in the counties. For example, the Duke of Newcastle complained bitterly
about the omission of Samuel Eyres in Northumberland.
Newcastle, who had nominated Eyres, felt himself insulted.[4]
When Parliament met on 21 October 1680 after its year-long
prorogation, it was expected that there would be strong
objections to the waves of changes. It was in the House of
Lords that the main assault on the Court over the commissions of the peace developed. This may, in conjunction with
Newcastle's protest, reflect a change of emphasis in the
opposition's attitude to the regulation. The country gentry
certainly resented the admission of new and unsatisfactory
colleagues, or their own fall from local grace; but the magnates, who saw their control of the counties they dominated
vanishing into the hands of the central government, took the
lead in criticizing the Court. The Lords ordered that a committee be appointed to inquire into 'abuses' in altering the
commissions. This was composed largely of Whig magnates,
some of whom had been allotted counties in the abortive
Whig regulation in May 1679. Shaftesbury, Monmouth,
Essex, Macclesfield, Lord Grey of Warke, Lovelace, Wharton,
and Delamer were all members.[5] This committee was supplied with a *liber pacis* by the Crown Office, and between 9
and 22 November 1680 it diligently studied the lists.[6] After

[1] H.M.C., Twelfth Report, Appendix V, *Rutland MSS.* ii. 54.
[2] P.R.O., C. 231/8, pp. 29ff.
[3] P.R.O., P.C. 2/69, p. 24: 29 June 1680; C. 231/8, p. 32: 10 July 1680.
[4] H.M.C., *Finch MSS.* ii. 82.   [5] *L.J.* xiii. 655.
[6] During this period, the Exclusion bill was passed in the Commons and defeated in the Lords.

the second day, Shaftesbury himself was in the chair. The committee's deliberations ended abruptly on 22 November after it had considered about half the counties, though it is possible that it convened again on 9 December. It never reported, but had it done so there is no doubt that it would have drawn attention to the large number of M.P.s and men of substance put out, and to the unsatisfactory character of those put in or kept in.[1]

The Commons does not seem to have debated the subject formally, although members expressed their views on several occasions. In a debate ostensibly about Tangier on 17 November, Whig spokesmen argued that the King had re-modelled the bench to serve his purpose of preventing Exclusion. Sir Henry Capel saw the hand of the Duke of York in the changes.[2] On 18 December, the leading Whigs insisted on the need for 'good justices'; according to Sir William Jones, the Court had put in clergymen and 'men of mean quality', and had put out M.P.s who had voted for Exclusion and active magistrates zealous against Popery. Boscawen hinted again at the sinister influence of the Duke.[3] It was possibly in this debate that Henry Booth, M.P. for Cheshire, argued persuasively that the county he represented had been greatly harmed by the dismissal of Sir Thomas Mainwaring, an experienced and popular justice of the peace. Booth declared ironically that he himself was glad to have been put out. He saved money; he was protected from assassination by Papist plotters; his neighbours thought more highly of him for having so manifestly incurred the Court's displeasure. But justices of the peace, as a class, were honest men, and to

[1] H.L.R.O., Main Papers, H.L., 9 Nov. 1680. This manuscript consists of the Crown Office lists of justices for the several counties (except Nottinghamshire), and the minute book of the committee in a pocket of the cover of the modern binding. It is calendared, though unreliably, in H.M.C., Eleventh Report, Appendix II, *House of Lords MSS., 1678–88*, pp. 172–93. A paper headed 'List of the Justices lately ordered to be left out and inserted in the Commissions of the Peace of the several counties in the Oxford Circuit' and endorsed 'Alterations in the Commissions of the Peace in the Oxford Circuit. March 1679[/80]' adds some names to the House of Lords' findings and confirms that the Lords ignored the omission of dead justices. B.L., Loan 29/183, ff. 5–6.

[2] Grey, *Debates*, viii. 10, 13; H.M.C., *Portland MSS.* viii. 17.

[3] Grey, *Debates*, viii. 187–8, 190, 194–5, 197; H.M.C., Twelfth Report, Appendix IX, *MSS. of the Duke of Beaufort and others*, pp. 99–100.

put any one of them out unheard was a great reflection on their character. 'God be thank't', he said, 'the nation sees very plainly who and what sort of persons rule the rost; by all the enquiry I can make I do not find that any man is put out but such as were very active against the Papists, such as are against arbitrary power, and such as approved the bill against the Duke.'[1] These sentiments (assuming that the speech was, in fact, delivered) must have appealed more strongly to the squires in the House than Garroway's assertion that the office of justice of the peace was burdensome, brought no honour, and was beneath consideration at a time of national crisis; this view was repudiated by later speakers.[2] An address to the King on 27 November hinted that 'Jesuits' had secured the dismissal of worthy justices. Another address on 20 December referred to the dismissal of eminently qualified justices and the inclusion of 'countenancers of Papists' and 'men of arbitrary principles'. It requested that justices might in future be men who were well-affected to the Protestant religion, and of estates and interest in their counties.[3]

It was certainly true that many justices were dismissed for the reasons Booth gave. Between forty-five and fifty of the M.P.s who had voted for Exclusion in May 1679 were put out for their counties in the winter and spring of 1679/80.[4] Among them were such prominent figures as Hugh Boscawen in Cornwall, Colonel Birch in Herefordshire, Silas Titus in Hertfordshire, Sir Trevor Williams in Monmouthshire, Sir John Hotham in the East Riding, Thomas Wharton in Buckinghamshire, and William Williams in Shropshire and Denbighshire. The purge of Exclusionist M.P.s was not, however,

---

[1] *The Works of Henry, late Lord Delamer and Earl of Warrington*, ed. J. Delaheuze (London, 1694), pp. 129–32. Sir Richard Newdigate reacted with similar ironic pleasure when put out for Warwickshire in November 1679. B.L., Add. MSS. 34730, f. 54: Newdigate to Thomas Marriot, 12 Jan. 1680.

[2] Grey, *Debates*, viii. 192, 194.

[3] *C.J.* ix. 665–6, 685; H.M.C., *Finch MSS*. ii. 99.

[4] This calculation, and the information following, is based on a comparison of the lists in H.L.R.O., Main Papers, H.L., 9 Nov. 1680, and the division list printed by A. Browning and D.J. Milne, 'An Exclusion Bill Division List', *B.I.H.R.* xxiii (1950), 207–25. Further information on the affiliations of M.P.s is derived from J. R. Jones, 'Shaftesbury's "Worthy Men": a Whig view of the Parliament of 1679', *B.I.H.R.* xxx (1957), 232–41.

comprehensive; more than sixty remained in commission, and certain inconsistencies reveal that the Court's system of synthesizing local recommendations was not foolproof. Hector Philips, M.P. for Cardigan borough, who had voted for Exclusion, was actually put into the Pembrokeshire commission *de novo*, and kept in that for Cardiganshire. In Devonshire, three Exclusionist M.P.s were put out, including two baronets, one of whom was the county member; seven were allowed to remain. In Hampshire three Exclusionists were put out, two kept in. Elsewhere, six justices were put out who had actually voted against Exclusion in May 1679.[1] Admittedly, one of these, Sir John Guise, may have been disgraced because he had killed his opponent in a duel.[2] These cases suggest that it would be an over-simplification to regard the changes as a ruthless campaign against the Exclusionists. Most of the M.P.s were put out in the first of the Court's purges in January and February 1680, and it is at least possible that a carefully calculated distinction was being made between intransigents and men who might be won over, although this is never explicitly stated. It is however more probable that, while the regulation appeared to be well organized and simultaneous, local influence at Court still played a large part in the remodelling of individual county benches. In particular, a number of Whigs of great social prominence were left in. The Court undoubtedly felt that the omission of certain magnates would be dangerous, and, for example, Lord Russell remained in commission for Bedfordshire, Lord Sherrard for Leicestershire, Lord Fairfax for the West Riding, Lord Townshend for Norfolk, and Lord Fitzwilliam for Northamptonshire.

Booth was also right when he said that some justices had been put out because of their zeal against Catholics. Henry Probert, one of the Monmouthshire justices who had been put out and then restored after giving evidence to the Commons in 1678, was put out again.[3] Two notoriously anti-Catholic justices, Sir William Waller and Sir Gilbert Gerard,

---

[1] Earl of Ancram (Berkshire, Surrey, and Buckinghamshire); Sir John Guise (Gloucestershire); Edward Hales (Kent); William Harbord (Hertfordshire); Walter Kendall (Cornwall); and Sir Francis Winnington (Worcestershire).

[2] W. R. Williams, *Parliamentary History of Gloucestershire* (Hereford, 1898), p. 60.

[3] H.L.R.O., Main Papers, H.L., 9 Nov. 1680, f. 38.

were dismissed in Middlesex; admittedly, the Council had further reasons for putting both out, since Waller had committed a prisoner without preferring any charges against him, while Gerard was discrediting himself by an ostentatious search for a 'black box' allegedly containing a certificate of marriage between the King and the Duke of Monmouth's mother.[1] Booth claimed to have been dismissed himself because he had secured the conviction of five thousand recusants in Lancashire.[2]

Others put out had been active in the promotion of petitions to the King in the winter of 1679/80, requesting that Parliament be allowed to sit. This was why, for instance, Broome Whorwood was put out in Oxfordshire.[3] One of the few counties where changes in the Whig interest had taken place in the early summer of 1679 was Kent; the new justices, led by Sir John Darell, petitioned that Parliament should sit, and promptly all of them lost their places on the bench.[4] One contemporary later wrote that the petitioning movement had been carried on in each county by some hot-headed, busy justice of the peace, a significant association of ideas.[5] Also, the trouble-makers in local disputes were put out. Two of the Kendal justices in Westmorland, Sir George Fletcher and Daniel Fleming, were dismissed for Cumberland, illustrating the continuity between such disputes and the growth of party during the Exclusion crisis. Animosities lingered on when first causes had been forgotten.[6]

Notwithstanding Booth's opinion that the changes were uniformly anti-Whig, not all the alterations were politically inspired. William Barnesley, left out of the Surrey commission, had endeavoured to corrupt a witness against the Duke

---

[1] P.R.O., P.C. 2/68, p. 471; *The Hatton Correspondence*, ed. E. M. Thompson (Camden Soc., N.S. xxii, xxiii, 1878), i. 216, 225.

[2] *Works of Henry Lord Delamer*, p. 130.

[3] *Life and Times of Anthony Wood*, ed. A. Clark (Oxford Historical Society, 1891–1900), ii. 476–7.

[4] Longleat MSS., Coventry Papers vi, f. 230: [Sir] Thomas Peyton to Coventry, 23 Jan. 1680; H.L.R.O., Main Papers, H.L., 9 Nov. 1680, f. 27.

[5] Ailesbury, *Memoirs*, i. 45; and see also H.M.C., *Ormonde MSS.*, N.S. v. 276, 502.

[6] In Roger North's account of the quarrels in 1676, he described the Musgraves as Tories and the Fletchers and Lowthers as Whigs, although he admitted that this was an anachronistic distinction. *Lives of the Norths*, i. 291.

of Buckingham on a sodomy charge.[1] Equally, it would have been hard to criticize the Chancellor for leaving out Philip Champernoone in Devonshire, since that gentleman was, according to the Bishop of Exeter, derided by the county for notorious incest with his wife's sister.[2] About a quarter of those ordered to be put out in April 1680 are described as 'dead' in the Privy Council register, and the operation could have been represented as one of rationalization, as well as manipulation, of the commissions of the peace. However, Finch could not have denied that Booth's analysis of the nature of the changes was, though over-simplified, substantially correct. The purge of factious men varied in intensity from county to county, but everywhere it had a clear end in view: each county was to have a preponderance of magistrates who were sympathetic towards the Court.

Charles dissolved Parliament on 18 January 1681 and summoned another to meet at Oxford in March. The changes in the commissions of the peace in 1680 did not assist the Court party in the elections of February and early March, to judge by results. The new House of Commons was to be as Exclusionist as the last.[3] Indeed, the Court made some concessions, suggesting a new timidity, during the election period. Henry Booth and Sir Thomas Mainwaring were restored to the Cheshire commission, and Booth once again became *custos*. He drew attention to the fact, saying that he had not desired the favour, in a speech to the freeholders after his election.[4] However, some changes seem to have been designed to encourage the supporters of the Court, rather than to conciliate its opponents; for example, Bridstock Hartford, 'a worthy member of the last Parliament', already in the Herefordshire commission, was added to that for Worcestershire.[5]

The next major changes took place after the Oxford Parliament was dissolved after sitting for only a week. Sir Leoline

---

[1] P.R.O., P.C. 2/68, p. 466; H.M.C., *Ormonde MSS.*, N.S. v. 296–7.
[2] Bodl. MS. Tanner 37, ff. 17, 47: Bishop of Exeter to Archbishop Sancroft, 24 Apr., 6 June 1680; H.L.R.O., Main Papers, H.L., 9 Nov. 1680, f. 16.
[3] Jones, *The First Whigs*, pp. 159ff.
[4] P.R.O., P.C. 2/69, p. 207: 4 Feb. 1681; C. 231/8, p. 42: 12 Feb. 1681; *The Speech of the Hon. Henry Booth Esq. . . . 2 March 1681, at his being elected one of the Knights of the Shire . . .* (1681).
[5] *Cal. S.P. Dom., 1680–1*, p. 176.

Jenkins and the Earl of Conway, who had replaced Coventry and Sunderland respectively as the Secretaries of State, endeavoured, in the spring and summer of 1681, to push to a logical conclusion the policy of removing from the commissions of the peace those men who had shown themselves to be disaffected to the government of the Court. Unfortunately, the process remains obscure; there was no parliamentary inquiry into the methods employed as there had been in 1680. Some light is shed on the Court's tactics by a letter from Jenkins to the Marquess of Worcester, in which he refers to a general review of the English commissions of the peace made before the summer circuit of 1681 by a committee chaired by Finch (who was created Earl of Nottingham in May) and including Halifax, Conway, Laurence Hyde, and Edward Seymour. Nothing, wrote Jenkins, was then done about the Welsh counties because Worcester had not then been present, and he drew Worcester's attention to some suggestions made by a well-affected gentleman from Denbighshire.[1] Presumably a similar operation of local recommendation and consultation had earlier taken place in England.

There is a little evidence to suggest that the regulation was conducted rather hastily and inefficiently in some counties. For example, the Earl of Lindsey was told that the King would take notice of his list of nominations for the parts of Lincolnshire, being satisfied that he would recommend 'none but such as are of ancient, unblemished families and such who for their fortune and capacity will bring no disreputation on his Majesty's commission'.[2] Lindsey responded in August with a list of deputy-lieutenants and justices who had refused to join in a loyal address to the King.[3] He had, however, been forestalled. Commissions for the three parts of Lincolnshire had already been sealed on 8 July, presumably after recommendations from some source other than Lindsey had been received. One of the justices added in 1680, Sir William Ellis, was now put out in 1681.[4] Lindsey complained in 1683 that 'many

[1] *Cal. S.P. Dom., 1680–1*, pp. 476–7. The letter is dated 29 Sept. 1681.
[2] P.R.O., S.P. 44/62, p. 230: Jenkins to 'Lord Chamberlain' [Lindsey], 28 July 1681.
[3] P.R.O., S.P. 29/416, Nos. 107, 107 I: Lindsey to Jenkins, 20 Aug. 1681.
[4] P.R.O., C. 231/8, pp. 31, 51.

disaffected persons are still in power and commission' in Lincolnshire.[1]

The 1681 regulation, though imperfectly organized at any rate in some counties, was nevertheless wide-ranging. Between 8 July and 23 August, new commissions were sealed for every English county except Cambridgeshire, Dorset, and Norfolk.[2] Distinguished Parliamentarians not put out in 1680 now suffered disgrace: Sir Henry Capel in Surrey, for example, and Warwick Bampfield and Edward Strode in Somerset. Others, less well-known, were dismissed with their leaders. John Kelland was put out in Devonshire; so was Samuel Rolle. Sir John Cope, in Oxfordshire, and Sir John Bowyer, in Staffordshire, were among the rank and file Exclusionist M.P.s who lost their places on the bench. A number of the great Whig magnates kept in commission in 1680 now ceased to be magistrates: notably the Earls of Essex, Manchester, Bedford, and Macclesfield, in Hertfordshire, Huntingdonshire, Bedfordshire, and Cheshire respectively.[3] Sir Thomas Mainwaring, restored for Cheshire in February after Booth had defended his reputation in the Commons, was humiliated by a second disgrace in August. The extent of the changes, and the disregard shown for considerations of social standing, almost justify one contemporary description of this purge: 'None were left either on the bench or in the militia, that did not with zeal go into the humour of the court.'[4]

IV

If the Court's intention was to be absolutely comprehensive, it did not succeed. The eleven gentlemen who, according to Lindsey, had not signed the loyal address from Lincolnshire, were still in the various Lincolnshire commissions in 1685.[5] The Northumberland bench was still dominated by men hostile to the 'King's interest', when a furious dispute, similar in character to the quarrel in Westmorland in the 1670s, broke out in 1683 over the management of the sheriff's county court. The justices on the bench split into parties for

---

· [1] *Cal. S.P. Dom., Jan.–June 1683*, p. 367.
[2] P.R.O., C. 231/8, pp. 51–4.   [3] Ibid., pp. 44, 45, 51, 54.
[4] G. Burnet, *History of His Own Time* (Oxford, 1833), ii. 285.
[5] P.R.O., C. 193/12/5, ff. 65–85.

and against the Tory sheriff. The factious men were in a majority of twelve to ten, and they actually succeeded in blackening the reputation of two of the Tory justices so that they were put out of the commission — this at the height of what is often called the 'Tory Reaction'. The loyal party was horrified by the willingness of the opposite party to carry matters in dispute by voting at quarter sessions, and they appealed for a 'speedy regulation' of the bench.[1] The matter was of real importance, since the sheriff had been active in packing juries to secure the conviction of Dissenters. The factious party countered by acquitting persons charged on what the loyal party considered to be clearly proved evidence of sedition.[2] Elsewhere, Whig justices were less active, but there were a handful of men whose past or future careers showed them to be, broadly speaking, Whig in sympathy in many county commissions of the peace at the end of Charles's reign.[3]

Nevertheless, the view that the county benches were controlled by Tory justices by 1685 is substantially correct. The 'Tory Reaction' was not complete in all counties by the autumn of 1681. Further adjustments took place, not by collective regulation, but by removals or additions for single counties on recommendations from local sources or assize judges. For example, nine Hertfordshire justices were supplanted on the bench by five well-affected gentlemen in May 1682; the fiat for this quite severe alteration also contained orders for the omission of one justice each in Surrey and Essex.[4] In 1683, the Bishop of Chichester thought that the factious party in Sussex retained its vigour because Henry Shelley and Robert Palmer were still in the commission of the peace; Shelley certainly, and Palmer probably, were

---

[1] P.R.O., S.P. 29/422, No. 95: eleven Northumberland justices to Jenkins, no date [Feb. 1683?]; No. 107: 'I.B.' [Isaac Basire] to Widdrington, 26 Feb. 1683; No. 129: Basire to Jenkins, 6 Mar. 1683; S.P. 44/66, p. 214: the King to the Northumberland justices, 16 Apr. 1683; S.P. 29/424, No. 146: Widdrington to Jenkins, 6 June 1683.

[2] P.R.O., S.P. 29/424, No. 154: declaration by several Northumberland justices, 8 June 1683.

[3] P.R.O., C. 193/12/5, *passim*; and see *Warwickshire Quarter Sessions Records, 1674-82*, p. xxvii n. 3.

[4] *Cal. S.P. Dom., 1682*, p. 218; P.R.O., C. 234/16, Hertfordshire: 31 May 1682. This is the only surviving fiat for Charles II's reign.

dismissed.[1] Some Exclusionist M.P.s were belatedly put out, like Bussy Mansell for Glamorgan and Arthur Onslow for Surrey, both in 1682.[2]

The Rye House Plot in 1683 does not seem to have had much effect on the composition of the magistracy, perhaps because the plotters were committed Whigs who had already been put out. However, there were occasions when the Court felt obliged to make sweeping changes in individual counties. The Duke of Monmouth's triumphal progress through the North Midlands, ostensibly to a race-meeting, in September 1682 was one such occasion. The Secretaries of State investigated, with scrupulous attention to detail, the names of those who had entertained Monmouth at their homes, formed part of his entourage, or incited the rabble to shout for him.[3] The results of their investigations were changes in the commission for Cheshire. One of those dismissed was Henry Booth; the Court seized the opportunity to deprive him of his local power for the second time. Seven reliable Court party supporters were added to take the places of the disgraced followers of Monmouth.[4]

The Cheshire commission for removing Booth as *custos* was dated 14 December 1682. Nottingham died four days later. Sir Francis North, the Lord Chief Justice of the Common Pleas, received the great seal as Lord Keeper on 20 December. He was raised to the peerage as Lord Guilford in 1683. Guilford's political views were similar to those of Nottingham, although he never enjoyed the same reputation as a lawyer or the same influence with other ministers.[5]

Perhaps surprisingly, there is little evidence of any willingness on the part of either Nottingham, or, towards the end of Charles's reign, Guilford, to conciliate by restoration gentlemen who were anxious to recover their lost local influence by repudiating their past. Thomas Herbert regained his place in the Monmouthshire commission in November 1683, but he had been dismissed in 1679, not for political disaffection, but

[1] Cal. S.P. Dom., July–Sept. 1683, p. 380; P.R.O., C. 231/8, p. 106.
[2] Cal. S.P. Dom., 1682, p. 548; P.R.O., C. 231/8, p. 62.
[3] P.R.O., S.P. 29/420, passim.
[4] Cal. S.P. Dom., 1682, p. 441; P.R.O., C. 231/8, pp. 74, 75.
[5] Holdsworth, History of English Law, vi. 531, 534–5.

for obstructing bail granted by an assize judge.[1] Sir Richard Brooke was reappointed to the Cheshire lieutenancy after confessing that he had erred in voting for Henry Booth in the 1681 county election, but he does not seem to have been put back in the Cheshire commission of the peace.[2] The only really clear-cut example of restoration was in Holland in Lincolnshire, where Daniel Rhodes and Walter Johnson were put back in September 1681 after disgrace by the Privy Council in April 1680.[3] As a general rule, however, the Whigs were kept out of the magistracy once they had been dismissed.

V

The commission of the peace emerged during the Exclusion Crisis as a weapon in politics controlled by the Court. Nottingham and Guilford exercised a considerable degree of influence in making suggestions and vetoing unsatisfactory nominations.[4] The tardy issue of commissions after the attempted Whig regulation in May 1679, and the speed with which the Crown Office translated the regulation of the Secretaries of State into omissions and inclusions in the countryside in February and March 1680, illustrate the practical power of the great seal. In the last resort, however, the King himself supervised changes that were serious departures from routine. He intervened in person in Norfolk in July 1679. Francis Gwyn, a Clerk of the Council, wrote that the King attended all the meetings of the Council committee of regulation in February 1680, and again that 'the King intends to take a new review of the commissions' in April of the same year.[5] Secretary Jenkins generally began his letters to the Chancellor with the phrase 'His Majesty has commanded me to signify his pleasure' that names be added to or subtracted from the commissions of the peace.[6] Control of the commission, then, never passed out of the hands of the Court.

[1] P.R.O., P.C. 2/68, pp. 224, 271; C. 231/8, p. 15; *Cal. S.P. Dom., 1683–4*, p.101.

[2] *Cal. S.P. Dom., July–Sept. 1683*, pp. 289, 350; P.R.O., C. 193/12/4, f. 13; C. 193/12/5, ff. 14–16.

[3] P.R.O., P.C. 2/68, p. 483; C. 231/8, p. 55.

[4] For Guilford, see North, *Lives of the Norths*, i. 240–1; and also *Cal. S.P. Dom., 1682*, p. 145.

[5] H.M.C., *Ormonde MSS.*, N.S. v. 270, 301–2, 306.

[6] P.R.O., S.P. 44/62, several letters.

The same was true of two other areas of local government which were regulated during the Exclusion Crisis and the Tory Reaction of 1681–5: the militia and the corporations.[1]

This vigorous manipulation of local government by the Court had serious disadvantages. The regulation of the commission of the peace left the ministers vulnerable to attack in Parliament. If the opposition politicians could represent to the gentry that zealous anti-Catholics and honest squires had been disgraced through sinister and obscure influence, then they had a formidable weapon. The commission of the peace was a matter close to the hearts of the country gentlemen in Parliament; it was a 'great affliction' to a justice to be dismissed.[2] The traditional view that all gentlemen of substance should be appointed whatever their opinions was still strong. In some parts of the country the omission of active justices led to administrative inconvenience. For instance, the clerk of the peace for Holland wrote to the *custos* that the county was greatly embarrassed by the lack of active justices, and that no sessions had been held at Spalding for six months. He added that the replacements for the active justices who had been left out were inadequate, since 'either conscious of their own imbecility, or out of a wilful humour', they refused to act or even to be sworn.[3] This was probably the reason for the untypical restoration of Rhodes and Johnson in that part of Lincolnshire.[4]

Another target for Parliamentary attack was the allegedly low social status of those put in commission by the Court. Sir William Jones's attack on clergymen and 'persons of mean quality' was echoed elsewhere.[5] The House of Lords committee

[1] For the militia, see J. R. Western, *The English Militia in the Eighteenth Century* (London, 1965), pp. 81–2. The independence of the lords-lieutenant in choosing militia officers was curtailed by a Council order that disgraced justices of the peace should also lose their commands in the militia. P.R.O., P.C. 2/69, p. 295: 2 June 1681. For the corporations, see J. Levin, *The Charter Controversy in the City of London, 1660–1688, and its Consequences* (University of London Legal Series, ix, 1969), pp. 82–9.

[2] *Letters of Humphrey Prideaux*, ed. E. M. Thompson (Camden Soc., N.S. xv, 1875), 89.

[3] P.R.O., S.P. 29/415, No. 15: Nathaniel Smyth to Earl of Lindsey, 22 Jan. 1681.

[4] See above, p. 57.

[5] See, for instance, Narcissus Luttrell, *A Brief Historical Relation of State Affairs from September 1678 to April 1714* (Oxford, 1857), i. 37.

discovered several of small estate or ill repute, some younger brothers or sons living at home who would be 'justices in the house of their fathers', and other varieties of unfit person: a brewer in Cambridgeshire, for instance, and a prisoner in the King's Bench in Leicestershire.[1] In counties where large additions were made, the new justices were often men without a family tradition of justice-ship.[2] It is hard to tell how many clergymen were put in. They were the natural choices of the party of Church and prerogative, but even in Oxfordshire only two justices held the degree of doctor between May 1680 and July 1683.[3] By 1685 they had been joined by two more, but these additions took place after Jones's criticisms.[4] One of the three clergymen in the Norfolk commission, Dr Hylyard, was represented even by the loyal party to be troublesome. 'Exceedingly ambitious', he made disturbances everywhere by his 'pragmaticalness and unskilfulness in the laws'.[5] Hylyard, however, had already been in commission in 1676; his inclusion was not the result of the Court's policy in 1680. In spite of his unpopularity, he survived a massive purge of the Norfolk bench in March 1682 when no less than fourteen justices were put out.[6] The old Cavalier gentry would not necessarily disapprove of clergymen in commission on social grounds, but other cases of Royalist doubts about the credentials of new justices occur during the years after the dissolution of the Oxford Parliament. Jenkins received a letter in the spring of 1683 describing a campaign by the justices of an unspecified county or liberty against a Mr Duck, who was allegedly of inferior birth, or 'an upstart in point of fortune'. Jenkins had to explain that, if other counties followed their example, 'the greater men would jostle out the lesser', to the disquiet of the county and the prejudice of the King's service.[7] These examples suggest that

[1] Most of the committee's comments are printed in H.M.C., Eleventh Report, Appendix II, *House of Lords MSS., 1678-88*, pp. 172-93.

[2] This was especially true in Essex, Hampshire, and Wiltshire.

[3] P.R.O., C. 193/12/4, ff. 94-5. One was a doctor of medicine.

[4] P.R.O., C. 193/12/5, ff. 113-14.

[5] P.R.O., S.P. 29/418, No. 67: account of affairs in Norfolk, 2 Feb. 1682; *Letters of Humphrey Prideaux*, pp. 123-4.

[6] H.M.C., Sixth Report, Appendix, *Ingilby MSS.*, p. 382; P.R.O., C. 231/8, p. 63.

[7] *Cal. S.P. Dom., Jan.-June 1683*, p. 164.

it is possible that well-affected men in the counties may have felt that their loyalty was beginning to be somewhat devalued by the Court's policy.

Perhaps more serious than the doubts of the squires were the complaints of the grandees. The Commons, after all, had no constitutional grounds for their attack on the Chancellor; commissions of the peace were letters patent and the names inserted therein were a matter for the King. The House of Lords was concerned for a different reason. Lords-lieutenant, *custodes*, and other magnates enjoyed constitutionally unrecognized but conventional surveillance over the magistracy. They may well have been disconcerted by the changes made by the Secretaries of State and the Privy Council in 1680 and 1681, even if they agreed with these changes in principle. A typical example was Viscount Fitzhardinge's complaint, as *custos* of Somerset, that one John Harington had been put off the Somerset bench in the summer of 1683 for having the same name as one of Shaftesbury's supporters.[1] This happened not to be true,[2] but the episode illustrated how even a loyal Courtier like Fitzhardinge could convince himself that Whitehall was capable of the most ignorant mistakes when it began to tamper with county affairs.

There were thus serious disadvantages for the government arising from the manipulation of the commission of the peace for political purposes during the Exclusion Crisis. These disadvantages were balanced by advantages. Open expressions of discontent were firmly opposed by legally constituted authority. A loyal bench meant a campaign against nonconforming Protestants of questionable political allegiance, rather than against Catholics, of whose allegiance to the Stuart monarchy there was no doubt.[3] The propaganda weapon of the charge to the grand jury was in reliable hands. Henry Booth scandalized the loyal gentlemen of Cheshire at Michaelmas sessions in 1682 by a charge defending Monmouth's claim to the succession. After he was dismissed, the

---

[1] *Cal. S.P. Dom., July–Sept. 1683*, pp. 238–9, 272.

[2] Som. R.O., Q/JC 92: commission of the peace, 20 July 1683, in which Harington's name appears.

[3] Several letters to Archbishop Sancroft from the Bishops of Norwich, Exeter, Bristol, and Peterborough illustrate this. Bodl. MS. Tanner 37, f. 114; MS. Tanner 36, ff. 11, 214, 218; MS. Tanner 35, ff. 67, 107.

charge could only have been delivered by men of impeccable loyalty.[1]

Most important, the Court demonstrated, by its handling of the commissions of the peace, that it was not going to abandon its supporters, and in so doing it gave the commission a significant role in the formation of the embryo Whig and Tory parties. Family rivalries, differing views on religion, the distinction between politicians and stay-at-homes, and the careers of family representatives in the Civil War, had all tended to split county communities after the Restoration. During the Exclusion Crisis, these inchoate divisions crystallized. The poles of party conflict were Loyalty and Faction. Faction, in the eyes of the loyal or Tory party, meant intemperate hostility towards recusants and a leaning to Dissent. It also meant unconstitutional pressure on the royal government reminiscent of 1641. It expressed itself in opposition to the Duke of York, and it led to turbulence in county affairs. Factious men should not be kept in commission; they were not sound or reliable servants of the King. A correspondent of Jenkins summed up the attitude of the Tories immediately after the dissolution of the Oxford Parliament: 'Many of the best subjects hope there will be great care throughout the nation for good justices of the peace and for the militia and indeed that none but persons of known integrity be preferred to any office in the King's dispose and that those who behave themselves best be advanced as opportunity serves and not a sort of men for affronting the Crown as has too often been done. . . .'[2] This was not sycophancy, but the expression of a widespread opinion. It is arguable that the Tory party had been, if not created, at least knit together, by the Court itself through the medium of the commission of the peace. The Duke of York wrote to William of Orange that '. . . The judges and all that are come to towne do say they find . . . the greatest alteration for the better that can be imagined, and what his Ma[jesty] has done in purging the commissions of the peace of all disaffected people to him has contributed very much to it by encouraging her [sic] old

[1] P.R.O., S.P. 29/420, ff. 307–8, 311, 313: three letters to Jenkins, all dated 7 Oct. 1682.
[2] P.R.O., S.P. 29/415, No. 121: Thomas Langham to Jenkins, 11 Apr. 1681.

freinds, the Cavalere or Church party. . . .'[1] Lord Chief Justice
Jeffreys observed after the Western Circuit in March 1684
that the Cornish gentry were reassured in their loyalty on
learning that the King proposed to be loyal to them.[2] The
Tory Reaction was possible because of this loyalty in the
counties; loyalty in the counties was stimulated by the Tory
Reaction.[3] At the end of Charles's reign, the party committed
to the support of Church and King was firmly in control of
county government.

---

[1] *Archives de la Maison d'Orange-Nassau*, 2nd Ser., ed. G. Groen van Prinsterer
(Leyden, 1857-62), v. 393.
[2] *Cal. S.P. Dom., 1683-4*, p. 328.
[3] Plumb, *The Growth of Political Stability in England*, pp. 54-7.

THE COMMISSION OF THE PEACE IN
THE REIGN OF JAMES II

I

Charles II died on 6 February 1685. James announced almost immediately the summoning of Parliament, and the first six weeks of his reign were marked by intense activity in the constituencies, where the Court was endeavouring to secure the return of loyal members.[1] At the same time, the demise of the Crown made it necessary to seal new commissions of the peace. By the end of March this had been done for every English county. Some of the Welsh counties had to wait until April, and Flintshire did not receive its new commission until June.[2] Even so, there was an opportunity to review nearly all the lists of county justices, immediately before and during an election in which the Court was making unprecedented efforts to 'pack' the Commons.

The evidence that the Court made use of this opportunity is rather slight. Certainly, changes were made for political reasons in a very few counties. Guilford possessed local influence in Suffolk, and it is probably more than a coincidence that Suffolk received as many as three commissions while the election was still in progress; Guilford seems to have contented himself with adding the names of supporters.[3] In Northamptonshire, too, three commissions were sealed during the election period. In one of these a justice was left out. This was Edward Harby, who had set up as the 'factious' candidate in the county election in opposition to Sir Roger Norwich and Sir John Egerton, the candidates of the loyal gentlemen.[4] These counties seem to have been exceptional, however, and there is reason to believe that relatively few of the commissions

---

[1] C. J. Fox, *History of the Early Part of the Reign of James II* (London, 1808), Appendix, pp. xviii, xliv.

[2] P.R.O., C. 231/8, pp. 116 ff.   [3] Ibid., pp. 117, 125-6.

[4] Ibid., pp. 119, 125, 126; *Cal. S.P. Dom., 1685*, p. 115.

of the peace sealed at this time were designed to influence the elections. The entries describing the first commissions of the reign in the docquet book mention the reappointment of *custodes rotulorum*, but do not in many cases refer to any other changes. It is a plausible supposition that the last commission of Charles's reign was simply renewed, or at most that the routine additions, pending immediately before Charles's death, were incorporated without any more drastic alterations. After the remodelling that had followed the dissolution of the Oxford Parliament, further regulation would in many counties have been superfluous, if not actually counter-productive. The principal manager of the 1685 election was Sunderland, reappointed as one of the Secretaries of State in 1683. He worked by advising lords-lieutenant and other prominent Court supporters in the constituencies to promote the interest of candidates of approved loyalty, and by assisting Court candidates and their supporters in their tactical manœuvres.[1] There are, however, no examples in Sunderland's surviving correspondence of orders to Guilford to add or omit county justices. Guilford's relations with Sunderland, who was the patron of his rival Jeffreys, were bad,[2] and it is unlikely that such instructions were transmitted verbally.

These inferences are not conclusive, but they can be supported by further evidence. The commission of the peace was not remodelled for electoral purposes even in those counties where some moderate Whigs survived on the bench. An obvious case where manipulation might have been desirable was Buckinghamshire, where the elections for the county and for several of the boroughs were vigorously fought by a strong Whig opposition.[3] The extreme Whig candidates, like Thomas Wharton, Richard Hampden, and Richard Ingoldsby, had long been omitted from the commission of the peace, but the less violent Whigs, such as Sir Thomas Lee, Sir

[1] R. H. George, 'Parliamentary Elections and Electioneering in 1685', *Trans. Roy. Hist. Soc.*, 4th Ser. xix (1936), 168–73; Kenyon, *Sunderland*, pp. 113, 114.
[2] North, *Lives of the Norths*, ii. 127; G. W. Keeton, *Lord Chancellor Jeffreys and the Stuart Cause* (London, 1965), pp. 244–5.
[3] R. H. George, op. cit., pp. 186–94; Frances P. and Margaret M. Verney, *Memoirs of the Verney Family during the Civil War and from the Restoration to the Revolution* (London, 1892–9), iv. 321–48.

Richard Temple, and Sir Ralph Verney, and their supporters Sir Peter Tyrrell, Sir Francis Leigh, and Alexander Denton, were still justices of the peace at the start of James's reign.[1] Lee was defeated at Aylesbury, but Temple and Verney were successful at Buckingham as were Wharton for the county and Hampden, apparently, at Wendover. Jeffreys, whose interest had been thrown into the elections in his dual capacity of Buckinghamshire landowner and Lord Chief Justice, was furious at Wharton's success, and threatened to inform Guilford of Verney's activities on Wharton's behalf.[2] Notwithstanding this hint that he would be dismissed from the commission of the peace, Verney remained on the county bench both during and after the election, as did the other moderate Whigs.[3]

Another county where a regulation of the bench would have been valuable, and was, indeed, recommended, was Hampshire. Sunderland received a note that Dr Harrison and two other unspecified names should be left out of the Hampshire commission for abusing Court supporters at Winchester, but this was too late to take effect in the commission sealed on 26 February, the next Hampshire commission was delayed until May, and in any case Harrison was still in commission in October.[4]

Thus it is by no means clear that the election of 1685 was the occasion for a remodelling of the magistracy in more than a very few counties. Equally, there is almost no evidence that the rebellion of the Duke of Monmouth in the West of England in the summer of 1685 had any effect on the commissions of the peace. Monmouth had stayed at the houses of several of the West Country Whigs in late 1680, and all of these had then been dismissed from the bench. In 1685 only a handful of gentry of the justice class joined in the rebellion.

[1] P.R.O., Assizes 16/49/1: Buckinghamshire *nomina ministrorum*, Lent 1685.
[2] *Memoirs of the Verney Family*, iv. 338.
[3] It should be added, however, that the commission of the peace for the borough of Buckingham, which like that for the county was issued under the great seal, was altered substantially during the election, probably through Jeffreys's influence. Two commissions were sealed in eight days, on 16 and 24 April 1685, and a Whig alderman, George Dancer, was left out in a third commission dated 12 May, three days before the election. P.R.O., C. 231/8, pp. 126, 127, 128; *Memoirs of the Verney Family*, iv. 343-5.
[4] *Cal. S.P. Dom., 1685*, pp. 96-7; P.R.O., C. 231/8, pp. 119, 128; C. 193/12/5.

Of these, Lord Grey of Warke had been put out for Northumberland in 1680, and the Somerset commission had been
purged of John Speke, William Strode of Barrington and his
brother Edward of Downside, and Warwick Bampfield in
1680 and 1681.[1] There is no evidence that any of the other
figures prominent during the rebellion, such as Edmund
Prideaux, Thomas Dore of Lymington, or Nathaniel Wade of
Bristol, were in any county commissions of the peace in
1685; 'for the Honour of the Gentry of England', wrote one
observer, 'I doe not hear of one Gentleman amongst them
but such Tagg Ragg Rogues scarce worth a hanging.'[2] Thirty-
five commissions of the peace were sealed in May, June, and
July 1685, but there is nothing to suggest that these were not
routine commissions in preparation for the summer assizes.
Twelve more counties, among them Devonshire, Dorset,
Hampshire, Somerset, and Wiltshire, received new commissions in August. The purpose of the new commissions for
these West Country counties was probably to include Jeffreys
and his colleagues, who were about to set out on the 'Bloody
Assizes', rather than to make substantial alterations in the
local names.[3]

II

It is surprising that as many as forty-seven commissions were
sealed between May and August, since Guilford was taken ill
before Parliament rose on 2 July and retired to his house at
Wroxton, in Oxfordshire, apparently taking the great seal and
the administrative staff of Chancery with him.[4] He died there
on 5 September, and the great seal was brought back to London, where the King retained it until 28 September, when

[1] H.L.R.O., Main Papers, H.L., 9 Nov. 1680; P.R.O., C. 231/8, pp. 25, 53. For
the gentry supporters of Monmouth, see B. Little, *The Monmouth Episode* (London, 1956), especially pp. 47–58. Another William Strode remained a Dorset
deputy-lieutenant and justice during and after the rebellion.

[2] Som. R.O., Sanford MSS. DD/SF 3109: William to Edward Clarke, 29 July
1685.

[3] P.R.O., C. 231/8, pp. 127 ff; Som. R.O., Q/JC 94–6: commissions of the
peace, 12 Feb., 14 May, 14 Aug. 1685; Devon R.O., Q/JC: commission of the
peace, 23 May 1685, compared with P.R.O., C. 193/12/5. Monmouth had landed
on 11 June, and was executed on 15 July. The assizes began at Winchester on
24 August.

[4] North, *Lives of the Norths*, ii. 134–5, 144.

Jeffreys returned from the West Country.[1] Although Halifax and Sir Robert Sawyer seem to have been mentioned as possible candidates,[2] Jeffreys was the natural successor, and he received the seal with the full title — denied to Guilford — of Lord Chancellor.

'Judge' Jeffreys was portrayed as a brutal, ignorant drunkard after his death in 1689, and Campbell and Macaulay perhaps followed hostile authorities too uncritically in their estimates of his career.[3] One reassessment argues that Jeffreys was generous, warm-hearted, and witty; an exceptionally handsome man of cultured conversation, a charming and accomplished host, and a judge conspicuously fair in political trials, though regrettably prone to a weakness for bullying witnesses.[4] The case that Jeffreys has been underestimated as a lawyer is perhaps more plausible. His promotion after being called to the bar at the age of 24 was remarkably rapid. He was Recorder of London at 34, Chief Justice of Chester at 36, and Lord Chief Justice of the King's Bench at 39. His rise was the reward of industry and competence and he seems to have been an able judge in the courts in which he presided.[5] His role in politics was straightforward. Like most contemporary lawyers, he took the view that judges were agents of the royal administration. He had been active in the Court interest in London politics during the Exclusion Crisis, and he played a leading part in the surrender of several municipal charters between 1683 and 1685. In James's reign, his respect for the prerogative and his loyalty to his patron Sunderland overrode his otherwise unshakeable Anglicanism.[6] In spite of his estates in Shropshire, Leicestershire, and Buckinghamshire,

[1] During this interregnum, the King himself supervised the sealing of two commissions of the peace, for Warwickshire and Leicestershire. Both were dated 3 September, so the fiats had presumably been signed by the dying Lord Keeper. P.R.O., C. 231/8, p. 135.

[2] Bodl. MS. Rawl. Letters 48, f. 41: Sir Edmund Warcup to Hugh Jones, 14 Sept. 1685.

[3] Campbell, *Lives of the Chancellors*, iii. 495, 580–95; Lord Macaulay, *History of England* (ed. C. H. Firth, London, 1913–15), i. 444–9.

[4] Keeton, *Lord Chancellor Jeffreys and the Stuart Cause*, pp. 469–70, 496–8.

[5] Lord Birkenhead, *Fourteen English Judges* (London, 1926), pp. 71–4, 83–98; H. Montgomery Hyde, *Judge Jeffreys* (London, 1940), pp. 153, 253–61; Keeton, op. cit., pp. 218–29, 377–95.

[6] H.M.C., *Ormonde MSS.*, N.S. vi. 441; Levin, *The Charter Controversy in the City of London, 1660–1688*, pp. 55, 82, 90; Kenyon, *Sunderland*, pp. 89, 124.

he was always a London lawyer rather than a country gentleman. He never sat in the House of Commons. He did, however, attend quarter sessions in Middlesex and Surrey; indeed,
he gave the charge at Middlesex sessions in Michaelmas 1684
when Lord Chief Justice.[1] A final point of some relevance to
Jeffreys's career as Chancellor is that he was periodically
handicapped by illness, especially by crippling attacks of the
stone.

During Jeffreys's first twelve months of office, that is
until October 1686, he neglected most of the county commissions of the peace. Naturally, he ordered a *liber pacis*
from the Crown Office; this survives.[2] Although he corrected
the names of Privy Councillors and assize judges as late as the
summer of 1686, he left the local names mostly untouched.[3]
This does not mean that no changes were made at all in the
local names until after the summer assizes in 1686; only that
Jeffreys kept his *liber pacis* up to date in a somewhat cursory
fashion. In fact, there was a substantial alteration in the commission of the peace for at least two counties: Middlesex,
which received six commissions in seven months between
November 1685 and May 1686, and Surrey, which received
three commissions in February, March, and April 1686.[4] The
details of the changes are obscure, but Jeffreys was probably
employing his own local knowledge in a regulation of the
county benches close to London, on which he had himself
sat. Rather strangely, however, he neglected Buckinghamshire
until July 1686, and there is little evidence of changes that
were more than routine in most of the commissions which he
sealed for the English and Welsh counties in his first year of
office. Only two entries in the docquet book in the whole of
1686 record the omission of a justice from a county commission.[5] Most of the commissions probably added local
gentlemen in ones and twos. One reason for this rather slow

[1] Keeton, op. cit., pp. 124, 187.
[2] P.R.O., C. 231/8, p. 136; C. 193/12/5.
[3] In Jeffreys's list for Warwickshire, the two assize judges put in on 6 July
1686 are inserted, but a local name, Robert Feilding, put in on 17 November
1685, is not. P.R.O., C. 231/8, pp. 139, 158.
[4] P.R.O., C. 231/8, pp. 139 ff.
[5] Thomas Earsby for Middlesex in May and John Willoughby for Northamptonshire in June. P.R.O., C. 231/8, pp. 153, 154.

start to the manipulation of his local patronage is that in February 1686, and again in July, Jeffreys was suffering severely from the stone, on the first occasion apparently as the result of spectacular debauchery.[1]

This seeming indifference to the commission of the peace was exceptional. In other areas of patronage, James's government was in 1686 beginning to favour Catholics in the distribution of place and office. In November 1685, the King informed Parliament that in view of the utility of some army officers who were Catholics he proposed to retain them in his service.[2] Four judges were dismissed in the following April to prepare for the collusive judgement in the case of Godden versus Hales, which would enable office-holding Catholics to plead, if prosecuted, the King's power of dispensing with the Test Act which required all office-holders to receive the Anglican sacrament. One of the replacements, Sir Christopher Milton, was himself a Catholic.[3] The judgement in Godden versus Hales in June was followed in July by the admission of four Catholic peers to the Privy Council, and by the establishment in August of a Commission for Ecclesiastical Affairs. At Oxford University, two Catholics became heads of houses. The King's policy of bringing Catholics into office in both church and state was thus under way by the autumn of 1686.[4] In Ireland, moreover, Catholics and Dissenters were added to the commissions of the peace in the summer and autumn of 1686, in spite of the misgivings of the Lord-Lieutenant, the Earl of Clarendon.[5]

There is only very slight evidence that, as yet, avowed Catholics were being admitted to the active county magistracy in England and Wales. This judgement is based on a comparison of the notices of new justices in the docquet book, with a list of Catholics residing in the several counties drawn up

[1] *Memoirs of Sir John Reresby*, p. 411; Luttrell, *Brief Relation*, i. 371; *Cal. S.P. Dom.*, *1686–7*, p. 204.

[2] *C.J.* ix. 756; Fox, *Early Part of the Reign of James II*, Appendix, pp. cxxxiii–cxxxv, cxl.

[3] Milton became one of the Barons of the Exchequer. Foss, *Judges of England*, vii. 255–8.

[4] Feiling, *History of the Tory Party, 1640–1714*, pp. 212–15; D. Ogg, *England in the Reigns of James II and William III* (Oxford, 1955), pp. 167–8.

[5] H.M.C., *Ormonde MSS.*, N.S. vii. 428, 456, 460; viii. 347; *Cal. S.P. Dom.*, *1686–7*, p. 182; J. G. Simms, *Jacobite Ireland, 1685–91* (London, 1969), p. 27.

five years before for the House of Commons.[1] The only trace
of a Catholic appointment before the winter of 1686/7 is in
Derbyshire, where the recusant Sir Henry Hunlock is alleged
to have sat on the bench at Michaelmas sessions in 1686. If
this was so, he can only have been appointed in the Derbyshire commission sealed in June. Otherwise, the changes
ordered in the summer and autumn of 1686 seem to have
been unremarkable.[2] However, Sunderland's close contact
with the Catholic advisers of the King, his drift to conversion
in the autumn of 1686, and his struggle for ascendancy over
Lord Treasurer Rochester, the remaining Protestant minister
opposed to the King's policy, meant that a review of the
English and Welsh magistracy by the Secretary and his ally
the Chancellor could not be long delayed.[3]

Such a review was conducted by a committee of the Privy
Council appointed on 22 October 1686. This was headed by
Jeffreys and Sunderland and contained, among others, the
Protestant peers Craven, Dartmouth, and (surprisingly)
Rochester, the Catholics Powis and Arundell of Wardour, and
the crypto-Catholic Peterborough.[4] There is very little evidence to illustrate the committee's methods of working.
Presumably its members employed their own local knowledge
in conjunction with recommendations from senior Catholic
gentry and Catholic sympathizers in the counties. This seems
to have been the procedure in Northamptonshire, where
Peterborough recommended names and obstructed the suggestions of the *custos*, Viscount Hatton. Elsewhere, the lords-
lieutenant and *custodes* were apparently bypassed.[5] The
committee had been briefed to report to the King in Council
such alterations in the commissions as were requisite for his
service, and it is quite possible that the King himself supervised at any rate the final stages of the work.

---

[1] H.L.R.O., Main Papers, H.L., 3 Dec. 1680, ff. 15-131.
[2] Cox, *Three Centuries of Derbyshire Annals*, i. 307; P.R.O., C. 231/8,
pp. 159 ff.
[3] Kenyon, *Sunderland*, pp. 128, 137-9.
[4] P.R.O., P.C. 2/71, pp. 325, 332; and C. 231/8, p. 162, for the issue of a *liber
pacis* for the use of the King and the Privy Council.
[5] B.L., Add. MSS. 29594, ff. 6, 9: Nottingham to [Hatton], 19 Nov., 9 Dec.
1686; J. P. Kenyon, *The Nobility in the Revolution of 1688* (Hull, 1963), p. 8;
Miller, *Popery and Politics in England, 1660-1688*, p. 209.

There was an inexplicable delay in implementing the recommendations of this committee. Its proceedings were the subject of gossip in November and December, the lists of changes were entered in the Council register after the record of a meeting on 17 December, and accurate reports about the proposed changes were circulating in the counties before the end of the year.[1] Sunderland wrote to Jeffreys that the new justices should be included in the commissions before the next sessions, and that they should be advised of their inclusion so that they might attend.[2] Only in Middlesex, however, did this prove possible. The commission for that county was entered in the docquet book on 3 January 1687 and the new Middlesex justices attended Hilary quarter sessions.[3] The other commissions were delayed. Jeffreys's fiat for Northamptonshire survives, and this too is dated 3 January, but the docquet book entry is dated 23 February.[4] Sunderland's intention that the new justices should be active as soon as possible was thus frustrated. Reresby, who had received exact information about the extent of the Council's changes in the West Riding, noted that quarter sessions passed off at Doncaster without any unusual alterations in the commission.[5] It was not until February and March 1687 that the Crown Office set to work in earnest; in these two months a new commission of the peace was sealed for all but four of the English counties. The commissions for the Welsh counties were sealed in August 1687.[6]

While there is no reason to suppose that the Council's regulation, as recorded in its register, was not implemented in the commissions of the peace sent to the counties in February and March, there are some minor problems involved in

[1] *Cal. S.P. Dom., 1686–7*, p. 307; *Ellis Correspondence*, ed. G. A. Ellis (London, 1829), i. 197; P.R.O., P.C. 2/71, pp. 363–79; *Autobiography of Sir John Bramston*, ed. Lord Braybrooke (Camden Soc., 1st Ser. xxxii, 1845), 251; *Memoirs of the Verney Family*, iv. 425, where the marginal date '15 Dec. 1687' should almost certainly be '1686'.

[2] *Cal. S.P. Dom., 1686–7*, p. 325.

[3] P.R.O., C. 231/8, p. 165; Luttrell, *Brief Relation*, i. 390, 391–2.

[4] P.R.O., C. 234/27, Northamptonshire; C. 231/8, p. 167.

[5] *Memoirs of Sir John Reresby*, pp. 440–1.

[6] P.R.O., C. 231/8, pp. 166 ff. The four English exceptions were Cheshire where the new commission was delayed until August, Ely, Peterborough, and Westmorland.

regarding the changes authorized by the Privy Council as an exact reflection of the changes actually made. In the first place, the few names recorded unsystematically in the docquet book do not always correspond to the names in the Council's list.[1] In the second place, some of the names that the Council ordered to be included were already in.[2] In the third place, some justices were left out whose exclusion had not been ordered by the Council.[3] However, these anomalies are not of great significance. In those counties for which confirmatory evidence is available, the changes ordered by the Council were actually carried out, while the alterations which had not been so ordered were not of a kind greatly to affect the character of the regulation.

It is apparent that the primary purpose of the Council's regulation was to add Roman Catholic gentlemen to the commissions of the peace. The four Catholic Privy Councillors were to be included over the whole country.[4] A total of 498 local inclusions was ordered for the counties supervised by Jeffreys.[5] A recent estimate by Dr John Miller suggests that about 64 per cent of the new names were Catholics.[6] Of the 498 inclusions, 134 were peers, baronets, or knights. Many of the remaining names were those of heads of armigerous families entitled to the designation 'esquire'. Thus the King was giving to the Catholic aristocracy and gentry the position in

[1] Daniel White and Samuel Tomlyn were put in for Kent, George Evans for Surrey, William Fynmore for Berkshire, and William Clarke for Somerset, but these inclusions do not appear to have been ordered by the Council.

[2] The Council ordered that '— Wood' be put in for Devonshire, but Thomas Wood had been a justice at least since 1685, and he remained the only Wood in the commission. Devon R.O., Q/JC: commissions of the peace, 18 Feb. 1685, 2 Mar. 1687.

[3] Two of the Middlesex justices described as disgraced by Luttrell do not appear in the Council list. In Somerset five local names were omitted, along with seven ordered to be dismissed by the Council. Som. R.O., Q/JC 97: commission of the peace, 22 Feb. 1687.

[4] P.R.O., P.C. 2/71, p. 379.

[5] This figure excludes thirteen Commissioners of the Navy who were to be added to the commissions of the peace for seven counties in the South-East, and also twelve new names for Lancashire. The total number of gentlemen who became justices was rather less than 498, as some were added for more than one county.

[6] *Popery and Politics in England, 1660–1688*, Appendix 3, pp. 269–72. Dr Miller's figures differ slightly (and unimportantly) from mine, since he does not count some of the local peers added by the Council, he includes Lancashire, and he treats Lincolnshire as one county rather than three.

local government to which their social status entitled them, and which they had not enjoyed, as a class, since the reign of Queen Mary. Some were put in commission in all the counties in which they had estates. Lord Clifford, for instance, was added in Devonshire, Middlesex, and Warwickshire, Lord Herbert of Montgomery in Middlesex, Northamptonshire, and Montgomeryshire, and the wealthy Catholic baronets Sir Walter Blount in Devonshire, Herefordshire, Shropshire, and Worcestershire, Sir Thomas Haggerston in Durham, Northumberland, and Middlesex, and Sir John Webb in Dorset and Wiltshire. In such cases, the Catholic magnates were presumably not expected to be ubiquitously active. A place in the commission was a courtesy to which they were entitled by rank. Other Catholic squires, put in only for the county in which they resided, were clearly expected to act.

While the majority of the names were those of Catholics, there were exceptions. The Middlesex commission, which contained forty-one new names, was stocked with officers in the regular army. Nine colonels and two majors were among the names to be added, and the Protestant generals, the Earl of Feversham and John Churchill, were to be included too.[1] Also, some persons not identifiable as Catholic gentry were put in for a number of counties; this was especially true in Bedfordshire, Hampshire, Merionethshire, Staffordshire, Sussex, and Surrey.[2] However, the Catholic character of the changes ordered by the Council was clear enough. The regulation was a logical and predictable extension of the Court's policy of Catholicizing the administration at both the central and the local level. Indeed, only one feature of the Council regulation, in so far as it involved a policy of adding names, can have aroused much surprise, and that was that the opportunity was not taken to include more Catholics. Several Catholic gentry of high status were not included in the commissions of the peace. The inclusion of Sir Philip Hungate, Sir Thomas Gascoign, John Middleton, and other noted Yorkshire Catholics in the West Riding commission was reasonable, but it is odd that Thomas Tempest of Broughton, of an old and famous Catholic family, should not be put in when John

[1] P.R.O., P.C. 2/71, pp. 369–70; Luttrell, *Brief Relation*, i. 388.
[2] Miller, *Popery and Politics in England, 1660–1688*, pp. 270–2.

Ryder, who was described in 1680 as 'gentleman' rather than 'esquire', became a justice. Equally, it is odd that Richard Crofts, possessed of £50 a year in Monmouth in 1680, should be included for that county when Francis Hall, with £400, Thomas Jones, with £700, and several others with £100, should be ignored.[1]

The Council regulation was also a purge. The number of justices put out amounted to less than half of the number of justices put in: 245 as against 498. Even so, a living justice was put out in all but six of the new commissions.[2] Again, the justices put out were often of high social status. Among them were two peers: Viscount Swords in Leicestershire and Lord Willoughby in Holland, Kesteven, and Lindsey. No fewer than sixty-six individual knights and baronets were left out of the commission of the peace. The Council was especially severe on Buckinghamshire, where four of the five justices disgraced were baronets or knights. One, Sir Ralph Verney, was M.P. for Buckingham; another, Sir Peter Tyrrell, had been a Whig M.P. in the Exclusion Parliaments. The Whig candidate for Aylesbury in the 1685 election, Sir Thomas Lee, was also dismissed. Arguably, Buckinghamshire was unusual in that a purge of the county's 'men of faction' was long overdue, but similar alterations took place elsewhere. In Essex, every one of the six justices dismissed was either a knight or a baronet. In Devonshire, ten justices were put out; three were sitting M.P.s,[3] Richard Hillersden had voted for Exclusion in 1679, and a fifth was Sir Henry Fane, Knight of the Bath. John Coke, M.P. for Derby, who had been sent to the Tower in 1685 by the Commons for words reflecting on the King,[4] was put out for Derbyshire. Altogether, nineteen M.P.s were put out for the counties in which their constituencies were situated, and several more who had sat in the Exclusion Parliaments were belatedly dismissed. In many

[1] H.L.R.O., Main Papers, H.L., 3 Dec. 1680, ff. 68–9, 116. The list of Catholics in Monmouthshire was annotated with notes about size of estates and degree of zeal by Lord Herbert of Cherbury.

[2] The counties which were not purged were Cambridgeshire, Cumberland, Huntingdonshire, Merionethshire, Rutland, and Warwickshire.

[3] Edward Yarde, William Stawell, and Edmund Walrond, whose name is mistakenly given as Edward in the Council register.

[4] C.J. ix. 760.

counties, the disgraced justices were of the leading families
in the shire. Three Pelhams were dismissed in Sussex, a
Bulkeley in Anglesey, and a Bertie and a Whitlock in Oxfordshire. Two future archbishops were left out of commission:
John Tillotson, then Dean of Canterbury, for Kent, and John
Sharp, then Dean of Norwich, who had recently been suspended for an anti-Catholic sermon, for Norfolk. This purge
was, of course, very far from complete, and the great majority
of Anglican justices in commission in 1686 remained on the
bench. The high social status of those dismissed suggests a
policy of selectivity on the part of the Council committee. It
seems a not impossible hypothesis that so many prominent
figures were disgraced *pour encourager les autres*. James's
government was demonstrating to gentlemen who were
doubtful about the increasing influence of Catholicism at
court that a firm line would be taken towards those wavering
in their loyalty to the King's Catholic regime, irrespective of
social rank or local position.

There seems to have been little comment when the names
of the new justices were made known in the counties. It was
difficult to argue that the King had acted in any way uncon-
stitutionally. The Test Act still applied. The King had given
certain loyal subjects an opportunity to qualify themselves to
serve him if they chose to do so. If they were prevented from
doing so by their religion, this was the King's misfortune, but
at least there was no constitutional impropriety in adding
their names to the commissions sealed in February and March
1687, which did not contain a clause dispensing the justices
from taking the oaths and the Test. It was impossible for the
Catholic gentlemen whose names appeared in the commissions
of the peace to act as justices until they had taken the oaths
and secured a certificate that they had taken the Anglican
sacraments in accordance with the Test Act of 1673 for civil
office-holders. Thus James's first attempt to bring the Catholic gentry into the county magistracy misfired.

The Court remedied this deficiency as speedily as possible.
In April the Chancellor received a warrant from Sunderland
to insert a clause of dispensation in the commissions of the
peace. This was to exempt all the gentlemen named in the
commission from taking the oaths and from the sacramental

qualification required by the Test Act.[1] In the months from June to September 1687, the commission of the peace was renewed to add the dispensation clause for every county except four.[2] The Welsh counties and Cheshire all received new commissions in August embodying both the Council alterations for the first time, and also the clause of dispensation. However, as far as can be judged, this mass renewal was not made the occasion for further large-scale changes in the lists of justices. The Duke of Beaufort, for example, recommended one name for each of six counties; at least two of these were Catholics, but this was hardly a striking revision, although it is possible that changes from other sources were implemented.[3] Dr Miller has calculated that seventy-one Catholics were added between the spring of 1687 and the winter of 1687/8, and many of these were probably included at the renewal of the commissions to add the dispensation clause.[4] The docquet book does not record any dismissals at this time.

In spite of the dispensation clause, there was still no guarantee that the Catholic justices could act. At the end of March 1688, the King was incensed at the discovery that the Clerk of the Crown had neglected to issue writs of *dedimus potestatem* to swear the new justices in 'several' counties. Consequently few justices of the peace remained in these counties to execute the laws. Jeffreys, to whom the matter was referred, found something like wilful obstruction of the government's intentions. The Clerk of the Crown, Henry Barker, had disobeyed a direct order to issue the necessary writs. Barker was instantly replaced by a more subservient official.[5] It is not clear how many counties were affected by

[1] P.R.O., S.P. 44/337, p. 421: placed out of sequence in a series of entries dated April 1688 and subsequently corrected to 10 April 1687.
[2] P.R.O., C. 231/8, pp. 173 ff. The exceptions were Bedfordshire, Ely, Peterborough, and Rutland.
[3] N.L.W., MSS. 11020E, Nos. 12, 13: recommendations of Duke of Beaufort, 18 May, 26 June 1687.
[4] *Popery and Politics in England, 1660–1688*, pp. 270–2. The highest number of inclusions was nine in Northumberland. I have subtracted Lancashire from Dr Miller's total of eighty-six.
[5] G. W. Sanders, *Orders of the High Court of Chancery and Statutes of the Realm relating to Chancery, from the Earliest Period to the Present Time* (London, 1845), pp. 381–2; Luttrell, *Brief Relation*, i. 436.

Barker's inefficiency (or his Protestant intransigence), but it seems that in some, at least, of the counties, Catholic justices were not able to act until the summer of 1688, although they had been named in commissions sealed as much as eighteen months before.

III

Leaving aside the question of whether or not the Catholics could act as justices, the commission of the peace had by the autumn of 1687 been brought into line with other areas of local and central government where similar changes were taking place. Lord Belasyse, the new head of the Treasury commission following Rochester's dismissal, was a Catholic. In the early months of 1687, the King conducted a series of interviews with office-holders and peers to ascertain their views on the repeal of the penal laws imposing penalties on Catholics, and the Test Act. Subsequently, the royal household was remodelled in February and March. In April and May the ecclesiastical commission established in 1686 began to attack the Universities, and the long campaign to install a President of Magdalen College in Oxford favourably disposed to Catholicism began.[1] The correspondence, newsletters, and diaries of the first six months of 1687 are full of descriptions of removals from office in the armed forces, the Customs, and the law courts.[2] By the end of the year, fourteen counties had new lords-lieutenant.[3] Meanwhile, James was taking steps towards removing the disabilities on Catholics. On 4 April he issued a Declaration of Indulgence in which the penal laws were suspended by an exercise of prerogative, and the oaths and the sacramental test imposed on office-holders

---

[1] Kenyon, *Sunderland*, pp. 145–9, 153–4; Feiling, *History of the Tory Party, 1640–1714*, pp. 217–18.

[2] For instance: Luttrell, *Brief Relation*, i. 391 ff.; *Ellis Correspondence*, i. 219 ff.; North, *Lives of the Norths*, iii. 179–82; *Memoirs of Sir John Reresby*, pp. 444–5.

[3] Buckinghamshire, Cumberland, Hampshire, Lancashire, Leicestershire, Oxfordshire, Shropshire, Somerset, Staffordshire, Warwickshire, Westmorland, Worcestershire, Yorkshire East and North Ridings. Jeffreys himself became lord-lieutenant of Buckinghamshire and Shropshire, and Sunderland lord-lieutenant of Warwickshire. The changes in the lieutenancy in James's reign are printed in Sir G. F. Duckett, *Penal Laws and Test Act* (London, 1882–3), i. 3–18.

were declared unnecessary.[1] After a tour of the West Midlands and the Welsh border in August and September, the King's confidence in the popularity of his Catholic policies seemed greater than that of his ministers; but the political situation changed in November with the announcement that the Queen was pregnant, a development that held out the hope for the Catholics that a permanent Catholic dynasty would be established on the throne. Sunderland privately committed himself to Catholicism in December.[2] Against this background, the alterations in the commissions of the peace in 1687 had followed a regular course in which a clear pattern can be discerned. The counties had received commissions roughly simultaneously in February and March 1687 to embody the Council changes, and again in July–September 1687 to incorporate the dispensation clause. The extent of the changes varied from county to county, no doubt because of differing degrees of local pressure, but the central government had apparently retained an over-all view. The pattern of tidy national regulation prevailing in 1687 gave way in the winter of 1687/8 to a more confused pattern, persisting until the autumn of 1688, in which the composition of the magistracy even in neighbouring counties took on different characters.

The reason for this was the dissolution of the Parliament elected in 1685 on 2 July 1687, and the decision to embark on preparations to secure a new Parliament which would comply with the King's intention of repealing the penal laws and the Test Acts. In the counties, these preparations took the form of an inquisition to ascertain the attitude of the political nation towards the King's proposals. The lord-lieutenant of each county was to ask every justice of the peace, and every militia officer

1. If in case he shall be chosen Knight of the Shire, or Burgesse of a town, when the King shall think fit to call a

---

[1] The Test Acts were not explicitly suspended, and the Declaration promised that the King would continue to issue dispensations. The Declaration is conveniently printed in W. C. Costin and J. S. Watson, *The Law and Working of the Constitution: Documents 1660–1914* (2nd edn., Oxford, 1961–4), i. 343–5.

[2] Kenyon, *Sunderland*, pp. 159–68; Sir J. Dalrymple, *Memoirs of Great Britain and Ireland* (London, 1771–3), ii, Appendix, Part I, 272.

parliament, whether he will be for taking off the Penal laws, and the Tests.

2. Whether he will assist, and contribute, to the election of such member, as shall be for taking off the Penal laws, and Tests.

3. Whether he will support the King's declaration for liberty of conscience, by living friendly with those of all persuasions, as subjects of the same Prince, and good Christians ought to do.

This operation presaged a regulation of the commissions of the peace, since, although it was not explicitly stated that those who returned uncompromising negatives to these questions would be dismissed, the lord-lieutenant was directed to write down the answers. He was further required to recommend to the King 'what Catholicks, and what dissenters are fit to be added either to the list of the deputy-lieutenants, or to the commission of the peace' throughout his lieutenancy.[1]

These orders were not given to the lords-lieutenant by the formal Privy Council, but by a 'Cabinet Council' in which the King, Sunderland, and Jeffreys sat. It seems likely that the original intention had been to summon the lords-lieutenant personally to London in order to interview them about the character of the militia officers and the justices, but that this idea was abandoned in favour of the 'questionnaire' method at some point between 13 and 25 October.[2] By November and December the more active lords-lieutenant began to put the questions and to send their returns to London. The Earl of Lindsey was the first to send in his account from the three parts of Lincolnshire; he had met the gentry of the county on 10 November at Sleaford. The majority of the returns were dated December 1687 and January and February 1688, but some lords-lieutenant were more dilatory. The Earl of Bristol did not send in his report for Dorset until May 1688. In a few counties the delay was the result of a change in the lieutenancy. The questions do not seem to have been put to

---

[1] Dalrymple, op. cit. ii, Appendix, Part I, 223–4; also printed several times in Duckett, *Penal Laws and Test Act.*

[2] Kenyon, *Sunderland*, p. 171 and note; H.M.C., Twelfth Report, Appendix IX, *Beaufort MSS.*, p. 91.

the West Riding gentry until August 1688 after Lord Thomas Howard replaced the Earl of Burlington in March.[1]

The returns survive for about three-quarters of the English and Welsh counties.[2] There have been several attempts to analyse them.[3] A numerical calculation of the extent and distribution of support for James's policy presents certain difficulties, however. The returns take different forms reflecting the different methods of the lords-lieutenant. For example, the Duke of Newcastle canvassed the gentlemen of Northumberland by post and simply forwarded the letters he received in reply to London. The Duke of Berwick reported the replies he had received from Hampshire in the third person. The Earl of Huntingdon entered the names of the justices of Leicestershire under appropriate headings. Also, lords-lieutenant presented the questions to the justices in different ways. Lord Yarmouth, for instance, cajoled reluctant Wiltshire justices into giving affirmative answers, but the Earl of Northampton announced to the Warwickshire gentlemen that he did not intend to comply with the King's proposal to repeal the penal laws and the Test Act himself. His replacement as lord-lieutenant of that county, Sunderland, does not seem to have found time to canvass the Warwickshire gentry at all.[4] The answers themselves are also difficult to assess. The plain

[1] Duckett, *Penal Laws and Test Act*, i. 84, 152; ii. 39.

[2] Bodl. MS. Rawl. A. 139A, from which they were printed by Duckett, op. cit. Duckett's editorial methods were highly idiosyncratic; however, although there are some minor errors, his version is basically a full and accurate transcript.

[3] The most recent of such attempts are at J. Carswell, *The Descent on England* (London, 1969), pp. 238-43; J. R. Western, *Monarchy and Revolution: The English State in the 1680s* (London, 1972), pp. 211-22.

[4] The circumstances in which the questions were put to the gentry are described by Duckett, *Penal Laws and Test Act*, as a preface to the transcriptions of the county returns. There are several accounts of the methods followed by the lords-lieutenant in individual counties, notably: Ailesbury, *Memoirs*, i. 163-4; *Memoirs of Sir John Reresby*, pp. 478-9, 494; *The Autobiography of Sir John Bramston*, pp. 306-7; J. Nicolson and R. Burn, *History and Antiquities of the Counties of Westmorland and Cumberland* (London, 1777), i. 167-70; H.M.C., Twelfth Report, Appendix VII, *Le Fleming MSS.*, pp. 205-9; Lord Lonsdale, *Memoirs of the Reign of James II* (York, 1808), pp. 15-19; Burnet, *History*, iii. 193-4, especially Dartmouth's note; Bodl. MS. Tanner 259, ff. 52 ff.: series of letters to and from Sir John Holland relating to the canvassing of the gentry of Norfolk, from 10 Dec. 1687; Bodl. MS. Rawl. D.851, ff. 34-6: 'A Short Relation of the Queries Maliciously dispersed up and down under the notion of the Bishop [*recte* Dean] of Durham's Queries', 6 May 1688; B.L., Add. MSS. 33923, diary of Sir John Knatchbull, ff. 430-3: Jan.-Apr. 1688.

acceptances are simple enough, but only one justice in the whole country (Thomas Boothby in Leicestershire) returned an uncompromising negative to all three questions.[1] Analysis of the temporizing answers is difficult. It was common for a gentleman to reply that the first question was irrelevant since he had no intention of standing for Parliament. Another common reply, this time for potential M.P.s, was that they would listen to the debates of the House before committing themselves. Some were in favour of repealing the penal laws, but wanted to retain the Tests; some were willing that both be repealed, but insisted on a security for the Protestant religion.

In a number of counties, the answers were manifestly collusive. For example, Sir Edward Seymour in Devonshire was doubtful about repeal until Parliament had debated the security of the Anglican church, and he promised non-committally to contribute to the election of loyal subjects who would faithfully serve the King. Forty-eight Devonshire gentlemen, and fifteen gentlemen from Cornwall, answered word for word the same.[2] The fine shades of equivocation which appeared when the justices' answers were sent to London direct were obscured when the lords-lieutenant returned a condensed account or when the identity of the gentlemen was submerged in a collective answer. Moreover, the opinions of many justices were not ascertained, because they were absent, ill, resident in another county, reluctant to meet the lord-lieutenant, or, occasionally, for some more bizarre reason. Richard Lyster of Leicestershire had absconded for debt, Richard Tolson was so little known to his colleagues on the Cumberland bench that they did not know how to direct a letter to him, and Dr Lamphire of Oxfordshire was not asked for his answers since he was 'not well in his senses'. These considerations make it difficult to make use of the returns for any assessment of national public opinion, although some conclusions about individual counties can be drawn from the justices' answers.[3]

The relevance of the returns is that they were associated

---

[1] Duckett, op. cit. ii. 104.   [2] Ibid. i. 49, 333; ii. 103.

[3] Of the counties in which a reasonably high proportion of the total number of justices gave answers, Kent, Worcestershire, and Herefordshire were most disposed to favour repeal. Dorset, Shropshire, and Norfolk were least co-operative.

with a regulation of the commission of the peace which began in December 1687 and continued fitfully until the summer of 1688. A committee of regulation had been established to remodel the corporations in November 1687, and in December this committee, usually described as the 'Board of Regulators', began to consider the county commissions of the peace as well. On 12 December an announcement appeared in the *London Gazette* that the King proposed to review the commission of the peace in order to maintain and strengthen his Declaration of Indulgence. The committee was not the same as the Council committee of a year earlier. Its members were Sunderland, Jeffreys, Sir Nicholas Butler, the Jesuit Father Petre, and two Catholic peers, Castlemaine and Powis. The obscure Butler seems to have been influential; he had kept his place as one of the Customs Commissioners in April by a timely conversion to Catholicism, and he had recently been admitted to the Privy Council.[1] The first substantial alterations seem to have been made in Cambridgeshire and Ely on 29 December. Although there are no extant replies from either county to the Three Questions, it seems clear that in Cambridgeshire eight justices headed by Sir Christopher Hatton were left out and six came in, on the recommendation of the Catholic lord-lieutenant Lord Dover.[2] Jeffreys was ill in December and January, which perhaps accounts for a lull in January when only one commission — for Middlesex — was sealed, but in the three months from February to April 1688 the commissions for forty-two counties were renewed. There was another lull in May, although again several Middlesex justices were dismissed. Then in June and July another series of commissions was sealed, so that by the end of July every county except five — Peterborough, Rutland, Warwickshire, Westmorland, and the East Riding — had received a new commission since the *Gazette* announcement in the previous December.[3]

The docquet book entries for these commissions are

---

[1] Luttrell, *Brief Relation*, i. 400, 420-1; *Autobiography of Sir John Bramston*, pp. 301-2; Ailesbury, *Memoirs*, i. 164, 174.

[2] P.R.O., C. 231/8, p. 184; Duckett, *Penal Laws and Test Act*, i. 321-2.

[3] P.R.O., C. 231/8, pp. 186 ff. The Regulators produced a list for the East Riding in March 1688 (Duckett, op. cit. ii. 256-7) but the commission does not seem to have been sealed.

uninformative; few names are given and a common formula was that the commissions had been renewed 'for leaving out of several persons, placing therein several others'. However, one important source remains for ascertaining the extent and scope of the changes made during these months: the lists approved by the Board of Regulators itself.[1] These lists are arranged under four headings for each county: 'Persons proposed to be Deputy-Lieutenants', that is, existing deputy-lieutenants to be retained; 'New Ones', that is, new deputy-lieutenants; 'Justices of the Peace', that is, existing justices to be retained; and 'New Ones', that is, new justices. Jeffreys sent copies of these lists directly to the Crown Office as the fiat for a new commission. The old and new deputy-lieutenants were included in the commission of the peace as well as the old and new justices.

This conclusion, at first sight a dangerous one since there is nothing in the manuscript of the Regulators' lists to suggest that their proposals were ever implemented, rests on an examination of these lists for certain counties for which other evidence is available. The list for Northamptonshire is dated December 1687 and was apparently based on a careful sifting by the Board of recommendations sent by the lord-lieutenant, Peterborough.[2] The fiat for this commission is dated 12 December 1687, although, probably because of Jeffreys's illness, the commission itself does not seem to have been sealed until 11 February 1688.[3] The Regulators' list, and the fiat signed by Jeffreys, are identical. One gentleman whose name appears twice in the Regulators' list, as a 'new deputy-lieutenant' and as a justice of the peace to be retained, also appears twice in the fiat and presumably, twice in the Northamptonshire commission of the peace. This evidence is supported by the example of Leicestershire. Two of the Regulators' lists survive. One is an earlier draft with five names crossed out, the other is a fair copy dated 16 February

[1] Bodl. MS. Arch. f. c. 6 (formerly MS. Rawl. A. 139B): printed in Duckett, op. cit. i. 228-9, 320-1, 327-9, 346-50, 403-5, 419-20, 435-7, 443-51; ii. 254-99. The lists survived the Revolution in the possession of one of the clerks of the Privy Council, William Bridgman, and they were probably purchased by Rawlinson in 1743 from Bridgman's daughter.

[2] Duckett, op. cit. ii. 90-1, 275-6.

[3] P.R.O., C. 234/27, Northamptonshire; C. 231/8, p. 186.

1688.[1] The Leicestershire commission of the peace dated 28 February 1688 corresponds exactly to the fair copy except that the order of names is rearranged and that ten local peers, with whom the Regulators were not concerned, are included.[2] Similarly, the Regulators' list for Devonshire, dated 2 July 1688, was embodied in a commission for that county sealed on 7 July 1688; seven local peers and, in this case, two extra local names, were included in the commission, but otherwise the Regulators' list was followed exactly.[3] It thus seems a reasonable conclusion that the Regulators' lists give at least a close approximation to the names of the justices in the commissions sent to the counties following the remodelling in the winter of 1687 and the spring and summer of 1688.

The names of the justices had been changed by the summer of 1688 on an extraordinary scale. One reason for the extent of the changes was that the Regulators were not revising the existing commissions of the peace.[4] They were constructing completely new lists on the basis of the answers to the Three Questions and the response of the lords-lieutenant to the order to recommend Catholics and Dissenters. The scope of the remodelling is illustrated by a comparison between the names of the justices in commission in late 1685 with those in commission in 1688 after the activities of the Regulators, for a group of counties selected at random.[5]

The justices who survived from 1685 to 1688 were, for the most part, men who had given favourable answers to the Three Questions.[6] By the summer of 1688 they had been joined on the bench by three groups. The Catholic squires added in 1687 were, on the whole, entitled in social terms to

[1] Duckett, op. cit. ii. 98–101, 294–6.

[2] Leics. R.O., QS 1/1; P.R.O., C. 231/8, p. 187.

[3] Duckett, op. cit. ii. 298–9; Devon R.O., Q/JC: 7 July 1688. One of the additional names in the commission was that of a Catholic added in 1687 and probably missed out in the Regulators' list by a mistake corrected between 2 and 7 July.

[4] There is no record in the docquet book that the Regulators were ever issued with a *liber pacis*.

[5] See table at p. 85.

[6] There were a very few exceptions to this rule. Richard Bishopp in Hampshire, Sir William Pennington in Cumberland, and Sir James Long and John Wyndham in Wiltshire, for instance, were retained although they had returned equivocal answers. Possibly they were retained because their homes were remote from those of any plausible alternative magistrates.

Comparison of justices of the peace in commission 1685-8

Column A Number of local justices in commission, October 1685*
Column B Number of local justices in commission by the summer of
          1688
Column C Number of local justices surviving from 1685 to 1688
Column D Number of local justices put out between 1685 and 1688

	A	B	C	D
Cumberland (May)†	35	17	7	28
Devonshire (July)	69	42	15	54
Hampshire (April)	72	44	18	54
Leicestershire (February)	33	24	5	28
Lincolnshire — Kesteven (February)	39	23	6	33
Norfolk (February)	79	49	11	68
Northamptonshire (February)	49	30	10	39
Oxfordshire (March)	41	40	8	33
Wiltshire (June)	64	40	7	57

*P.R.O., C. 193/12/5. The local peers are ignored, since the Crown Office seems to have taken the view that they should be reincluded notwithstanding omission from the Regulators' lists. The local names are thus taken to begin with the first baronet.

†The month is that in 1688 in which the commission based on the Regulators' list was sealed in the Crown Office: P.R.O., C. 231/8.

be justices, although possibly their legal education and experience was inclined to be faulty. The second group consists of the Catholics added by the Regulators in 1687-8, who tended to be of lesser status. Although some were respectable enough, others were members of cadet branches of Catholic gentry families and a few were younger brothers or sons of fathers who were still living. Dr Miller estimates that by the summer of 1688, these two groups of Catholics together made up about 24 per cent of the total number of deputy-lieutenants and justices of the peace.[1]

The third group is perhaps the most interesting. A number of names were of Protestant Dissenters and former Exclusionist Whigs. The King took the view that the Dissenters were

[1] *Popery and Politics in England, 1660-1688*, pp. 270-2; since the deputy-lieutenants in the Regulators' lists were also in the commission of the peace, the total of 'deputy-lieutenants' plus 'justices' equals the total of justices of the peace. The absence of the local peers from the Regulators' lists, and their appearance in the commissions of the peace sent to the counties, may possibly lower the percentage of Catholic justices very slightly.

likely to support his Declaration of Indulgence for the same reasons as the Catholics, and that their support was worth having as a counterbalance to the Anglican squires.[1] Some Dissenters had received deputy-lieutenancies at the King's request during his western tour in the summer of 1687.[2] The lords-lieutenant had been required to recommend Dissenters for the commission of the peace in the instructions which accompanied the Three Questions. The commission in almost every county which the Regulators remodelled contained some identifiable ex-Whigs and Dissenters.[3] Exclusionists such as Sir William Courtenay in Devonshire, William Trenchard in Wiltshire, John Swynfen in Staffordshire, Thomas Foley in Worcestershire, and Richard Hampden in Buckinghamshire; elderly ex-Parliamentarians and Cromwellians such as Edward Herle and Edward Nosworthy in Cornwall, Sir John Fagg and John Bremen in Sussex, and Thomas Reynell in Devonshire; rebels of 1685 such as John Speke, Warwick Bampfield, and William and Edward Strode in Somerset; these and several more were added or restored to the commissions of the peace. The Duke of Beaufort obediently recommended about twenty-five Dissenters for the Welsh commissions, and Jeffreys canvassed Sir William Williams, the Recorder of Chester, for the names of more Welsh Dissenters.[4] Edward Harley wrote in February 1688 that 'in Northampton, Nottingham, Norfolk, and Somersetshire are put in commission all the old Whigs' and Narcissus Luttrell observed

---

[1] Lacey, *Dissent and Parliamentary Politics in England*, pp. 175 ff.; J. R. Jones, 'James II's Whig Collaborators', *Hist. Journal* iii (1960), 65.

[2] H.M.C., Fourteenth Report, Appendix II, *Portland MSS.* iii. 402.

[3] Duckett, *Penal Laws and Test Act, passim* (sometimes gentlemen are described as Dissenters in the recommendation that they be put in); Lacey, op. cit., Appendix II, biographical notes on M.P.s with probable or possible dissenting sympathies, pp. 373 ff.

[4] A. H. Dodd, *Studies in Stuart Wales* (Cardiff, 1952), pp. 221–3; T. Richards, 'Declarasiwn 1687: Tipyn o'i Hanes a Barn Cymru am Dano', *Cymdeithas Hanes Bedyddwyr Cymru* (Trafodion, 1924), pp. 40–1, 46 (this study was kindly translated for me by the Revd. Geraint Jones). Dodd follows Richards in concluding, from the absence of evidence that the Dissenters acted, that most of them were not put in at all, and that consequently the changes of James's reign had little effect in Wales. However, their names appear in the Regulators' lists for the Welsh counties dated 23 February 1688 (Duckett, op. cit. i. 443–50), and they were presumably added in the Welsh commissions sealed in April, even if they chose not to act.

that 'those that were in former times the tories are turn'd out, and the then Whiggs are put in'.[1]

The traditional magistracy, the Anglican squires 'that were in former times the tories' lost their places on the bench. In each of the nine counties chosen to illustrate the activities of the Regulators, three-quarters or more of the justices in commission in 1685 had ceased to be justices by the summer of 1688. In Cumberland, the rulers of the county were almost without exception dismissed: Sir Christopher Musgrave, Sir George Fletcher, Sir John Lowther of Lowther, Sir John Lowther of Whitehaven, Sir Daniel Fleming, and Sir John Ballantyne. The Bishop of Carlisle noticed that only eight of the 'old justices of the county' remained.[2] The two county members in Norfolk in 1685, Sir Thomas Hare and Sir Jacob Astley, had both been dismissed, as were squires as locally prominent as Sir William Cooke, Sir Christopher Calthorp, Sir Neville Catelyne, William de Grey, and Colonel Robert Walpole, the father of the future Prime Minister. The Bishop of Norwich commented on the changes: 'indeed', he wrote 'all the most considerable gentry in the county are out of the commission'.[3] In Northamptonshire, Sir Justinian Isham and Richard Reynesford, the two M.P.s for Northampton in 1685, were out, as was Sir Roger Norwich who had been knight of the shire; while, in a complete reversal of fortune, the factious Whig candidate who had been disgraced in 1685, Edward Harby, was now restored. The heads of the colleges were put out of the commission for Oxfordshire along with squires such as Sir Robert Jenkinson, Sir Fairmedow Peniston, Sir Edward Norris, Sir Robert Dashwood, and Sir William Walter.[4] The Devonshire Anglicans who had survived the Privy Council's purge in 1687 remained on the bench in a commission sealed as late as 1 June 1688, but on 7 July they too were displaced in a commission which contained fewer than half as many names as that of five weeks before. Fifty-two gentlemen were dismissed. Sir Arthur Northcott had died, but Sir Edward Seymour, Sir Coplestone Bampfield,

[1] H.M.C., Fourteenth Report, Appendix II, *Portland MSS.* iii. 405; Luttrell, *Brief Relation*, i. 429, 431.
[2] H.M.C., Twelfth Report, Appendix VII, *Le Fleming MSS.*, p. 212.
[3] Bodl. MS. Tanner 29, f. 135: Bishop of Norwich to Sancroft, 20 Feb. 1688.
[4] *Life and Times of Anthony Wood*, iii. 260.

Sir Courtenay Poole, Sir Peter Prideaux, Sir Hugh Acland, Sir John Rolle, Richard Annesley the Dean of Exeter, Sir William Drake and many more were still alive. Sir Ames Pollard, Sir Bourchier Wray, William Cary, and one or two others who had been added by the Council in 1687 were now put out. The Anglican squires in Devonshire must especially have resented the retention of a small group of justices, headed by Sir William Bastard and Sir John Davy, apparently because of their connections with Dissent, even though their answers to the Three Questions had been as equivocal as their own had been. In Leicestershire, only one of the eight knights and baronets in commission in 1685, Sir Henry Beaumont, re-turned a favourable answer to the Three Questions. He was retained in February 1688, but the other seven, headed by Sir Thomas Hesilrige and Sir Beaumont Dixie, had gone, and they were accompanied in disgrace by twenty out of the twenty-four rank and file squires. There is no reason to sup-pose that the changes in most other counties did not follow broadly the same pattern. In Essex, for instance, six of the county's eight members of Parliament in 1685 were not in the regulated commission. In Derbyshire, in spite of appeals for moderation even from Catholic sympathizers,[1] only a handful of Protestant justices survived regulation in March 1688; of the ten names not described as 'new justices' in the Regulators' list, four were Catholics, one was an officer in the army, and another lived in Nottinghamshire. Nor were the changes confined only to wealthy counties plentifully sup-plied with gentry families. In North-West Wales, thirteen justices were turned out in Anglesey, fourteen in Caernarvon-shire, and fourteen in Merionethshire. Richard Bulkeley, the head of a powerful Welsh family, and Sir John Wynne, *custos* of Merionethshire, were among those disgraced. In their places, persons variously described by an admittedly hostile pen as 'a drover of cattle', 'a furious Independent', 'Indepen-dents of no considerable estate or quality' became justices of the peace, along with a number of 'Papists', the son of the regicide John Jones, and the agent to Lord Powis.[2] Perhaps

[1] H.M.C., *Hastings MSS.* ii. 182–3.
[2] Leics. R.O., Finch MSS. Law Papers 15: 'An Account of Such Justices of the Peace . . . as were turned out of Commission upon the Regulation made in the late

Kent suffered less severely than elsewhere; as many as sixty justices seem to have survived the Regulators' purge in February 1688, and only a small proportion of these were Catholics added in 1687. Also, the Anglican magistracy would obviously remain relatively intact, except for those dismissed in 1687, in five unregulated counties; Rutland, Warwickshire, Westmorland, and the East Riding did not receive a new commission in 1688, while Peterborough was unique in that no commission was sealed at all in James's reign after the necessary renewal in May 1685. Even so, a purge of unprecedented thoroughness had clearly taken place in the great majority of counties.

In the spring of 1688 the Regulators began another campaign of adjustment to the commissions of the peace. This was based, not on the recommendations of lords-lieutenant and the answers to the Three Questions, but on the reports of the agents who were touring the countryside in order to assess the prospects of packing a House of Commons to repeal the penal laws and the Test Acts.[1] The instructions issued to these agents did not include any reference to the county commissions of the peace,[2] but the agents recommended some alterations in the spring and summer of 1688 for about twenty counties, and possibly more.[3] These suggestions were presumably sent to the government's election manager, Robert Brent of the Middle Temple, who forwarded them to Jeffreys. Most, though not all, of their recommendations seem to have been acted upon.[4]

Commissions continued to be sealed throughout the summer: sixteen in July, eight in August. Wiltshire received a commission in August after two in June; the two commissions

Reigne after the 3 questions about the penall Laws and Test had been proposed . . .' [1689].

[1] Lacey, *Dissent and Parliamentary Politics in England*, pp. 202, 218; Kenyon, *Sunderland*, pp. 192-3, 202; Jones, 'James II's Whig Collaborators', pp. 67-8, 70-2.

[2] Duckett, *Penal Laws and Test Act*, i. 194-9.

[3] Ibid. ii. 233, 251-2, 300-1.

[4] P.R.O., C. 231/8, pp. 197 ff. Some alterations were suggested for Norfolk and Surrey in July 1688; Surrey did not receive a new commission until November, and Norfolk not until after the Revolution. But most of the counties concerned received new commissions making changes among which are those recommended by the agents.

for the West Riding in August and September both left out some justices; Devonshire and Gloucestershire each received two commissions in June and July; Dorset received no less than three; while Sussex and the North Riding each received two commissions in July and August. It is worth remarking that those commissions of the peace sealed in the summer of 1688 which survive are more than usually untidy documents, with numerous erasures, insertions, and blottings, suggestive both of haste and of second thoughts at a late stage in their manufacture.[1]

There is very little evidence to show what the sources of these changes were. Probably the frequent commissions reflected overlapping recommendations from the government agents, the Court's candidates in the impending elections, lords-lieutenant, and opportunist local politicans eager to exploit the state of flux in the composition of the magistracy. Three persons appointed to the Privy Council in July 1688, Christopher Vane, Silas Titus, and Sir John Trevor, were thought to have had some influence.[2] The Board of Regulators still seems to have been exercising a general supervision, but the changes in the summer of 1688 were not really part of a national, government-controlled remodelling. Rather, they reflected government willingness to respond to local pressure. In late July it was rumoured that yet another regulation would shortly take place that would again be tightly controlled from the centre.[3]

James's programme of incorporating Catholics and Dissenters into the political nation had advanced in other areas: the court, the law, the corporations, the London companies, the armed forces, and the administration in Scotland and Ireland. The King's second Declaration of Indulgence, issued in April 1688, was to be read in churches to the congregations, and the Case of the Seven Bishops, tried for seditious libel in petitioning the King not to insist that the clergy read the Declaration, occupied attention in June. In the same month the Queen gave birth to a son, an event which signified to

---

[1] The Wiltshire commission sealed on 6 Aug. 1688 is a particularly choice example of deplorable Crown Office engrossing. Wilts. R.O., A 1/1/1.

[2] *Autobiography of Sir John Bramston*, p. 311.

[3] H.M.C., Fourteenth Report, Appendix IV, *Kenyon MSS.*, p. 196.

Catholics and Protestants alike that the Counter-Reformation in the British Isles would be permanent, not temporary; and Sunderland openly declared himself a Catholic. On 30 June, the day on which the seven bishops were acquitted, William of Orange, the husband of the King's elder daughter, was invited to land in England to 'protect' an unspecified change in the conduct of the government desired by 'much the greatest part of the nobility and gentry', who were 'much dissatisfied'.[1] William began to make preparations to invade. The news that he intended to do so reached James and Sunderland at some time in mid-September.[2]

IV

There can be no doubt that the massive changes made in the commissions of the peace in 1687 and especially in 1688 played a significant part in the 'Glorious Revolution' of the winter of 1688/9.[3] The loyalty of 'much the greatest part of the nobility and gentry' to the Stuart monarchy had been vindicated in 1660 and had remained a fundamental feature of their political philosophy ever since. It was not necessarily broken altogether in 1688, but James's programme strained it severely. A political revolution had taken place on a huge scale in 1687 and 1688, and it is reasonable to regard the subsequent 'Glorious Revolution' essentially as a counter-revolution. The general admission of Catholics to the county magistracy in 1687, less than ten years after the Commons had taken fright at the thought of a small handful of Catholics in the Monmouthshire and Northumberland commissions and the populace had given way to the hysterical fears of the Popish Plot, was naturally unwise. The further admission of Dissenters in 1688 raised the ghost of the Cromwellian 1650s. But the crucial fact was that the appointment of these new and uncongenial justices was coupled with the dismissal and

[1] Kenyon, *Sunderland*, pp. 194–202; Feiling, *History of the Tory Party, 1640–1714*, pp. 224–8; Browning, *Danby*, i. 384–91; Ogg, *England in the Reigns of James II and William III*, pp. 198–204. The invitation has been reprinted many times from the original, which is at P.R.O., S.P. Dom., King Williams's Chest, S.P. 8/1, ff. 226–9.

[2] Kenyon, op. cit., pp. 214–15.

[3] Plumb, *The Growth of Political Stability*, pp. 60–1; Feiling, op. cit., pp. 219–20; L. Pinkham, *William III and the Respectable Revolution* (Cambridge, Mass., 1954), p. 132.

disgrace of the Anglican squires. The threat to property, liberty, and the Church posed by a Catholic King was associated by the traditional rulers of the counties with a more mundane concern for the loss of the offices which conferred authority and status within their local community.

Two further considerations increased the gentry's antagonism to the Court's policies. One was that the changes were inefficiently carried out. Those of 1687 were backed by Privy Council authority, but the absence of the dispensing clause and the delay in issuing the writs of *dedimus* suggested that the Court had bungled its regulation. Those of 1688 were carried on in a confused welter of commissions, in such a way that by the early autumn of 1688 it must have been a matter of serious difficulty, both in the counties and at the centre, to discover who was in the commission of the peace and who was not. The ineptitude of the Court led to embarrassment. Some gentlemen only learned of their dismissal at sessions or at assizes, when the whole county witnessed their humiliation. Some, like Henry Lambton in Durham who gracefully withdrew from the bench, disguised their resentment, but they are unlikely to have been as indifferent to the tactlessness of the King as they pretended.[1] The second consideration, which applies especially to the alterations of 1688, was that the purge of the squires had been conducted by sinister figures at the centre such as Father Petre, the converts Sunderland and Butler, and the obscure Robert Brent; by Catholic magnates and subservient Anglicans in the counties; and, worst of all, by peripatetic royal agents of humble origin who could not possibly appreciate the complexities of county hierarchy. In particular, the reappearance of Nathaniel Wade, the Bristol lawyer who had been pardoned after playing a leading role in Monmouth's rising, as one of the agents for Somerset and Devonshire,[2] can only have antagonized the gentlemen who had prided themselves on their loyalty in 1685.

The real effect on local government of this revolution among those holding county office is difficult to measure. If

[1] H.M.C., Twelfth Report, Appendix VII, *Le Fleming MSS.*, p. 210. The Leicestershire justices were treated more courteously. H.M.C., *Hastings MSS.* ii. 183.

[2] Duckett, *Penal Laws and Test Act*, i. 101 n.

it is true that in some counties the issue of writs of *dedimus* was delayed until early April 1688, Catholic and dissenting justices cannot have begun to act until the early summer of 1688, and the Catholic magistracy must have been a short-lived phenomenon. This may have happened in, for instance, Wiltshire, where no Catholic justices attended quarter sessions until July 1688 when Lord Stourton sat on the bench at Warminster.[1] In other counties, Catholic justices were active earlier. Lord Carrington and another Catholic attended Warwickshire sessions in the autumn of 1687. In the West Riding, where the Catholic justices apparently sent for their own writs of *dedimus*, two Catholics attended sessions in August 1687. One of the justices put in for Oxfordshire by the Privy Council in 1686-7 attended quarter sessions as early as Easter 1687, and in 1688 the majority of justices attending each sessions in that county were recent appointments.[2] There is a little evidence to suggest that a body of opinion among the Catholic and dissenting gentry was less than enthusiastic about elevation to public office. The Catholic Sir William Goring in Sussex, for instance, warned his co-religionists against the 'folly and vanity' of acting as justices. The Earl of Clarendon dined in August 1688 with a 'rigid fanatic' who declined to act and asked to be put out. On the other hand, Reresby found so many 'papists and fenaticks' at Middlesex quarter sessions in July 1688 that he remained aloof from business.[3]

As far as can be judged, there was no radical change in the administration of the counties, beyond the obvious fact that the prosecution of Catholics and Nonconformists ceased from early 1687 onwards.[4] The transference of local power was not, of course, always smooth. In Somerset, where in

[1] Wilts. R.O., Q.S. Great Rolls, Minute Book, Order Book.

[2] *Warwickshire Quarter Sessions Records, Trinity, 1682, to Epiphany, 1690*, ed. H. C. Johnson (Warwick County Records, viii, 1953), p. liv; *Memoirs of Sir John Reresby*, pp. 449-50, 451 and note, 463; *Oxfordshire Justices of the Peace in the Seventeenth Century*, ed. M. S. Gretton (Oxfordshire Record Society, xvi, 1934), 121-3.

[3] Ailesbury, *Memoirs*, i. 152; *The Correspondence of Henry Hyde, Earl of Clarendon* . . . , ed. S. W. Singer (London, 1828), ii. 186; *Memoirs of Sir John Reresby*, p. 502; and see Miller, *Popery and Politics in England, 1660-1688*, pp. 223-5.

[4] *Cal. S.P. Dom., 1686-7*, pp. 345, 389.

January 1688 the former Monmouth rebel Edward Strode was sheriff and the ex-Tories were still in a majority on the bench, a quarrel broke out at quarter sessions in which insults were exchanged at dinner and Strode arrested the deputy clerk of the peace as an outlaw. Even so, at the next sessions in April, most of the Anglicans had gone, more than a dozen justices approved by the Regulators attended, the dissenting Recorder of Ilchester delivered a Ciceronian charge, and business was conducted without 'the usual clashing and violence'.[1] There may have been doubts about the authority of justices who acted without having qualified themselves according to law, and in Norfolk, where the Bishop vainly exhorted the dismissed gentry to swallow their pride and co-operate with the new regime, some of the new justices displayed a certain ignorance of legal procedures.[2] Nevertheless, there does not seem to have been anything in the nature of a 'breakdown' of local government until the winter of 1688/9. In Kesteven, for instance, the average number of justices attending sessions fell after regulation in February 1688, but those who did attend were the few experienced justices retained by the Regulators and the newcomers seem to have been almost entirely inactive.[3] It is possible that the clerks of the peace, who do not seem to have lost their office in more than a very few counties, supplied a continuity of tradition and routine.

V

The news in September 1688 that William's naval and military preparations were directed towards an invasion of England led to further changes in the county commissions of the peace, which aggravated the confusion into which they had fallen. In October as many as thirty-five commissions were sealed, among them two each for Bedfordshire, Herefordshire, Hertfordshire, and Huntingdonshire. Another seventeen

---

[1] Duckett, *Penal Laws and Test Act*, ii. 19-29; E. Green, *The March of William of Orange through Somerset* (London, 1892), pp. 33-43; *Cal. S.P. Dom., 1687-9*, pp. 191-2; Som. R.O., CQ 2 2/3(3), ff. 3, 11.

[2] Luttrell, *Brief Relation*, i. 432; H.M.C., Eleventh Report, Appendix VII, *Le Strange MSS.*, p. 107; Bodl. MS. Tanner 259, ff. 61-5: correspondence between Sir John Holland and Sir Francis Jerningham, Mar.-Apr. 1688.

[3] *Minutes of Proceedings in Quarter Sessions held for . . . Kesteven . . . 1674-95*, ii. 334 ff.

followed in November.[1] Gloucestershire received two after one in October, Bedfordshire, Herefordshire, and Huntingdonshire each received a third commission, and several counties, including some of the smaller ones like Anglesey and Cardiganshire, received a second commission to follow that sealed in October.[2] These commissions constituted an incomplete reversal of the political revolution of the preceding twenty months. In the third week in September there were several reports that Jeffreys was proposing to restore the justices who had been dismissed.[3] Some lords-lieutenant were invited to notify Jeffreys of the names of justices who would be willing to act if restored; it is, however, significant that they were not also invited to suggest names that might profitably be omitted.[4] The Earl of Bath thought that the news of a mass restoration of justices had had a good effect in Cornwall. Other lords-lieutenant were less sanguine. It was reported from Norfolk that the King's offer to restore disgraced justices had not been well received, although the gentry were thought to be basically loyal.[5]

The lists of justices in the commissions sealed in October and November must have been hastily compiled. The docquet book records that, for a number of counties, the justices 'who were in commission in 1687' were put in;[6] but Jeffreys probably found it difficult to ascertain who these persons were. Even so, many Anglican squires seem to have found their way back into commission; for instance, Sir Christopher Musgrave in Cumberland, Sir Thomas Hussey in Kesteven, Sir Richard Everard in Essex, Sir Charles Rawleigh in Wiltshire, and Sir William Twisden in Kent. Recently appointed justices — the Catholics and Dissenters — seem not to have been dismissed in these panic commissions, except perhaps in a very few counties for which the docquet book records the omission

---

[1] The total number of commissions sealed in October and November in the early years of James's reign had been: 1685, three; 1686, four; 1687, six.

[2] P.R.O., C. 231/8, pp. 199 ff.

[3] H.M.C., *Downshire MSS.* i. 301; Luttrell, *Brief Relation*, i. 463; *Ellis Correspondence*, ii. 219; Ailesbury, *Memoirs*, i. 177–8; *Autobiography of Sir John Bramston*, p. 316.

[4] *Cal. S.P. Dom., 1687–9*, pp. 280, 293–4, 302; H.M.C., *Hastings MSS.* iv. 220.

[5] *Cal. S.P. Dom., 1687–9*, pp. 286–7, 304–5, 316.

[6] P.R.O., C. 231/8, pp. 200–4; *Ellis Correspondence*, ii. 246–7.

of justices.[1] In the last commission of the peace sealed in James's reign, on 30 November, 'Sir Edward Hales and other Roman Catholics' were left out for Middlesex.[2]

The haphazard nature of the panic restorations is well illustrated by what happened in the West Riding. Sir Henry Goodricke, a prominent member of William's party in Yorkshire,[3] was restored on 17 November. Only two days earlier, the Yorkshire gentry had received news of a commission sealed in September, in which Goodricke and twenty more of 'the most eminent for quality and estates', had been left out. Among those put in were a landless illiterate and the bailiff of the Duke of Norfolk's mother. This commission is often quoted in accounts of the Revolution, but it was not really typical. It must have been one of the last to be sealed before the panic began, and its arrival in Yorkshire was delayed for nearly two months. Yet when the commission restoring Goodricke reached the county, which it did on 26 November, it was discovered that, of all people, Sir John Reresby, who was still clinging to his loyalty to James, had now been put out.[4] Possibly something similar happened in other counties receiving two or more commissions during this period of panic, with the time-lag between the sealing of a commission and its arrival in the county introducing further complications.

The reversal did not take place in every county. No commissions of the peace were sealed at this time for eighteen counties, and the Catholics and Dissenters added in 1687 and 1688 remained justices of the peace throughout the period of the Revolution, while the Anglican squires remained in the wilderness.[5] One explanation for this might be that senior magnates took the initiative in some counties, but not in others. The Duke of Beaufort apparently supervised the restoration of Welsh justices, and he wrote to them

---

[1] Bedfordshire, Hertfordshire, Huntingdonshire, and Shropshire. It is, however, possible that, in those counties which received more than one commission during this period, the first restored the Anglicans and the second dismissed the Catholics and the Dissenters.

[2] P.R.O., C. 231/8, p. 204.   [3] Browning, *Danby*, i. 390.

[4] *Memoirs of Sir John Reresby*, pp. 526, 533, 584.

[5] Berkshire, Cambridgeshire, Cheshire, Derbyshire, Ely, Hampshire, Leicestershire, Norfolk, Northamptonshire, Northumberland, Nottinghamshire, Suffolk, and Worcestershire; plus Peterborough, Rutland, Warwickshire, Westmorland, and Yorkshire East Riding, which did not receive commissions at all in 1688.

individually to inform them that they were restored.[1] Bedfordshire and Huntingdonshire, where Ailesbury was lord-lieutenant, experienced a violent reshuffling of the magistracy, while the neighbouring counties of Cambridgeshire and Northamptonshire, where the lords-lieutenant were the discredited Catholics Dover and Peterborough respectively, were left untouched.

In view of the impending invasion, the militia was thought to be more important than the commission of the peace. The militia, too, was in a state of confusion. James's appointment of Catholic lords-lieutenant had been intended as a social and political manoeuvre rather than as an attempt to monopolize military power, and the fighting capacity of the militia had been allowed to run down.[2] Ailesbury had been compelled to give militia commissions in his two counties to gentlemen he did not know and could not trust, and he found in the autumn of 1688 that the 'prime gentry' of Bedfordshire were unwilling to accept their commissions again. The Earl of Oxford experienced similar difficulties in Essex. The Lincolnshire militia was in grave disorder. The Earl of Bristol had unofficially retired as lord-lieutenant of Dorset, and the Dorset militia had virtually ceased to exist. The militia in Staffordshire and Kent had also almost vanished.[3] Another area of county government where confusion prevailed was the shrievalty. The sheriffs had been 'pricked' (that is, selected) on 5 November. The choices reflected an attempt to conciliate the Protestant gentry, but the new sheriffs had not time to take out their patents and in many counties the Catholics chosen in late 1687 had not been replaced as sheriffs until well into 1689.[4]

In some cases, the Anglican squires did not respond to the offers of restoration, either to the commission of the peace or to the militia. They refused to act as magistrates alongside Catholics and Dissenters. The Norfolk gentry explained with great clarity in October 1688 that they did not conceive that

[1] H.M.C., Third Report, Appendix, MSS. of Whitehall Dod, p. 259.
[2] Kenyon, The Nobility in the Revolution of 1688, p. 7.
[3] Ailesbury, Memoirs, i. 166–7, 181–2; Autobiography of Sir John Bramston, pp. 325–6; Cal. S.P. Dom., 1687–9, pp. 284, 287–8, 302–3, 325–6.
[4] P.R.O., P.C. 2/72, p. 789; Warwickshire Quarter Sessions Records, 1682–90, pp. lxii, 249–50.

it was possible to serve the King by acting in conjunction with persons disqualified by law in the administration of that law.[1] In attempting to restore the *status quo*, the Court was manifestly acting from panic; the gentry recognized this, and they were understandably reluctant to co-operate. After William had landed, however, the squires reasserted a sense of responsibility, and even the recalcitrant gentry of Norfolk were issuing orders in December to disarm Catholics who were still technically justices of the peace for the county.[2]

Thus, in the winter of 1688/9, local government was in a state of chaos appropriate to a revolutionary situation. On 8 December James received from Jeffreys the great seal and the writs for a Parliament which was to have been summoned in January. He burned the writs and on 11 December he left London, dropping the great seal in the Thames as he went. After his departure, a meeting of peers at Guildhall assumed temporary powers of civil government and issued a Declaration which, among other things, continued all Protestant justices in office until further notice.[3] Subsequently, James, having been recaptured on the Kent coast, escaped a second time to France in late December. William summoned a Convention Parliament, which met on 22 January 1689. This Parliament offered the English throne to William and his wife Mary jointly, and they accepted on 13 February. The period between 11 December 1688 and 13 February 1689 was thus one of uncertainty. The King had effectively thrown up his responsibility for the administration of civil government, and it was by no means clear whether any legally constituted civil authority existed at all. In the counties, little notice was taken of the last commission of the peace sealed by Jeffreys. Protestant gentlemen of experience and established social position simply assumed office as 'Keepers of the Peace', whether they were technically in the commission of the peace or not.[4] In those counties for which quarter sessions

[1] H.M.C., *Lothian MSS.*, pp. 132-3.
[2] *Norfolk Lieutenancy Journal, 1676-1701*, ed. B. Cozens Hardy (Norfolk Record Society, xxx, 1961), 95.
[3] R. A. Beddard, 'The Guildhall Declaration of 11 December 1688 and the Counter Revolution of the Loyalists', *Hist. Journal* xi (1968), 404-6.
[4] Bodl. MS. Rawl. Letters 48, f. 70: Sir Edmund Warcup to Hugh Jones, 22

were held in January 1689, business was confined to a brief meeting of gentry, the transaction of commonplace business of a kind that could not be postponed, and an adjournment. A principal duty of the new regime would therefore be the re-establishment of the routine of county government.

Dec. 1688; W. L. Sachse, 'The Mob in the Revolution of 1688', *Journal of British Studies*, iv (1964), 37-9.

4

THE COMMISSION OF THE PEACE AND THE ESTABLISHMENT OF THE REVOLUTION REGIME, 1689–1700

I

Jeffreys, on his deathbed in the Tower, was replaced on 1 March 1689, not by a new Lord Chancellor, but by three Commissioners of the Great Seal.[1] Before 8 March a committee of the Privy Council was appointed to 'make lists of justices of the peace' to submit to these Commissioners. Unfortunately, no record survives of the membership or method of working of this committee, which was also responsible for replacing James's sheriffs.[2] It is probable that it received recommendations from the lords-lieutenant, who had been appointed in nearly every county by the end of March. The knights of the shire in the Convention, who had already been asked to supply the names of gentlemen to act as commissioners for levying an aid in the counties, also played a prominent part. In Kent, for instance, the members for the county constructed a list of justices by going through a much longer list they had already drawn up for 'the tax'.[3] Whatever the method of nomination, the lists had been received and assessed by the Privy Council as early as 15 March, when the Earl of Shrewsbury, appointed Secretary of State the month before, forwarded them to the Commissioners of the Great Seal with a note that the King desired the commissions of the peace to pass forthwith.[4] On the following day, the King told Parliament, with some justification where the county magistracy was concerned, that vacancies in offices and places of trust were rapidly being filled.[5]

---

[1] P.R.O., C. 231/8, p. 209. [2] P.R.O., P.C. 2/73, p. 30.

[3] *Cal. S.P. Dom., 1689–90*, pp. 20–1; *C.J.* x. 41, 57; B.L., Add. MSS. 33923, f. 464.

[4] P.R.O., S.P. 44/97, p. 42: Shrewsbury to [Commissioners of the Great Seal]. The lists themselves have not been traced.

[5] *C.J.* x. 51.

So far the operation had proceeded smoothly, but at this point it broke down. Only six commissions of the peace were sealed in March, and three in April.[1] The King considered that the delay was prejudicial to his service, and on 18 May he ordered in Council that the Commissioners of the Great Seal should issue the others as quickly as possible.[2] Twenty-six were sealed in May, and most of the remainder in June, but even so a number of counties remained without a commission dated after the Revolution until July 1689 or later.[3] Furthermore, the earlier commissions were so imperfect that as many as thirty-three counties needed another before the end of the year.[4]

There were a number of reasons for these delays. One was that Sir John Maynard, Sir Anthony Keck, and Sir William Rawlinson, the Commissioners of the Great Seal, were not men of sufficient stature to take much part in the selection of new justices of the peace. They were not even Privy Councillors. They operated, in a subordinate position, the machinery by which the commissions were passed. A single Chancellor would have provided the contact between Privy Council and Crown Office that would have enabled the Clerk of the Crown to produce commissions more quickly. The Crown Office was overburdened anyway, with patents for judges, patents for peers, and commissions for lords-lieutenant. Also, some serious delays in the appointment of *custodes rotulorum* held back the engrossment of commissions of the peace, since the *custos* normally appeared in the *assignavimus denique* clause. The Commissioners of the Great Seal had informally 'appointed' *custodes* as early as March 1689, but their choice and the King's did not always coincide.[5] The Commons proposed to vest in the Commissioners the power

---

[1] Derbyshire, Huntingdonshire, Leicestershire, Northamptonshire, Sussex, and the West Riding in March; Dorset, Durham, and the East Riding in April. P.R.O., C. 231/8, pp. 211 ff.

[2] P.R.O., S.P. 44/97, p. 77: Shrewsbury to Commissioners of the Great Seal, 15 May 1689; P.C. 2/73, p. 118.

[3] Buckinghamshire, Ely, and Peterborough did not receive new commissions until July 1689; Anglesey and Caernarvonshire, not until September 1689; Flintshire and Merionethshire, not until January 1690.

[4] Twelve counties needed more than one more, and Middlesex received six commissions between May and December.

[5] B.L., Add. MSS. 29594, f. 143: Nottingham to Hatton, 30 Mar. 1689.

to appoint *custodes*, but the Lords took the view that the nomination of *custodes* belonged to the King, and a compromise had to be worked out whereby the appointments made by the Commissioners before 1 May 1689 were confirmed, but thereafter the King's nominations stood.[1] The King was obliged to disappoint some peers. The Earl of Rutland, who had been promised the office of *custos* of Leicestershire, nearly threw up the lord-lieutenancy in disgust when the Earl of Stamford (the Commissioners' choice) was continued. The *custodes* of the English and Welsh counties were not all certain of their appointment until late September. These difficulties delayed not only the reconstitution of the magistracy, but also, in some counties, the appointment of clerks of the peace.[2]

The revision of so many commissions during the summer and autumn of 1689 was necessary because local recommendations were still coming to the notice of the government.[3] Consequently, a stream of corrections to the original lists of 15 March poured from the offices of Shrewsbury and Nottingham, the two Secretaries of State.[4] This *ad hoc* process of reconstructing the magistracy left the central government itself confused. Shrewsbury, on receiving a complaint from one of the Welsh judges about a Herefordshire justice, had to write to ask the lord-lieutenant whether he was in commission or not; he did not know and there was no quick way of finding out.[5] It was natural enough that those who had constructed the lists in the confusion of the early months of 1689 should have overlooked obvious names; more serious than such second thoughts, however, was the uncertainty about who was willing to serve. Not all the 'old gang' of Tory justices, placed in the commissions of the peace by optimistic

---

[1] 1 William & Mary, c. 21; *C.J.* x. 153, 193.

[2] H.M.C., Twelfth Report, Appendix V, *Rutland MSS.* ii. 125-6; *Cal. S.P. Dom., 1689-90*, pp. 32, 35, 164, 171, 173, 210, 271; B.L., Add. MSS. 29594, ff. 147, 157, 180: Nottingham to Hatton, 4 Apr., 2 May, 8 Oct. 1689.

[3] P.R.O., State Papers Domestic, William and Mary, S.P. 32/2, ff. 182 (Leicestershire), 184 (Nottinghamshire); S.P. 32/13, f. 118 (Staffordshire); H.M.C., Thirteenth Report, Appendix II, *Portland MSS.* ii. 162 (Middlesex).

[4] P.R.O., S.P. 44/97, pp. 43 ff.: Shrewsbury to Commissioners of the Great Seal, several dates; S.P. 44/98, pp. 5 ff.: Nottingham to same, several dates.

[5] P.R.O., S.P. 44/97, p. 109: Shrewsbury to Macclesfield, 22 June 1689; p. 110: same to Hopton, 22 June 1689.

lords-lieutenant in the early months of the year,[1] were prepared to endorse the Revolution to the extent of accepting office under the new regime. A justice of the peace had to take the revised oath of allegiance. Admittedly, the oath could be taken by anyone who accepted William and Mary as *de facto* monarchs, as the phrase 'rightful and lawful' was deliberately omitted from the description in its wording of the nature of their authority. Even this aid to tender consciences could not persuade some of the Tory squires to act as justices. In Wales, where the problem of inactive justices was aggravated by the revival of the statutory limitation of the number of justices in each county to eight,[2] the gentlemen of Merionethshire declined to act with the 'Whig collaborator', Sir William Williams, who was *custos*, while in Anglesey the *custos* himself refused to act.[3] When similar difficulties arose in England, they were met in the course of 1689 by the recruitment of more justices to fill the gaps.

In spite of the activities of the Secretaries of State, the appointment of justices of the peace was carried on with less central control in the months after the Revolution than ever before. King William could hardly be expected to distinguish between the merits of English squires. The Commissioners of the Great Seal were merely lawyers, though the octogenarian Maynard might have enjoyed some local influence in the West Country. The Privy Council committee and the Secretaries of State seem simply to have transmitted recommendations to the Commissioners of the Great Seal. Consequently, the local magnates who drew up the lists had the field to themselves. By 1689 there were seven classes of gentlemen available to be placed in the commissions of the peace. The 'men of faction' put out in the early 1680s divide into two categories: some had not been restored since their omission during the Exclusion Crisis, others had collaborated with James II and had been restored in 1687 or 1688. The 'men of loyalty' of the Tory Reaction, who had dominated the bench in 1685, also divide into two types: those who had been put out for

[1] H.M.C., Fourteenth Report, Appendix II, *Portland MSS.* iii. 435.
[2] See above, p. 16.
[3] Leics. R.O., Finch MSS. Law Papers 15: lists of justices put in for Anglesey, Caernarvonshire, and Merionethshire in 1689.

refusing to comply with James's intentions respecting the
Test Act, and those who had remained continuously in commission throughout James's reign. Next there were the
Protestant justices put in during James's reign. These might
be either Anglicans put in during the early part of the reign,
or Dissenters added in 1687 and 1688. Finally there were
gentlemen who had not been named in the commission
before the Revolution. The proportions in which these seven
classes of justice were mingled in the commissions sealed in
1689 varied from county to county in a bewildering fashion.

In Northamptonshire, for instance, the lord-lieutenant,
Lord Mordaunt, who was created Earl of Monmouth in 1689,
was presumably responsible for the commission sealed in
March 1689. This contained a relatively high proportion of
Exclusionist Whigs put out during the Tory Reaction: at least
eight, and possibly ten, out of a total of seventy. At the same
time, the number of Tory squires who were not restored after
dismissal in 1687 and 1688 was surprisingly large.[1] In Devonshire, rather more of those dismissed under James were
restored, and the proportion of those in commission in 1689
who had been in commission in 1685 was higher than in
Northamptonshire. At least some of the Devonshire Whigs
put out between 1680 and 1685 reappeared, and so too did
as many as nineteen of the forty-eight justices put in under
James, but there was an abrupt break at the Revolution, since
only sixteen of the 119 justices in the Devonshire commission in 1689 had been in the last commission sealed in 1688.[2]
Five of the 'Whig collaborators' of Somerset, notably Warwick
Bampfield, John Speke, and William Strode, were retained
for that county; however, the justices appointed for the
first time during James's reign were not so much to the fore
in Somerset as in Devonshire.[3] James's justices were ignored
completely in Kesteven, where, on the evidence of the first
post-Revolution commission to survive, the category most
strongly represented in the list was that of the newcomers to

---

[1] P.R.O., C. 234/27, Northamptonshire: 23 Mar. 1689.
[2] Devon R.O., Q/JC: commissions of the peace, 11 July, 27 July 1689. The
second, used as the basis for calculation, added thirty-four names to the first.
[3] Som. R.O., Q/JC 99: commission of the peace, 17 May 1689.

the bench.[1] Warwickshire had suffered less from regulation in 1687 and 1688 than other counties, and the moderate Tory lord-lieutenant, the Earl of Northampton, was unwilling to bring back two of the four surviving Whigs put out in the early 1680s, while nearly half the Tory justices of 1685 were back in the Warwickshire commission in 1689 compared with fewer than a quarter in Northamptonshire.[2] The Earls of Rutland and Stamford, respectively lord-lieutenant and *custos* of Leicestershire, produced a balanced commission for that county, in which those of James's inclusions who were retained roughly equalled the Whigs restored from before 1685, and more than half of the 1685 justices supplied an experienced nucleus of about 40 per cent of the 1689 commission.[3] This quite small sample suffices to illustrate one general point: when the lists of justices were reconstructed after the Revolution, there were evidently great differences, arising from local rather than central pressures, in the character of the bench even in neighbouring counties.

Nor was this all. Everywhere except in Wales, the number of local justices seems to have risen, and the percentage of completely new men was surprisingly high. One-third or more of the justices in all of the six counties so far analysed were recruits to the bench, a figure which bears incidental comparison to the proportion of newcomers to the House of Commons — 172 out of 513 — in the Convention. If the experience of these six counties was repeated elsewhere, the qualification for a place in the commission must have been lowered to include men of less status, if not necessarily of less wealth, than the heads of the established families whose ancestors had recorded pedigrees at heraldic visitations. It is a platitude that the Revolution ushered in an oligarchic

[1] Lincs. A.O., commission of the peace, Kesteven, 18 July 1691. Though this is rather late, the only changes since 1689, according to the docquet book, had been to include the Earl of Lindsey as *custos* and to alter the assize judges. P.R.O., C. 231/8, pp. 249, 274.

[2] *Warwickshire Quarter Sessions Records, 1682-90*, pp. xxix-xlix. The first two post-Revolution commissions do not survive, and the calculations are based on a commission sealed in March 1690.

[3] Leics. R.O., QS 1/2, 1/3: commissions sealed 25 Mar., 1 Aug. 1689. The second, used as the basis for calculation, added fifteen names to the first, and omitted one, probably as the result of the discovery of a misnomer.

regime, but its immediate effect in the localities was to complete the destruction of the old oligarchy of the county families. However, it was clearly desirable to appoint more justices of the peace. More people were within the scope of the treason laws than at any time since the 1650s. The country was committed to a European war in which a French invasion receiving support from within the British Isles was a real possibility. The demands of security thus made for an expansion of numbers, while the weakness and inexperience of the government meant that the composition of the bench became a matter for local rather than central politics.

II

William's first ministry, which contained both Whigs and Tories, had been constructed on the principle that a mixture of politicians in office would win moderate support and divide the opposition between unemployable extremists on both sides. This 'trimming' at the centre had some curious effects in the localities. One of the methods used to establish equilibrium was the impartial distribution of lord-lieutenancies.[1] Thus, for instance, the Earl of Abingdon, who had voted with the Tories for a Regency in the Lords' debate of 29 January 1689, and who was lord-lieutenant of Oxfordshire, was sandwiched between two peers who had spent James's reign at The Hague: the Earl of Macclesfield in Gloucestershire, and the Earl of Monmouth in Northamptonshire. Except in Wales, where every county was entrusted to Macclesfield, this fragmentation was repeated elsewhere. It could have been argued that, while the parties might be balanced over the country as a whole, the authority thus delegated was to be exercised within a smaller area by a single individual, and the influence of party in that area might be strengthened rather than diminished. However, in some counties at least, this objection was met by the appointment of a *custos* on the principle that he would balance the lord-lieutenant. Danby, now Marquess of Carmarthen, hated his rival Halifax, yet the two were respectively lord-lieutenant and *custos* of the West Riding. In Worcestershire, where the Earl of Shrewsbury was lord-lieutenant, the *custos* was Lord Coventry,

[1] Feiling, *History of the Tory Party, 1640–1714*, p. 257.

who, like Abingdon, had voted for a Regency. The office of county vice-admiral offered another opportunity of neutralizing a lord-lieutenant. For example, the Earl of Shaftesbury in Dorset and Sir Henry Hobart in Norfolk were Whig vice-admirals who were politically out of step with, respectively, the Earl of Bristol and the Duke of Norfolk.

The effects of such a 'trimming' policy were unsatisfactory, both at the centre and in the localities. At the centre, the Whigs were indignant at the employment of those who had regulated charters and beheaded Lord Russell, while the Tories in the ministry, especially Carmarthen, were constantly pressing for a greater share of the spoils of office. Politicians with nothing in common were expected to work together at, for example, the Treasury, where James's servant Godolphin was yoked to Monmouth and Delamer. The result was conflict in Parliament and paralysis in government.[1] In the localities, 'trimming' meant that the English counties became a patchwork. In some places, the influence of a dominating magnate was too overpowering to be balanced, and this influence might be exploited freely in the absence of rivals of equal status in high county office. Two examples were the Tory Earl of Lindsey in Lincolnshire and the Whig Earl of Manchester in Huntingdonshire. Elsewhere, two peers of different views shared the offices, as in Northamptonshire where the Whig Monmouth as lord-lieutenant and the Tory Hatton as *custos* cancelled each other out.

The Commissioners of the Great Seal were incompetent to supervise the nominations of justices of the peace produced by such diverse county grandees. It was the King himself who prevented an outbreak of party warfare involving the lower levels of local office in 1689. Admittedly, at one point in the summer William was considering the compilation of a black list of non-juring and disaffected justices, possibly with a view to their elimination from the bench.[2] A list of Somerset justices, annotated by an unknown Whig with such comments as 'T[ory]-ignorant' against individual names,

[1] E. L. Ellis, 'The Whig Junto in relation to the development of Party Politics and Party Organisation, from its inception to 1714' (Oxford University D.Phil. thesis, 1961), pp. 134-40; H. Horwitz, *Parliament, Policy and Politics in the reign of William III* (Manchester, 1977), p. 95.
[2] *Cal. S.P. Dom., 1689-90*, p. 148.

possibly stemmed from this, but the next two Somerset commissions together merely added a total of three names and
left out two who were dead, and nothing more was heard of
the projected purge elsewhere.[1] Notwithstanding complaints
about disaffected justices like Mr Lechmere in Herefordshire,
who was 'much alienating the hearts of true Protestants and
loyal subjects',[2] the commissions sealed late in 1689 were to
add gentlemen who were willing to act, not, as far as can be
judged, to remove those who were disaffected. When, in the
winter of 1689/90, William decided to rely more openly on
the 'Church party' and to dissolve the Convention, he explicitly told Carmarthen that he was willing to reform the commissions of the peace by inclusions, but not by a purge.[3]

Early in 1690 the King turned to a ministry of moderate
Tories and Court politicians, with a number of Whigs who did
not regard Whiggery as the doctrine of permanent opposition
in minor office. This combination lasted, with variations,
until 1693, when its inability to do the King's business in the
Commons discredited it in the Closet and its mismanagement
of the war discredited it in the country. Carmarthen, the
dominant figure in the ministry after the resignations of Halifax as Lord Privy Seal and Shrewsbury as Secretary of State,
might have been expected to attempt to strengthen it by
judicious manipulation of the offices of power and status in
the localities. The replacement of Maynard as one of the
Commissioners of the Great Seal by Sir John Trevor, who
combined the Speakership of the Commons with the role of a
leading manager of the Court party there, was possibly
designed to assist in such manipulation. However, royal
moderation continued to guide policy with regard to local
office. It is true that the London lieutenancy was changed —
this remained a Whig grievance for some time — but Tories
were added to swamp the Whigs.[4] Also, some Tory lords-
lieutenant occasionally considered a regulation of the militia.

---

[1] Som. R.O., Sanford MSS. DD/SF 1749; Q/JC 100-1: commissions of the
peace, 11 July 1689, 1 Jan. 1690.
[2] P.R.O., S.P. 32/1, f. 234: H. Pughe to Shrewsbury, 3 Aug. 1689.
[3] Shrops. R.O., Attingham MSS. 112/3: Carmarthen to [Abingdon], 15 Feb.
1690.
[4] Burnet, *History*, iv. 72-3; Luttrell, *Brief Relation*, ii. 21, 25; Horwitz, *Parliament, Policy and Politics in the reign of William III*, pp. 52, 56, 57.

Carmarthen was reported to have dismissed some 'Whiggishly inclined' gentlemen from their deputy-lieutenancies in Yorkshire. The Duke of Ormonde and the Earl of Lindsey were said to have remodelled the lieutenancies of Somerset and Lincolnshire respectively. Six of the reputedly disgraced deputy-lieutenants had voted for the 'factious' Sacheverell Clause, debarring persons named in corporation charters issued after *quo warranto* proceedings in the 1680s from holding office for seven years.[1] Even so, these rumours were unreliable,[2] and this limited purge of the lieutenancies did not extend to the commissions of the peace. It would, of course, have been absurd to have expected changes in support of the Court's policy in, for instance, Hampshire, where the lord-lieutenant's son voted for the Sacheverell Clause, or in Cambridgeshire, where the *custos* voted for it himself.[3]

There were, from time to time, reports that the ministers planned a revision of the commission of the peace. For instance, in April 1691 it was rumoured that the Commissioners of the Great Seal had directions to make lists of the names of justices of the peace who refused to act.[4] Only one commission of the peace, for Montgomeryshire, was issued in the following two months, and although thirty-two commissions were sealed in July and August, this was only slightly above the average, since commissions were normally revised in the summer to put the assize judges in. The entries in the Crown Office docquet book — admittedly an unreliable source — suggest that the changes at this time were routine. The Devonshire commission, which left out one justice who had died and added his heir and one other, was probably typical.[5] Warwickshire, where the justices of 1685 had been strongly represented in 1690, was neglected altogether in 1691, and when a new commission eventually passed in 1692 it left out one justice for 'stealing horse-traces', while one

[1] B.L., Loan 29/185, ff. 81, 86: Robert Harley to Sir Edward Harley, 19 May, 23 May 1691; Luttrell, *Brief Relation*, ii. 230; Browning, *Danby*, iii. 164–72.

[2] Only one gentleman was dismissed in Yorkshire. B.L., Loan 29/185, f. 89: Robert Harley to Sir Edward Harley, 29 May 1691.

[3] Lord William Paulet and Edward Russell.

[4] Northern Ireland Public Record Office, De Ros MSS. 13/52: John Pulteney to Lord Coningsby, 23 Apr. 1691. I am grateful to Miss Beth Rainey for transcribing this letter for me.

[5] Devon R.O., Q/JC: commission of the peace, 24 July 1691.

local name was added.[1] Only in Hampshire were justices dismissed.[2]

If little change took place in 1691, there undoubtedly was a regulation of the magistracy in Wales in 1692, when 'several' justices in six counties were put out.[3] Some gentlemen in Radnorshire blamed Robert Harley, complaining that their omission branded them as 'criminals or malefactors'. Harley, who as a leader of the Country Whigs had little reason to defend the ministers, argued that the changes that had been made were an unavoidable result of the need for active justices combined with the limitation of the Welsh commissions to eight names.[4] Even Harley's observation that he had recommended the dismissal of his own father did not mollify his opponents, and the affair of the Radnorshire justices was to recur, but Harley was justified in pointing out that circumstances in the Welsh counties were unusual.

There is no reason to suppose that the English commissions of the peace were significantly altered in 1692 except in one county — Middlesex. When the Earl of Bedford replaced the Earl of Clare as lord-lieutenant in March 1692, he urged that sixteen justices be put out as 'not proper to be continued'. Among them was Sir James Smith, one of London's foremost Tories, who was described as a Nonjuror in a hostile newssheet on the subject of the London lieutenancy. The Tories fought back; the Bishop of London asked Queen Mary to reconsider Bedford's suggestions. A month later Nottingham wrote that the tardiness of the Commissioners of the Great Seal in passing the commission had enabled Bedford to change his mind. Six of the sixteen justices formerly ordered to be left out were now to be continued, including Sir James Smith.[5]

Middlesex, as so often, was an untypical case, and in general there is no real evidence in the early 1690s of any very systematic policy of remodelling the magistracy. The

---

[1] *Warwickshire Quarter Sessions Records, Easter 1690 to Michaelmas 1696*, ed. H. C. Johnson and N.J. Williams (Warwick County Records, ix, 1964), pp. xvi-xvii.
[2] P.R.O., C. 231/8, p. 275.   [3] P.R.O., C. 231/8, p. 293.
[4] B.L., Loan 29/186, ff. 193–4: Harley to Samuel Morgan, 3 Nov. 1692 (copy).
[5] *Cal. S.P. Dom., 1691-2*, pp. 165-6, 220-1, 250; Luttrell, *Brief Relation*, ii. 399, 437; *A List of the Commissioners of Lieutenancy of the City of London as constituted in 1690* [1693?]; P.R.O., C. 231/8, pp. 281, 288.

central government seems neither to have flooded the bench with supporters, nor to have purged it of opponents. New justices were recruited in small numbers. Those dismissed had generally committed some misdemeanour, like Julius Deeds in Kent, whose servants had assaulted the customs officers and taken part in the rescue of his contraband.[1] Nottingham was accused in 1692 of hindering the appointment of Whig gentlemen to the commissions of the peace,[2] but otherwise the county magistracy was an inconspicuous theme in parliamentary and governmental politics.

The King's well-known dislike of the exploitation of ministerial power in the interests of party was one reason for this perhaps rather unexpected stabilization of the membership of the county bench after the upheavals of 1688/9. Another was the lack of initiative displayed by the Commissioners of the Great Seal. Their conduct of business was slow and cautious. When the King wanted them to discover more about the character of some persons recommended to be added to the Essex commission, the result was a delay of over eighteen months before an order was given to include them.[3] The reluctance of the Commissioners to act without some higher authorization was sometimes laudable, as when they refused to dismiss certain justices whose loose moral principles were represented to them by the early Societies for the Reformation of Manners,[4] but their true status was revealed in a brusque Council order that they explain why they had not passed a commission for Northumberland in accordance with recommendations forwarded by the clerk of the peace on the instructions of the *custos*.[5] It is hard to imagine a Lord Keeper, still less a Lord Chancellor, suffering the humiliation of such discipline. The experiment of putting the great seal in commission was a failure in other ways, since suits were slower and more expensive and the Commissioners' judgements

---

[1] P.R.O., P.C. 2/74, pp. 396, 425: 12 May, 23 June 1692.
[2] B. W. Hill, *The Growth of Parliamentary Parties 1689–1742* (London, 1976), p. 54.
[3] *Cal. S.P. Dom., 1690–1*, p. 11; *Cal. S.P. Dom., 1691–2*, p. 157.
[4] *Letters illustrative of the Reign of William III . . . Addressed to the Duke of Shrewsbury by James Vernon*, ed. G. P. R. James (London, 1841) [hereafter cited as *Vernon Correspondence*], ii. 133.
[5] P.R.O., P.C. 2/75, p. 99: 23 Feb. 1693.

were not respected.[1] When at last the King appointed the Whig Sir John Somers as Lord Keeper in March 1693, it was generally expected that Somers would reinvigorate the patronage powers attached to the great seal which the Commissioners had permitted to lapse.

III

Somers, the son of a Worcestershire attorney, had written Exclusionist pamphlets as a young man, and he appeared as junior counsel for the seven bishops in 1688. He was elected M.P. for Worcester in 1689, when he associated himself with the group of younger Whigs who, unlike most of Shaftesbury's followers in the early 1680s, were ambitious for office — the future Whig Junto. Solicitor General in 1689 and Attorney General in 1692, Somers was in his early forties when he accepted the great seal, and he is generally acknowledged to have been a cultivated man of wide interests and an outstanding lawyer-statesman.[2] The choice of an able Whig for a post commanding extensive local patronage was to some extent accidental, as William had originally thought of Nottingham as a possible Chancellor.[3] Nevertheless, the appointment, together with that of the former Exclusionist Sir John Trenchard as the second Secretary of State, marked a change in politics at the centre. Since early 1692 Sunderland, now reconverted from Catholicism and acting as William's adviser after a period in exile, had been urging that the Whigs were more committed than the Tories to the Revolution and the war. William was not yet fully convinced by Sunderland's political strategy, but the elevation of Somers and Trenchard meant that the Cabinet, which had recently emerged as the focus of executive government, now contained a vigorous Whig element.[4]

[1] Campbell, *Lives of the Chancellors*, iv. 51–3; H. C. Foxcroft, *A Supplement to Burnet's History of My Own Time* (Oxford, 1902), pp. 381–2.

[2] The most recent biography in W. L. Sachse, *Lord Somers, A Political Portrait* (Manchester, 1975); see also *Memoirs of the Life of Lord Somers* (London, 1716); Holdsworth, *History of English Law*, iv. 535–7; and Ellis, 'The Whig Junto', pp. 58–77.

[3] H. Horwitz, *Revolution Politicks; The Career of Daniel Finch, Second Earl of Nottingham, 1647–1730* (Cambridge, 1968), p. 141.

[4] Kenyon, *Sunderland*, pp. 250–5; Ellis, 'The Whig Junto', p. 218; Horwitz, *Parliament, Policy and Politics in the reign of William III*, pp. 114–15.

Moreover, the Privy Council had been planning a revision of the county magistracy immediately before Somers's appointment. The assize judges were required to compile lists of non-juring and inactive justices of the peace in which those who were disaffected were to be distinguished from those who were merely idle. The judges were also to report on the general state of the commissions of the peace in their circuits.[1] The Council was concerned to eliminate disaffection and provide for a more active enforcement of the law. Somers would doubtless have subscribed to this, but he was also a leading member of a group of politicians anxious to build up a position of strength in the countryside from which to demand their own advancement at the centre and the proscription of their political enemies. One of Sancroft's correspondents hinted at this when he wrote that Somers would remodel the commissions of the peace 'till all is made fit for a Parliament'.[2]

The first phase of Somers's tenure of office, as far as his handling of local patronage was concerned, lasted for almost three years, from his appointment to the end of February 1696. In this period he sealed 103 commissions of the peace. However, the docquet book reveals that he did not undertake a simultaneous regulation of the bench dealing with all or nearly all of the counties together, as had occurred in 1680 or 1687.[3] There were rumours that such a comprehensive revision was intended and even that it had taken place,[4] but in fact the number of commissions passing the great seal actually dropped. The highest number sealed in any one month was ten, a figure achieved in July 1694 and July 1695, whereas the Commissioners of the Great Seal had issued twelve or more in fourteen of the forty-nine months between March 1689 and March 1693. However, Somers did produce at least one commission for every county in England and Wales except four: Breconshire, Shropshire, Warwickshire, and the North Riding.

[1] P.R.O., P.C. 2/75, p. 97: 23 Feb. 1693.
[2] Bodl. MS. Tanner 25, f. 21: [Sir Henry North] to Sancroft, 27 Mar. 1693.
[3] P.R.O., C. 231/8, pp. 304 ff.
[4] Luttrell, *Brief Relation*, iii. 237, 272, 274, 305; H.M.C., Seventh Report, Appendix, *Denbigh MSS.* iii. 218; B.L., Loan 29/187, f. 105: Robert Harley to Sir Edward Harley, 24 June 1693; Lincs. A.O., Monson MSS. 7/12/84: newsletter, 13 Oct. 1694.

The Whigs would hypothetically have wanted to put out justices who refused to recognize the Revolution regime, declined to act, or were troublesome in local politics because of strong Tory sympathies. They would equally have wanted to add gentlemen not already in, who were reliably reported to be well-affected Whigs. There were undoubtedly changes along these lines in a number of counties at different times between April 1693 and February 1696, mostly in the summer of 1694. Devonshire received as many as four commissions in 1694 and 1695, in which ten names were added; many of the thirty-two put out had died, but at least one crypto-Jacobite, Thomas Hele, was dismissed, probably on the report of the assize judge. Similarly, Sir Haswell Tynt was left out in Somerset in 1693 for not taking the oaths. Sir John Cotton, Sir Anthony Chester, and several others in Bedfordshire, and Sir Edward Bromfield in Surrey, were probably omitted for the same reason. The Middlesex magistracy, predictably, was reshuffled severely in July 1693 and again in December the same year. Among the living justices disgraced in Leicestershire in 1694 were two prominent Tory squires, John Verney and Sir Wolstan Dixie, while ten new names were added, among them Sir William Ellis and Sir William Yorke, both M.P.s of Whig sympathies for constituencies in neighbouring Lincolnshire. Sir William Monson, who had refused the oaths in 1689, was sacked in Kesteven, where eleven gentlemen were recruited.[1]

The commissions for most of the Welsh counties were also reshaped following the repeal of the statute limiting the number of justices to eight, and conflicting local interests suggested different sets of names. In Radnorshire, for instance, Robert Harley produced what he thought was an unexceptionable list, but probably the recommendations of Sir Rowland Gwynne, the *custos* and a supporter of the Junto, carried more weight with Somers. One of the Radnorshire justices put out in 1692, Thomas Lewis of Harpton Court,

---

[1] Devon R.O., Q/JC: commissions of the peace, 23 Jan. 1694, 25 July 1695; *The Diary of Mr Justice Rokeby* (privately printed, 1887), p. 30; Som. R.O., Sanford MSS. DD/SF 1747: list of justices put in and out by Somers since 1693, [April 1700]; Luttrell, *Brief Relation*, iii. 131, 134, 274; Leics. R.O., QS 1/7: commission of the peace, 24 July 1694; Lincs. A.O., commission of the peace, Kesteven, 15 Dec. 1694.

was so incensed by well-founded rumours of his continued exclusion that he attempted to murder Harley in the street. The composition of the bench of magistrates was clearly a matter which aroused strong passions in Radnorshire, and Somers was obliged to omit several names in November 1693.[1]

Another county where changes not only took place but also attracted contemporary attention was Suffolk. One of those dismissed in a commission dated July 1694 was Edmund Bohun, a target for Whig hostility when he was deprived of his place as licenser of the press by the Commons for licensing a book entitled *King William and Queen Mary Conquerors*. Also disgraced were Sir Robert Bacon, four more baronets, and at least eight other gentlemen. Bohun, an active Suffolk justice, stated explicitly that the object of the regulation in Suffolk was to 'lift up a party' of inconsiderable Whigs at the expense of the Church of England squires. The initiative came from below, from the Whig party in the county. Bohun blamed Sir Robert Rich, M.P. for Dunwich, Charles Whitaker, the Recorder of Ipswich, and Henry Heveningham, while Somers himself later said that the lord-lieutenant, Lord Cornwallis, had wanted even more drastic changes in the Whig interest.[2] Probably it was the weakness of Suffolk Toryism that encouraged the local Whigs to press for such a severe regulation, and it is noticeable that Whitaker and Heveningham joined Rich in the House of Commons after the 1695 election.

The evidence so far presented suggests that Somers was actively reshaping the bench in the Whig interest during his first three years in office, and certainly this conclusion holds good for several counties and matches developments in other areas of government during the period. Nottingham was dismissed as Secretary of State in November 1693, and Shrewsbury was eventually persuaded to take the seals. Somers's Junto associate Charles Montagu became Chancellor of the Exchequer in the spring of 1694 amid a number of

[1] Surrey R.O., Somers MSS. A.2, 2B: Harley to Somers, 3 Sept. 1693; J. A. Downie, 'The Attack on Robert Harley, M.P., by the Lewis brothers of Harpton Court, in the streets of New Radnor, 2 October 1693', *National Library of Wales Journal*, xx (1977), 41-4.

[2] *Diary and Autobiography of Edmund Bohun*, pp. 120-2, 124; *Vernon Correspondence*, ii. 436.

concessions to the Whigs. Meanwhile, the old Whig grievance of the London lieutenancy had been remedied in February 1694, and Somers took a leading part in remodelling the Customs and Excise Commissions the following June. There was plenty of advance warning of the election held in the autumn of 1695.[1] However, there are some indications that Somers's revision of the county magistracy was incomplete, and that cases like that of Suffolk were not necessarily typical.

The number of counties in which substantial changes are definitely known to have taken place is about twenty-five.[2] The true figure is probably higher, since the docquet book entries are unreliable. Even so, several other counties were let off lightly. The four for which Somers did not seal a commission at this time were obviously neglected, and there was little change in, for example, the West Riding, where Somers added three new justices and left out none.[3] Moreover, when living justices were dismissed, the reason was not always political disaffection. Henry Cooper, of Sussex, had taken part in a riot; George Vernon, of Derbyshire and Staffordshire, had caused disturbances in Needwood Forest; Sir James Butler, put out in four counties, had not recaptured an escaped pirate.[4] The oddest case was that of Richard, Viscount Wenman, who was left out for Oxfordshire because he was seven years old and an imbecile. His name was the same as that of his father, whose death in 1690 had passed unnoticed at the Crown Office. Somers actually gave in on one occasion to Tory requests to put a Whig justice out. Abraham Trout, of Devonshire, was described by the assize judge as a sober, well-affected man of a good estate, but Sir Hugh Acland and other Devonshire squires alleged that his low origins and mean understanding disqualified him. Although this was reported

---

[1] Luttrell, *Brief Relation*, iii. 265, 266, 269; *Cal. S.P. Dom., 1694–5*, pp. 179–82, 184–6; Horwitz, *Parliament, Policy and Politics in the reign of William III*, pp. 128, 132–3, 156–7.

[2] In addition to those counties already mentioned, alterations that were more than routine can be traced in Cardiganshire, Cheshire, Derbyshire, Dorset, Ely, Essex, Glamorgan, Hampshire, Hertfordshire, Kent, Northamptonshire, Oxfordshire, Peterborough, Rutland, Staffordshire, and Sussex.

[3] P.R.O., C. 234/44, West Riding: 6 Feb., 13 Feb., 30 Nov. 1694.

[4] Luttrell, *Brief Relation*, iii. 199, 558–9; *Cal. S.P. Dom., 1694–5*, p. 493; P.R.O., P.C. 2/76, p. 225.

to be a Tory complaint against a Whig, the unlucky Trout was displaced.[1]

The safest interpretation, therefore, is that while Somers did make alterations involving in some cases a purge in a number of counties, most notoriously in Middlesex and Suffolk, these alterations did not amount to a full-blooded regulation covering the whole country. Somers was either too cautious, or too handicapped by circumstances, to embark on a thorough remodelling of the county magistracy on his own initiative. The judges had failed to carry out the Council's instructions, early in 1693, to investigate the justices, when only Lord Chief Justice Holt, who had ridden the Norfolk circuit, submitted a satisfactory return; and Somers, noticing various categories of disaffected justices in the imperfect reports of the other judges, still found it necessary to ascertain the King's views on the proper action to take towards them.[2] This dependence on royal authorization led to delays, while Godolphin's opposition to the revision of the Customs and Excise Commissions in 1694 possibly extended to the revision of the commissions of the peace as well. In a letter mostly devoted to Godolphin's complaints, written in May 1694, Sunderland observed that 'the . . . affaire of Justices will be done with Moderation'. Fourteen months later he was still writing that 'all things concerning justices of peace and the commissions of Customs and Excise are Posponed to the King's return',[3] and in general it is likely that William's well-known distrust of faction inhibited the wholesale removal of Tory gentlemen from the county magistracy.

Also, most counties in the years after the Revolution had a stubborn group of magistrates of Tory sympathies who were firmly entrenched by virtue of family and status in the commission of the peace, and who were willing to act with the new regime just so far as to give no clear grounds for dismissal. They were, in many cases, too indispensible in county administration to be removed, and it was reasonable that

[1] *Diary of Mr Justice Rokeby*, p. 30; H.M.C., Thirteenth Report, Appendix VI, *Fitzherbert MSS.*, p. 34; Devon R.O., Q/JC: commission of the peace, 25 July 1695.
[2] N.U.L., PwA 1171, 1172: Somers to Portland, 20 June, 25 July 1693.
[3] N.U.L., PwA 1234, 1248: Sunderland to Portland, 28 May 1694, 28 July 1695. It is tempting to think that Sunderland was remembering the results of lack of moderation in 1687 and 1688.

such men should be conciliated with local office rather than permanently alienated by exclusion. Not only this; the disgrace even of genuinely disaffected or Jacobite justices still had to be recommended by some responsible source, and the differing political character of the official hierarchy of lords-lieutenant and *custodes* in the English counties after 1689 further hampered Whig attempts to remodel the commissions. Several of the counties where a purge of justices is known to have taken place were under the direction of a Whig lord-lieutenant, the most obvious example being Cornwallis in Suffolk, and it is at least a plausible conjecture that what happened in the first three years of Somers's tenure of office was that counties in which there was already a sturdy Whig element in local politics experienced a strengthening of that element among local office-holders. Counties like Yorkshire, where Carmarthen, now Duke of Leeds, was lord-lieutenant of all three Ridings, found little change in their commissions of the peace. It is likely, therefore, that the Whigs welcomed with something like relief an opportunity for a more systematic regulation that arose at the beginning of Somers's fourth year in office.

IV

On 24 February 1696 the King reported to Parliament the discovery of a conspiracy to assassinate him. Instantly, Parliament and the Privy Council took emergency measures.[1] Enthusiasm for William's escape, and fear lest a Jacobite conspiracy was about to blow up into armed revolt, found expression in the Commons in an Association to defend the person of the 'rightful and lawful' King and if necessary to avenge his death. The Association was subsequently promoted at assizes and quarter sessions by M.P.s and others in a display of conspicuous loyalty.[2] The leaders of the Junto were quick to see that the Association provided an opportunity to expose men whose commitment to the Revolution was equivocal, since the phrase 'rightful and lawful' was unacceptable to those who, while agreeing that William was

---

[1] *C.J.* xi. 465–7; P.R.O., P.C. 2/76, pp. 293 ff.
[2] B.L., Loan 29/147: Edward Howarth to Robert Harley, 15 Mar. 1696; Add. MSS. 36913, f. 221: Sir John Mainwaring to Sir Willoughby Aston, 29 Feb. 1696.

King *de facto*, still believed that the 'rightful and lawful' King was in exile. On 21 April 1696 the Act for the Security of the Crown, which made subscription to the Association obligatory for all office-holders, received the royal assent.[1] Nine days later, the Privy Council required every *custos rotulorum* to forward the names of justices of the peace who had refused the Association. The lords-lieutenant were given similar instructions with regard to defaulting deputy-lieutenants and militia officers.[2] A nationwide regulation of local officials was thus under way, and as the returns from the *custodes* came in between July 1696 and March 1697, the Council issued orders to Somers to put 156 specified gentlemen out of thirty-three county commissions of the peace. There was a further isolated case of the dismissal of two justices in Flintshire by Council order for obstructing subscriptions to the Association as late as July 1698.[3]

This exercise was the first centrally controlled revision of the commissions of the peace on a large scale since the Revolution.[4] However, it was a cumbersome administrative operation: inconsistent, haphazard, and, above all, slow. There were several reasons for this. The most obvious is that the remodelling was conducted by the unwieldy Privy Council, not by Somers or the Secretaries of State. The King was doubtless reluctant to give the Whig politicians a free hand in a purge of their political opponents.[5] He evidently preferred to invoke the traditional authority of the Council, where decisions were recorded; but the Council proved incapable of speedy action. It is not clear whether it even appointed a committee to deal with the returns from the *custodes*. When,

[1] 7 & 8 William III, c. 27.   [2] P.R.O., P.C. 2/76, p. 417: 30 Apr. 1696.
[3] P.R.O., P.C. 2/76, pp. 458-598: P.C. 2/77, p. 208. The counties involved, with the number of justices to be dismissed following in parentheses, were Anglesey (7), Bedfordshire (1), Buckinghamshire (2), Cambridgeshire (11), Cardiganshire (4), Cheshire (7), Denbighshire (3), Derbyshire (2), Devonshire (18), Dorset (5), Durham (4), Ely (1), Flintshire (2 + 2), Gloucestershire (16), Herefordshire (5), Holland (5), Huntingdonshire (2), Kesteven (5), Lindsey (5), Middlesex (2), Monmouthshire (2), Montgomeryshire (8), Norfolk (3), Northamptonshire (1), Nottinghamshire (1), Oxfordshire (1), Shropshire (9), Suffolk (6), Surrey (1), Sussex (4), Westmorland (5), Worcestershire (5), and the West Riding (3).
[4] There was at the same time a comparable purge of the militia, involving in many cases the same persons.
[5] E. L. Ellis, 'William III and the Politicians', in G. S. Holmes (ed.), *Britain after the Glorious Revolution, 1689-1714* (London, 1969), p. 127.

in November 1696, some tardy magnates had to be reminded that the Council was expecting lists of non-subscribers, the letters were signed by a small group of Councillors,[1] but another Councillor left fragmentary notes on the discussions, and rumours that the lists of justices had been considered referred to days when the full Council met.[2] Whatever the procedure, it cannot be said to have produced dynamic results. The atmosphere in which, for example, the Earl of Pembroke was signing letters to defaulting lords-lieutenant and *custodes* which were identical to those that he himself received in respect of his neglected duties in Cardiganshire and Breconshire was redolent of inefficiency and muddle.

Another reason for the clumsiness of the remodelling of the commissions of the peace after the Association move-ment was that the local agents with whom the Privy Council was compelled by traditional practice to do business were in some cases less than enthusiastic about the Association them-selves. The Association signed in the House of Lords employed the phrase 'by right of law' rather than the phrase 'rightful and lawful', but, even so, some *custodes* were reluctant to sign. Viscount Weymouth, *custos* of Wiltshire, refused on 31 March 1696. Viscount Hatton, *custos* of Northamptonshire, pleaded illness, without much conviction, as an excuse for not signing. The Earl of Oxford, *custos* of Essex, never signed in the House of Lords, though he subscribed a form of Asso-ciation for the Bedchamber. Sir Richard Middleton and Andrew Newport, *custodes* respectively of Denbighshire and Montgomeryshire, both refused in the House of Commons.[3] Many of the subscribing *custodes*, too, were incompetent. Some forgot to send lists of non-Associating justices altoge-ther. Others sent returns that did not distinguish between those who refused, and those who merely neglected, to sign;

[1] Dukes of Norfolk and Bolton, Earls of Pembroke, Stamford, Dorset, and Montagu, Sir William Trumbull, Sir Henry Goodricke, and Sir Joseph Williamson. The composition of this group modifies the hypothesis that the 'active' members of the Council on this occasion were men of Junto sympathies.

[2] *Recusant Documents from the Ellesmere Manuscripts*, ed. A. G. Petti (Catho-lic Record Society, lx, 1968), 305–9; *Cal. S.P. Dom., 1696*, p. 320; Bodl. MS. Carte 233, ff. 1A, 7, 16, 26A: [Vernon to Wharton], 4 July, 16 July, 4 Aug., 29 Sept. 1696; Luttrell, *Brief Relation*, iv. 88, 91, 99, 110.

[3] H.M.C., *House of Lords MSS.*, N.S. ii. 212–13; Browning, *Danby*, iii. 188–213; P.R.O., C. 213/365.

mixed up justices and militia officers; or were otherwise imprecise. Moreover, some counties were temporarily without a *custos*, and the Council's letter had to be addressed to the clerk of the peace or to 'the justices'.[1]

Also, the Association itself was not a satisfactory basis for a purge. The rolls lodged in the Tower of London as a memorial to the loyalty of the nation were often too bulky to use to discover whether a particular individual had signed. Some of them contained above 10,000 signatures.[2] In addition, the Act for the Security of the Crown paradoxically weakened the value of the Association as a political weapon, since some Tories, although reluctant to subscribe voluntarily, were prepared to do so under legal compulsion. For instance, three M.P.s who had refused the Association in Parliament signed in Oxfordshire, ostentatiously dating their signatures to show that they had waited until after the passage of the Act.[3] Shrewsbury was driven to suggest to William in June 1696 that justices who were 'notoriously disaffected' might be put out with the rest even though they had signed, and, while William is unlikely to have approved of this idea, it indicated that the Whigs had ceased to have much confidence in the Association as a formal test for office-holders.[4]

Lastly, there was a lack of liaison between the Privy Council and Somers, or alternatively between Somers and the Crown Office. There is no evidence in the docquet book that Somers ever passed commissions embodying the changes required by the Council for seven of the thirty-three counties. In these cases, the next commission was recorded some months or even years after the Council's order.[5] It did sometimes happen that a commission was overlooked in the compilation of the docquet book,[6] but it is unlikely that seven such mistakes in a period of twelve months would occur. If

---

[1] Derbyshire, Herefordshire, Monmouthshire, Nottinghamshire, and the West Riding had no incumbent *custos*; Lord Paget, *custos* of Staffordshire, was abroad.
[2] P.R.O., C. 213.
[3] H.M.C., Fourteenth Report, Appendix II, *Portland MSS.* iii. 575; P.R.O., C. 213/207 (the three were Lord Norris, Sir Edward Norris, and Simon Harcourt).
[4] *Cal. S.P. Dom., 1696*, pp. 213-14, 216.
[5] Anglesey, Cambridgeshire, Cardiganshire, Cheshire, Monmouthshire, Montgomeryshire, and Suffolk.
[6] See below, p. 137 n.4.

the docquet book is correct on this occasion, then the Council's purge is reduced to one of 111 justices in twenty-six counties.

The revision of the magistracy by the Council after the Association movement was therefore condemned to a slow start and to frustrating delays. The investigation of disaffected justices dragged on long after the excitement of the Association had faded into apathy. At least twenty-four counties escaped regulation by the Council altogether, including some of electoral importance like Cornwall, Hampshire, Somerset, and Wiltshire. It is, of course, possible that in at least some of these counties the *custos* had reported that every justice had signed the Association, but this was not the case in, for instance, Warwickshire, where six out of eight M.P.s refused the Association of the Commons. Four of them were county justices and not one was dismissed.[1] Sir John Bolles, who refused the Association as M.P. for Lincoln, appeared 'disordered' on the bench at Lincoln assizes in 1699, so he was in the commission of *oyer and terminer* and therefore almost certainly in the commission of the peace for Lindsey as well. On this occasion he insulted the judges and kicked the sheriff. The other justices tried to excuse his conduct by saying that when drunk and tired he tended to be distracted. Even after this accumulation of political and personal misdeeds, Bolles still does not seem to have been dismissed.[2] Evidently, where the local Whigs were weak, or where a purge of Tory justices would have left too few active magistrates, the Council was reluctant to meddle.

Notwithstanding these reservations, the changes ordered by the Council were not negligible. The displaced justices were Tory squires who were unhappy with the monopolisation of power at the centre by ambitious Court Whigs, and with the sinister influence of the traitor Sunderland. They were men who grumbled at high taxes, a debased coinage, Dutch favourites, insolent Dissenters, and the conduct of the war, and who demonstrated their discontent in local politics.

[1] Andrew Archer, William Bromley, Lord Digby, and Francis Greville. *Warwickshire Quarter Sessions Records, 1690–6*, pp. xv–xvi.

[2] Luttrell, *Brief Relation*, iv. 545; *Vernon Correspondence*, ii. 337–8; B.L., Add. MSS. 40774, f. 137: Vernon to the King, 8 Aug. 1699.

Twenty-three of those definitely known to have been put out were members of the House of Commons.[1] One of them, Anthony Hammond, wrote that he had been dismissed in Huntingdonshire, where he was knight of the shire, for 'voting against the Court'.[2] In a handful of counties the purge of justices was in numerical terms quite severe, and the gentlemen put out were figures of consequence. In Gloucestershire, sixteen justices were dropped, including Viscount Tracy, an Irish peer, and three M.P.s, among them the prominent Country party politician Jack Howe. In Shropshire, four M.P.s and five others were discarded. The most striking regulation, however, was that for Devonshire. Baron Powys, one of the assize judges, had discovered that several Devonshire justices, influenced by the clergy, were reluctant to accept the words 'rightful and lawful' in the Association, and that they had framed a 'loyal address' for separate presentation. In spite of the politically unsophisticated attempts of moderate squires like Sir Francis Drake to compose the quarrels on the bench, the evidence that eighteen justices could not accept 'rightful and lawful' was strong enough to secure their disgrace. Among those left out were the knight of the shire, Francis Courtenay; the Dean of Exeter, Richard Annesley; and Sir George Chudleigh, who had been 'insufferably insolent'. The Whig Earl of Stamford replaced the Earl of Bath as lord-lieutenant.[3] Moreover, Sir Edward Seymour, a powerful figure in the West Country, was also automatically left out of the Devonshire commission of the peace, as he was for every county following his dismissal from the Privy Council.

In 1696 and 1697, therefore, the Whigs made a gallant if

[1] Edward Brereton, Robert Byerley, William Cary, Sir John Conway, Francis Courtenay, Gilbert Dolben, Montagu Drake, Sir Thomas Dyke, Anthony Hammond, Simon Harcourt, John Howe, Richard Howe, Edward Kynaston, John Kynaston, John Lewknor, Sir Richard Middleton, Sir William Morley, Sir Christopher Musgrave, Sir Robert Owen, William Try, George Weld, Sir Michael Wentworth, and Sir William Williams. In addition, Price Devereux was omitted for Montgomeryshire if Somers in fact sealed a commission for that county. To complete the list, Thomas Brotherton and Peter Shakerley were left out for Lancashire (see below, p. 282).

[2] Bodl. MS. Rawl. A. 245, Hammond's autobiographical notes, f. 62.

[3] H.M.C., Thirteenth Report, Appendix VI, *Fitzherbert MSS.*, pp. 38–41; N.U.L., Pw2 Hy 486: paper headed 'Justices Out', no date but clearly relating to Devonshire in 1696.

only partially successful attempt to purge the bench of dis-
loyal justices (and also incidentally to discredit disaffected
M.P.s) in those counties where they felt that it was feasible
to support their local adherents by an assertion of the patronage powers of the central government. Even as the Privy
Council conducted its laborious inquiries, however, the
strength of the Whigs in ministerial politics was being under-
mined. Shrewsbury remained in the background following
disclosures about his Jacobite connections and a bad illness
in October 1696. Sunderland had already become estranged
from the Junto before the Assassination Plot, and he now
opposed the Whig-supported attainder of the conspirator Sir
John Fenwick. The Junto had thus lost two of their links
with the King, and they became isolated in the Cabinet. As
the peace negotiations developed in 1697, William relied on
Portland and Sunderland, now Lord Chamberlain; and he
appointed James Vernon instead of the Junto candidate
Wharton to the Secretaryship of State vacated by Trumbull
in December. Although Sunderland's nerve broke at the end
of the year and he resigned, Whig influence had become pre-
carious. Meanwhile, the Junto was beginning to lose ground
in Parliament. Montagu was still able to pilot the King's
financial business through the Commons, but after the end of
the war in 1697 the independent gentry, assisted by some
Whig defectors, embarrassed the ministers on the issues of the
retention of a standing army and the King's grants of land to
his Dutch followers.[1] The Junto was thus on the defensive by
the winter of 1697/8, and much depended on the general
election due in 1698. The King could hardly dispense with
his Whig ministers if they maintained their parliamentary
strength. It was therefore likely that Somers would make
some attempt to exploit his powers of local patronage to
assist the Whigs in the countryside.

V

Somers, who was promoted to Lord Chancellor and elevated
to the peerage as Baron Somers in 1697, made an attempt to
follow up the regulation of the commission of the peace

[1] Horwitz, *Parliament, Policy and Politics in the reign of William III*, pp. 182–94,
222–37; Kenyon, *Sunderland*, pp. 281–300; Ellis, 'The Whig Junto', pp. 323–51.

conducted by the Council after the Assassination Plot with another remodelling based on Junto interests. This private re-shuffle was contemporaneous with the later stages of the wearisome Privy Council operation. From September 1696 to July 1698, commissions leaving justices out were sealed for twenty counties without Privy Council authorisation.[1] Admittedly, some of these were issued as a matter of routine, as in the East Riding where the alterations had been planned before the Assassination Plot.[2] Elsewhere, the displaced jus-tices might have committed some misdemeanour. Sir Edward Phelips was put out in Somerset following a complaint from the Admiralty.[3] A Leicestershire gentleman, Roger Rooe, was put out by Somers on instructions from the Lords Justices entrusted with domestic affairs during William's absence abroad in 1697 for using the emotive word 'sequestrators' to describe the tax commissioners.[4] Somers and Harley co-operated over the Radnorshire commission in what may have been a routine revision. At least two of those put out were dead, and it seems that the county itself was anxious to have more justices appointed for administrative reasons.[5] But some of Somers's changes were of significance. For example, whereas the *custos* of Nottinghamshire had reported to the Council that all the justices had signed the Association except John Digby, who was accordingly the only name left out in 1696,[6] Somers was prepared to dismiss the wealthy Francis Molyneux of Tevershall and several others in February 1697. Somers supplemented the much more extensive Council purge in Devonshire by leaving out fourteen additional names,

[1] Breconshire, Cornwall, Devonshire, Ely, Essex, Herefordshire, Hertfordshire, Leicestershire, Middlesex, Northumberland, Nottinghamshire, Oxfordshire, Pem-brokeshire, Radnorshire, Shropshire, Somerset, Surrey, and all three Ridings of Yorkshire. P.R.O., C. 231/8, pp. 358 ff.

[2] H.M.C., *Downshire MSS.* i. 620–1.

[3] Som. R.O., Sanford MSS. DD/SF 1747.

[4] *Cal. S.P. Dom., 1697*, p. 170; B.L., Add. MSS. 40777, ff. 182–3: Vernon to Somers, 27 May 1697; Leics. R.O., QS 1/8: commission of the peace, 1 June 1697. The omission of Rooe was the only change made in Leicestershire between 1694 and 1700.

[5] B.L., Loan 29/188, f. 141: Robert Harley to Sir Edward Harley, 15 Sept. 1696; ff. 148–51: presentment of grand jury of Radnorshire, 21 Sept. 1696, enclosed in a letter to Robert Harley, 2 Oct. 1696.

[6] B.L., Loan 29/237, f. 637: Duke of Newcastle to the Privy Council, 13 June 1696 (draft); P.R.O., P.C. 2/76, p. 487.

though some of these were dead, and adding fifteen, among them three M.P.s.[1] The Oxfordshire bench was also reshaped, probably on the advice of Wharton, who replaced the Earl of Abingdon as lord-lieutenant and *custos* in May 1697. Four gentlemen who had signed the Association only after the passage of the Act for the Security of the Crown were put out, along with the contentious Sir Edmund Warcup and another elderly gentleman who never acted. In the course of 1697, more than twenty new names were added to the Oxfordshire commission.[2]

In carrying out this regulation — that is, the regulation not authorized by the Privy Council — Somers was faced with two serious difficulties. In the first place, the King was as hostile as ever to any attempt to win party advantage through the excessive use of patronage; for instance, he expressly desired that the militia should not be altered before the elections.[3] Although Somers issued twenty-two commissions of the peace in the two months, June and July, before the elections of July and August 1698, more than for any two consecutive months since he became Lord Keeper, these commissions seems to have put gentlemen in rather than left them out; indeed, the only justice dismissed at this time was William Skyrme in Pembrokeshire.[4] Somers may well have been restrained from exploiting the resources of his patronage to strengthen the Junto's hand in the elections by the will of the King, implied if not explicit.

The second handicap under which Somers was labouring was a partial breakdown in the procedure by which commissions of the peace were passed under the great seal. In September 1696 Somers pointed out that the commissions of the peace embodying the Council's purges had been delayed because the counties scrupled the payment of the necessary fees to Thomas Chute, the Clerk of the Crown. It had then been ordered that Chute should be compensated from the

[1] Devon R.O., Q/JC: commission of the peace, 4 Mar. 1697. The three M.P.s were Henry Henley, Sir Charles Rawleigh, and Charles Trelawny.

[2] Bodl. MS. Carte 79, ff. 702, 706: lists of justices put in and out of the Oxfordshire commission since 1693, annotated by Wharton [1700]; Luttrell, *Brief Relation*, iv. 298.

[3] H.M.C., Twelfth Report, Appendix V, *Rutland MSS.* ii. 163.

[4] P.R.O., C. 231/8, pp. 389–93.

Hanaper, but in June 1698 Chute and Thomas Engeham, Somers's Secretary for Commissions, were again petitioning that the fees customarily received at the Crown Office had not been paid.[1] Two years later, Chute again claimed that his arrears of fees for putting 454 names in the English and Welsh commissions of the peace between 1694 and 1698, when the King's service had required exceptional haste and speed, amounted to over £800. He was allowed half of this by the Treasury.[2] This was in 1700; in 1698 Chute and probably Engeham were disconsolate at their losses, incurred because of their zeal in the King's service, and they were presumably grudging in their co-operation with Somers in the speedy issue of further commissions.

The remodelling of the commissions of the peace since the Assassination Plot, both officially by the Privy Council and privately by Somers and the Junto leaders, produced some effect on the elections of July and August 1698, but it was hardly decisive one way or the other. Of the twenty-three M.P.s who had been put out of the commission for not subscribing the Association, fifteen were returned in 1698 for the same constituency, and two more were elected elsewhere. Jack Howe's reputation in Gloucestershire was so little affected by his omission that he was returned as knight of the shire. At least two justices put out in the period after the Association, who had not then been M.P.s, were returned in 1698 for their counties. These were Sir John Packington in Worcestershire, put out by the Privy Council, and Sir Edward Phelips in Somerset, put out by Somers at the request of the Admiralty. It is tempting to think that at least part of the reason for their success was that they were able to claim that they were the victims of Court hostility. Against this must be set the cases of three M.P.s who had been put out of the commission of the peace in 1696 and 1697, and who were not re-elected in 1698.[3] It is possible

[1] B.L., Add. MSS. 40777, f. 139: Vernon to Somers, 18 Sept. 1696; *Cal. S.P. Dom., 1696*, p. 392; *Cal. S.P. Dom., 1698*, p. 285.

[2] P.R.O., S.P. 44/100, pp. 443–5: Jersey to the Treasury, 17 June 1700, enclosing Chute's petition; *Cal. Treas. Books*, xv. 107, 387, 421.

[3] H. Horwitz, 'Parties, Connection, and Parliamentary Politics, 1689–1714: Review and Revision', *Journal of British Studies*, vi (1966–7), 68–9. The three were Gilbert Dolben, Richard Howe, and William Try.

that omission from the magistracy had blighted the chances of a few M.P.s.

It is more likely, though difficult to prove, that Somers's supervision of persons to be put into the commission since 1694 bore more fruit than his endeavours to put persons out. The commission of the peace had been used as a means of binding together the families disposed to support the Whigs. The inclusion in 1698 of Sir Thomas Alston for Bedfordshire and Sir John Phillips for Pembrokeshire, shortly before their respective elections for Bedford and Pembroke boroughs, may have been calculated either to assist their candidature or to gratify them in the hope of winning supporters in the event of their success. But it is noticeable that in, for instance, Oxfordshire, where the bench had been quite severely regulated in September 1697, only three new members were elected in 1698, of whom only one, James Isaacson, was thought to be a supporter of the Court, and he was expelled the House shortly after the election anyway. Also, the use of the commission of the peace as an instrument of patronage was not always successful. Eleven days before the election of Sir Brian Stapylton for Boroughbridge in Yorkshire, Somers signed a fiat to add him to the West Riding commission. The commission was sealed four days after the election, but Sir Brian was, and remained, an opponent of the Whigs.[1] The limitations of the commission of the peace as an aid to electoral and parliamentary management are further illustrated by the fact that of the ninety-two county members returned in 1698, fifty-eight — nearly two-thirds — were not expected to support the Court, while the counties that returned at any rate one knight of the shire thought to be a potential supporter of the Court do not correspond significantly to those counties in which the bench had been purged or otherwise remodelled.[2] It is clear that other influences on county elections were more important.

Somers thought that the election had been unfortunately timed and mismanaged, and he viewed the future with foreboding.[3] There were several reasons for the Junto's lack of

[1] P.R.O., C. 234/44, West Riding: 15 July 1698.
[2] Horwitz, 'Parties, Connection, and Parliamentary Politics', pp. 62-7.
[3] *Miscellaneous State Papers, 1501-1726*, ed. Philip Yorke (London, 1778), ii. 435-6.

success at the polls. Taxes remained heavy in spite of the peace. There was a general distrust of placemen. A pamphlet controversy on the issue of the standing army highlighted the recent regulation of local office by advancing arguments for and against an efficient militia. The outcome was that the Court could not prevent the passage of a bill for disbanding most of the army in the winter of 1698/9. William was thoroughly disappointed by the bill, and he even spoke of abdication.[1] Somers thought that he might accept a mixed ministry if this would be more effective.[2] In the event, the Cabinet colleagues of Somers and Montagu by the autumn of 1699 were inoffensive Courtiers who performed routine duties without arousing the wrath of the Commons. The French ambassador thought that domestic government in England was breaking down altogether, and the bleak tone of some of Secretary Vernon's letters echoed this view.[3] The Whigs could not hope to restore themselves with the King unless their fortunes improved in the Commons, now dominated by a Country opposition in which Robert Harley was the leading figure. It was not likely that mass changes in the commissions of the peace would do much good, but as long as Somers retained the great seal there was a possibility that discreet and conciliatory adjustments in the county magistracy might bolster up the Whigs in central politics.

VI

Somers was certainly active in issuing commissions of the peace. Fifty-nine were sealed in 1699 for thirty-eight counties, more than in any one year since 1692.[4] He was principally concerned to put gentlemen in. More than five names

---

[1] Horwitz, *Parliament, Policy and Politics in the reign of William III*, pp. 247–56; Ellis, 'The Whig Junto', pp. 381–409.

[2] *Private and Original Correspondence of Charles Talbot, Duke of Shrewsbury*, ed. W. Coxe (London, 1821), pp. 559–61.

[3] *Letters of William III and Louis XIV and of their Ministers*, ed. P. Grimblot (London, 1848), ii. 316–17; Duke of Manchester, *Court and Society from Elizabeth to Anne* (London, 1864), ii. 49–50.

[4] P.R.O., C. 231/8, pp. 401–16. The docquet book entries at this time generally indicate the numbers added and left out in each commission, a temporary improvement on the practice of the early 1690s which is perhaps explained by Chute's attempts to calculate his fees.

were added for at least twelve counties, among them Buckinghamshire, where Wharton was *custos*, and Dorset, where the
Duke of Bolton had recently replaced the dead Earl of Bristol
as lord-lieutenant. There were eleven inclusions in Radnorshire, although the details are obscure and it is not clear
whether Somers was acknowledging Harley's influence in that
county or attempting to thwart it.[1] The allegiance of committed or potential Whig M.P.s and local placemen was consolidated, either by putting them into the commission of the
peace for the first time, or by adding them for counties other
than those in which their main influence lay.[2] A very few
persons who had been dismissed for misdemeanour before
1698 were restored where there seemed to be a possibility
of gaining political advantage. For instance, George Vernon,
put out for Derbyshire and Staffordshire in 1695 after the
quarrels in Needwood Forest, was elected to the 1698 Parliament as M.P. for Derby, and, after his profession of honest
intentions, Somers reincluded him in the Derbyshire commission of the peace. He voted with the ministry in a division on
the bill for disbanding the army in 1699, and was, shortly
afterwards, restored in Staffordshire also.[3] The number of
justices who were restored after having been put out by the
Council during the Association regulation was very small
indeed, however.[4]

Somers did not put justices out on a large scale. The most
publicized case of omission in 1699 was that of Sir Harry
Dutton Colt for Middlesex in July, but Somers was not really
responsible for this. Colt was a 'busy justice' who had embarrassed the Whigs in 1696 by agitating for a witch-hunt among
Jacobite justices far beyond what even the Junto thought

---

[1] In addition to the counties mentioned, five or more gentlemen were added in
Breconshire, Cheshire, Flintshire, Gloucestershire, Kent, Middlesex, Staffordshire,
Surrey, and the North Riding. Elsewhere names were added in ones and twos.

[2] Examples of such inclusions are Lord William Paulet for the three parts of
Lincolnshire, James Isaacson for Essex (after his expulsion from the Commons),
and Thomas Mansell for Breconshire, shortly before he fought a successful by-
election in Glamorgan; and, at a lower level, the receiver of taxes in Berkshire,
for Hampshire.

[3] B.L., Add. MSS. 40771, f. 323: James Vernon to George Vernon, 13 Aug.
1698; Browning, *Danby*, iii. 217.

[4] There are no certain cases in 1699; Cyprian Thornton had been restored for
Kesteven in 1697. Lincs. A.O., commission of the peace, Kesteven, 6 July 1697.

reasonable. He opposed Montagu and Vernon in the Westminster election of 1698 with extraordinary factiousness, and he was put out by the King's order at the request of the Commons.[1] Otherwise, those put out were either dead, or persons guilty of misdemeanour, like Thomas Smith, a minor official dismissed for fraud in February 1699 and put out of the Middlesex commission of the peace in the same month.[2]

Somers was the subject of vigorous attacks in the Commons in the winter of 1699/1700. The main targets were his use of the great seal to pass grants of Irish land to royal favourites and his sponsorship of Captain Kidd, the pirate, but his alleged manipulation of the commissions of the peace in a spirit of party was a useful secondary issue which appealed strongly to the country gentry who made up a majority of the opposition.[3] The squires' discontent in the matter had been apparent as early as 1696, when Sir Edward Seymour had objected to the sacking of members of the House of Commons from the commission of the peace in their counties.[4] By 1699 the time was ripe for Seymour's grievance to be examined at length. On 28 November the Commons appointed a committee to examine the commissions of the peace and the lieutenancy as they then stood, with power to examine also the lists of those added and left out over the past seven years. After the inclusion of all the knights of the shire a week later, this committee contained at least eight gentlemen who had themselves been dismissed from the commission of the peace during this period.[5] The committee reported on 4 March 1700, and the lists were ordered to lie upon the table. After taking three weeks to ponder them, the

---

[1] Vernon Correspondence, i. 268–70, ii. 135–7, 139–40; N.U.L., PwA 1468A: Vernon to Portland, 3 Sept. 1697; Cal. S.P. Dom., 1698, pp. 430, 434; C.J. xii. 365–7; Luttrell, Brief Relation, iv. 465, where Colt's dismissal is attributed, rather oddly, to his hindering the quartering of soldiers in inns.

[2] Cal. Treas. Books, xiv. 40, 58, 275.

[3] J. Oldmixon, History of England during the Reigns of King William and Queen Mary, Queen Anne, King George I . . . (London, 1735), pp. 192–3; C. Roberts, The Growth of Responsible Government in Stuart England (Cambridge, 1966), pp. 292–4; Horwitz, Parliament, Policy and Politics in the reign of William III, pp. 261–70; Sachse, Somers, 157–67.

[4] Vernon Correspondence, i. 34–5.

[5] C.J. xiii. 8, 39. The eight were Sir John Conway, Francis Courtenay, John Howe, Edward Kynaston, Sir Richard Middleton, Sir Christopher Musgrave, Sir John Packington, and Sir Edward Phelips.

members produced a motion for an address to the King that it would be for the good of the nation that 'Gentlemen of Quality and good Estates' be put in, and restored to, the commissions of the peace and lieutenancy, and that 'Men of small Estates' be neither continued in, nor put in.[1] The Country party had won a clear victory. It was implied that Somers had tampered with the magistracy to deprive honest gentlemen of the local powers to which their status, property, and wealth entitled them. The Commons thus echoed the Lords' criticism of Lord Chancellor Nottingham nearly twenty years before, but William did not support Somers as Charles II had supported Nottingham. On 1 April he returned the conciliatory answer 'I am of the Opinion that Men of the best Quality and Estates are most proper to be intrusted in the Commissions of the Peace, and Lieutenancy; and Directions shall be given accordingly.'[2] It was rumoured that several justices had been removed only a fortnight after the King's answer to the Commons, while Somers was still in office.[3] This is not, however, borne out by the facts. Twelve commissions of the peace were issued for ten counties between the appointment of the Commons' committee in November 1699 and the end of April 1700, and these left out two justices: Sir Nicholas Toke in Kent and Thomas Wrentmore in Somerset. The highest number of new justices was six in the West Riding, and the total number of recruits was thirty, none of whom seem to have been gentlemen who had formerly been purged.[4]

Somers had a good case against his critics. It would have been difficult to prove the accusation that his justices were men of low calibre. Moreover, in leaving gentlemen out of the commissions after April 1696, Somers was following the

[1] *C.J.* xiii. 264, 301-2; B.L., Add. MSS. 30000D, f. 116: Bonet's dispatch, 2 Apr. 1700 (Bonet's gloss on the phrase 'Men of small Estates' was 'des gens pauvres et corruptibles et d'une naissance basse'); D. Rubini, *Court and Country, 1688-1702* (London, 1967), p. 200, quoting Shrewsbury MSS. at Boughton House.

[2] *C.J.* xiii. 308.

[3] Luttrell, *Brief Relation*, iv. 634, followed by Sachse, *Somers*, p. 166.

[4] P.R.O., C. 231/8, pp. 419-20; C. 231/9, pp. 1-3. The counties involved were Breconshire, Carmarthenshire (two commissions), Cumberland, Essex, Glamorgan (two commissions), Kent, Lindsey, Somerset, Wiltshire, and the West Riding. The fiats for all the commissions except those for Breconshire and Glamorgan survive at P.R.O., C. 234/7, /12, /18, /22, /33, /40, /44, and /81.

principle laid down in the Act for the Security of the Crown, that those who did not sign the Association should not hold office. The real significance of the Commons' address lies in its parliamentary context, as part of the Country party's attack on a leading Junto minister. The Irish land grants, Kidd, Somers's own fruits of office, the commission of the peace — all were means to an end, that end being the overthrow of the Chancellor. The defeat on 10 April of a motion for his permanent removal from the ministry seemed to vindicate Somers's courage in resisting attack, but this success was illusory. Sunderland was arguing that the King must join hands with the Tories.[1] Although there was no obvious Tory candidate for the great seal, the King became convinced that he could not persevere with a Chancellor so unpopular in the Commons. Somers, in Whig eyes a martyr to a conspiracy of Sunderland and a Tory clique, was dismissed on 27 April 1700.

VII

Somers had been a leading member of an organized and disciplined party which had dominated the King's ministry. Other prominent members of his party took a strong interest in local affairs with a view to influencing elections. The King was absent from the country for long periods, and in any case he knew little of provincial England. Yet Somers's achievements were, perhaps, rather limited where the commission of the peace was concerned. In the years 1693-5 he seems to have depended on local recommendation rather than on the implementation of a central policy. The result was that while some counties like Suffolk were vigorously remodelled, others, perhaps more than half the total number, were left alone. The opportunity to go further, created in 1696 by the Assassination Plot, was only partially taken. The initiative was taken out of Somers's hands, and the Privy Council performed a laboured and inefficient purge of justices whose enthusiasm for the Revolution was lukewarm. In a few counties, it was probably the energy of magnates sympathetic to the Junto that enabled a more thorough regulation to take place in 1697 and early 1698, but the ministers were on the

[1] Kenyon, *Sunderland*, pp. 314-16.

defensive from the election of 1698 onwards, and the last eighteen months of Somers's Chancellorship saw little change in the commissions of the peace beyond the inclusion of supporters on a modest scale.

There were several reasons for this curiously unimpressive record. The legacy of the Commissioners of the Great Seal was a set of county commissions differing in character according to the political complexion of the lords-lieutenant and the *custodes rotulorum*. Political and administrative expediency dictated the nature of the changes that could be made thereafter. The Junto magnates could only act decisively in areas which they either dominated or hoped to dominate. In some of the more remote counties it was not always feasible to dismiss justices willing to act. The Secretaries of State had been active in collecting information in 1680 and 1687, but in the 1690s they were of little help to Somers. A final factor was the restraining influence of the King, who distrusted party distinctions in the abstract and the ambitions of the Whigs in particular. He wanted to be kept informed of projected purges; it was probably his wish that the Association regulation should be conducted by the Council; he was reluctant to permit the exploitation of local patronage before the 1698 election. In 1680 and again in 1687, the Crown's weight had been firmly behind the efforts of successive Chancellors to regulate the county bench. In the 1690s this was not the case, and the Whigs were never able to set in motion the systematic, comprehensive revision of local office, involving a really substantial purge, that probably they would have desired.

5

THE COMMISSION OF THE PEACE AND PARTY CONFLICT, 1700-5

I

After Somers had been dismissed in April 1700, Sunderland still hoped that a mixed ministry of moderate Tories, Country party leaders, and Whigs might be practicable. This scheme fell to the ground, largely because Harley held out against a 'patched' administration and because Shrewsbury pleaded ill health, but also because of the difficulty of finding a successor to Somers who might fit into what would have been a strangely assorted Cabinet.[1] Lord Chief Justice Holt was approached, but he refused on the grounds that he was not familiar with the law of equity. The Attorney General, Sir Thomas Trevor, declined. The Junto pressed the claim of Sir John Powell, a judge in the Common Pleas. The Earl of Nottingham was rumoured to be a serious candidate.[2] After three weeks of negotiation, during which Chancery business was executed by the three senior common-law judges and no commissions of the peace at all were sealed, the King fell back on a sergeant-at-law, Sir Nathan Wright, who received the great seal on 21 May 1700.

Wright is generally thought to have been an obscure figure, a High Church Tory forced on the King through inability to find anyone else.[3] His career at the bar had been moderately distinguished, and in early life he was, if anything, a Whig in politics. He had been Recorder of Leicester since 1680, having been put out in 1684 and restored in 1688. He was

[1] Kenyon, *Sunderland*, pp. 316–17; Sachse, *Somers*, pp. 171–3.

[2] Luttrell, *Brief Relation*, iv. 639; B.L., Add. MSS. 34730, f. 227: Richard Pusey to [John Marriot], 30 Apr. 1700; N.U.L. PwA 833: Lonsdale to Portland, 1 May 1700; B.L., Add. MSS. 30000D, ff. 164, 174: Bonet's dispatches, 3/14 May 1700, 14/25 May 1700; Leics. R.O., Finch MSS. Box VI, Bundle 22: Edward Southwell to Nottingham, 11 May 1700; unsigned memorandum dated 14 May 1700.

[3] See, for instance, Feiling, *History of the Tory Party, 1640–1714*, p. 340; Roberts, *Growth of Responsible Government*, p. 296.

knighted in 1697 for his arguments in support of the attainder of Sir John Fenwick, which apparently raised his reputation considerably. The Prussian ambassador still described him as a Whig when he was appointed Lord Keeper. Wright's reputation as a judge is low, but it is hard to say why; although his conduct of business was slow, he was allowed to have been prudent and fair.[1] He suffered from almost complete lack of personality — the single recorded example of his judicial wit is colourless in the extreme — and his political influence is thought to have been small.[2]

A regulation of the county commissions of the peace had been planned and half completed when Wright was sworn Lord Keeper. This regulation was carried on by the Privy Council in response to the King's promise to the Commons to order an investigation of the composition of the commissions.[3] As in 1696, William felt that the proper place for this to be done was the Council, and Somers was ordered to supply lists of justices for its inspection shortly before his dismissal.[4] On 25 April the whole Privy Council was constituted a committee to investigate the lists of justices. In effect this entrusted the regulation to the great officers of state and a handful of other active members, meeting at Whitehall rather than in the presence of the King at Hampton Court or Kensington. The committee reported on 29 April that all persons put out by order of the Council since 30 April 1696 should be restored, if they had in the interval taken the oaths and signed the Association. The committee further recommended that lists of justices in commission for the appropriate counties, and lists of justices put out since 1696, be sent to the lords-lieutenant, the *custodes*, and the assize judges, for their comments, and that they be invited to make suggestions

---

[1] Campbell, *Lives of the Chancellors*, iv. 242-5; Foss, *Judges of England*, vii. 408-10; Burnet, *History*, iv. 446; v. 224, and note by Onslow; B.L., Add. MSS. 30000D, f. 179: Bonet's dispatch, 21 May/1 June 1700; R. W. Greaves, 'The Earl of Huntingdon and the Leicester Charter of 1684', *H.L.Q.* xv (1952), 389-90.

[2] Holmes, *British Politics in the Age of Anne*, p. 370, where he is described as a 'passenger' in the Cabinet. His one joke is described by Campbell, op. cit. iv. 254: he returned a watch offered as a bribe with the remark, somewhat less than sparkling, that 'it has one motion too much for me'.

[3] B.L., Add. MSS. 30000D, f. 116: Bonet's dispatch, 2/13 April 1700.

[4] *Vernon Correspondence*, iii. 19.

as to new names to be put in. These lists were prepared within three days, and the returns began to come in from the counties before the end of May.[1] The Lords of the Treasury and those *custodes* and lords-lieutenant who were in London were called in to advise.[2] The changes to be made had been decided by the end of June, and were entered in the Privy Council register.[3] Wright was entrusted with an investigation into cases of fathers and sons being named in the same commission, but otherwise he was not involved until he sealed the revised commissions. Except for Carmarthenshire, where no changes were thought to be necessary, every county in England and Wales received a new commission of the peace in July or August 1700.[4] As in 1696, there was a simultaneous examination of the militia.

The regulation of the county magistracy in 1700 was a smooth and speedy operation. It was not linked, as that of 1696 had been, to a test involving complicated research by unenthusiastic local magnates. The Council eased the administrative problem in 1700 by sending lists of justices to the *custodes*. This was not difficult, as lists had already been laid before the Council in March, and only needed to be recopied by the Council's clerks. The address of the Commons and the King's answer had made the composition of the county benches an issue of public interest, and the *custodes* were receptive to the idea of changes. The judges showed themselves efficient agents of the government on this occasion; even before the regulation had begun, Lord Chief Baron Ward reported from the Western circuit on the inadequacy of the Cornwall bench, where only twenty gentlemen condescended to act.[5] Finally, the regulation was not carried on by the

---

[1] P.R.O., P.C. 2/78, pp. 13, 16, 17-19, 32. The active committee consisted of the Archbishop of Canterbury, Pembroke (Lord President), Lonsdale (Lord Privy Seal), Devonshire (Lord Steward), Bridgwater, Marlborough, and James Vernon (Secretary of State).

[2] Luttrell, *Brief Relation*, iv. 655, 659.   [3] P.R.O., P.C. 2/78, pp. 58, 63-9.

[4] P.R.O., C. 231/9, pp. 8-10. There is no entry in the docquet book for a new commission for Shropshire, although changes had been ordered by the Council, but this was an oversight, since a commission, embodying the changes and dated 15 July 1700, survives at Shrops. R.O., Quarter Sessions Records, Box 292. I am grateful to Dr David Cox for drawing my attention to this.

[5] P.R.O., Privy Council Miscellaneous Papers, P.C. 1/1/50: Ward's account from Cornwall, 18 Apr. 1700.

whole Council in the ordinary course of its meetings, as in 1696, but by an active committee.

There is some evidence that the Council's regulation in 1700 was executed in a mechanical way. It authorized the restoration of all the justices put out for Cambridgeshire by its own order recorded in the register under the date 15 July 1696. The order for their restoration in 1700 follows that for their omission exactly — the names are in the same sequence — except for one clerical error, corrected three weeks later. It seems possible that the clerk simply copied out the list from the earlier register. The fact that Cambridgeshire had not received a commission since before the original order of 1696 was ignored. The justices had been in commission all the time.[1] A similar example concerns the three parts of Lincolnshire. In 1696 five justices had been left out for 'Lincolnshire'. In 1700 the Council ordered that three of them be restored to the commission 'for the division in which they formerly served'. The task of discovering precisely where these gentlemen were to be justices was left to the Crown Office. One of the three, Cyprian Thornton, had actually been restored for Kesteven in 1697.[2] It seems, therefore, that on this occasion the Council sacrificed precision to speed; the exact opposite of what had happened in 1696.

The regulation reflected a conscious decision to reverse the changes made by the Junto Whigs in their heyday. Nevertheless, it was essentially non-party in character. The great officers of state who composed the active committee conceived their task to be to settle the commission of the peace in response to complaints from the King's high court of Parliament. The proper persons to advise on the matter were the *custodes* and the judges, and their wishes were scrupulously observed. The *custodes* had not changed much since 1696.[3] Consequently the Council accepted, apparently with impar-

[1] P.R.O., P.C. 2/76, p. 470; P.C. 2/78, pp. 63, 71.

[2] P.R.O., P.C. 2/78, p. 65; C. 231/8, p. 372; Lincs. A.O., commission of the peace, Kesteven, 6 July 1697.

[3] The Duke of Bolton had replaced the Earl of Bristol in Dorset; the Duke of Newcastle and the Earl of Burlington had replaced the Duke of Leeds in the East and West Ridings respectively (Leeds having been 'dismissed' on a mistaken rumour that he was dead, for which see Browning, *Danby*, i. 548). Sir Robert Cotton had replaced Sir Richard Middleton in Denbighshire, and the office in both Lincolnshire and Montgomeryshire was vacant.

tiality, the reports of Junto politicians like Wharton, *custos* of Buckinghamshire and Oxfordshire, the Earl of Orford, *custos* of Cambridgeshire, and the Duke of Bolton, *custos* of Dorset and Hampshire, as well as those of Tories like the Duke of Norfolk, *custos* of Berkshire and Norfolk, and Viscount Weymouth, *custos* of Wiltshire. All Wharton's recommendations for his two counties were accepted. The assize judge made nine further recommendations for Oxfordshire, of which Wharton agreed to two.[1] In some counties, the non-party character of the ministry resulted in a similarly non-party approach. Thus, for example, the Court Whig Coningsby left the list he had been sent as *custos* of Herefordshire with the Country party leader Harley for his suggestions.[2]

The operation was manifestly a 'putting-in' rather than a 'putting-out' exercise. The Council ordered the inclusion of 919 new justices, and the omission of 72.[3] Thirty or more justices were added for five counties;[4] but ten or more were left out for only three counties.[5] Inevitably, some of the new men were either members of families which, a generation before, would not have aspired to a place in the commission, or members of cadet branches of established families. Some justices had, in the years since 1689, neglected their duties, because of political discontent, unwillingness to associate with socially inferior gentlemen, or laziness. It was doubtless hoped that the new men would supply the want of active justices; this, for instance, was explicitly the principle behind the Duke of Newcastle's recommendations for Nottinghamshire.[6]

Members of the Parliament elected in 1698 who were not already justices were also added, apparently as a conscious policy. Nearly one-fifth of the total number of inclusions —

[1] Bodl. MS. Carte 79, ff. 694, 696, 698-9; P.R.O., P.C. 2/78, pp. 63, 66.
[2] H.M.C., Fourteenth Report, Appendix II, *Portland MSS.* iii. 619.
[3] These figures are based on the entries in the Council register. No adjustment is made to take account of anomalous or ambiguous orders like those relating to Cambridgeshire and Lincolnshire.
[4] Gloucestershire (44), Suffolk (42), Leicestershire (41), Cornwall (33), Oxfordshire (32).
[5] Suffolk (14), Leicestershire (11), Kent (10).
[6] B.L., Loan 29/237, f. 7: Newcastle to Privy Council (draft), 5 June 1700.

176 out of 919 — were M.P.s. Admittedly, it had in the past been a polite convention, irregularly observed, that newly elected M.P.s should be included if they were not already justices. However, about 60 per cent of the M.P.s added in 1700 had been members at least since the 1695 elections. In Hampshire, for instance, eight of the ten members to be put in had been members since before 1698. Not surprisingly, a number of the M.P.s now put in were Tories and Country party supporters. Among them were Sir Edward Seymour, put in for Devonshire and Wiltshire; Sir Christopher Musgrave, put in for Cumberland, Westmorland, and Durham; Jack Howe, put in for Gloucestershire; and Edward Harley, Robert Harley's younger brother, put in for Herefordshire. However, the non-party character of the 'putting-in' operation is illustrated by the appearance of a number of committed Whig Junto supporters: for example, Henry Blaake for Wiltshire, Christopher Montagu, the Junto leader's brother, for Northamptonshire, and Lord William Paulet for Hampshire. In view of the complaints about inactive justices, it is perhaps surprising that the Council should have chosen to fill up the commissions with members of Parliament who could not be expected to be consistently active. It was, however, characteristic of the whole tone of the operation that the Council should have felt it to be desirable to make comprehensive, irrespective of politics, the courtesy of making members of Parliament justices of the peace.

Of the justices put out of the commission between 1696 and 1698 because of non-subscription to the Association, either by the Council or by Somers acting independently of the Council, at least 120, about two-thirds of the total, were restored.[1] In addition, several of those put out by Somers on his own initiative before 1696 were put back.[2] This high proportion of restorations suggests that the Council was taking seriously the advice of its committee, to put back those dismissed on account of non-subscription to the Association. Some of those not so restored had, of course, died

[1] These figures cannot be precise because of uncertainty as to the exact numbers put out by Somers independently of the Council in 1696–7.

[2] For instance, six of the gentlemen put out in Suffolk in 1694 were restored in 1700.

or sold their estates. It is possible that, in some counties, Whig *custodes* succeeded in preventing the return of gentlemen who had not died, but this was exceptional.[1] It would be easy to see, in this restoration of justices left out by Somers, evidence of political motivation, but this would be a misinterpretation. The gentlemen involved were of high social status; they were by tradition entitled to a place on the bench. The danger of a Stuart restoration was temporarily remote. Louis XIV had tacitly recognized William III's claim to the English throne at Ryswick, and the dominant issue in foreign politics was the Spanish, not the English, succession. Consequently the proscribing spirit of the Association movement was dormant, and there was no reason why those who tolerated William as *de facto* King should not serve him in the local magistracy.

Little need be said about the seventy-two justices dismissed by the Council in 1700. Some of them had died, and the Council was carrying out the routine duties of the Chancellor's office during the period when the great seal was in commission.[2] Otherwise the Council seems to have been acting in response to the Commons' complaint that 'men of small estates' had been put into the commissions. Again, the advice of the *custodes* was scrupulously observed. Wharton, perhaps out of loyalty to his Junto colleague Somers, reported that all the justices in Buckinghamshire and Oxfordshire were fit to be continued, and all of them were.[3] In Somerset the report on justices put in by Somers was, on the whole, favourable, with three exceptions: Henry Reynon, originally put in on the advice of the Duke of Ormonde, was now 'a beggar'; George Fenn, also put in by the Duke, had married Viscount Fitzhardinge's widow, but apparently had no other claim to be a justice of the peace; John Dutton Colt had been in Parliament when first put in, and was the Collector of Customs at Bristol, but he had not been elected to the 1698 Parliament. These three were put out, the rest left in.[4]

[1] In Devonshire, ten of the seventeen justices put out in the purge of July 1696 were not restored in June 1700. The Earl of Stamford was the *custos*.
[2] For instance, two of the three put out in Berkshire, and seven of the eleven in Leicestershire, were dead.
[3] Bodl. MS. Carte 79, ff. 698–9.
[4] Som. R.O., Sanford MSS. DD/SF 1747.

During July a number of adjustments were made in several counties. Misnomers and Crown Office errors were corrected. Some names ordered to be added in June were now left out again.[1] Late reports from negligent lords-lieutenant like Shrewsbury, who was told by Vernon that the Council had proceeded to regulate the commissions for Herefordshire and Worcestershire without his advice, were dealt with.[2] These adjustments were without much political significance. However, the settlement of the commission of the peace on a 'broad bottom' had become out of date in the context of politics at the centre almost before it had been achieved.

II

During the summer it had become plain that Sunderland's scheme to patch up a reconciliation between the Court and the Whigs had failed. The death of the Duke of Gloucester, Princess Anne's only son, at the end of July, made a strong ministry with reliable parliamentary support necessary to confirm the Protestant Succession. This meant that the King had to trust himself to the Tories, and in particular to Harley. In the course of the autumn the ministry was reconstructed along Tory lines, and Harley persuaded the King to agree to a dissolution. The influence of Godolphin and Rochester had revived, even before their appointments as First Lord of the Treasury and Lord-Lieutenant of Ireland respectively.[3] The new ministers were dissatisfied with the regulation of the commission of the peace by well-meaning Courtiers in the spring. Harley belied his avowedly non-party attitude by his assertion to Vernon that the regulation had not gone far enough, while Vernon hinted that the Commons would object to the part played in the regulation by the Whig lords who had kept their local offices.[4]

The immediate consequence of these developments at the

---

[1] P.R.O., P.C. 2/78, pp. 71, 74: 18 July, 25 July 1700.

[2] *Vernon Correspondence*, iii. 109–10. Shrewsbury was lord-lieutenant but not *custos* of these counties. One name was added for Herefordshire a fortnight after Vernon's reminder.

[3] Feiling, *History of the Tory Party, 1640–1714*, pp. 340–2; Roberts, *Growth of Responsible Government*, pp. 296–7; Kenyon, *Sunderland*, pp. 318–20; Horwitz, *Revolution Politicks*, p. 160.

[4] *Vernon Correspondence*, iii. 91, 110.

centre was another, small-scale, regulation of the commission
of the peace by the Privy Council in September 1700. Though
it took place only a few weeks after the last set of changes
ordered in Council, it was clearly distinguished from those
changes by the fact that it was not described, as they had
been, as clarifying the alterations ordered in late June. Ten
counties were involved.[1] The greatest changes were made in
three counties where the *custodes* were 'inner ring' Junto
lords. Fifteen gentlemen were put in for Oxfordshire, including six recommended by the judge in June, when they had
been vetoed by Wharton. Rochester, Simon Harcourt, and
Harley took an interest in this commission.[2] Four gentlemen
were added for Buckinghamshire, and six for Cambridgeshire.
The other changes were measured in ones and twos; only one
county justice, Civet Rich in Norfolk, was left out. The
Tories could not, as yet, afford to offend potential enemies
by a purge on a larger scale. The intention of this regulation
was to undermine the strength of the local Whig parties, built
up during the years of Junto supremacy, in those counties
where the Council had failed to do this decisively in the
summer.

These changes were planned too early to have been con-
sciously designed to assist an election. The decision to dissolve
the Parliament elected in 1698 was not made public until the
middle of December.[3] The new Parliament, which assembled
in February 1701, was little affected by recent manipulation
of the commissions of the peace, except perhaps in a handful
of cases like Rutland, where Sir Thomas Mackworth was
elected knight of the shire for the first time following his
addition to the Rutland bench in October. Only two commissions of the peace were issued in November and December
1700 — apparently routine ones for Caernarvonshire and
Westmorland — and none at all in January and February.
Eighteen commissions, some of which left justices out, were

[1] Buckinghamshire, Cambridgeshire, Essex, Norfolk, Oxfordshire, Rutland,
Staffordshire, Surrey, Wiltshire, and the West Riding. P.R.O., P.C. 2/78, p. 83:
26 Sept. 1700. The commissions were sealed on 29 October 1700. P.R.O., C.
231/9, p. 12.

[2] Bodl. MS. Carte 79, f. 696; H.M.C., Fifteenth Report, Appendix IV, *Portland MSS.* iv. 2.

[3] Rubini, *Court and Country*, p. 205.

sealed in the spring, but many of those left out were described in the docquet book as dead.[1] The Devonshire commission, with 119 local names in 1700, lost seven by death and acquired eight recruits in April 1701, and it is likely that this unremarkable pattern prevailed elsewhere.[2]

Possibly the Tories would ideally have liked to have done more in the counties to consolidate their position, but circumstances were against them. Wright had run into the same difficulty with the Crown Office that Somers had done. The Privy Council had ordered that the new justices added in June and July 1700 should not be required to pay fees, in order to induce them to qualify themselves to act. No compensation was provided, and the grievance of the Crown Office clerks was renewed.[3] Moreover Thomas Chute, the Clerk of the Crown, died in early May 1701. Wright secured the appointment of his son George to the place, but there was probably some temporary disorganization in the Crown Office.[4]

In any case, it could have been argued that drastic changes in the commissions of the peace in the Tory interest would have been premature. The King was in England, and his well-known dislike of purges may have exercised a restraining influence. The Tory ministers were divided between the 'Church Party', led by Rochester, which was opposed to the King's preparations for war, and the moderate men, led by Harley, who were anxious to prove to the King that they could do his business in the Commons by securing the Protestant Succession and suitable supply.[5] While Parliament was sitting, the overriding need was to placate the Commons, which throughout the session was engaged in violent party conflict over foreign policy and the impeachment of the Whig lords. In March and April the Commons considered the lists of justices of the peace as they stood after the Privy Council's operation of 1700, and apparently pronounced themselves satisfied; at any rate the issue of the composition of the bench

---

[1] P.R.O., C. 231/9, pp. 14 ff.

[2] Devon R.O., Q/JC: commissions of the peace, 19 July 1700, 19 Apr. 1701.

[3] P.R.O., P.C. 2/78, p. 84; B.L., Loan 29/29/11: case and annexed petition of Thomas Edwards, no date, but clearly relating to this period.

[4] Luttrell, *Brief Relation*, v. 45; *Cal. S.P. Dom., 1700–2*, pp. 312–13.

[5] Roberts, *Growth of Responsible Government*, pp. 298–9.

was dropped.[1] It was replaced by the parallel issue of the militia, where the Commons hoped to secure a similarly non-party approach to the appointment of deputy-lieutenants by attacking lords-lieutenant for their recent partisan choices.[2] The Commons evidently took the view that all gentlemen qualified by wealth and status should serve as magistrates, both military and civil. The more extreme Tories introduced a bill to raise the property qualification of justices of the peace to £500 in land — an indirect way of supporting the impeachment of Somers — and the country gentlemen readily supported it.[3] They could not, however, have been relied upon to maintain this support if the Tory ministers had proscribed the Whigs in local politics as the Whigs were alleged to have proscribed the Tories. Harley and the moderates, anxious to minimize divisive issues in the Commons, may well have felt that a general purge of the commissions of the peace would have been out of place.

However, the events of the spring and summer made regulation of the bench absolutely necessary if the Tories were to maintain their influence in the ministry. At the beginning of 1701, the bench in most counties was constructed on a 'broad bottom'. The gentlemen put in by Somers had not been put out in any numbers except in a handful of counties, but the Whigs had been joined by new men, chosen for the most part, though this was not a deliberate policy, from among the country gentlemen of Tory sympathies. Therefore, the balance of power within the counties was determined by the degree of activity of the two parties on the bench. In most counties the Whigs seem to have stirred themselves to combat the danger of numerical domination. For a short time the activity of the justices at quarter sessions became a matter of European concern. The Whig grand jury and justices in Kent petitioned the Commons from Easter quarter sessions at Maidstone that the King might be supported by grants of supply to enable him to assist his allies. The Commons treated

[1] *C.J.* xiii. 377, 378, 384, 390, 489. The *liber pacis* ordered by the Commons on 5 March 1701 survives at N.L.W., MS. 17071E.
[2] B.L., Add. MSS. 33084, f. 165: Newcastle to Thomas Pelham, 15 Mar. 1701.
[3] *C.J.* xiii. 516, 523, 627; Roberts, *Growth of Responsible Government*, pp. 316–17. Such bills had been proposed in the 1698/9 and 1699/1700 sessions, and were to be proposed at regular intervals in Queen Anne's reign.

the petition as a breach of privilege, and recommended that five offending justices be dismissed. Accordingly they were put out in a commission sealed on 31 May.[1] The Whigs recognized the value of such addresses in embarrassing the ministers, and they promoted more petitions from summer quarter sessions in counties where a Whig majority of active justices could still be found, and from summer assizes in counties where a Whig sheriff could pack the grand jury.[2] Consequently, it became necessary for the ministers to forestall such manœuvres, either by swamping the 'factious' justices, or by putting them out. Such a regulation could not be conducted by the Council. The King, apart from his general aversion to dismissals, could hardly have been expected to have agreed to the disgrace of justices who supported his foreign policy.

Thirty-four commissions of the peace, involving twenty-nine counties, were sealed in June and July 1701. The character of these is not always clear from the docquet book,[3] but a comparison between two *libri pacis* drawn up in March 1701 and April 1702 indicates the extent of the alterations in at least those counties which received commissions only in the summer of 1701 during the intervening period.[4] It seems clear that a fairly high proportion of these commissions were merely routine. For instance, one dead justice was left out for Herefordshire, and one new name was added; the Bishop of Bristol was included for Dorset, but no other changes were made; three were put in for Nottinghamshire, and some dead justices were omitted. However, there were more substantial alterations in a small number of counties. These changes had a political content and were apparently conducted in a manner which can almost be described as clandestine by Rochester before his departure for Ireland, in conjunction with the leading Tory gentlemen in the counties.[5] In Warwickshire, six gentlemen who were still alive were left out; in Hampshire and Wiltshire, five; in Durham, three. Eleven

---

[1] *C.J.* xiii. 518, 538–9, 550; P.R.O., C. 231/9, p. 25.
[2] Feiling, *History of the Tory Party, 1640–1714*, p. 351; Rubini, *Court and Country*, p. 219.
[3] P.R.O., C. 231/9, pp. 25–9.
[4] N.L.W., MS. 17071E; B.L., Harl. MSS. 7512.
[5] B.L., Add. MSS. 30000E, f. 313: Bonet's dispatch, 25 July/5 Aug. 1701.

names were missing from the Norfolk commission sealed in July. Eight had died, but the other three were still alive, and as many as twenty-nine new justices were appointed. Four living justices at least were dismissed in Hertfordshire, and eleven were added. In Middlesex, Sir Joseph Tilly and 'several' others were put out; Luttrell says that 'several' amounted to more than thirty. Tilly was the defendant in an impending forgery trial, but it is improbable that all the others were open to accusations of misdemeanour.[1] No living justices were certainly left out in the North Riding, but seven new justices were added.

The cases of Westmorland and Cumberland were peculiar. Rochester and Sir Christopher Musgrave secured the disgrace of Dr Henry Fleming, Thomas Hebblethwaite, and Thomas Pullin for Westmorland in June, but in July they were mysteriously restored.[2] Sir Christopher, 'out of humour', appealed for assistance to Rochester, who delayed his journey to Ireland to help. Harley thought that Musgrave's wishes in the matter should be gratified to keep his parliamentary support. The outcome of the affair is obscure. Westmorland's next commission was not sealed until June 1702, yet Fleming and the others had inexplicably disappeared from the list drawn up in April 1702, possibly by some irregular method. Meanwhile, seven new Westmorland justices had been appointed.[3] The neighbouring county of Cumberland received no fewer than three commissions in three weeks in July 1701, although, whatever the hypothetical pattern of inclusion, exclusion, and restoration, the net effect was only to leave out three dead justices and put in two new names.

It seems, therefore, that the Tories were engaged in a quite extensive (though far from comprehensive) operation covering, perhaps, between a quarter and a third of the counties,

[1] P.R.O., C. 231/9, p. 27; Luttrell, *Brief Relation*, v. 73, 104.
[2] P.R.O., C. 231/9, pp. 25, 28.
[3] B.L., Add. MSS. 40775, ff. 47, 57: Vernon to the King, 1 Aug., 5 Aug. 1701; Loan 29/186, f. 81: Musgrave to Harley, 11 Aug. 1701, misplaced among papers dated 1692; H.M.C., Fifteenth Report, Appendix IV, *Portland MSS.* iv. 19; Leics. R.O., Finch MSS. Box VI, Bundle 22: Normanby to Nottingham (in very cryptic terms, but hinting that Rochester and Musgrave had secured the expulsion of the justices against the King's explicit orders), 4 Sept. 1701; B.L., Harl. MSS. 7512, f. 56, where in the Westmorland list the names of Fleming and Hebblethwaite are crossed out.

designed principally to add Tory squires to the commission.
To a lesser extent, it was also designed to eliminate a very
few Whigs. One curious feature was that in many counties
the bishop of the diocese, who would normally expect to be
in commission anyway, was added. The part played by
Wright in the changes is obscure. Rochester, though he was
not certainly involved in every county, seems to have played
a more important part, and Wright may passively have followed the lead of his more forceful colleague. In some cases
the alterations probably owed a great deal to the initiative of
local men. This quite promising start to a campaign of regulation in the Tory interest was, however, not destined to be
carried very much further.

III

It became clear by the autumn that the Tories in the Cabinet
were on the defensive. European tension during the spring
and summer became acute in the autumn after Louis XIV
had recognized the Pretender. Sunderland and Somers advised
the King to dissolve Parliament. They argued persuasively
that the Whigs, backed by public opinion, would support him
during the inevitable war, and that the Tories' promises were
not to be trusted while their growing unpopularity, demonstrated by the Kentish petition and its consequences, made
them useless for the King's service. They also suggested a
renewal of the Association, possibly in the form of an oath
abjuring the Pretender.[1] William was convinced, dissolving
Parliament in November. The Tory ministers were clearly
discredited, though the King preferred not to dismiss them
until after Parliament had been elected.

Between Rochester's offensive against Whig justices in June
and July, and the elections of November and December 1701,
only five county commissions of the peace were issued. The
Tory squire Sir George Barlow was put in with seven others for
Pembrokeshire: in Anglesey, Carmarthenshire, and Gloucestershire one or two gentlemen were added, but that was all.[2] The

---

[1] *Miscellaneous State Papers, 1501–1726*, ii. 443–61; Kenyon, *Sunderland*,
pp. 322–4; G. V. Bennett, *The Tory Crisis in Church and State, 1688–1730: The
Career of Francis Atterbury, Bishop of Rochester* (Oxford, 1975), p. 60.
[2] P.R.O., C. 231/9, pp. 30–1; N.L.W., MS. 17071E; B.L., Harl. MSS. 7512.

Middlesex commission did, however, represent an attempt to influence the election. Sir Harry Dutton Colt was restored only days before his election for Westminster. But there was no very serious attempt to influence the second election of 1701 by remodelling the commissions of the peace in the months immediately beforehand.

The changes of June and July had been made before the decision to dissolve. They did have at least one unexpected consequence. In Westmorland, Sir Christopher Musgrave lost his seat for the county, partly through the animosity of Thomas Pullin, one of the displaced justices.[1] Over the rest of the country, the summer regulation seems to have had little discernible effect. The Whigs did rather better than in the previous election, but apart from the Westmorland case this cannot be shown to have been linked to gentry discontent at unwarrantable omissions from the commission of the peace. Among Tory knights of the shire who might have co-operated with Rochester in remodelling the commissions in their counties, and who lost their seats, were Jack Howe in Gloucestershire, Sir Jacob Astley in Norfolk, and Lord Cheyne in Buckinghamshire; it would be pure conjecture to say that these were comparable cases to that of Sir Christopher Musgrave, but it is at any rate possible that resentment at changes in the commission of the peace was a contributing factor. There are only two cases of a newly elected member having been recently made a justice in the same county as his constituency.[2] On the whole, the safest conclusion is that the composition of the county bench played no decisive part one way or the other in the over-all course of the election.

The ministry with which William met his last Parliament was no longer Tory. Godolphin had gone, and Rochester was to follow in January. The Cabinet was now heavily weighted with Court party politicians who held the great offices of state: men like Carlisle, Somerset, Manchester, and Pembroke. The Junto had high hopes of infiltrating this administration when, as they anticipated, the need for vigorous prosecution

---

[1] Rubini, *Court and Country*, p. 246, quoting a letter from Pullin to Lord Irwin in Leeds Public Library.

[2] Sir Harry Dutton Colt (see above) and also Henry Thynne, elected for Milborne Port after inclusion in the Somerset commission in July.

of war discredited the ornamental grandees at the head of it.[1] The Commons proved to be balanced equitably, with the Courtiers able to carry on the King's business, though debates on matters other than supply were hotly contested, and majorities on both sides were small.[2] The new Cabinet, with its non-party flavour, would not, presumably, have been anxious for any violent changes in the commission of the peace. Moreover, the Tories were shrewd enough to provide for compulsory subscription of the new test for office-holders — the oath of abjuration of the Pretender — to quiet the consciences of justices of the peace and others who would have scrupled voluntary subscription.[3] This meant that the Whigs, had they been given the opportunity to enforce abjuration as a political test, would have run into the same difficulties as they had done with the Association in 1696.

Thus, after the change of ministers, no very significant alterations were to be expected in the commissions of the peace beyond the routine ones associated with the approach of the Lent assizes. Newly elected M.P.s were put in irrespective of party. The Junto supporter Richard Hampden, M.P. for Wendover, was put in for Buckinghamshire; at the other end of the spectrum, the Tory Sir Thomas Hanmer, elected for Flint borough though he preferred to serve for Thetford, was put in for Flintshire.[4] Otherwise, the changes in the admittedly quite large number of commissions of the peace issued in the early months of 1702 do not seem to have been politically motivated. The only justices known to have been left out were dead. There is little or no evidence that the Whigs had enough weight in the new government to make any attempt to begin the reversal of Rochester's remodelling of the commission of the peace in the previous summer. Some of the counties receiving new commissions were among those for which justices had then been put out, but it is not clear that any of these justices were restored.[5] It is noticeable

---

[1] Ellis, 'The Whig Junto', pp. 455–6; Sachse, *Somers*, pp. 215–16.

[2] Feiling, *History of the Tory Party, 1640–1714*, pp. 356–8; Roberts, *Growth of Responsible Government*, pp. 323–5.

[3] 13 & 14 William III c. 6; Rubini, *Court and Country*, pp. 255–6; Horwitz, *Revolution Politicks*, p. 164.

[4] P.R.O., C. 231/9, pp. 38, 39.

[5] This conclusion is based on a comparison of the admittedly incomplete lists

that the great majority of the counties that received new commissions had Whig *custodes* or lords-lieutenant or both, which suggests that the Whig lords were taking advantage of the decline of Tory influence at the centre to reassert their control of the localities. In this case, however, the changes might have been expected to have been more spectacular. One might, for instance, ask why the heroes of the Whig opposition to Sir Christopher Musgrave in Westmorland were not restored; why Wharton was able to secure a new commission for Buckinghamshire, but not for Oxfordshire; or why the Duke of Bolton did not restore any of the five living justices put out for Hampshire during 1701 in either of the commissions issued in January or March 1702.

The commission of the peace was thus in a state of some confusion. After Somers's dismissal it had been rationalized by the Privy Council on an all-inclusive basis. The Whig lords-lieutenant and *custodes* had found their wishes, not over-ruled, but at any rate supplemented. In the summer of 1700 the principle of 'broad bottom' had triumphed in an effi-ciently executed regulation. Thereafter the commissions for many — but not all — of the counties had been subjected for twenty months to the stresses of party warfare. The changes of ministries, at the centre, and the exigencies of two general elections and the division of opinion on the desirability of assisting the King to prepare for war, in the localities, made for changes in the composition of the bench. These changes were not uniform over England and Wales, and no valuable geographical pattern emerges. Wales remained relatively un-touched after the Privy Council regulation in the summer of 1700, and so too did certain English counties, including such widely separated examples as Northumberland, Berkshire, Cheshire, and the three parts of Lincolnshire. On the other hand, Middlesex received seven commissions in eighteen months, and in fact most English counties experienced some change. Lords-lieutenant and *custodes* pulled one way, mini-sters another; leaders of county society like Sir Christopher Musgrave took a hand, sometimes in conjunction with,

of justices known to have been left out in 1701 with the equally incomplete lists of justices known to have been put in early in 1702, from the docquet book and from the *liber pacis* at B.L., Harl. MSS. 7512.

sometimes in opposition to, the Court. The King himself
clung to his 'broad bottom' ideal. His death on 8 March 1702
stabilized the situation, paradoxically, by creating a state of
flux. All commissions were determined, though as usual they
were held to be in force until new ones could be issued.[1] In
spite of Queen Anne's professed antipathy to party, no one
could doubt at the beginning of her reign that the loaves and
fishes of power would be distributed to the 'Church Party', in
local as well as central politics.[2] The Whigs resigned themselves to a period in the wilderness. The combination of
freshly commissioned lords-lieutenant and *custodes*, the need
for a new commission of the peace in every county, and the
lapse of royal reluctance to remove persons from office, gave
the Tories an opportunity to establish a more complete
dominance of local society than had been possible at any
time since the early 1680s.

IV

A reshaping of the Cabinet took place shortly after the
Queen's accession. Godolphin and Marlborough, who both
had great personal influence with the Queen, and who were
supported by those who conceived their political role to be
faithful service to the Crown, were joined in office by the
High Churchmen. Rochester received a new patent as Lord-
Lieutenant of Ireland. Sir Edward Seymour replaced Wharton
as Comptroller. Nottingham and Sir Charles Hedges became
the two Secretaries of State, displacing Vernon, with his
lingering Junto connection.[3] The Queen's Privy Council
included the new holders of high office, and also a handful of
leading Tories without important office, notably Abingdon,
Weymouth, John Granville, and Jack Howe. Shrewsbury,
Portland, Somers, Charles Montagu (now Lord Halifax), and
Trumbull were dropped.[4] The new abjuration oath did not

---

[1] P.R.O., P.C. 2/79, p. 8: 8 Mar. 1702.
[2] H.M.C., *Various Collections*, viii. 86.
[3] Feiling, *History of the Tory Party, 1640–1714*, pp. 364–5; R. Walcott,
English Politics in the Early Eighteenth Century (Oxford, 1956), pp. 96–9;
Roberts, *Growth of Responsible Government*, p. 330; Horwitz, *Revolution Politicks*, p. 166. Minor offices went to the Tories as well. A. Boyer, *History of Queen
Anne's Reign digested into Annals, Year the First* (London, 1703), pp. 50–3.
[4] P.R.O., P.C. 2/79, p. i.

prove an obstacle to the acceptance by the High Churchmen of place and power.[1] In the midst of these changes, Wright was continued as Lord Keeper, simply because there was no one else. The Queen told him, when he surrendered the great seal just after William's death, that it would not have been restored to him if she had known a fitter person in the kingdom — a curiously ungracious tribute, which Wright apparently took as a compliment.[2]

This ministry grew progressively weaker until its downfall in the spring of 1704. Briefly stated, the reason was the lack of any common ground between the Queen's friends — pre-eminently Godolphin and Marlborough, the 'duumvirs' — and the Tory leaders.[3] During the two years from 1702 to 1704, the composition of the commissions of the peace was an issue dividing the two elements in the Cabinet and contributing to the downfall of the ministry, as much as the war or religion.[4] The Tories wanted to drive the Whigs from all offices of trust. Rochester, in particular, was anxious to complete in 1702 the interrupted purge begun in 1701. The Occasional Conformity Bills of these years were intended to give statutory sanction to this policy of proscription. The duumvirs, on the other hand, were anxious to keep the Queen out of the grip of the ruthless men of party, and they deprecated the estab-lishment of a Tory monopoly of place. Godolphin was fight-ing the same battle against the Tories that he had fought against the Whigs in 1694.[5]

The Queen reappointed all but a handful of the lords-lieutenant who had served under William, and a Tory was substituted for a Whig in only four counties, in one of which the incumbent lord-lieutenant was on his deathbed anyway.[6]

[1] Horwitz, *Revolution Politicks*, pp. 165-6; G. S. Holmes and W. A. Speck, *The Divided Society: Party Conflict in England* (London, 1967), p. 101: Wey-mouth to James Thynne.

[2] C.U.L., Baker MSS. 29, pp. 189-90: account of Lord Keeper Wright, sent by Dr Thomas Littel to Laurence Echard.

[3] Holmes, *British Politics in the Age of Anne*, pp. 198-9.

[4] G. M. Trevelyan, *England under Queen Anne* (London, 1948), i. 207-8.

[5] Feiling, *History of the Tory Party, 1640-1714*, p. 367; Bennett, *The Tory Crisis in Church and State, 1688-1730*, pp. 63-4.

[6] John Granville for Radnor in Cornwall; Poulet for Stamford in Devonshire; Abingdon for Wharton in Oxfordshire; and Normanby for Irwin, who died a fort-night after his removal, in the North Riding.

A Tory was substituted for a Whig as *custos* in six counties.[1] Several Whig magnates thus retained their county offices: for instance, the Duke of Bolton in Dorset and Hampshire, the Earl of Orford in Cambridgeshire, and Lord Cornwallis in Suffolk. However, it is clear that the surviving Whig lords-lieutenant were subjected to heavy pressure from the ministers in making militia appointments. The Earl of Berkeley, lord-lieutenant of Gloucestershire, was told that the approbation of his choices would not be a formality.[2] The Earl of Carlisle's list for Cumberland was vetted by Nottingham, who took out two names.[3] When the Earl of Rutland protested about the nomination of some Tory squires as deputy-lieutenants for Leicestershire, it was explained to him that the Queen was resolved to be 'Queen of all her Subjects', and that party considerations would not weigh with her. In effect the Queen was recommending deputy-lieutenants to Rutland, rather than the reverse, and Rutland contemplated resignation in protest.[4] The lists of the deputies appointed by the lords-lieutenant between May and December 1702 show how the Whig magnates had been persuaded to appoint men of decidedly Tory complexion. For instance, Berkeley had to accept Jack Howe in Gloucestershire, and the Duke of Bolton named two Jacobites, Sir Nathaniel Napier and George Pitt, in Dorset.[5]

As with the militia, so with the commissions of the peace. Tories were added, and Whigs, who could be represented to the Queen as Dissenters, were put out. The well-documented case of Derbyshire illustrates how the commission of the peace was reconstructed during the summer of 1702. It was not the *custos*, the Whig Duke of Devonshire, who made up

[1] Ashburnham for Herbert of Cherbury in Breconshire, and Cheyne for Wharton in Buckinghamshire, in addition to changes corresponding to the changes in the lord-lieutenancies. Also, Wharton was dismissed as *custos* of Westmorland and Stamford as *custos* of Leicestershire, though their respective replacements (the Earls of Carlisle and Rutland) cannot be described as Tories.

[2] P.R.O., S.P. 44/104, pp. 40, 46–7: Nottingham to Berkeley, 4 June, 9 June 1702.

[3] Ibid., p. 124: Nottingham to Carlisle, 3 Oct. 1702.

[4] Ibid., pp. 179–80: Nottingham to [Sir John Leveson Gower], 14 Dec. 1702; H.M.C., Twelfth Report, Appendix V, *Rutland MSS.* ii. 173.

[5] P.R.O., S.P. 44/170, p. 119; S.P. 44/171, p. 78. For Napier and Pitt, see Duke of Manchester, *Court and Society from Elizabeth to Anne*, ii. 115–16.

the list. The work was done by the Tory knights of the shire in William's last Parliament, Thomas Coke and John Curzon, with a view to establishing a numerical majority to counter the Whig justices, headed by Sir Philip Gell. Among other changes, they added Brooke Boothby and John Beresford, and left out two gentlemen called Spateman and Cotchett, notwithstanding a chorus of protests that Mr Cotchett was an amiable man who 'would not give trouble in elections'; even his replacement, Beresford, spoke up for him. The commission was sealed in July. The Tory magnate Lord Scarsdale warned Coke in August to tell the Queen and Wright, through Nottingham, that Spateman was a Dissenter, whereas Beresford was in every way qualified, before the disgruntled *custos* could represent his grievances to either. Scarsdale was too late, however. Devonshire had already protested to Wright, who, caught off his guard, wrote to Coke to say that he was unacquainted with the gentlemen involved, that he could not explain to Devonshire what was happening, and that Coke and Curzon should send him a description of the persons put in and left out. This did little good. The bewildered Devonshire later told the Duke of Somerset that Wright had ignored him completely in altering the Derbyshire commission. The new justices were Jacobites, men of no estates, and 'violently of a party', while some of the 'usefullest men' had been left out.[1]

What happened in Derbyshire, happened elsewhere. Devonshire decided to let the matter of the Derbyshire commission drop, because, as he told Somerset, 'his' (that is, Wright's) 'practice has been the same in most places'. This is borne out by other evidence. For instance, in Northamptonshire the Tory squire Sir Justinian Isham suggested that two justices be left out 'to put the rest in awe'.[2] Jack Howe recommended the exclusion of four clergymen who were willing to act with Dissenters for Gloucestershire.[3] In Suffolk, Sir Richard Gipps was convinced that he had been disgraced by the malevolence of Sir Edward Seymour, and he let fall some injudicious

[1] H.M.C., Twelfth Report, Appendix III, *Cowper MSS.* iii. 10-15; P.R.O., C. 231/9, p. 56; Holmes and Speck, *The Divided Society*, p. 47.

[2] B.L., Add. MSS. 29568, ff. 67-8: Sir Justinian Isham to Mr Griffin, no date but bound with papers dated May 1702.

[3] B.L., Add. MSS. 29588, f. 257: Howe to [Nottingham], 6 May 1702.

remarks on the Queen's government.[1] Fifty-seven justices were reported to have been dismissed for Middlesex — almost a quarter of the total — and forty-three were added, among them several Tory M.P.s.[2] The new commission for Kesteven contained eighteen new names, and six gentlemen who were still alive were dropped.[3] In Worcestershire, only three justices were left out, but one of them was the ex-Lord Chancellor Somers, and swords were drawn over an election quarrel at the quarter sessions at which this commission was published.[4]

It is difficult to say whether changes took place in every county. However, every county did receive a new commission of the peace during the summer of 1702. The balance of probability is that the bench was purged to a greater or lesser extent in all but a very few counties during the months after the Queen's accession. This conclusion rests on the evidence of lists of justices put out between 1700 and 1704, presented to the House of Lords in 1704.[5] A comparison between these lists and the *liber pacis* dated April 1702[6] gives the names of those put out between April 1702 and March 1704. The names in the House of Lords' lists are arranged in 'sequences' corresponding to the order of names in the *liber pacis* in such a way that the fiats from which these lists were compiled can be distinguished. On the basis of this evidence, it seems that, to take the West Country as a specimen area, four living justices were left out at this time for Cornwall, five for Devonshire, and eleven for Dorset. In Wales, as many as eleven justices were left out for Denbighshire and nine for Cardiganshire. A very few counties did escape. Only one gentleman was dismissed in Bedfordshire, and none at all in Northumberland and the East Riding, but these counties were exceptional.

[1] *The Letter Books of John Hervey, First Earl of Bristol* (Wells, 1894), pp. 170-8. Hervey told Sir Richard that he was not among those to be put out, but, in fact, he was to be dismissed.

[2] Luttrell, *Brief Relation*, v. 204; Oldmixon, *History of England*, p. 293. Among those put out were Sir Harry Dutton Colt, for the second time, and Luttrell himself.

[3] Lincs. A.O., commission of the peace, Kesteven, 7 July 1702; compared with the list for April 1702 at B.L., Harl. MSS. 7512, ff. 32-3.

[4] B.L., Add. MSS. 29579, f. 400: Sir Charles Littleton to Hatton, 18 July 1702. Somers was probably left out by the Crown Office without Wright's warrant as a dismissed Privy Councillor.

[5] H.L.R.O., Main Papers, H.L., 20 Mar. 1704; see below, p. 160.

[6] B.L., Harl. MSS. 7512.

There are, however, one or two indications that the Tories
did not have everything their own way. Weymouth complained
to Nottingham that his list of Wiltshire justices to be dismissed
had been overlooked, and that the *dedimus potestatem* for
the county did not include the newly appointed justices who
were therefore required to pay £4 each for a separate *dedimus*.[1] If the same thing happened elsewhere, the cupidity of
the Crown Office may well have taken the edge off the Tory
regulation. Less serious than this, but still important, was the
difficulty of finding Tory gentlemen fit and willing to undertake the troublesome duties of a country justice. Two gentlemen recommended by Coke for the Derbyshire bench asked
him to take their names off the list.[2] On the whole, however,
there seems no reason to doubt that the Tories in most counties took advantage of the changes at the centre and the
warm support of the new ministers (and their anxiety for a
'good Church of England Parliament') to remodel the magistracy in accordance with their wishes.

The Tories were materially assisted by these changes in the
election of 1702. The Queen's High Church sympathies, the
revised Privy Council, and the vigorous exercise of government patronage, combined to produce a swing towards the
Tories compared with the balanced House of Commons
elected some months before.[3] The commissions of the peace
were received in most counties while the elections were in
progress — indeed, the Whigs thought that this was a deliberate
stratagem by the ministry.[4] The reading out of the new
names at quarter sessions must have contributed to an
impression in the minds of voters that the High Churchmen
were all-powerful at court, and that the Whigs were disgraced.
It is, admittedly, difficult to prove that Whig candidates for
parliamentary seats were themselves left out as a systematic
policy, but it is plain enough that the relations and supporters
of Whigs were, in many counties, omitted before the elections,

---

[1] B.L., Add. MSS. 29588, ff. 83-4: Weymouth to Nottingham, 7 July 1702.
[2] H.M.C., Twelfth Report, Appendix III, *Cowper MSS.* iii. 10, 12.
[3] Walcott, *English Politics in the Early Eighteenth Century*, Chapter VI, especially p. 109.
[4] P.R.O., P.R.O. 30/24/20/65: Shaftesbury to Furley, 10 Aug. 1702. The commissions for Middlesex, Northamptonshire, and, possibly, some of the Welsh
counties, were sealed too late to affect the elections. P.R.O., C. 231/9, p. 68.

and that the relations and supporters of Tories replaced them. Unlike the changes in favour of the Tories in 1701, when the ousted justices might combine to defeat at the polls those like Sir Christopher Musgrave whom they blamed for their disgrace, the changes in 1702 took place in a radiant atmosphere of Tory optimism. Moreover, the Tories had by now conformed to public opinion by committing themselves to the war. Hence the reconstruction of the commission of the peace contributed to, rather than detracted from, the Tory success at the election.

The Tory ministers were not satisfied by the changes of 1702, extensive as these probably were, and they continued to work for more changes in individual counties in the course of the next two years. Rochester, it is true, was forced out of office in February 1703, but Nottingham and Hedges, especially the former, retained control of domestic government. In March 1703 some of the Whig peers who had retained office as lords-lieutenant and *custodes* were replaced. Rutland, no doubt disgusted by his inability to choose his own deputy-lieutenants, was supplanted by the Tory Earl of Denbigh in Leicestershire; the Whig Lord Cornwallis lost both positions to the Tory Earl of Dysert in Suffolk. These alterations were accompanied by the issue of twenty-eight commissions of the peace in February and March 1703, an unusually high number for any two months even in view of the approaching Lent assizes. In the summer of 1703, another batch of commissions was sealed; fifteen in June alone, nine of which explicitly left justices out. Thirty-six English counties received commissions at one or both of these times.[1]

It seems fairly clear that the changes made in 1703 followed the pattern of those made in the summer of 1702. Local Tory leaders represented to Nottingham, or to Hedges, the desirability of removing Whigs and adding gentlemen whose credentials were respectable in Tory terms. Thus, for instance, in Devonshire it is likely that the commission of February 1703 left out upwards of twenty local names.[2] Elsewhere,

---

[1] P.R.O., C. 231/9, pp. 89–90, 97–8.
[2] Devon R.O., Q/JC: commission of the peace, 18 Feb. 1703; compared with B.L., Harl. MSS. 7512, ff. 13–15. This conjecture assumes that only five were omitted in the commission dated June 1702, which does not survive.

the changes were perhaps less spectacular than those of the previous summer. No M.P.s seem to have been dismissed, and one Whig M.P. was actually put in. This was Horatio Walpole, who sat for Castle Rising, and who was elevated to the Suffolk bench. More naturally, a number of government supporters in the Commons were added: Henry St. John for Berkshire, William Gifford for Hampshire, and John Wicker for Sussex, for example.[1]

However, there are signs that the Courtiers were, by the summer of 1703, uneasy at the progress of Tory proscription. A Tory attempt in Flintshire misfired. Two Tory squires, Sir Thomas Hanmer and Sir Roger Mostyn, had recommended names to Nottingham, which were forwarded to Wright. Wright sealed the commission, but the entry in the Crown Office docquet book is marked 'stopped'. Godolphin had been moved to protest. He was prepared to take the matter to the Queen for her decision on the merits of the Flintshire recommendations. The next commission for Flintshire was not sealed until twelve months later, and the rest of Wales remained almost completely untouched in 1703.[2] Godolphin also complained of the extravagance of Sir Christopher Musgrave's recommendations in the North, and though he added 'I shall meddle in it as little as I can', Nottingham had to write to James Grahme, one of Musgraves's Westmorland friends, that he had been 'unsuccessful in the case of your two justices'. Meanwhile, Grahme lamented the inactivity of the Tory justices, who had only just managed to block a petition to the Queen from assizes specifying the changes desired by the grand jury in the commission of the peace.[3] These difficulties in Flintshire and Westmorland, and also the addition of Walpole in Suffolk, suggest that the High Churchmen were beginning to meet with obstructions in the pursuit of their local ambitions.[4]

---

[1] P.R.O., C. 231/9, pp. 89, 91, 103.

[2] Cal. S.P. Dom., 1702–3, p. 536; P.R.O., C. 231/9, p. 86; B.L., Add. MSS. 29589A, ff. 95–6: Godolphin to Nottingham, 19 Aug. 1703.

[3] H.M.C., Fifteenth Report, Appendix IV, Portland MSS. iv. 65; Tenth Report, Appendix IV, Bagot MSS., p. 337; B.L., Add. MSS. 29588, ff. 480–1, Add. MSS. 29589A, ff. 101–2: Grahme to Nottingham, 5 June, 22 Aug. 1703.

[4] Horwitz, Revolution Politicks, pp. 188–9.

V

The reason for the uneasiness felt by Godolphin and others was that the magistracy was in disrepute. In Monmouthshire, Michaelmas sessions could not be held in 1703 because so few justices condescended to act.[1] The recruitment of soldiers, a matter of importance in 1703, was obstructed by justices of the peace in several counties.[2] A much publicized case of misdemeanour by a Middlesex justice helped to discredit the magistracy. Mr Tracy was tried in the Queen's Bench for encouraging the Gatehouse gaoler to put a gentleman accused of highway robbery in irons, so that he would offer bribes to have them taken off.[3] Other complaints about individual justices were sent to Wright.[4] Such complaints were not unusual in themselves, but they could be used to cast doubts on the character of the gentlemen in the commissions of the peace under the Tory ministry. The Whigs began to mount a campaign on this issue in the House of Lords in the 1703-4 session, as part of a wider campaign against the High Tories in office, especially Nottingham.[5] Thus, when an act to authorize justices to deliver able-bodied vagabonds to the press was debated, it was argued that the justices of the peace had been appointed in so strange a manner recently that they could no longer, as a body, be entrusted with such great powers.[6]

The climax to this campaign came in March 1704. The Lords ordered that complete lists of justices for every county, and lists of those justices dismissed since Wright had been appointed, be laid before them.[7] When these were debated, the Lord Keeper was roughly handled, particularly over the

[1] *Cal. S.P. Dom.*, *1703-4*, p. 183. Most of those put out in Monmouthshire since 1702 had died, but it might have been argued that Whig replacements had not been included in the commission.

[2] *Cal. S.P. Dom.*, *1702-3*, pp. 542, 573-5, 626.

[3] Luttrell, *Brief Relation*, v. 292, 296-7, 309, 426-7.

[4] *Cal. S.P. Dom.*, *1703-4*, pp. 373, 580.

[5] Horwitz, *Revolution Politicks*, pp. 191-6. The main charge against Nottingham was his conduct over 'the Scotch Plot', a matter involving Jacobite intrigues.

[6] Burnet, *History*, v. 137-8.

[7] *L.J.* xvii. 482, 483, 484, 489; the list of disgraced justices is at H.L.R.O., Main Papers, H.L., 20 Mar. 1704; the complete list of justices for each county has not been traced.

case of his distinguished predecessor Somers in Worcester-shire.[1] The first name on the list of those dismissed was a Berkshire justice called Medlicott. Wright alleged that he had been put out because he was a practising attorney who took bribes. He may have prepared similar reasons for the whole list, but he was abruptly cut short, and it was proposed to declare in general that no one should be continued who had not taken the oaths to King William. An address to the Queen to this effect was prepared. This further advised the Queen to order a general review of all the commissions, so that no persons but men of quality and estates, of known affection to the Queen's title, the Protestant Succession, and the Church of England, might be continued; and that men so qualified who had been unjustly turned out, might be restored. The Queen's answer agreed with the Lords on the character of the gentlemen who should ideally be in the commissions, and she promised to give directions accordingly.[2]

The Whigs in the Lords had made out a strong case against Wright, and they were supported by some Courtiers. Indeed, the Duke of Somerset, who was in the Cabinet, seems to have been the chief manager of the attack on his colleague. The accumulated purges since 1700 had certainly been extensive. In crude figures, the House of Lords' lists showed that the names of 1,176 justices had been dropped from the commissions. Of these, 528 were dead, so Wright had dismissed 648 living justices, an average of more than eleven per county.[3] Middlesex had, predictably, suffered most with sixty-two exclusions; Devonshire, Essex, Kent, and Suffolk each lost more than thirty justices. Since the triumph of the Tories following the death of King William, to take a handful of counties at random, Wright had dismissed nineteen justices in Oxfordshire, eight in Warwickshire, fourteen in Cheshire, six in Kesteven, ten in Northamptonshire, eight in Somerset, and twenty-three in Gloucestershire. Pockets of Whig resistance such as Hampshire and Northumberland, where the Whig peers Bolton and Scarborough were the respective *custodes*,

[1] *Vernon Correspondence*, iii. 256-7.
[2] H.L.R.O., MS. Min., H.L., 30 Mar., 31 Mar. 1704.
[3] The House of Lords included in their lists the justices left out by order of the Privy Council in 1700, although Wright was not really responsible for the changes then made.

were exceptional, and they were overlooked in the outcry over Tory iniquity.[1]

Wright was thus the victim of parliamentary hostility in 1704 as Somers had been in 1700. His case was different from that of Somers in two respects. In the first place, the attack (as on Nottingham in 1680) came in the Lords, not in the Commons. The Whigs' strength lay in the Lords. They could rely on the support of aggrieved *custodes* and of non-party peers who had subscribed to William's ideal of a county magistracy founded on a 'broad bottom'. The Commons might have been expected to have objected strongly to an attack on the county status of the country gentry, but they remained relatively indifferent. This suggests that the squires had not yet accepted the view that the Tory remodelling had gone beyond bounds. In the second place, Wright could not justify the dismissals by appealing to the authority of recent statute, whereas Somers had been able to point to the Act for the Security of the Crown of 1696. Wright defended himself by quoting the advice of the *custodes* and the Tory squires that individual justices, like Medlicott in Berkshire, were unfit, but this only shifted the spotlight away from Wright to the Tory party in the localities. The Whigs still considered the Tories guilty of a campaign of partisan proscription.

The principle laid down in the Lords in March 1704, that the county magistracy was no longer to be trusted, intensified the flow of complaints to the Court. Sir Richard Cocks wrote from Gloucestershire that since 'the Papists' had remodelled the bench, the justices had not acted for the Queen's service.[2] Richard Duke complained from Exeter that the Devonshire justices put out by Sir Edward Seymour had not been restored since the Lords' address; he enclosed a formidable list of ex-sheriffs, ex-Parliament men, and other gentlemen of unimpeachable integrity and enormous estates who had been put out, to the detriment of the popularity of the Queen's government.[3] A Westmorland gentleman wrote to Wharton,

[1] Hampshire had lost six living justices since 1700, and Northumberland only one.

[2] H.M.C., Fifteenth Report, Appendix IV, *Portland MSS.* iv. 86–7.

[3] B.L., Loan 29/191, ff. 235–6, 274, 276: Richard Duke to Harley, two letters and an enclosure, Sept. 1704. Another annotated list of the dismissed Devonshire justices, and also of those for Northamptonshire, is at Blenheim MSS., Box VIII,

the former *custos* of that county, describing the insolence of the Nonjurors of the last reign on the bench. He said that he was the only magistrate left active who had owned William's government.[1] More complaints about justices of the peace who discouraged recruitment were received at Whitehall.[2]

Wright, now self-convicted of, at best, a kind of unworldly gullibility, was in a difficult position in the Cabinet. In April, Seymour was dismissed and Nottingham resigned. The High Churchmen were now planning to force Occasional Conformity through the Lords by the 'Tack'. The ministry had assumed a moderate Tory character, and Harley, who had reluctantly accepted the Secretaryship vacated by Nottingham, was brought into the forefront.[3] By July, Godolphin and Harley were already conspiring to force Wright out of office.[4] However, Wright refused to be intimidated by the House of Lords' address, by the fall of the High Churchmen in the ministry, or by the hostility of his remaining colleagues. During the 1704/5 session the Whigs in the Lords found it necessary to renew their attack on his abuse of local patronage. They ordered a list of the justices who had been put in and out since the last sessions of Parliament to be submitted, and a committee was appointed to consider them.[5] Again, the Duke of Somerset managed the business of this committee, which came to the conclusion, by a vote of eighteen to one, that the well-qualified gentlemen left out since 1700 had not been restored, and that the unfit gentlemen complained of the previous year had been continued.[6] The Lords accepted this report, and another address was presented to the Queen asking for a review of the commissions. The Queen had not, she said, expected to be troubled again in the matter, but she

Bundle 22; this was possibly compiled for, or by, Charles, third Earl of Sunderland, a youthful Whig attached to the Junto.

[1] Bodl. MS. Carte 109, ff. 67–8: Westmorland justice to Wharton, 29 Apr. 1704.

[2] H.M.C., *Portland MSS.* viii. 123–4; Luttrell, *Brief Relation*, v. 429, 485.

[3] A. McInnes, 'The Appointment of Harley in 1704', *Hist. Journal* xi (1968), 266–8.

[4] *The Marlborough-Godolphin Correspondence*, ed. H. L. Snyder (Oxford, 1975), i. 334–5.

[5] *L.J.* xvii. 659, 665; H.L.R.O., Main Papers, H.L., 16 Feb. 1705.

[6] H.L.R.O., Committee Book, H.L., 22 Feb. 1705, pp. 76, 85.

promised to give such directions as would seem to be necessary.[1]

Meanwhile the Commons contributed to the pressure on Wright by introducing a bill for qualifying justices of the peace similar to that introduced to discredit Somers in 1701.[2] This marked a new development since the previous session, but too much significance should not be attached to it. Among those who brought in the bill was the Tacker Sir Thomas Hanmer, whose recommendations for the Flintshire bench had been thwarted in January 1703. He, no doubt, saw in the measure an alternative to the Occasional Conformity Bill as a means of keeping Dissenters out of the commission of the peace. It was to some extent a Country party measure, analagous to a place bill. There is no evidence that the Whigs approved of it as intensifying the attack on Wright.

Was the critical report of the Lords' committee in February 1705 justified? On the surface, the evidence of the Crown Office docquet book suggests that Wright had made a conscientious effort to reorganize the magistracy. No commissions at all had been sealed in April, May, and June 1704, the months following the Queen's answer to the first Lords' protest in March 1704. It was rumoured at this time that new commissions making the required changes were being prepared.[3] Then in less than five weeks, in July and August, a new commission of the peace was sealed for every English and Welsh county except the 'counties' of Ely and Peterborough; a simultaneous issue almost without precedent.[4] Thereafter no new commissions were issued until January 1705. Notwithstanding Wright's apparent willingness to cooperate by comprehensive regulation, the evidence submitted to the House of Lords indicates that the changes made did not correspond to those implicitly promised in the Queen's answer to the Lords' protest four months before. The total number of new justices for fifty-five counties was 129, a little over two per county on average, and in only three

---

[1] *L.J.* xvii. 671, 672, 673.
[2] *C.J.* xiv. 465, 508, 548; H.M.C., *House of Lords MSS.*, N.S. vi. 260–1.
[3] Luttrell, *Brief Relation*, v. 416.
[4] P.R.O., C. 231/9, pp. 113–15. Most of the commissions were described as renewed 'for placing therein the several justices'.

counties did the number of inclusions reach double figures.[1] Wright, with what can be interpreted as courage, innocence, or folly, had restored justices put out between the summer of 1700 and March 1704 in only fourteen counties. Even in these, the number of restorations, in proportion to the numbers of living justices put out, was so small as to be derisory. The only county where the Whigs might feel that their wrongs had been righted was Cheshire.[2] In several counties where removals since 1700 had been extensive, like Devonshire and Kent, where thirty-four and thirty-eight living justices had been left out respectively, no restorations at all were made. Moreover, although 206 justices were put out in the summer of 1704, many of these were dead, and Wright dismissed only a handful of those he had himself added during the period from 1700 to March 1704. Nor was this all. The local influence of the Tackers Orlando Bridgeman and Sir John Packington had been extended by including them, respectively, for Suffolk and Pembrokeshire. In short, in spite of Wright's conscientious issue of new commissions for almost every county simultaneously in 1704, he could hardly be said to have remedied the defects in the magistracy to which the House of Lords had drawn attention in March.

It is surprising in the circumstances that Wright remained in office until after the election of May and June 1705. The triumvirs -- the duumvirs plus Harley — wanted his immediate dismissal so that the county commissions could be manipulated to assist the proscription of the Tackers. Their candidate was Lord Chief Justice Trevor, who was approached in March. The Queen approved, but Trevor declined. Less plausible was the rumour that the Duke of Buckinghamshire would be appointed.[3]

---

[1] Cheshire (14), Middlesex (13), and, oddly, Pembrokeshire (14).

[2] The figures following the counties in the list are, respectively, the number of living justices put out between 1700 and March 1704, and the number of these who were restored between March 1704 and February 1705: Anglesey, 12, 1; Buckinghamshire, 18, 5; Cheshire, 14, 12; Cumberland, 7, 1; Derbyshire, 5, 1 (the popular Mr Cotchett); Glamorgan, 2, 1; Gloucestershire, 28, 3; Middlesex, 62, 2; Nottinghamshire, 6, 1; Pembrokeshire, 8, 2; Sussex, 18, 1; Westmorland, 7, 1; Wiltshire, 23, 1; and Worcestershire, 5, 1 (Somers). H.L.R.O., Main Papers, H.L., 20 Mar. 1704, 16 Feb. 1705.

[3] Holmes, *British Politics in the Age of Anne*, p. 204; *The Marlborough-Godolphin Correspondence*, i. 418 nn. 2, 3; H.M.C., Tenth Report, Appendix IV, *Bagot MSS.*, p. 339.

The election therefore took place when Wright was still in office, and there is little evidence that the Whigs received any assistance from the remodelling of county commission of the peace. Admittedly, changes among office-holders were expected after the dissolution.[1] A general shift in the balance of local power seemed foreshadowed by the replacement of five Tory lords-lieutenant in April.[2]

Thirty-eight commissions of the peace were sealed in February and March 1705, and another twenty followed in the summer. Altogether forty-two counties were covered.[3] Wright was nothing if not industrious, and he gave himself at least the opportunity to remodel the bench in most of the counties in accordance with the wishes of the House of Lords and the Queen. The nature of the changes is rather obscure, but some scattered evidence survives. A few fiats in the form of a complete list of justices occur for early 1706, so, by discounting the changes made by these fiats, it is possible to reconstruct the commissions sealed by Wright between February and October 1705 for about a dozen counties. In these months, Wright made a relatively generous restoration of justices he had dismissed between 1700 and 1704 in two of these counties: Devonshire and Gloucestershire, where eight and nine justices respectively reappeared after earlier disgrace. This was, however, less than a third of the total of living justices Wright had previously left out in each case. Elsewhere, there were a very few similar restorations: two in Northamptonshire, six in Essex, four in Suffolk, three in Surrey, and one in Worcestershire, but these restorations were always small in proportion to the total number of justices put out between 1700 and 1704. Eighteen gentlemen were hypothetically available for restoration in Buckinghamshire, thirteen in Hertfordshire, and ten in Carmarthenshire, but Wright only restored one or two in each; it is improbable that all the

[1] H.M.C., Fifteenth Report, Appendix IV, *Portland MSS.* iv. 169–70.

[2] Godolphin for Granville in Cornwall; Rivers for Guilford in Essex; Grafton for Dysert in Suffolk. Winchelsea and Buckinghamshire resigned as lords-lieutenant of Kent and the East Riding respectively, and they were replaced by Rockingham and Newcastle.

[3] P.R.O., C. 231/9, pp. 122 ff. The counties neglected in 1705 were Caernarvonshire, Cardiganshire, Denbighshire, Ely, Glamorgan, Herefordshire, Kesteven, Merionethshire, Montgomeryshire, Northumberland, Oxfordshire, Pembrokeshire, Peterborough, Rutland, and Sussex.

others had died or left the county.[1] A very heavily corrected fiat for April 1705 survives for Anglesey — one of only five signed by Wright that has been traced — but this only gives two names, both new men, to be put in.[2]

Those put out in these commissions seem in many cases to have died, and there is some evidence to suggest that Wright was still not prepared to dismiss the Tackers and their supporters, despite appeals from 'great men in posts of honour'.[3] Burnet said that the Whigs had received no help from the ministers in the 1705 election.[4] One of the reasons alleged in July for Wright's impending dismissal was that he had not complied with Wharton and other Whig peers, in the matter of country justices.[5] During the summer and autumn of 1705, Defoe was sending to Harley reports on the political complexion of the county magistracy; he found that Tories were still in commission in most places, and that they were a great obstruction, next to the clergy, to the Queen's service in the countryside. He observed, for instance, that nothing would help future elections in Wiltshire more than the dismissal of the Tacker Henry Chivers.[6] It is true that Wright did, in fact, put Chivers out in September 1705, shortly before a by-election for Chippenham which Chivers lost, but this was probably on the representation of Burnet, as Bishop of Salisbury, who had a clearly proved case of *scandalum magnatum* against him.[7] In general, therefore, the magistracy was

[1] P.R.O., C. 234/9, Devonshire: 14 Feb. 1705/6; C. 234/13, Gloucestershire: 6 Apr. 1706; C. 234/27, Northamptonshire: 12 Feb. 1705/6; C. 234/12, Essex: 23 Feb. 1705/6; C. 234/35, Suffolk: 5 Mar. 1705/6; C. 234/36, Surrey: 7 May 1706; C. 234/41, Worcestershire: 9 Dec. 1706; C. 234/3, Buckinghamshire: 25 Feb. 1705/6; C. 234/16, Hertfordshire: 28 Feb. 1705/6; C. 234/81, Carmarthenshire: 25 Jan. 1705/6; in each case corrected backwards and compared with H.L.R.O., Main Papers, H.L., 20 Mar. 1704, 16 Feb. 1705. In the case of Devonshire the findings are confirmed by the survival of the commission of the peace for 27 Feb. 1705 at Devon R.O., Q/JC.

[2] P.R.O., C. 234/78, Anglesey: 5 Apr. 1705.

[3] H.M.C., Fifteenth Report, Appendix IV, *Portland MSS.* iv. 189-90.

[4] Burnet, *History*, v. 223.

[5] Margaret, Lady Verney, *Verney Letters of the Eighteenth Century* (London, 1930), i. 227.

[6] *The Letters of Daniel Defoe*, ed. G. H. Healey (Oxford, 1955), pp. 103-4, 108, 113.

[7] P.R.O., C. 231/9, p. 132; Luttrell, *Brief Relation*, v. 565, 614. The Earl of Peterborough was able to secure the dismissal of a Northamptonshire justice for the same reason. Luttrell, op. cit. v. 546.

probably left much as it had been during the period of Tory dominance, throughout the 1705 election and into the early autumn of 1705.

Before the election, the triumvirs had hoped that a ministry could be supported in the Commons without concessions to the Junto Whigs. The return of more Tackers than had been expected — possibly because of the Court's refusal to deprive them of local office — made it necessary to prevent a Country party combination of Tories and Whigs in opposition. Consequently, the triumvirs backed the Whig John Smith for the Speakership of the new Commons, and undertook to have Wright dismissed at last.[1] It was rumoured in June that he would be replaced by William Cowper, a prominent Whig leader in the Commons.[2] The only difficulty was that the Queen wanted a moderate Tory in the office. She was reluctant to put herself into the hands of the Junto. A Whig Lord Keeper, she explained to Godolphin, would be 'an inexpressible uneasiness and mortification to me'.[3] Notwithstanding this appeal, Godolphin urged Cowper's claims, and the Duchess of Marlborough brought her influence to bear, against Wright as much as on behalf of Cowper.[4] Wright was finally dismissed in October, to the general satisfaction of the Whigs.

VI

It is difficult to come to a final conclusion about Wright's handling of the commission of the peace. Burnet and Marlborough, whose verdicts are usually followed, both thought of him as a Tory zealot,[5] although he had begun his career as a Whig. He had held the great seal in successive ministries of different character, when he seemed to have accepted uncriti-

---

[1] Trevelyan, *England under Queen Anne*, ii. 25-32; Roberts, *Growth of Responsible Government*, pp. 334-5; Horwitz, *Revolution Politicks*, pp. 203-4; W. A. Speck, 'The Choice of a Speaker in 1705', *B.I.H.R.* xxvii (1964), 21-46; G. Elisabeth Cunnington, 'The General Election of 1705', *B.I.H.R.* xvii (1939-40), 145-6.

[2] Luttrell, *Brief Relation*, v. 566.

[3] B.L., Add. MSS. 28070, f. 12: Queen Anne to [Godolphin], 11 July 1705; Holmes, *British Politics in the Age of Anne*, p. 253.

[4] *Account of the Conduct of the Duchess of Marlborough* (London, 1742), p. 159.

[5] Burnet, *History*, v. 137, 223-5; *The Marlborough-Godolphin Correspondence*, i. 376.

cally the names forced on him by politically committed colleagues. Naturally the gentlemen anybody chose to recommend would be distinguished for 'loyalty', 'integrity', or
'estates'; naturally any gentleman recommended to be put
out would be 'disaffected', 'corrupt', 'impoverished', or
otherwise unfit. Wright, like every Chancellor, had no obvious
means of checking the characters of country squires in every
corner of the kingdom. Unlike most Chancellors, he accepted
in good faith assurances from every quarter that they were
fit, or otherwise, to be in commission. This led him into
trouble with Tories as well as Whigs. He had to write an
apologetic letter to Nottingham in the summer of 1702 after
leaving out a Northamptonshire justice on local recommendation. He explained ingenuously that he knew nothing about
this gentleman and bore him no ill will; he had been advised
to dismiss him, and had thus done so.[1]

Admittedly, he seems to have shown a certain obstinacy in
neglecting to put in, or restore, well-affected Whigs following
the censure of the House of Lords in March 1704. It may
have been that conflicting recommendations from different
party sources transformed his earlier naivety into caution in
the face of parliamentary criticism. Harley, for instance,
thought that he would have to be bullied to implement Newcastle's recommendations for Nottinghamshire in 1704.[2] On
the other hand, if this sprang from Tory conviction on
Wright's part, why did he restore twelve gentlemen in Cheshire
in 1704? It is possible that the Whigs blackened his character
in general terms and then gave him no specific help in putting
the commission of the peace in order. He could not have
restored all those put out before March 1704 without any
authorization from local sources — how was he to know if
they were still alive? The Cheshire case is perhaps to be explained by the hypothesis that some kind-hearted Whig,
possibly Sir Joseph Jekyll, who had retained the Chief Justice-
ship of Chester throughout the Tory regime, had submitted
suggestions as to the gentlemen to be put back, while the

---

[1] B.L., Add. MSS. 29588, f. 135: Wright to Nottingham, 19 Aug. 1702.
[2] B.L., Loan 29/191, f. 164: Sir Willoughby Hickman to Sir Christopher Musgrave, 17 July 1704, sent by Musgrave to Harley; Loan 29/237, f. 80: Harley to
Newcastle, 29 July 1704.

Whigs in other counties had either maintained silence or had concentrated on persuading him to put Tory gentlemen out; but this is pure conjecture.

Whatever justification is urged in Wright's defence, it is clear enough that, when he surrendered the seal, he had totally lost the esteem of all parties. Godolphin said that it would have been 'ridiculous' to have kept him in office.[1] He retired to his estates in Leicestershire, where he was elevated, somewhat belatedly, to the commission of the peace in 1712, as the last in the list of knights.[2] He re-emerged briefly from obscurity in 1715 to support the Tory candidates in the Leicestershire county election,[3] and he died in 1721. His successor as Lord Keeper, Cowper, was not much more distinguished in the legal profession than Wright had been at the time of his appointment. Unlike Wright, however, Cowper was trusted by his colleagues in the Cabinet. One of his first tasks was to establish the stability of the ministry of the triumvirs by judicious manipulation of the patronage of the great seal.

---

[1] H.M.C., *Bath MSS.* i. 64 (misdated 1704).
[2] P.R.O., C. 234/19, Leicestershire: 17 Mar. 1711/12.
[3] Verney, *Verney Letters of the Eighteenth Century*, i. 329, 333.

6

THE COMMISSION OF THE PEACE AND THE WHIGS, 1705-10

I

The new Lord Keeper's background was impeccably Whig. His father, Sir William Cowper, had supported Exclusion, and was concerned with Shaftesbury in the indictment of the Duke of York as a recusant in 1680. In 1689 he had voted for the Sacheverell Clause. He was still alive in 1705. The son had been elected M.P. for Hertford in 1695. He voted consistently along Junto lines, and rapidly acquired a high reputation in the Commons as a Whig spokesman. He played a part in the prosecution of the Assassination Plot conspirators in 1696, supported Somers in 1701, and defended Halifax against the accusation of malpractices as Auditor of the Exchequer in 1704.[1] Cowper's personal reputation was rather dubious. He was rumoured to have contracted a bigamous marriage. There were stories of illegitimate children. His brother had been the defendant in a sensational murder trial in 1700. His second marriage, though respectable, was conducted in secrecy before he had held the great seal a year.[2]

Unlike Wright, Cowper was a man of great personal distinction; he was eloquent, witty, and polished in manner. He immediately won the applause of laymen, if not of lawyers, by his lofty refusal of the 'New Year Gifts' traditionally made to the Keeper or Chancellor by the subordinate officers of Chancery.[3] He overcame the Queen's initial dislike of him fairly quickly by permitting her to nominate to all ecclesiastical appointments in the gift of the great seal worth more than £40 a year.[4] After his appointment, Cowper lost some of his

[1] Jones, *The First Whigs*, p. 118; Browning, *Danby*, iii. 167; Ellis, 'The Whig Junto', Appendix G, p. 6; *V.C.H., Hertfordshire*, Genealogical Volume (1907), 133-9.

[2] Campbell, *Lives of the Chancellors*, iv. 260-1, 274-83, 290-1.

[3] Ibid., pp. 296-9.

[4] B.L., Loan 29/263: Harley to Cowper, 23 Sept. 1706; Blenheim MSS., B

Junto connections, and became, to some extent, a Court Whig. Admittedly, his social circle included some high-spirited Whig ladies: his wife; the Duchess of Marlborough, who had pressed for his appointment and who was a close friend; and particularly his formidable sister-in-law, Anne Clavering, whose partisan Whiggishness led her to badger him to put Tories whom she disliked out of the commission of the peace.[1] Notwithstanding this domestic background, Cowper was quite capable of taking a different line from his Junto colleagues.

Cowper was expected to exercise the patronage of the great seal in the interests of the Whigs in the localities, and in particular to balance the Tory ascendancy in the commission of the peace that had marked the Queen's accession. Years later he described his programme to George I:

> . . . as the two partys grew more & more set & violent against one another . . . Gentlemen well qualify'd wer put out of that Commission [of the peace] without formal hearings or even so much as proof ex parte of any misbehaviour in their Duty. When I had the Honour of the Great Seale the first time, I cannot accuse my self of that last mention'd practise, & yet by perseverance in putting in those who wer best inclind to the Protestant Succession & leaving out, as fast as I could discover them, those who wer of too inferiour a Condition ['as well as ill intentioned' crossed out] & taking all just advantages of proof against those who discovered a disaffection to the true interest of their country, I can truly say, the Commissions of the Peace wer at my surrendring the Seale in a very good state with a sufficient balance in favour of the honest interest.[2]

Cowper's description makes the remodelling sound like a long-term policy rather than a comprehensive, simultaneous purge. The evidence, now much more complete after the new Lord Keeper's laudable decision to preserve the fiats for every commission he issued,[3] suggests that this is a correct impression. Fifteen months after Cowper had accepted the seal, at some time between 14 January and 4 February 1707,

I-23: Cowper to Marlborough, 13 Oct. 1709, apologizing for not appointing Marlborough's candidate to a great seal living with the remark 'Your Grace knows I am particularly obliged to obey the Queen in things of that kind.'

[1] *The Correspondence of Sir James Clavering*, ed. H. T. Dickinson (Surtees Society, clxxviii for 1963, 1967), 8, 12, 27–8, 29, 80, 81, 88.
[2] Herts. R.O., Cowper (Panshanger) MSS. D/EP F152: Memorandum for George I.
[3] P.R.O., C. 234/1–95, *passim*.

he drew up an analysis, county by county, of the justices of the peace whom he had ordered to be put in and out since his appointment.[1] During this period, new commissions had been sealed for forty counties, nearly all of them during the months from February to June 1706.[2]

Cowper was not, at this time, simply reversing the changes made by his predecessor. Of the total of 355 gentlemen put in, only forty-seven were restorations of justices who had been left out by Wright during the period from the summer of 1700 to 20 March 1704; and only one was the restoration of a justice left out by Wright during the period from the end of the 1703/4 session to 16 February 1705. Oxfordshire had most restorations, with nine out of twenty-six put in; Cardiganshire had the highest proportion of restorations to gentlemen put in *de novo*, with five restorations out of nine to be added. Dr Henry Fleming and Thomas Hebblethwaite, the two Westmorland justices who had caused so much difficulty in 1701, were restored for that county. In general, however, Cowper was not principally concerned at this time to put back into the commission those gentlemen whom Wright had put out at the height of the Tory ministry's influence.[3] This is rather surprising. In Devonshire, for instance, where in 1704 Richard Duke had lamented the omission of twenty-nine wealthy and respectable gentlemen since 1702, only four of those put in by Cowper during his first fifteen months of office were restorations, and they were among the least distinguished of those who had been put out by Wright.

[1] Herts. R.O., Cowper (Panshanger) MSS. D/EP F152. This list complements the fiats; there are some minor discrepancies, but in general the list and the fiats tally. The most serious inaccuracy is that Cowper thought that changes had been effected in the East Riding, but no commission was sealed for that county during this period. In the numerical calculations which follow, the figures are adjusted to take account of this slip.

[2] P.R.O., C. 231/9, pp. 135 ff. The seventeen neglected counties were Anglesey, Caernarvonshire, Cornwall, Derbyshire, Dorset, Flintshire, Glamorgan, Herefordshire, Leicestershire, Merionethshire, Pembrokeshire, Peterborough, Radnorshire, Rutland, Shropshire, Somerset, and the East Riding.

[3] The calculations are based on a comparison of the list at Herts. R.O., Cowper (Panshanger) MSS. D/EP F152, with: H.L.R.O., Main Papers, H.L., 20 Mar. 1704; and H.L.R.O., Main Papers, H.L., 16 Feb. 1705. It is possible that some more restorations, of justices put out between February and October 1705, may have taken place, but it is unlikely that these were significantly numerous. An attempt has been made not to confuse gentlemen of the same name.

More than thirty of those who were put in, were members of the House of Commons. Most of these had been elected for the first time in the election of 1705. These M.P.s were of several types. Some had strong Junto connections: for example, the two M.P.s for Lymington, Paul Burrard and the Marquess of Winchester, were now put in for Hampshire. Others were non-Junto Whigs of an independent type, like John Dibble, M.P. for Okehampton, who was put in for Devonshire, and Langham Booth, knight of the shire for Cheshire, who was put in for that county.[1] Some of the M.P.s were government servants, like Walter Whitfield, Paymaster of the Marines, and Josiah Burchett, Secretary to the Admiralty, who were put in for Middlesex and Kent respectively. However, few, if any, of these M.P.s now put into the commission were identifiable Tories; of those who had sat in the 1702–5 Parliament, none had voted for the Tack.

It is difficult to say much about those appointed to the magistracy during this fifteen-month period who were not M.P.s. Some were famous men. Sir Godfrey Kneller became a justice in Surrey, and Joseph Addison, recently made Under-Secretary of State, was included for Middlesex. Oxfordshire had twenty-six new justices; Middlesex, twenty-one; Surrey and Wiltshire, seventeen each; but with the exception of Ely, which received a commission adding thirteen names, the numbers added were not disproportionate to the relative size of the counties. In Wiltshire the intention seems to have been to put into commission a number of gentlemen of moderate political views who could be relied on to fulfil the duties of a justice of the peace. Of the seventeen added in that county in April 1706, three became regular attenders at quarter sessions during the following four years, five more became occasional attenders, at least two acted sporadically as justices out of sessions, and two more were active justices in neighbouring counties who, if nothing else, took out their writs of *dedimus* for Wiltshire.[2] The government was still receiving complaints, as when Wright had held the seal, about the lack

---

[1] Ellis, 'The Whig Junto', Appendix G, pp. 3, 17, 42, 47.
[2] Wilts. R.O., Q.S. Minute and Order Books for the years 1706–10; Q.S. Great Rolls, Trinity 1706–Michaelmas 1710; P.R.O., C. 193/43.

of active justices.[1] It is probable that one consideration in Cowper's programme was the need to restore the general reputation of the magistracy by providing counties like Wiltshire with resident justices willing to undertake the responsibilities of county administration.

The number of living justices left out at this time was eighty-four.[2] This was quite a high total for a fifteen-month period, but with the exception of two counties, Gloucestershire and Hertfordshire, the omissions were spread thinly among the counties. In Gloucestershire, twenty-two justices were put out in two commissions, much the highest number for any one county. Of these, three had been victims of the Association purge of 1696, having been restored in the summer of 1700; a fact which suggests a certain continuity of Whig-Tory animosity.[3] A significant shift in the balance of political power had clearly occurred in the Gloucestershire election of 1705, when the Junto supporter Sir John Guise had replaced the formidable Jack Howe as one of the knights of the shire, but this was not the immediate cause of the disgrace of sixteen Gloucestershire justices. They were dismissed on 14 January 1707 for 'refusing to act'. In Hertfordshire, fourteen gentlemen were left out in two commissions. These counties together made 40 per cent of the total number of omissions. The next highest numbers of dismissals for single counties were six, perhaps disproportionately, in Carmarthenshire, and five apiece in Middlesex, Essex, and Northamptonshire.[4] Only two of those put out anywhere were sitting M.P.s. Both were Tackers. One was Thomas Rowney, M.P. for Oxford, who was one of the sixteen put out in Gloucestershire for 'refusing to act'. The other case was more conspicuous. This was Charles Caesar, M.P. for Hertford, who had been sent to the Tower in October 1705 for hinting in Parliament

[1] See, for instance, B.L., Loan 29/193, f. 262: Baron Price to Harley (from the Midland Circuit), 2 Aug. 1706.

[2] In Cowper's list at Herts. R.O., Cowper (Panshanger) MSS. D/EP F152, dead justices are ignored.

[3] Robert Pleydall, Walter Estcourt, and Brereton Bourchier. P.R.O., P.C. 2/76, p. 463; P.C. 2/78, p. 68; C. 234/13, Gloucestershire: 6 Apr. 1706, 14 Jan. 1706/7.

[4] Carmarthenshire was an unusual case. No justices at all were put in, and of the six put out, three had been put in by Wright in July 1704. These were the only cases in any county of justices put in at that time now suffering dismissal.

at Marlborough's Jacobite tendencies. Eight months later he endeavoured to present an address to the Queen from Hertford. The Queen rejected it and issued a special order that Caesar be put out of the commission of the peace and the lieutenancy for Hertfordshire. This was accordingly done.[1] A handful of M.P.s in the 1702–5 Parliament who had voted for the Tack, and who had not been re-elected in 1705, were also put out.[2]

In many of the counties affected by these changes, it was not so much direct supervision by Cowper as a shift in the balance of power within the counties that influenced the alterations in the commissions of the peace. Hertfordshire was an exception. Cowper's own local connections were in that county, and his personal knowledge presumably dictated changes outstripping in intensity those made for most other counties. Elsewhere, it was a switch in the lord-lieutenant or *custos* in 1705 that was probably behind the revision of the commission of the peace. In Kent, where fourteen were put in, the Whig Lord Rockingham had replaced the Tory Earl of Winchelsea. In Oxfordshire, where twenty-six were put in, the Duke of Marlborough had replaced the Tory Earl of Abingdon. In Suffolk, where fifteen were put in and two left out, a Court Whig, the Duke of Grafton, had replaced the Tory Earl of Dysert. A change in the lieutenancy represents the operation of government influence, reflected at second hand in changes in the commission.

In other counties, the initiative for alteration came from below. One interesting example is Cardiganshire. In 1705 and 1706, Lord Lisburne, who lived in the county, was pressing Harley and Cowper for changes in the commission made urgently necessary by the 'insults and injuries' suffered by certain persons. Lisburne did not say whether this was because they had been left out, or because those who had been left in

[1] Luttrell, *Brief Relation*, v. 625–6; vi. 62; H.M.C., Thirteenth Report, Appendix II, *Portland MSS.* ii. 194; N.U.L., Pw2 Hy 617: Queen's warrant to Cowper, 26 June 1706; B.L., Loan 29/263: Harley to Cowper, 26 June 1706; P.R.O., C. 234/16, Hertfordshire: 12 July 1706; H.M.C., *Bath MSS.* i. 83.

[2] John Drake, M.P. Amersham 1702–5, put out for Buckinghamshire; William Levinz, M.P. East Retford 1702–5, put out for Hertfordshire (but not for Nottinghamshire); Sir Charles Barrington, M.P. Essex 1702–5, put out for Hertfordshire (but not for Essex). Sir Charles had been in trouble in June 1705 for listing a licensed pedlar. Luttrell, *Brief Relation*, v. 567.

were insolent. Cowper told him that he would obey the Queen's commands in the matter. Lisburne, dissatisfied, informed Harley that in the summer of 1702 several Non-jurors had been put in, and other faithful servants of King William had been left out, and that in consequence the people were subject to 'violent humours'. Lisburne, who was neither lord-lieutenant nor *custos*, presumably had his way. The new commission for Cardiganshire, sealed in February 1706, made the most sweeping changes in any Welsh county. Nine were put in, of whom five had been put out by Wright, and one, John Pughe, was M.P. for the county; two were left out.[1]

On balance, the changes made in the first fifteen months of Cowper's tenure of office were less spectacular than the Whigs had hoped for, and the Tories had feared. The reason for this is that the ministerial 'triumvirate' of Godolphin, Marlborough, and Harley exercised a restraining influence. Godolphin was, as always, averse to gratifying the wishes of a predominant party. He had himself replaced a Tory, Granville, as lord-lieutenant and *custos* of Cornwall in April 1705, but no commission of the peace was issued for that county between July 1705, when Wright still held the seal, and September 1709. Harley took a similar view, observing at the time of Cowper's appointment that the country gentry should not be embodied against the Queen's service, and that the ministry should guard against the Whigs' desire to proscribe their enemies. A year later, he thought that the independent gentry would support any government which left them alone.[2] As Secretary of State, Harley exercised some influence over the appointment of magistrates. In June 1706, for instance, he stopped the sealing of commissions for the parts of Lincolnshire, and Cowper had to write to ask him what alterations he wanted to make.[3] It was quite probably Harley, too, who moderated the demands of the Whig *custos*

[1] Herts. R.O., Cowper (Panshanger) MSS. D/EP F155: Lisburne to Cowper, 12 Nov. 1705; B.L., Loan 29/192, f. 394: Lisburne to Harley, 20 Dec. 1705; N.U.L., Pw2 Hy 834: list of Cardiganshire justices enclosed in a letter from Lisburne to Harley, 3 Jan. 1706; P.R.O., C. 234/80, Cardiganshire: 19 Feb. 1705/6.

[2] H.M.C., *Bath MSS.* i. 74–5, 110–11; Bennett, *The Tory Crisis in Church and State, 1688–1730*, pp. 85–6.

[3] B.L., Loan 29/132, f. L.157: Cowper to Harley, 21 June 1706.

of Worcestershire, the Earl of Coventry, who complained of
the 'arbitrary practices' of the justices, some of whom were
furious High Church zealots. Coventry's nominees were, with
one exception, put in, but only one of those he denounced
was put out.[1] Furthermore, the Whig peers might themselves
be divided on the merits of those they wanted put in or out.
In Suffolk, for example, the Duke of Grafton wanted the dismissal of a justice called Taylor, but the Whig Lord Hervey
persuaded him, in the interests of domestic tranquillity, not
to press the demand, as Sir Thomas Hanmer, Grafton's step-
father and a Tacker, objected.[2] In general, therefore, it seems
reasonable to conclude that the appointment of Cowper did
not make for an immediate take-over of local power by the
Whigs in the great majority of counties.

II

The situation at the centre was, however, changing, and Cowper's control of the patronage of the great seal moved into a
second phase at about the time — January 1707 — when he
reviewed his achievement in the alteration of the commissions
of the peace. The Whigs slowly increased their power in the
government. Charles, third Earl of Sunderland, became Secretary of State in December 1706, after long opposition from
the Queen and the beginnings of a quarrel between Harley
and Godolphin on the desirability of the appointment. Cowper himself was elevated to a peerage late in 1706, and after
the passage of the Act of Union he became the first Lord
Chancellor of Great Britain. In May 1707 the Privy Council
was remodelled. Fourteen Tory Councillors were displaced.[3]
Notwithstanding these concessions, the Whigs in Parliament
were discontented with their comparatively small share of the
places of profit and power, and in the 1707/8 session they
entered into factious opposition — of which Cowper, in his
continued disentanglement from the Junto, disapproved — in

[1] Herts. R.O., Cowper (Panshanger) MSS. D/EP F154: Coventry to Cowper, 13
Jan. 1706; P.R.O., C. 234/41, Worcestershire: 18 Feb. 1705/6, 9 Dec. 1706.
[2] *Letter Books of John Hervey, First Earl of Bristol*, i. 220-1.
[3] W. Coxe, *Memoirs of the Duke of Marlborough* (new edn. revised by John
Wade, London 1847-8), ii. 1-25; Trevelyan, *England under Queen Anne*, ii. 167-
71; S. Biddle, *Bolingbroke and Harley* (London, 1975), pp. 124-8; P.R.O., P.C.
2/81, p. 361: 20 May 1707.

the hope of increasing the value to the ministry of their support. During the winter of 1707/8, the government was under severe internal strain, as Godolphin was by now convinced of the need to woo parliamentary support, while Harley was dissatisfied with any tendency towards party faction.[1] The climax came in February 1708, when Harley, who had been approaching the younger Tories with a view to building a parliamentary majority independent of the Junto Whigs, was caught out in what looked like an intrigue to displace Godolphin. In spite of spirited resistance by the Queen, he was forced out of the ministry.[2] Against this background of events at the centre, Cowper's handling of the commission of the peace in 1707 and the early part of 1708 was of some relevance in the development of the political situation.

The evidence is that Cowper believed that manipulation of local patronage in the Whig interest should be kept to a minimum. During the period from the end of January 1707, when Cowper reviewed the achievements of his first fifteen months in office, and 13 February 1708, when Harley was dismissed as Secretary of State, Cowper sealed a total of fifty-two commissions spread over thirty-nine counties. Most of these were issued, as was usual, in the months before assizes, in February–March and in June–July 1707.[3] Of the counties which did not receive commissions, seven — Cornwall, Derbyshire, Dorset, Flintshire, Pembrokeshire, Peterborough, and Rutland — had not, by February 1708, received a commission at all since Wright had held the seal. In itself, this shows that Cowper had been unwilling or unable to carry on a completely comprehensive revision of the county commissions in the Whig interest.[4] Leaving aside Middlesex and Durham, for which the fiats do not survive, the commissions that were

[1] Holmes, *British Politics in the Age of Anne*, pp. 110-11, 242; A. McInnes, 'The Political Ideas of Robert Harley', *History*, N.S. 1 (1965), 318.

[2] G. S. Holmes and W. A. Speck, 'The Fall of Harley in 1708 Reconsidered', *Eng. Hist. Rev.* lxxx (1965), 673-98.

[3] P.R.O., C. 231/9, pp. 151 ff. These figures include Herefordshire, for which county Cowper signed a fiat dated 5 February 1707/8, although the commission was not sealed until March.

[4] The ambiguous case of the East Riding is an eighth such county. Besides these eight, Denbighshire, Ely, Gloucestershire, Hampshire, Holland, Huntingdonshire, Kesteven, Monmouthshire, Northumberland, and Worcestershire were neglected in 1707.

sealed during this period added 234 gentlemen and left 41
living justices out.[1]

The dismissals were concentrated in a few counties. Ten
were dismissed in Leicestershire, four in Warwickshire, and
two in Montgomeryshire, all for 'refusing to act'. Eight were
left out in Breconshire, but it is possible that some of these
had died, since their names are noted on the back of a list
serving as a fiat, not embodied in a specific order describing
the reason for their omission. The Tory family of Hatton suffered in Cambridgeshire with the exclusion of Sir Christopher
and Thomas Hatton, the only two justices left out in that
county. In about half a dozen other counties, justices were
left out in ones and twos. There seems, however, to have
been a feeling that Cowper was reluctant to dismiss justices.
When Charles Sergison, of the Admiralty, complained about a
justice in Sussex who had over-assessed him for the land tax,
he recommended another gentleman as a balance, on the
explicit assumption that his obnoxious neighbour could not
be removed.[2]

The bench in Leicestershire was quite substantially remodelled, since not only were ten left out, but also twelve
came in: the Earl of Gainsborough, Lord Rockingham, and
ten squires. The highest number added was twenty-three in
Surrey, followed by thirteen in Buckinghamshire and, rather
oddly, thirteen in Anglesey and eleven in Glamorgan. The
majority of the commissions were, however, of the most
routine kind, in which a few gentlemen of established county
families were added: five in Northamptonshire, three in
Cheshire, five in Staffordshire, eight in Norfolk, for example.

The political element in these changes was not strongly
marked. There was nothing in the nature of a Whig attack on
the Tory squires in Warwickshire, where the four gentlemen
who refused to act had all been put in by Cowper himself the
previous year. The Tories suffered a little more in Leicestershire, where Sir Wolstan Dixie and Sir Thomas Cave were
among those dismissed. Some of those added in several

---

[1] Twenty-one justices described as dead were also left out. P.R.O., C. 234/1–95,
passim.
[2] B.L., Loan 29/194, ff. 97–8: Sergison to George Tollett, 17 May 1707. Sergison observed that he did not trouble to act himself; his nominee was not added.

counties were local Whig leaders. For example, Josiah Diston, who was engaged in an intense and occasionally violent struggle for power in Devizes, was added for Wiltshire shortly after winning a by-election for that town in December 1706. He was, and remained, a firm Junto supporter.[1] Similarly, the inclusion of Sir Robert Marsham for Kent in 1707 brought to an end the temporary eclipse of his family's Whig interest at Maidstone, which had followed the death of his father in 1703, and the youthful Sir Robert was to be elected M.P. for Maidstone in 1708. There were some restorations of justices put out by Wright, including Medlicott, the Berkshire attorney who, according to Wright, took bribes, but in 1707 as in 1706 this was not a prominent feature of the commissions sealed. The over-all impression left by the alterations is that Cowper was, at this time, engaged in discreet adjustment in the Whig interest rather than in conspicuous and comprehensive regulation.

This is not to say that during this period of complex struggle at the centre, the commission of the peace was neglected as an instrument of politics. Though the changes were on a limited scale, Cowper had to tread warily, to avoid offending friends and driving enemies into committed opposition. Godolphin and Harley both resisted a full-scale purge of local office-holders in 1707, but Harley was more in favour of conciliating the Tories on local matters, a policy of which Godolphin disapproved lest the Whigs be made uneasy. The result was that a proposal to add names to the commissions for single counties led to a tug-of-war at the centre, with each side unwilling to allow advantages to the other. The changes eventually agreed on were non-committal, with both Whigs and Tories protesting from the county concerned that worthy men were kept out and unsatisfactory justices continued. When, for example, Harley's friend Lord Poulet complained about a Somerset justice, Henry Brett, who was an 'offitious drudg of the tacking party', Harley noted on the back of Poulet's letter 'H. Bret to be removed',

[1] H.M.C., Fifteenth Report, Appendix IV, *Portland MSS.* iv. 175-6, 486; *Letters of Daniel Defoe*, p. 104; Blenheim MSS., C I-35: papers relating to Devizes riots, 22 Apr.-25 Oct. 1707; P.R.O., S.P. 44/106, p. 125: Sunderland to Sir James Long, 28 Oct. 1707; Ellis, 'The Whig Junto', Appendix G, p. 6.

but Brett was not dismissed.[1] Again, Sir Robert Davers, the knight of the shire for Suffolk, was a High Churchman and a Tacker who was also on friendly terms with Harley.[2] When his nominations for the Suffolk bench were not included in a commission sealed in July 1707, in spite of a promise from Cowper that he would accept them, Davers turned to Harley, who agreed to speak to the Chancellor. It seems that Cowper had at first agreed to Davers's names, but subsequently objected that one had been an attorney and that the others were too young. Davers impatiently brushed these objections aside. Nothing further was done, but Harley was able to appear, in spite of a certain asperity in Davers's letters, as a sympathetic friend against the hypocritical Whig Chancellor.[3] In counties where Harley himself enjoyed influence, it was the Whigs who complained that their candidates were left out. Special interest attaches to Radnorshire, where Harley himself was *custos*. Lord Bradford, who lived at Wroxeter in Shropshire, and who was a staunch Whig, recommended two gentlemen for the commission of the peace for Radnorshire. Cowper wrote to Harley to say that he knew he would have no objection to one of the names, and asking him if he had any complaint against the other.[4] Before the commission could be sealed, however, Cowper received an infuriated letter from the octogenarian Bradford, alleging that Harley opposed the appointment of honest men as justices to maintain his own electoral interests, and that those who were in, were 'mean persons' included for the same reason. Bradford's own nominations, he said, were gentlemen of greater wealth in the county than Harley himself. He conceded that there was an unspecified accusation against one of his candidates, but countered with the curious argument that the gentleman should have been put in notwithstanding, as the disgrace would be greater if he had to be put out again.[5] The result was a compromise. One of Bradford's names was put in, but

[1] B.L., Loan 29/193, ff. 306-7: Poulet to Harley, 18 Sept. 1706.

[2] Holmes, *British Politics in the Age of Anne*, pp. 265, 327.

[3] B.L., Loan 29/194, f. 178: Sir Robert Davers to [Harley], 18 June 1707; f. 197: same to same, 6 Sept. 1707.

[4] B.L., Loan 29/132, f. L.180: Cowper to Harley, 20 June 1707.

[5] Herts. R.O., Cowper (Panshanger) MSS. D/EP F152: Bradford to Cowper, 30 June 1707.

the other was not included.[1] Thus, in Suffolk, Whig pressures prevented a Tacker from bringing his candidates on to the bench; in Radnorshire, Harley had partially blocked a Whig magnate's attempt to nominate new justices.

The ministry's attitude to the commissions of the peace was therefore typically that of a coalition. A place on the bench was a useful minor concession for potential supporters, but when leading ministers held different views on which set of potential supporters should be conciliated, the result was stalemate. Harley's role until his downfall was partly to resist overbearing Whig demands, and partly to use his position as Secretary as an indirect channel for nominations from potential parliamentary supporters. He was not always successful, but he was the champion of those who distrusted Whig ambitions to engross local power, and when in January 1708 he attempted to explore openly the possibility of accommodation with the Tories, one of the baits he offered was a bill for the qualification of justices.[2] This policy of conciliating the Tories through local office was in conflict with the Junto's ambition to establish Whig benches of justices in every county. The Junto conceived that this aim had been obstructed while Harley had been Secretary of State, and when he fell in February 1708 it seemed that the stalemate had been broken. It might reasonably have been expected that Cowper's tenure of office would move into a third phase, of the assertion of the Whig interest in the localities in time for the election due in 1708.

III

The fall of Harley in 1708 did not immediately result in a reconstitution of the government along Junto lines. 'Lord Treasurer's Whigs' rather than Junto Whigs were promoted to fill up the vacancies left by Harley and his friends. The Junto was supporting the Court in the House of Commons, but it had not, as yet, been admitted to supremacy in the ministry.[3] Consequently, the election of May 1708 was not fought by

---

[1] P.R.O., C. 234/90, Radnorshire: 10 July 1707.
[2] Holmes and Speck, 'The Fall of Harley in 1708 Reconsidered', p. 684.
[3] Walcott, *English Politics in the Early Eighteenth Century*, pp. 148-50; Holmes, *British Politics in the Age of Anne*, p. 199 n.

the Junto with the backing of ministerial patronage. Court and Junto candidates sometimes even conflicted.[1] Changes in the county commissions of the peace played some part in the election, but in a random fashion. Twelve English counties, and five Welsh counties, did not receive a commission at all during the twelve months before the election, among them the electorally important counties of Cornwall, Gloucestershire, Oxfordshire, and Somerset. In several more, the changes that were made before the elections were insignificant. For instance, in both Herefordshire and Norfolk, two gentlemen were put in and none put out in February 1708.[2]

The number of counties where large changes took place was relatively small. In some, more gentlemen were put in than was usual. As many as nine gentlemen were added in March 1708 for Cheshire, among them Charles Stanley, about to be re-elected knight of the shire in the neighbouring county of Lancashire. In Devonshire, twelve new justices were included. Twenty new justices were appointed for Peterborough, and two put out; admittedly, this was the first commission since the Queen's accession six years before.[3] In Wiltshire, nine gentlemen were added, among whom were Matthew Ducie Morton, about to be re-elected knight of the shire in Gloucestershire, and John Webb, shortly to be re-elected at Ludgershall. Fourteen gentlemen who refused to act were dismissed. On the same day, fifteen were added for Dorset, and ten were put out as refusing to act.[4] The coincidence of dates and of reasons for dismissal suggests that the proposals for Dorset and Wiltshire came from the same source. It is a reasonable conjecture, in the absence of further evidence, that this source was either the Marquess of Dorchester or the Duke of Bolton, two magnates of considerable local influence in both counties. It is difficult to relate the dismissals in these counties to the progress of the election. In Surrey, however, there was a possible connection between the removal of a justice and electoral success. Charles Cox,

[1] Ellis, 'The Whig Junto', pp. 609–18.

[2] P.R.O., C. 234/15, Herefordshire: 5 Feb. 1707/8; C. 234/27, Norfolk: 10 Feb. 1707/8.

[3] P.R.O., C. 234/5, Cheshire: 22 Mar. 1707/8; C. 234/9, Devonshire: 1 Mar. 1707/8; C. 234/92, Peterborough: 24 Feb. 1707/8.

[4] P.R.O., C. 234/40, Wiltshire; C. 234/10, Dorset: both 1 Mar. 1707/8.

the sitting member for Southwark, himself took an affidavit
that one John Lade, a Surrey justice, was unwilling to co-
operate in the summoning of suspected persons to take the
oaths, that he had dismissed the case of a Catholic who had
refused the oaths, that he had been a Nonjuror in King William's time, and that he still referred to William as a usurper.
Cox sent this to Sunderland, who showed it to the Queen.
Lade was promptly dismissed from the Surrey commission,
just twenty days before Cox was re-elected.[1]

In another case, a Whig attempt to remodel the commission for electoral purposes misfired. This involved John Gape,
M.P. for St. Albans in the 1705-8 Parliament and a strong
Tory. Sunderland wrote to Cowper that the Queen was
informed that Gape had 'misbehaved himself on several
occasions where her Majesty's and the publick service were
concerned'; he was to be turned out of the Hertfordshire
commission.[2] Cowper issued a fiat leaving Gape and four
others out, and putting ten gentlemen in.[3] However, the
docquet book does not record the sealing of a commission
for Hertfordshire between March 1707 and July 1709, and
Gape was re-elected for St. Albans in May 1708. The Duchess
of Marlborough lamented that he had been left with 'the
power of justice' in St. Albans since this, she thought, was
the reason for the defeat of her brother in that election.[4]

It is a reasonable conclusion that, broadly, there was no
very coherent attempt by the Court to use the commission
of the peace to influence the elections. The number of counties where the bench was remodelled was comparatively small.
One point may be of some significance. Harley, and his
friends Sir Simon Harcourt, formerly Attorney General, and

[1] Blenheim MSS., C I-36: affidavit of William Puryour, 27 Mar. 1708; Charles
Cox to Sunderland, 27 Mar. 1708; P.R.O., S.P. 44/106, p. 207: Sunderland to
Cowper, 31 Mar. 1708; C. 234/36, Surrey: 10 Apr. 1708; C. 231/9, p. 172. For
John Lade, see G. S. Holmes, *The Trial of Doctor Sacheverell* (London, 1973),
p. 56 n.

[2] P.R.O., S.P. 44/106, p. 213: Sunderland to Cowper, 10 Mar. 1708.

[3] P.R.O., C. 234/16, Hertfordshire: 11 Mar. 1707/8.

[4] *The Marlborough-Godolphin Correspondence*, ii. 966; *Correspondence of
Sarah, Duchess of Marlborough* (London, 1838), i. 116, 130. Sarah meant that
Gape had not been put out for either the town or the liberty of St. Albans, both
of which received commissions like counties. The Queen's order ⁚ ɪd been for
Hertfordshire. The confusion was not such as to defeat Cowper's purpose and the
reason for Gape's reprieve was probably a Crown Office muddle.

Henry St. John, formerly Secretary at War, ceased to be named *ex officio* in the commissions for all the counties after the loss of their offices in February 1708. This may have had some effect in a general sense. But the Harcourt counties of Berkshire and Oxfordshire did not receive a new commission at all in 1708, and it is difficult to trace a connection between St. John and the justices put out in Wiltshire. On the whole, the complaint of the Whigs that the ministers were reluctant to use their patronage seems to have been justified.[1]

The electoral success of the Whigs was really attributable to the Jacobite invasion of Scotland, and to a run on the Bank of England engineered by the Tories.[2] When Parliament reassembled in the autumn of 1708, the Junto was at last able to use its parliamentary strength to storm the Closet, in spite of a stubborn resistance by the Queen. Somers, as Lord President, and Wharton, as Lord-Lieutenant of Ireland, entered the Cabinet in November 1708. Orford replaced Pembroke as First Lord of the Admiralty in October 1709. At a lower level, Junto supporters were brought into minor office. Godolphin and Marlborough phlegmatically accepted the colleagues forced on them by parliamentary necessity, but both regretted the Queen's uneasiness, and Godolphin in particular was uncomfortably aware that the only Junto lord not in major office was Halifax, the natural Whig candidate for the Treasury.[3] It would be natural to expect that, during the period from the election of 1708 to the beginning of 1710, the Junto leaders would set themselves to complement their success at the centre with the consolidation of their power in the localities.

This, in fact, was what they did, but as far as the commission of the peace was concerned, they achieved their local aims by promoting supporters rather than by putting opponents out. After the ones and twos included in 1707, the

---

[1] Sir John Cropley to Shaftesbury, 15 Jan. 1708, quoted in Holmes, *British Politics in the Age of Anne*, pp. 351–2.

[2] *Letters of Joseph Addison*, ed. W. Graham (Oxford, 1941), p. 107; Trevelyan, *England under Queen Anne*, ii. 349–50; Holmes, *British Politics in the Age of Anne*, p. 219.

[3] Ellis, 'The Whig Junto', pp. 621–4, 625–38; Holmes, *British Politics in the Age of Anne*, pp. 377–8.

numbers added in late 1708 and 1709 were, in several counties, fairly high: for instance, sixteen in Derbyshire, twelve in
Kesteven, nine in Kent, nine in Herefordshire, seven in Hampshire, and six in Cumberland. Devonshire, which had received
twelve additional names in March 1708, received ten more in
March 1709.[1] However, the initiative for such additions was
not the result of planned policy at the centre. Cowper sealed
fewer commissions of the peace in each of the years 1708
and 1709 than had been sealed in any year since before 1675.
Most of the commissions he did seal were dated in the
routine period before the assizes. Several counties were
passed over, especially in Wales. It is a reasonable conclusion
that Cowper responded to requests, but that these requests
were unsolicited. It was natural that the Whigs in the localities should, at the zenith of their party's fortunes, desire the
Chancellor to include their supporters in the commission of
the peace, but it was not inevitable that this would happen in
every county. Moreover, even when Whig suggestions were
made, Cowper was not prepared to examine them uncritically. For instance, Sir Francis Drake wrote from Devonshire
that, though he was pleased that one of his recommendations
had been accepted, he was surprised that others whom he had
named were not included.[2] This was the one county where a
striking number had been added — twenty-two in twelve
months — and Cowper perhaps felt that he had sufficiently
gratified the Devonshire Whigs. Nor was this all. In Staffordshire a sound Whig, Brian Broughton, was actually put out in
July 1709. The blunder was quickly drawn to Cowper's
attention by Dr William Lloyd, and Broughton was restored
in August, but Lloyd's letter was couched in a revealingly
defensive tone. Staffordshire needed justices of 'good Revolution principles' to meet the threat from a local Toryism made
more, not less, vigorous by the triumph of the Whigs at the
centre.[3]

It was unusual for justices to be dismissed in 1708 and

[1] P.R.O., C. 234/8, /21, /18, /15, /14, /7, /9, respectively: various dates between
12 Feb. 1708/9 and 26 July 1709.
[2] Herts. R.O., Cowper (Panshanger) MSS. D/EP F54: Sir Francis Drake to
Cowper, 12 Dec. 1709.
[3] Herts. R.O., Cowper (Panshanger) MSS. D/EP F55: Lloyd to Cowper, 25
July 1709; P.R.O., C. 234/34, Staffordshire: 5 July, 22 Aug. 1709.

1709. There is some evidence that, after the fall of Harley in February 1708, the Queen herself took over his role as a moderating influence against Junto pressures. When William Lowther, the Junto M.P. for Pontefract, wrote that a West Riding justice, one of four in a single parish, had maliciously issued troublesome warrants and was, moreover, 'one of the Discontented Party', the Queen, in referring the matter to Cowper, charged him to 'hear both sides'. The next commission for the West Riding did not omit Lowther's enemy and was not, indeed, issued until eight months later.[1] Again, in November 1709 the Queen desired the Chancellor to investigate a complaint against a Surrey justice called Shem Bridges, but Bridges was not dismissed either.[2] It is also possible that Cowper, mindful of the fate of his predecessors Somers and Wright, was unwilling to arouse parliamentary antagonism. The fiats note more frequently than usual such acceptable reasons for the omission of living justices as 'at his own request' or 'left the county'.[3]

In only one county is there much evidence of a systematic purge at this time. This is Wiltshire, where in March 1708, before the election, fourteen living justices had been left out. Another was dismissed in March 1709 and fifteen more were dismissed from the commission in December 1709.[4] The reasons were probably the substitution of the Whig Marquess of Dorchester for the Tory Viscount Weymouth as *custos* in June 1706, and the exertions of Josiah Diston's caucus at Devizes. Possibly the Duke of Bolton took a hand. But Wiltshire is the only county where large numbers were put out. Admittedly, justices were dismissed in smaller numbers in other counties too, and these cases have sometimes been interpreted as evidence that the Junto exercised its local patronage in an arrogant way in 1708 and 1709.[5] Hertfordshire, where Cowper doubtless drew on his local knowledge

---

[1] P.R.O., S.P. 44/107, pp. 183–6: Henry Boyle to Cowper, 1 Mar. 1709, enclosing the petition of William Lowther.

[2] P.R.O., S.P. 44/108, f. 167: Sunderland to Cowper, 17 Nov. 1709. The complaints came from the contentious Sir Harry Dutton Colt.

[3] For instance: P.R.O., C. 234/35, Suffolk: 25 Mar. 1709; C. 234/31, Rutland: 8 Mar. 1708/9.

[4] P.R.O., C. 234/40, Wiltshire: 1 Mar. 1707/8, 17 Mar. 1708/9, 6 Dec. 1709.

[5] Ellis, 'The Whig Junto', p. 657.

again to dismiss four justices in two commissions in 1709, might be a valid example of such arrogance, especially as one of the four was Richard Goulston, who had been Tory M.P. for Hertford between 1701 and 1708.[1] But with the exceptions of Wiltshire and Hertfordshire, Cowper was generally acting on the authority of the Queen in Council in dismissing justices at this time, and the reason for omission was misdemeanour. In one case, involving a justice whose support for the Tory candidate in the Surrey election of 1708 had been too enthusiastic, the Queen signified that she was entirely convinced of his 'disaffection' before Cowper was permitted to put him out.[2] Three justices in Cambridge town — a corporation where justices were appointed by the Chancellor — were dismissed in January 1709. The decision to put them out was taken by the Cabinet after the Attorney General's report showed that they had taken bribes to release listed soldiers.[3] Five Suffolk justices, including Leicester Martin who had briefly sat as knight of the shire in 1708, were put out in March 1709 for similar reasons. They had not taken bribes, but they had obstructed the press in a riotous manner. William Churchill, the Whig M.P. for Ipswich, advised the government to discount their defence. Nevertheless, it was the Queen's order in Council that secured their dismissal.[4] The evidence for and against the disgraced gentlemen was weighed carefully by the Attorney General. His report was, on the whole, favourable to them, and in March 1710 the Queen decided that three of them should be restored to the Suffolk bench, which was accordingly done.[5]

[1] P.R.O., C. 234/16, Hertfordshire: 23 July 1709, 26 Nov. 1709.
[2] P.R.O., S.P. 34/9, No. 100: Sir John Buckworth to [Sunderland], 7 June 1708, enclosing affidavits that John Mitchell, justice for Surrey, insulted the supporters of Sir Richard Onslow and Mr Scawen; S.P. 44/106, p. 322: Sunderland to Cowper, 15 June 1708; C. 234/36, Surrey: 2 July 1708.
[3] Blenheim MSS., C I-6: minutes of Cabinet, 20 Dec. 1708, 30 Jan. 1709; C I-36: Sunderland to Cowper, 28 Jan. 1709, signifying the Queen's order that the justices be put out and noting that one of them was dead anyway.
[4] P.R.O., P.C. 2/82, pp. 277-8, 296, 299: 13 Mar., 31 Mar., 10 Apr. 1709; P.R.O., S.P. 34/10, No. 77: William Churchill to Sunderland, 27 Mar. 1709, enclosing No. 77/I: C. Grovenor, Bailiff of Ipswich, to William Churchill, 24 Mar. 1709; C. 234/35, Suffolk: 18 Mar. 1708/9.
[5] Bodl. MS. Rawl. D. 383, ff. 1-53: copies of affidavits referred to the Attorney General, and reports of the Attorney General and the Solicitor General, 2

The number of counties in which living justices were put out without royal authorization, for reasons that could be construed as party factiousness, was therefore small between the election of 1708 and the winter of 1709/10. One explanation for this is that it was more necessary in 1709 than it had been for many years past for the central government to have the full co-operation and support of its local agents. In the first place, the justices of the peace were still indispensable to the system of recruiting soldiers and sailors. Any threat to put justices out for neglect would lead to insolent bullying of the magistrates by the officers of the press.[1] In the second place, 1709 was a year of serious economic hardship.[2] The justices' functions of regulating prices and enforcing the statutes relating to forestalling and engrossing became of great importance, while distress in the parishes apparently led to an increase in the number of justices' indictments.[3] The Secretaries of State received numerous reports of corn riots. It was represented from some counties that the ordinary local authority of the justices had broken down.[4] The ministers possibly felt that a remodelling of the county benches would be inopportune. To put justices out of the commission of the peace, on account of their Tory principles only, would have been folly, if those justices were prepared to act. Consequently, with the possible exceptions of Wiltshire and Hertfordshire, Cowper was reluctant to purge the county magistracy for purely party reasons when no dereliction of duty could be proved.

IV

The ministerial alliance between the duumvirs and the Junto

July 1709; P.R.O., S.P. 44/108, f. 206: Sunderland to Cowper, 28 Mar. 1710; C. 234/35, Suffolk: 5 Apr. 1710.

[1] *The Marlborough–Godolphin Correspondence*, ii. 945, 1144-5; *Vernon Correspondence*, iii. 322.

[2] M. Beloff, *Public Order and Popular Disturbances, 1660–1714* (reprinted edn., London, 1963), pp. 68-70; Trevelyan, *England under Queen Anne*, iii. 33-8; Holmes, *The Trial of Doctor Sacheverell*, pp. 177-8.

[3] J. S. Cockburn, 'The North Riding Justices, 1690-1750. A Study in Local Administration', *Yorkshire Archaeological Journal*, xli (1966), 490-1.

[4] For instance: Blenheim MSS., C I-37: Sunderland's domestic correspondence, 1709-10, *passim*; C I-40: Lord Chief Justice Holt to Sunderland, 24 July 1709, describing disorder in Northamptonshire.

Whigs was outwardly strong. However, it was in reality a fragile political combination. Godolphin and Marlborough distrusted the ambition of the Whigs. They had reservations, for instance, about the replacement of Pembroke by Orford at the Admiralty in October 1709. Also, the waning of the Queen's affection for the Duchess of Marlborough had weakened their position. The Whigs resented the moderation of Godolphin and antagonized Marlborough by their reluctance to support his request to be made Captain-General for life.[1] Meanwhile, Harley was endeavouring to build an alternative Court party which he hoped would eventually be strong enough to undermine the influence of the duumvirs and their Whig allies. This party gathered weight as Harley drew Shrewsbury, Somerset, Newcastle, Argyll, Rivers, Queensberry, and several more into a loose alliance.[2] By the autumn of 1709, therefore, the ministry, its problems exacerbated by military and diplomatic difficulties and by economic distress, was on the defensive. In the course of the winter it lost its cohesion. Marlborough threatened to resign in January when the Queen proposed, without consulting him, to promote John Hill, the brother of her favourite companion Abigail Masham, to the colonelcy of a vacant regiment, and he resented the failure of his colleagues to support him on the issue. The more vehement Whigs did not endear themselves to the Queen by talking of a parliamentary address to dismiss Mrs Masham from the Bedchamber.[3] The impeachment of Dr Sacheverell in February and March for a sermon which, among other highly controversial matter, criticized the ministers' conduct of the Queen's government in Church and State, misfired badly; and the over-all outcome of this *cause célèbre*, in spite of the narrow vote for Sacheverell's guilt, was merely to illustrate how far opinion at all levels of society was hostile to the Whig-dominated regime.[4] In the spring of 1710 the Queen initiated an agonizingly slow reorganization of the Cabinet. The Duke of Shrewsbury was admitted in April, after replacing the Marquess of Kent, who

[1] Coxe, *Marlborough*, ii. 482-9, 491-2.
[2] A. McInnes, *Robert Harley, Puritan Politician* (London, 1970), pp. 116-21.
[3] Holmes, *The Trial of Doctor Sacheverell*, pp. 114-16.
[4] Ibid., Chapter X.

had not been of Cabinet rank, as Lord Chamberlain. Sunderland was dismissed in June, and in August Godolphin himself fell.

Harley, who had adroitly manipulated these events, was anxious not to find himself presiding over a new ministry dominated by Tories. His aim was to construct a coalition. The summer of 1710 saw a complex series of intrigues, as Harley and his allies tested the willingness of politicians of all parties to serve under the new regime. Even some of the senior Junto lords were approached, and Halifax and Somers were briefly receptive until they realized that a dissolution of the Whig Parliament elected in 1708 was an unavoidable part of the plan.[1] Politics at the centre, then, were in a state of turmoil throughout June, July, and August, as Harley strove to build a balanced administration and to prepare for an election that would undermine the Junto in the Commons without at the same time resulting in a Tory landslide.

It is sometimes said that this ministerial revolution was accompanied by changes among the lords-lieutenant. In fact, only two lieutenancies that were not vacant by death changed hands before the 1710 election. Rochester replaced Godolphin in Cornwall, and Beaufort replaced Bolton in Hampshire. These changes were not necessarily designed to mobilize Toryism in Cornwall and Hampshire in readiness for the election. If this had been so, Bolton would not have remained lord-lieutenant and *custos* of Dorset. Harley seems rather to have been trying to gratify those territorial magnates who had no Junto connections. He did not find this easy. Beaufort had set his heart, not on Hampshire, but on Gloucestershire, but the Earl of Berkeley was appointed to that county in succession to his father, who died in September 1710. The Earl of Scarsdale, who 'above all things' desired the lieutenancy of Derbyshire, was passed over.[2] Cowper himself became lord-lieutenant of Hertfordshire in 1710 in succession to the dead Earl of Essex, an appointment which admittedly caused mild surprise.[3] The lords-lieutenant of only two

---

[1] *The Marlborough–Godolphin Correspondence*, iii. 1509-10; Holmes, *British Politics in the Age of Anne*, p. 112; Sachse, *Somers*, pp. 291-3.

[2] H.M.C., Fifteenth Report, Appendix IV, *Portland MSS.* iv. 545-6.

[3] Ibid., pp. 563-4.

counties, therefore, were dismissed, and the opportunity to appoint Tories in other counties was neglected. As far as the magnates at the top of county society were concerned, it seems that, in the majority of cases, local politics did not, as yet, reflect the great changes taking place in the ministerial politics of Whitehall.

During the upheavals at the centre, Cowper retained the great seal. In this, the last phase of his Chancellorship, the commission of the peace became a hypothetical means of strengthening Junto influence, not to confirm the Whigs' central power, but to stave off the loss of it. The localities had become positively anti-Whig. A series of riots in London and the provinces, and a number of loyal addresses engineered by High Churchmen from assizes and quarter sessions, indicated that those in authority in the countryside were hostile to the Junto.[1] One possible answer was to carry out the purge of the county commissions of the peace that had been expected, but had never fully taken place, since Wright had been replaced in 1705. However, Cowper now felt himself unable to risk conducting such a purge. The opportunity had gone. From January 1710 to September he sealed twenty-five commissions of the peace. These were spread over twenty counties, so that more than half of the counties of England and Wales did not receive a new commission at this time.[2] The evidence of the commissions that were sealed suggests that in 1710, when the Junto was on the defensive, as in 1708, when it was at the height of its power, Cowper was willing to respond to demands from the counties themselves, but that there was no initiative from the centre to change the commission of the peace on a large scale. Consequently most of the commissions sealed in the first nine months of 1710 are of a routine character. Names were added in small numbers, and dead justices were left out. The most striking changes in the early part of the year were in the Huntingdonshire and Norfolk commissions. Huntingdonshire's

[1] H.M.C., Fifteenth Report, Appendix IV, *Portland MSS.* iv. 539; Beloff, *Public Order and Popular Disturbances*, pp. 51-4; Holmes, *The Trial of Doctor Sacheverell*, pp. 233-9; P.R.O., S.P. 34/12, No. 41: Jekyll to [Sunderland?], 4 Apr. 1710; No. 49: G. Parker to Lord Chief Justice Parker, 8 Apr. 1710.
[2] P.R.O., C. 231/9, pp. 197 ff.

first commission for two years added thirteen names. In Norfolk, seven were added, and Thomas de Grey, the Whig M.P. for Thetford, was added to the quorum.[1]

Later in the year, in June and July, Cowper ceased, to some extent, to be a free agent. Tory gentlemen began to be restored to the commission of the peace in some counties. A commission sealed for Oxfordshire in July 1710 restored Sir Simon Harcourt, left out of all commissions of the peace, including that for his home county, on losing office as Attorney General in 1708, and also added for the first time the Tory Sir Robert Jenkinson, who had been elected knight of the shire in succession to his deceased father in a by-election in February 1710.[2] At about the same time, the Queen herself ordered Cowper to put as many as nine gentlemen into the commission of the peace for Derbyshire, and Cowper obeyed.[3] He fought, deviously but unsuccessfully, against the Tory takeover of Hampshire. By a lapse of memory, the Queen forgot to order him to replace Bolton by Beaufort in the office of *custos* as well as in the lord-lieutenancy. The Whigs were anxious to place one Robert Foarder in the commission of the peace, and Cowper accordingly issued a fiat to include him. Harcourt rightly discerned a conspiracy to have the commission sealed and sent to the county with Bolton's name in the *assignavimus denique* clause as *custos*, 'that it may be understood by this stratagem that the D[uke] of B[olton] is since his being removed from the lieutenancy restored to her Majesty's favour'. Harley intervened in the nick of time. Cowper was ordered not to seal any commissions for Hampshire until further notice, and the fiat had to be corrected to ensure that it was Beaufort who was named as *custos*.[4]

The fact that Cowper was no longer a fully independent

[1] P.R.O., C. 234/17, Huntingdonshire: 22 Feb., 26 Feb. 1709/10; C. 234/26, Norfolk: 16 Mar. 1709/10.

[2] P.R.O., C. 234/30, Oxfordshire: 7 July 1710.

[3] P.R.O., S.P. 44/110, p. 8: Dartmouth to Cowper, 29 June 1710; C. 234/8, Derbyshire: 6 July 1710.

[4] B.L., Loan 29/312: [Harcourt] to Harley, 13 Sept. 1710; P.R.O., S.P. 44/110, p. 86: Dartmouth to Cowper, 13 Sept. 1710; P.R.O., C. 234/14, Hampshire: 18 Sept. 1710. The date of the fiat is changed from 9 September, and the instruction to put Beaufort in as *custos* is inserted, which confirms Harcourt's suspicions.

agent in the summer of 1710, is obscured by an episode open to misinterpretation. Harley himself was left out of the commission of the peace for Herefordshire. His name had originally been in the commission, but it had been scraped off the parchment, and he sent a stinging letter to Cowper, resenting the mortification he had received, and adding, in the best tradition of the Whigs of the early 1680s, that he was rather pleased to have been left out.[1] This affair caused a minor sensation. Letters of surprise and sympathy, comparing Harley's omission with that of his father, Sir Edward, in 1687, passed between the countryside and London.[2] Cowper was appalled. His first impulse was to think that Harley's name had been erased in Herefordshire. Then he tracked down the mistake to a Crown Office blunder. When Harley ceased to be Secretary of State he also ceased to be a Privy Councillor, and, like Harcourt, he had been put out of the commissions of the peace for all the English and Welsh counties. An unlucky clerk, seeing his name in the Herefordshire commission about to be sealed, crossed it out in ignorance of Harley's local claim to be included. Cowper's letters to Harley explaining this reflect extreme distress.[3] Harley was restored in a new commission issued in August, but bearing the date 17 July 1710 — that is, the date of the commission sealed without Harley's name. This was sent to the clerk of the peace with a covering letter explaining the cause of the mistake.[4]

Harley allowed himself to be mollified by Cowper's explanations about Herefordshire, because he had no alternative to Cowper as Chancellor. Harcourt was destined for the post of Attorney General. The Queen had overcome her initial dislike of Cowper, and Harley wanted to keep him as a balance in the Cabinet to the High Churchmen, who, he

---

[1] B.L., Loan 29/196, f. 58: Harley to Cowper, 2 Aug. 1710 (draft).

[2] B.L., Loan 29/196, f. 84: William Bromley to Harley, 12 Aug. 1710; f. 59: Edward Harley to an unknown correspondent, 3 Aug. 1710.

[3] B.L., Loan 29/196, ff. 63–4: Cowper to Harley, 4 Aug. 1710; ff. 68–9: same to same, 6 Aug. 1710. Cowper's draft of his second letter is at Herts. R.O., Cowper (Panshanger) MSS. D/EP F152. Numerous crossings out and insertions betray his agitation.

[4] P.R.O., C. 231/9, pp. 209, 210; B.L., Loan 29/196, ff. 68–9. No trace of the operation to restore Harley's name appears in the Herefordshire fiats. Cowper probably gave the instruction verbally.

feared, would swamp the new ministry.[1] Harley first approached Cowper in late August, and continued through September to persuade him to retain the seal. His quarrel with the Chancellor over the Herefordshire commission forgotten, he protested that 'a Whig game was intended at bottom'. The Queen added her influence.[2] During these two months Cowper issued two commissions of the peace in addition to the revised Herefordshire commission and the commission for Hampshire intended to disguise Bolton's dismissal as *custos*. That for Middlesex added two Under-Secretaries of State.[3] The commission for Cheshire is more interesting and may reflect a despairing attempt by Cowper to assert the Whig interest in the localities in time for the approaching election. In late August two Cheshire Tories complained to Harley that the bench was dominated by Whigs who in their charges to the jury 'preach up Resistance or anything to Poyson the People against an Election & in their private Acting declare they may expect to be dealt with, as they shall give their vote'. They enclosed a list of the changes they desired.[4] Cowper's fiat, dated 9 September, ignored these recommendations and put in four gentlemen, three of whom were to be removed after he had resigned the seal.[5] This is, however, the only case of Whig resistance.

Cowper was not attracted by the prospect of remaining in office in a Cabinet dominated by Harley, whom, in spite of his protestations of respect at the time of the Herefordshire incident, he regarded with dislike. Harley was under pressure from a number of Tories with local connections to change the commissions of the peace in readiness for the anticipated election, and Cowper was hardly the man to satisfy their demands.[6] As the Tories became more restless, Harley's

---

[1] Feiling, *History of the Tory Party, 1640–1714*, pp. 418–19; Trevelyan, *England under Queen Anne*, iii. 68; Holmes, *British Politics in the Age of Anne*, pp. 378–9.

[2] *The Private Diary of William, First Earl Cowper*, ed. E. C. Hawtrey (Roxburghe Club, Eton, 1833), pp. 42–6.

[3] P.R.O., S.P. 44/110, p. 8: Dartmouth to Cowper, 1 July 1710.

[4] B.L., Loan 29/196, f. 134: G. Warburton and C. Cholmondeley to Harley, 30 Aug. 1710.

[5] P.R.O., C. 234/5, Cheshire: 9 Sept. 1710.

[6] C. Buck and G. Davies, 'Letters on Godolphin's Dismissal in 1710', *H.L.Q.* iii (1939–40), 236; Biddle, *Bolingbroke and Harley*, pp. 183–4.

scheme for a balanced ministry became less plausible.[1] On 20 September the Queen at last administered the *coup de grace* to the old ministry, dismissing Somers, Devonshire, and Boyle. Within a few days Orford and Wharton resigned. Cowper went with them, ostensibly in protest at the proclamation to dissolve Parliament, but more probably because he could not remain as the only Whig in office, and because he disapproved of the policies and tactics of the new ministers: 'they carry on things', he said to Sir David Hamilton, 'by Trick and Contradiction and Shuffle, which will make the Queen lose her honnour and the affection of her People'.[2] He now retired to a dignified rural seclusion in Hertfordshire.

V

Cowper had held the great seal for three weeks short of five years. During this time, his manipulation of the county commissions of the peace had been inconspicuous. He never issued more than fifteen commissions in a single month, whereas his predecessor Wright had sealed forty, thirty-two, and forty-two commissions in consecutive Julys between 1700 and 1702.[3] Though there were some complaints about the composition of the bench in single counties, there were none relating to Cowper's over-all handling of the commission. There was no parliamentary demand for an inquiry into his conduct of local patronage, before or after his fall. It is true that he had been appointed as a Whig, with a view to redressing the balance between Whig and Tory in the localities which had been disturbed by Wright, and that he did not lose his Whig connection. He was not tempted by Harley's desire for a coalition of moderate men, in 1708 or in 1710. But he does not, on the surface, seem to have pursued a Whig policy of party proscription.

One explanation that has been advanced for this is that it was the Tories who were pre-eminently the party of the country gentry. The Whigs lacked supporters of sufficient calibre for the commission of the peace, and Tories had to be

[1] Bennett, *The Tory Crisis in Church and State, 1688–1730*, pp. 124–5.
[2] Roberts, *Growth of Responsible Government*, pp. 351–2; *Private Diary of William, First Earl Cowper*, pp. 44–6; *The Diary of Sir David Hamilton 1709–1714*, ed. P. Roberts (Oxford, 1975), pp. 17–18, 34.
[3] Cowper issued fifteen commissions in March 1707.

kept in perforce.[1] This argument is plausible, though it rests on a letter to the effect that in Surrey the Whigs could not muster enough respectable followers to fill the bench in 1710. This is very surprising in view of the fact that Wright had put out twenty-two living Surrey justices between 1700 and 1705, of whom only two were restored by Cowper.[2] Moreover, the Surrey freeholders had in 1705 and 1708 elected two knights of the shire, Sir William Scawen and Sir Richard Onslow, who are thought to have been among the 'friends and allies' of the Junto.[3] It might be argued, too, that the Whigs did not experience the same problem in 1714–15, when the commissions for most counties expanded in size, although Tories and Jacobites were put out.[4] A different, perhaps preferable, explanation is that Cowper's discreet handling of the commission creates a misleading impression. It is true that he did not approve of large-scale purges. In only six counties were more than ten living justices dismissed.[5] But it is also true that many counties received commissions which, in aggregate over the period from 1705 to 1710, added gentlemen to the bench in substantial numbers. Excluding Middlesex and Durham, for which the fiats do not survive, Cowper added 1,044 names to the commissions, and he left out about 195 gentlemen who were still living.[6] On average, therefore, Cowper added 18·9 justices and left out 3·5 justices per county. This is, of course, too crude. In Kent, for instance, fifty-two new justices were appointed, but the only justices put out were the deceased admirals Sir Cloudesley Shovell and Sir George Rooke.[7] On the other hand, Holland received one commission adding two

[1] Holmes, *British Politics in the Age of Anne*, p. 171.

[2] H.L.R.O., Main Papers, H.L., 20 Mar. 1704, 16 Feb. 1705; P.R.O., C. 234/36, Surrey.

[3] Ellis, 'The Whig Junto', Appendix G, pp. 32, 35.

[4] See below, Chapter 8.

[5] Dorset (10), Essex (10), Gloucestershire (22), Hertfordshire (24), Leicestershire (12), and Wiltshire (29).

[6] These figures look exact, but they can only be approximate. Although an attempt has been made to take account of duplication in consecutive fiats, cases in which fiats were not implemented in commissions, dead justices not so described in the order to leave them out, 'inclusions' which were merely the promotion of an esquire to a place among the baronets, and other ambiguities, a margin of error remains.

[7] P.R.O., C. 234/18, Kent: four fiats from 5 Mar. 1705/6 to 13 June 1710.

names,[1] and Flintshire did not receive a commission at all, while Cowper held the great seal. Even so, it is probably the case that in most counties, as Cowper subsequently claimed, his adjustments had created by 1710 a Whig preponderance of power at quarter sessions. Preponderance is not the same as monopoly. The Tories had not been ruthlessly excluded, except in a few counties where local initiative had demanded such exclusion, and the Whigs paid dearly for Cowper's moderation after the Sacheverell trial. However, there is no reason to suppose that Cowper's subsequent claim to George I, that in 1710 the commissions of the peace were 'in a very good state with a sufficient balance in favour of the honest interest', was unjustified.

On the day of Cowper's resignation, it was thought in Tory circles that the delays in preparing for the election had damaged the party's interests, and that speedy changes in the commissions of the peace would be necessary.[2] These did not occur. The great seal was put into commission while Harley cast about for a successor. During this interregnum, which lasted for four weeks during the height of the 1710 election campaign, no commissions of the peace were issued at all. Among the names bandied about were those of Sir Edward Northey, Sir Thomas Trevor, Lord Guernsey, and Baron Price. As term drew on, the Commissioners of the Great Seal grew alarmed at the prospect of sitting judicially, and Harley at last persuaded the reluctant Sir Simon Harcourt to accept office as Lord Keeper. He took the oaths before the Council on 19 October 1710.[3] Just as, five years before, the appointment of Cowper had seemed to foreshadow a Whig remodelling of the commission of the peace, the appointment of Harcourt now was expected to herald changes in the interests of the Tories.

[1] P.R.O., C. 234/21, Kesteven: 6 June 1706 (a combined fiat for all the divisions of Lincolnshire).

[2] *The Epistolary Correspondence, Visitation Charges, Speeches and Miscellanies, of the Right Reverend Francis Atterbury, D.D., Lord Bishop of Rochester,* ed. J. Nichols (London, 1783-7), i. 26-7.

[3] Luttrell, *Brief Relation,* vi. 633, 643, 644; *Letters of Joseph Addison,* pp. 233-4; W. S. Churchill, *Marlborough, His Life and Times* (edn. in two volumes, London, 1947), ii. 758-9; Roberts, *Growth of Responsible Government,* p. 352; B.L., Loan 29/196, f. 266: Harcourt to Harley, 17 Oct. 1710; P.R.O., P.C. 2/83, p. 123.

7

THE COMMISSION OF THE PEACE AND THE TORIES, 1710-14

I

Sir Simon Harcourt came from an ancient family settled in Oxfordshire. Like Cowper, Sir Simon had made his reputation in Parliament. In Fenwick's case, and in the impeachment of Somers, he was a prominent spokesman on the Tory side. In 1702 he was appointed Solicitor General, in 1707 Attorney General. In 1708 he resigned when Harley fell, and for a short time he was out of the House of Commons. When he was chosen for Cardigan at a by-election in the middle of the Sacheverell trial, the return was delayed to enable him to make an eloquent and effective speech for the defence before he was obliged to abandon his client to take his seat.[1] He accepted the great seal on 19 October 1710. Subsequently he was raised to the peerage as Viscount Harcourt in September 1711, and he was elevated from Lord Keeper to Lord Chancellor in April 1713. The verdict of legal historians is that he was a thoroughly able lawyer, without quite being one of the great Chancellors.[2] He was, like Somers and Cowper, but in contrast to the unfortunate Wright, a convivial man of presence and authority in polite society. In the early years of the Tory ministry of 1710-14, he was generally regarded as third to Harley and St. John. After the gradual split between the two senior ministers, Harcourt was aligned with St. John, and he was therefore associated with the Secretary's policy of the ruthless exclusion of Whigs from the civil administration, rather than with the Treasurer's desire for moderation and conciliation.[3]

[1] Holmes, *The Trial of Doctor Sacheverell*, pp. 143, 192-3.
[2] Campbell, *Lives of the Chancellors*, iv. 430-79; Foss, *Judges of England*, viii. 33-41; *The Harcourt Papers*, ed. E. W. Harcourt (privately printed, no date), ii. 1 ff.; Holdsworth, *History of English Law*, xii. 201-3.
[3] Jonathan Swift, 'An Enquiry into the Behaviour of the Queen's Late Ministry', *Jonathan Swift's Political Tracts, 1713-19*, ed. H. Davis and I. Ehrenpries

A wave of county commissions of the peace in the winter of 1710/11 represents Harcourt's first campaign to revive Tory strength in the localities. The first appeared in December 1710, when six were sealed; three more followed in January 1711, then twenty-six in February and eight in March. Thus, forty-three commissions, for forty-two out of the fifty-seven counties, were issued in four months.[1] After this activity, no more commissions were sealed until June 1711.

The most striking feature of the forty-three commissions sealed in the winter of 1710/11 was the large number of gentlemen put in. Harcourt added a total of 919 names.[2] In most of the forty-two counties which received a new commission, the number of gentlemen put in is significantly higher than would have been normal in a 'routine' commission. More than forty new names were added to the bench in three counties: there were seventy-three new justices in Kent, fifty-six in Gloucestershire, and forty-two in Sussex. Eight counties found between thirty and forty new names in their new commissions; eleven more had between twenty and thirty; and fifteen counties received between ten and twenty additions, among them some of the smaller counties.[3] Only five counties received commissions making less than ten additions, and these also were among those with the shortest lists of justices.[4]

It would be an obvious assumption that Harcourt was introducing Tory gentlemen who had been put out or kept out by his Whig predecessor. St. John, who had been Harcourt's ally

---

(Oxford, 1964), p. 144; G. S. Holmes, 'Harley, St. John, and the Death of the Tory Party', in Holmes (ed.), *Britain after the Glorious Revolution, 1689–1714*, p. 225; Bennett, *The Tory Crisis in Church and State, 1688–1730*, pp. 141, 165–6.

[1] P.R.O., C. 231/9, pp. 420 ff. The East Riding received two commissions. The neglected counties were Breconshire, Caernarvonshire, Cumberland, Derbyshire, Dorset, Durham, Flintshire, Glamorgan, Herefordshire, Leicestershire, Merionethshire, Northumberland, Peterborough, Radnorshire, and Wiltshire.

[2] P.R.O., C. 234/1–95, *passim*; not counting Middlesex for which the fiat does not survive. It was reported that twenty-five gentlemen were included in the new Middlesex commission at this time. Luttrell, *Brief Relation*, vi. 665.

[3] Small counties which received relatively large additions at this time to the number of justices in commission were Ely (18), Rutland (13), Anglesey, Carmarthenshire, Huntingdonshire (11), and Pembrokeshire (10).

[4] Denbighshire, Westmorland (8), Cardiganshire (7), Montgomeryshire (4), and Holland (3).

in 1711, later wrote that Tory policy was 'to break the body of the Whigs, to render their supports useless to them, and to fill the employments of the kingdom, down to the meanest, with tories'.[1] Possibly this represents Harcourt's intentions with regard to the commission of the peace fairly accurately. However, there are some qualifications to the view that Harcourt was putting gentlemen into the commission of the peace in large numbers in the winter of 1710/11 in order to wrest local power from the Whigs by mobilizing all the available resources of grass-roots Toryism.

The first point is that Harcourt was not as eager as might have been expected to replace justices who had been dropped by Cowper. In the forty-two counties for which Harcourt sealed a commission in this first campaign, Cowper had dismissed 131 justices. Harcourt restored forty-four of these.[2] Admittedly, in a few counties where Cowper's purges had been on a small scale, Harcourt did partially or wholly reverse them: in Buckinghamshire, for example, four out of seven justices who had incurred Cowper's disfavour were brought back along with twenty-three newcomers, and Harcourt's eleven additions for Carmarthenshire included three out of the four gentlemen whom Cowper had omitted. Cowper had left out one gentleman apiece in Monmouthshire, Oxfordshire, and Worcestershire, and in each case the solitary scapegoat was readmitted to the bench. These cases were unusual, however, and, in counties where Cowper's purges had been more substantial, Harcourt was not automatically putting back those whom Cowper had displaced. Only nine out of the twenty-four dismissed in Hertfordshire in 1706–9 came back into the commission in December 1710, and Harcourt was even less generous in Gloucestershire, where, of the twenty-two left out in 1706–7, only three returned to the bench, along with fifty-three new faces. Moreover, Harcourt's forty-four restorations make up less than 5 per cent of his total number of additions to the magistracy in the winter of 1710/11. Harcourt was not, therefore, conscientiously

---

[1] Bolingbroke, *A Letter to Sir William Wyndham* (1753), pp. 21–2.

[2] This figure is if anything likely to be an over-estimate, although an attempt has been made to rule out cases in which Harcourt put in someone of the same name as a justice dismissed by Cowper.

searching out the victims of his Whig predecessor's displeasure in order to re-elevate them to their former place in county society.

A second qualification to the hypothesis that Harcourt's additions were simply Tory changes reversing Cowper's Whig changes emerges from consideration of those members of the Parliament elected in the autumn of 1710 and now added to the commissions of the peace. Of Harcourt's 919 additions, 119 were sitting M.P.s. The number of M.P.s put into one or more commissions of the peace was ninety-four.[1] It is true that as many as forty-nine of these had sat for the same constituency in the 1708–10 Parliament, having, presumably, been kept out by Cowper. It is also true that among them were some of the leading Tories in the House of Commons. For example, Sir William Wyndham came in for Somerset where he was knight of the shire; Allen Bathurst, who sat for a Gloucestershire constituency and lived in Bedfordshire, became a justice for both counties and also for Oxfordshire; George Granville, Secretary at War and M.P. for Cornwall, was put in the Cornwall, Berkshire, and Surrey commissions. Forty-eight of the ninety-four M.P.s who now became magistrates were 'members' of the October Club, a Tory pressure group which was already embarrassing the ministry by its Country party tactics in February 1711. The October Club was composed largely of landed gentry, and it may be that Harcourt was initiating a Cabinet policy, later to be modestly successful, of toning down the excesses of extreme Toryism by gratifying its exponents with the kind of minor and local office that was dear to their hearts.[2] In general, it was natural enough that Harcourt should include identifiable Tories in the commission of the peace for the counties in which their constituencies or their residences were situated. However, not all of the M.P.s added to the commissions of the peace were reliable Tory supporters. Of the ninety-four M.P.s put into the commissions in the winter of 1710/11, as many as twenty-six cast 'opposition votes' in the course of the 1710–13

---

[1] Again, this figure is likely to be imprecise, though not significantly so. Several doubtful but possible cases have been omitted.

[2] A. Boyer, *The Political State of Great Britain* (2nd edn., London, 1718–19), iii. 117–21; H. T. Dickinson, 'The October Club', *H.L.Q.* xxxiii (1970), 155–61, 164–5, 167, 169.

Parliament, according to the three surviving division lists.[1] Opposition votes did not necessarily mean Whig votes. The third of these divisions was on an issue, the French Commerce Bill, which divided the Tories. The reasons for the later defection of such persons as Lord Finch and Sir Thomas Hanmer are well known; they could not have been regarded as anything but Tories when Harcourt was remodelling the commissions early in the life of the new Parliament.[2] Even so, it seems significant that more than a quarter of the ninety-four M.P.s were not won over to consistent support for the ministers by their inclusion in the commission of the peace. The point is given further weight by the fact that as many as nine of the ninety-four M.P.s were described as either 'Whig' or 'Doubtful' in an analysis of the political character of the new House of Commons drawn up shortly after the 1710 election.[3] It is probable that Harcourt was not only distributing the loaves and fishes of local power to loyal supporters, but that he was also tempting persons who were not loyal supporters to change their allegiance, and persuading others whose sympathies were unknown to align themselves with the Tories. An extension of this hypothesis would be that Harcourt was prepared to gratify the uncommitted gentry outside as well as inside Parliament by putting them in the commission of the peace. It is thus by no means certain that the 919 gentlemen placed in commission at this time were all committed Tories.

The case that Harcourt's inclusions were ruthlessly Tory is

[1] J. G. Sperling, 'The Division of 25 May 1711 on an amendment to the South Sea Bill; a note on the reality of parties in the Age of Anne', *Hist. Journal* iv (1961), 193, 198–9; G. S. Holmes, 'The Commons' Division on "No Peace without Spain", 7 December 1711', *B.I.H.R.* xxxiii (1960), 233–4; *A Collection of White and Black Lists* (4th, corrected, edn., London, 1715), pp. 23–30.

[2] Horwitz, *Revolution Politicks*, pp. 234, 239. Finch and Hanmer became justices for Rutland and Surrey respectively in February 1711.

[3] B.L., Stowe MSS. 223, ff. 453–6. The 'Whigs' were Richard Harnage, M.P. for Bishops Castle (put in for Shropshire), and Edward Jeffreys, Brecon (Surrey). For Jeffreys's connection with Surrey, see W. R. Williams, *Parliamentary History of the Principality of Wales* (Brecknock, 1895), pp. 24–5. The 'Doubtfuls' were John Drake, Amersham (Buckinghamshire); Leonard Gale, East Grinstead (Sussex and Surrey); Francis Gwyn, Totnes (Somerset); James Herbert, Queenborough (Kent, and also, probably, Buckinghamshire and Oxfordshire); Sir Thomas Lee, Chipping Wycombe (Buckinghamshire); Philip Rashleigh, Liskeard (Cornwall); and Samuel Robinson, Cricklade (Hertfordshire).

weakened further by a third qualification, that apparent at every substantial addition to the lists of names in the commissions. Harcourt could not have checked the character of every one of his 919 new justices, any more than his predecessors in similar circumstances. The new names had to be recommended. It is unlikely that those persons in each of the several counties who were making suggestions were conducting a consistent campaign. Unfortunately, it is not clear who was sending nominations in the winter of 1710/11. Beaufort, the new lord-lieutenant of Hampshire, may have had a hand in the appointment of thirty-two new justices in that county in January 1711. In two more counties, the appointment of Tory *custodes rotulorum* — the Earl of Cardigan in Northamptonshire and the Earl of Plymouth in Worcestershire — perhaps had some significance; they replaced dead, not disgraced, incumbents. Elsewhere, the recommendations possibly came from caucuses of gentlemen within the counties. In Cornwall, for example, the Tory knight of the shire, George Granville, was a likely source of suggestions; he had certainly remodelled the Cornish stannaries by October 1711.[1] Lack of evidence means that an assessment of the process of recommendation cannot be made for every county, but it seems probable that, whoever did make the suggestions, there was some variation in the criteria of choice from county to county. It is implausible that the policy of 'filling the employments of the kingdom . . . with tories' was wholly dominant in all areas.

Another striking feature of the commissions of the peace sealed between December 1710 and March 1711 is the high number of living justices dismissed. The fiats gave orders to leave out 183 gentlemen who were not specifically described as dead, and who were, so far as can be ascertained, still alive.[2] Harcourt was apparently conducting a substantial purge among justices of the peace. Ninety-seven of the dismissed justices — more than half the total — had been put into the commission over the previous five years by Cowper, and this suggests that Harcourt was eliminating the Whig element on the county bench introduced by his predecessor. However,

[1] H.M.C., *Portland MSS.* v. 97.
[2] 135 dead justices were ordered to be left out. These figures do not include Middlesex.

just as there are qualifications to the view that Harcourt's inclusions were all inspired by considerations of Tory supremacy, so there are qualifications to the view that all his dismissals represented a desire to put the Whigs to the sword.

In the first place, Harcourt conducted a really substantial purge in only two counties, Kent and Surrey, where thirty and twenty-four justices were omitted respectively. The remaining 129 dismissals were spread evenly over twenty-seven of the forty other counties for which a new commission was sealed.[1] In only one county apart from Kent and Surrey were more than ten justices dismissed: eleven in Cheshire. The number of justices put out in some counties with lengthy commissions was quite small. For example, seven were put out in Devonshire, eight in Essex, seven in Hertfordshire, and only three apiece in Gloucestershire and Hampshire.[2] The aggregate total of justices dismissed in more than twenty-five modest purges thus gives a possibly misleading impression of the severity of Harcourt's campaign in counties other than Kent and Surrey. The point is strengthened by a piece of negative evidence: the apparent absence in the following months of protest about Harcourt's willingness to disgrace so many honest Whig squires.

Also, while it is true that over half of Harcourt's dismissals were of justices put in by his Whig predecessor, Cowper, it is also true that Harcourt did not put out at this time the vast majority of all the justices put in by Cowper. Cowper had authorized the inclusion of 1,044 justices in counties other than Middlesex and Durham. Harcourt put out ninety-seven of these who were still living and twenty-two more who had died. A few of Cowper's early inclusions had been put out by Cowper himself, and some, having died, may have been left out without appearing in the fiats. Neither of these categories is likely to have been large, and it is probable that at least 80 per cent of the justices put in by Cowper between 1705 and 1710 remained in commission during and after Harcourt's campaign in the winter of 1710/11.

[1] No living justices at all were left out in Buckinghamshire, Cardiganshire, Carmarthenshire, Denbighshire, Holland, Huntingdonshire, Montgomeryshire, Nottinghamshire, Rutland, Shropshire, Staffordshire, or the East and North Ridings.

[2] Luttrell noticed five dismissals in Middlesex. *Brief Relation*, vi. 665.

Finally, the dismissed justices were not, for the most part, gentlemen of outstanding social or political prominence. The exceptions to this rule can be counted briefly. Three sitting M.P.s were dismissed, one of whom — John Dibble, M.P. for Okehampton, put out for Devonshire — was actually described as a Tory just after his election, although he had voted on the Whig side in the Sacheverell trial.[1] Six more justices who had been M.P.s in the 1708–10 Parliament, but who had not been re-elected in 1710, were put out for the county in which their constituency had been situated. One of them, David Polhill, was the former knight of the shire for Kent.[2] A very few other gentlemen of consequence were dismissed. The Tory Sir John Bolles was dropped for Kesteven, perhaps more because his violent temperament had at last exhausted the tolerance of his fellow-magistrates in Lincolnshire than for any political reason.[3] Sir John Elwell, the leader of the Exeter Whigs, whose earlier disgrace at the hands of Sir Nathan Wright had caused a stir in the West Country, was left out again for both Devonshire and Surrey.[4] George Booth, the uncle of the Earl of Warrington, and Sir Robert Duckinfield, an influential Presbyterian baronet, were dismissed for Cheshire. In Northamptonshire, the senior baronet, Sir Robert Hesilrige, and the second name in the list of esquires, Christopher Montagu, were both put out. But these cases were exceptional. Again in Northamptonshire, the four gentlemen dismissed besides Hesilrige and Montagu were among the lowest names in the list.[5] No lay peers were left out at all. The great majority of the justices dismissed by Harcourt in the winter of 1710/11 were squires of relatively humble status.

[1] B.L., Stowe MSS. 223, f. 454; *A Collection of White and Black Lists*, p. 19. The other two were John Cater, M.P. for Bedford (Surrey) and Walter Whitfield, M.P. for New Romney (Hertfordshire).

[2] The other five were George Balch (Somerset), John Borlase and Anthony Nichol (Cornwall), Nicholas Carew (Surrey), and William Lowther (West Riding).

[3] See above, p. 122.

[4] At the time of his dismissal in 1704, Elwell had been chairman of Devonshire quarter sessions for some years, and was 'the most necessary justice in the county'. B.L., Loan 29/191, ff. 235–6: Richard Duke to Harley, Sept. 1704.

[5] Edmund Bateman, John Clendon, John Weaver, and John Winston. P.R.O., C. 234/27, Northamptonshire: fiats in the form of a complete list, 12 Feb. 1705/6, and also 7 Oct. 1714.

The view that Harcourt was extending a Tory triumph and a Whig defeat in central politics and in Parliament into the counties, through the medium of the commission of the peace, can thus be hedged about with qualifications. Even so, these qualifications arguably arise from a rather mechanical counting of heads on a nationwide basis. When the changes for an individual county are considered in the context of that county's political society, a distinct party flavour is apparent even if these changes were less than comprehensive. For example, Cowper's old enemies in Hertfordshire politics, Charles Caesar and John Gape, were restored for Hertfordshire along with four more 'members' of the October Club in the 1710–13 Parliament, while four of the seven justices dismissed in that county had been put in by Cowper.[1] The eighteen new justices in Cheshire included representatives of the Tory families of Shakerley, Oldfield, Grosvenor, Warren, and Egerton of Tatton, and Harcourt left out at least three justices who had used their local influence in the Whig interest during the 1710 election, plus three more who had been put in by Cowper in the commission of the peace sealed in September 1710.[2] The fifty-six new justices in Gloucestershire included nine M.P.s described as Tories after their election, and although only three gentlemen were left out (all of them originally put in by Cowper in 1706 and 1707) the Gloucestershire commission was certainly swamped.[3] The pattern was the same in Hampshire, except that the three justices put out had first been put in by an earlier generation of nominating Whigs. Wolfran Cornwall and Robert Poyntz had been included by Somers in 1697. The third, Richard Cobb, is probably identical to a gentleman of the same name added as long ago as the time of the capture of the Privy Council by the Exclusion Whigs in 1679.[4] These examples indicate the general tendency of Harcourt's changes.

Furthermore, there is no doubt that Harcourt was making alterations on a more extensive scale than Cowper had ever attempted. Whereas Cowper had held the great seal for almost

[1] P.R.O., C. 234/16, Hertfordshire: 11 Dec. 1710.
[2] P.R.O., C. 234/5, Cheshire: 10 Mar. 1710/11; B.L., Loan 29/196, f. 134.
[3] P.R.O., C. 234/13, Gloucestershire: 2 Feb. 1710/11.
[4] P.R.O., C. 234/14, Hampshire: 16 Jan. 1710/11; C. 231/8, pp. 5, 382.

a year when he sealed his fortieth commission, Harcourt had
sealed more than forty within six months. Cowper had added
355 names in the first phase of his tenure of office, which
lasted for about fifteen months — and these figures include
Middlesex and Durham.[1] In less than half the time, Harcourt
added 919 names. Harcourt's total of 183 dismissals in six
months is not far short of the total of about 195 living justices
left out by Cowper during the whole period of just less than
five years when he had held the great seal. For these reasons,
it is quite possible that Harcourt was embarrassed in the
spring of 1711 by another bill to raise the property qualification of justices of the peace, which suggested that too many
gentlemen of low calibre had recently been appointed to the
bench.[2] Otherwise, however, the scale of Harcourt's alterations seems to have attracted little attention. The difference
in the degree of intensity with which the two Lord Keepers
conducted their initial campaigns is not necessarily to be
explained by an inherent difference between Whig and Tory
approaches to the local rewards of central power, or even by
the hypothesis that there were more Tories than Whigs
among the country gentlemen. In 1705–7 Cowper had been a
Whig in a non-party Cabinet, the leaders of which distrusted
party factiousness in local politics. Harcourt, on the other
hand, was an influential figure in a ministry with a strong
party bias and a large parliamentary majority.

II

Harcourt sealed no commissions of the peace at all during
April and May 1711, but a second wave of commissions followed in June, July, and August, when twenty were issued in
readiness for the summer assizes.[3] Thirteen of these twenty
were for counties which had already received a commission
in the winter of 1710/11, and in these counties the alterations
were for the most part unexciting. The highest number of
living justices put out was two in Northamptonshire, and
only in Kent and Norfolk were as many as ten put in. However, one interesting feature of five of the thirteen 'second

[1] Herts. R.O., Cowper (Panshanger) MSS. D/EP F152.
[2] *C.J.* xvi. 536, 609, 668, 674, 691; and see above, p. 17, n. 2.
[3] P.R.O., C. 231/9, pp. 235 ff.

commissions' is that Harcourt was restoring some justices whom he had dismissed earlier in the year. In Kent, five gentlemen put out in February reappeared in July, along with five new names, and Harcourt restored one of the justices whom he had earlier dismissed in each of Cheshire, Kesteven, Lindsey, and Norfolk.[1] In particular, the reprieve of George Booth in Cheshire suggests that Harcourt may have recognized the danger of disgracing Whigs of more than ordinary social status. Alternatively, the changes of mind may reflect conflicting advice given to Harcourt from the localities, or the problem of finding magistrates willing to act in remote or under-justiced areas. Whatever the reason, as many as nine gentlemen disgraced by Harcourt in the winter of 1710/11 were back in the commission of the peace by the following July, although at this very time Harcourt, with St. John, was pressing for a vigorous purge of Whig office-holders.[2]

Seven counties received new commissions in the summer of 1711 for the first time since Harcourt had accepted the great seal. In three of these, the changes were inconspicuous. The Flintshire commission had not been renewed since March 1705, when Wright had still been Lord Keeper. Cowper had neglected the county completely, and Harcourt was now content to add two names and leave out one. In Herefordshire, six were added, and the elevation of Robert Harley to the peerage in May as Earl of Oxford, and to the Lord Treasurership, was marked by the inclusion of his son Edward under the courtesy title of Lord Harley. Sixteen days later the new justice of the peace was elected to his father's vacated seat of Radnor borough. Seven names were put in for Glamorgan in a commission which also left out Sir Humphrey Mackworth, M.P. for Cardiganshire, whose fraudulent management of the Mine Adventurers' Company had been exposed in the House of Commons in March 1710.[3]

[1] P.R.O., C. 234/18, Kent: 4 July 1711 (Paul D'Aranda, Henry Deeds, Thomas March, John Stevens, and Snelling Thomas); C. 234/5, Cheshire: 9 July 1711 (George Booth); C. 234/21, Kesteven: 7 July 1711 (Gilbert Bury); C. 234/22, Lindsey: 7 July 1711 (John Disney); C. 234/26, Norfolk: 18 June 1711 (Edward Carter).

[2] Bennett, *The Tory Crisis in Church and State, 1688–1730*, p. 141.

[3] P.R.O., C. 234/84, Flintshire: 18 June 1711; C. 234/15, Herefordshire: 30 June 1711; C. 234/85, Glamorgan: 6 Aug. 1711. For Mackworth, see M. Ransome, 'The Parliamentary Career of Sir Humphrey Mackworth, 1701–13', *University of Birmingham Historical Journal*, i (1948), 233–4.

Thus four counties are left in which the alterations in the summer of 1711 were on a large scale. The Northumberland bench was swamped with additions.[1] No justices were left out, but forty-nine gentlemen were put in. Rather surprisingly, the list was headed by Algernon Seymour, son of the Duke of Somerset, who was M.P. for Northumberland and a consistent Whig. Moreover, Cowper's last fiat for Northumberland, dated the year before, does not seem to have been implemented by the sealing of a commission, and it is interesting to see that Harcourt included two names that Cowper had intended to add, one of them that of the stout Whig Sir John Delavall.[2] However, Harcourt also added the Tory M.P. for Newcastle, Sir William Blackett; a number of country squires whose political allegiance seems to have been Tory; a group of Newcastle coal-owners, such as Ralph Brandling, Robert Fenwick, and Matthew White; and the goldsmith and merchant, William Ramsey, who had recently bought a large estate at Gateshead.[3] The fiat for a Durham commission sealed in June does not survive, but it is highly probable that Durham followed the same pattern as Northumberland. The new commission for Leicestershire was along different lines, however.[4] Unlike Northumberland, Leicestershire had been purged by Cowper, who had put out twelve living justices, ten of them for 'refusing to act', in July 1707. Harcourt now restored nine of the twelve, and also added eighteen new names, headed by the Tory baronet Sir Justinian Isham from the neighbouring county of Northamptonshire. Seven justices were dismissed, among them four who had been put in to replace those who had 'refused to act' in 1707 and one who had originally been put in by Somers in 1697. These changes were perhaps the work of a new Tory lord-lieutenant and *custos*, the Earl of Denbigh, who had replaced the Whig Duke of Rutland after the latter's death in January 1711; although admittedly Denbigh's appointment was not confirmed immediately,[5]

[1] P.R.O., C. 234/28, Northumberland: 20 July 1711.
[2] For Delavall, see *The Correspondence of Sir James Clavering*, p. 81; the other name added in both fiats was Arthur Hepburne or Hebburne.
[3] For these gentlemen, see E. Hughes, *North Country Life in the Eighteenth Century: The North-East, 1700–1750* (London, 1952), *passim*.
[4] P.R.O., C. 234/19, Leicestershire: 7 July 1711.
[5] H.M.C., Fifteenth Report, Appendix IV, *Portland MSS.* iv. 694.

and it is equally possible that a Tory caucus led by Isham, Sir Thomas Cave, and Sir George Beaumont was active in selecting names. Finally, Caernarvonshire received a new commission making alterations which, for a Welsh county, were substantial.[1] Sixteen new names were added and three gentlemen, two of whom had been put in by Cowper in 1707, were dismissed.

Harcourt again rested on his oars after August 1711, producing only one commission — for Middlesex — before December. He had, after his first year in office, sealed at least one commission of the peace for forty-nine out of the fifty-seven counties. In a third wave of commissions in the winter and early spring of 1711/12 he dealt with four of the remaining eight.[2] Derbyshire was let off lightly, probably because some changes in the Tory interest had already taken place at the Queen's express desire in July 1710.[3] Now, eighteen months later, eleven inconspicuous squires were added, but no one was left out.[4] In Breconshire and Merionethshire the changes were also unremarkable, although in the former county, one Robert Rumsey, put in by Cowper in 1705, was left out, and in the latter, William Wynne, left out by Cowper in 1707, was restored.[5] However, in Dorset Harcourt remodelled the bench on a scale commensurate with earlier changes in other large counties.[6] Nineteen gentlemen were put in. The list was headed by three Tory M.P.s, Sir William Poole, Sir Jacob Bancks, and Thomas Strangeways junior, while further down come Nicholas Hardy and Harry Chafin, who had been put out for 'refusing to act' in 1708, and two more October Club M.P.s, Thomas 'Diamond' Pitt and Henry Whitaker.[7] Two gentlemen, Anthony Flyer and George South, were left out; both had been added by Cowper in

[1] P.R.O., C. 234/82, Caernarvonshire: 18 June 1711.
[2] Those still neglected were Cumberland, Peterborough, Radnorshire, and Wiltshire.
[3] See above, p. 194.
[4] P.R.O., C. 234/8, Derbyshire: 21 Dec. 1711.
[5] P.R.O., C. 234/79, Breconshire: 19 Mar. 1711/12; C. 234/78, Anglesey: a composite fiat for Anglesey, Merionethshire, and Caernarvonshire, 31 Mar. 1712.
[6] P.R.O., C. 234/10, Dorset: 14 Apr. 1712.
[7] Pitt had been classified as a Tory in 1710, and he was included in Boyer's list of October Club M.P.s, but he normally voted with the Whigs. B.L., Stowe MSS. 223, f. 453; Dickinson, 'The October Club', p. 156 n. 12.

that commission in which Hardy and Chafin had been disgraced.

In addition to these four 'first' commissions, Harcourt sealed twenty more commissions between December 1711 and April 1712 for counties which had already received at least one commission since he had accepted office. These were for the most part routine commissions, sealed in readiness for the Lent assizes, and they did not make alterations on a large scale. Setting aside Middlesex, Montgomeryshire (for which the fiat is missing), and the four 'first' commissions, the total number of gentlemen added to the lists in eighteen counties was only seventy-four. The number of justices omitted was twenty-four. Two gentlemen whom Harcourt had already put out in the winter of 1710/11 were restored.[1] Harcourt also dismissed two justices whom he had put in.[2] The highest number of inclusions was for Gloucestershire, where Harcourt had already added fifty-six names in February 1711; now, just over a year later, he put in ten more. The new Dean of Christ Church, Francis Atterbury, was included with two others for Oxfordshire, and the Dean of Lichfield with one other for Staffordshire. Sir Nathan Wright's retirement was enlivened by the opportunity to act as a country justice in Leicestershire. Among those dismissed from the bench were Robert Foarder, who had been included in that commission for Hampshire in which Cowper had tried to keep the Duke of Bolton's name as *custos* in September 1710; Robert Kercher, also for Hampshire, who had been put in by Somers in 1697; and Dr Robert Cox or Cocks, one of Wharton's nominees for the Oxfordshire commission in 1700. However, the highest number of dismissals in the winter of 1711/12 was in Shropshire, a county which had received a commission putting thirty-nine names in, but none out, in February 1711. Now, a year later, the Shropshire bench was purged with the omission of seven justices, of whom four had been put in by Cowper between 1705 and 1710.[3]

[1] P.R.O., C. 234/87, Monmouthshire: 25 Feb. 1711/12 (Henry Romsey); C. 234/16, Hertfordshire: 3 Mar. 1711/12 (David Hecksletter).

[2] P.R.O., C. 234/22, Lindsey: 10 Mar. 1711/12 (John Disney); C. 234/89, Pembrokeshire: 14 Apr. 1712 (John Warren).

[3] P.R.O., C. 234/13, Gloucestershire: 10 Mar. 1711/12; C. 234/30, Oxfordshire: 30 Jan. 1711/12; C. 234/34, Staffordshire: 7 Mar. 1711/12; C. 234/19,

Perhaps the most interesting feature of the twenty-four commissions sealed in the winter of 1711/12 is that there is some evidence that Harcourt was trying to use his patronage for the purposes of electoral and parliamentary politics. Several sitting M.P.s were put in, among them some who had been successful at by-elections during the previous year. Most of these M.P.s were identifiable Tories to whom inclusion in the commission of the peace was in the nature of a routine perquisite, although there were some exceptions such as William Dowdeswell, a Junto supporter elected for Tewkesbury in Gloucestershire in January 1712 and apparently put into the Worcestershire commission in the following March.[1] In this case, Harcourt was possibly advised to attempt to convert the new generation of Dowdeswells, who had a powerful interest at Tewkesbury, to Toryism after the death of the head of the family, Richard, a staunch Whig, in 1711. Also, some future candidates in by-elections, and, looking further ahead, in the next general election which was to be held in August and September 1713, were already being put in. Again, there are some exceptions to the rule that these were all reliable supporters of the ministry. For instance, Francis Lewis, to be elected for East Retford in April 1713, had been put in for Leicestershire a year earlier, but he voted with the Whigs against the French Commerce Bill in June 1713. It is easier to account for the inclusion of men like the Jacobite Sir Charles Kemys, who was to be elected knight of the shire for Monmouthshire in September 1713 after being put into the commissions of the peace for Glamorgan in August 1711 and Monmouthshire in February 1712.[2] However, the most striking example of the use of the commission of the peace at this time for electoral purposes, albeit unsuccessfully, was the omission of John Turner, Robert Walpole's friend and cousin, in Norfolk, one month before his election for King's Lynn in place of Walpole who had been expelled from the House.[3]

Leicestershire: 17 Mar. 1711/12; C. 234/14, Hampshire: 26 Dec. 1711; C. 234/32, Shropshire: 10 Mar. 1711/12.

[1] P.R.O., C. 234/41, Worcestershire: 3 Mar. 1711/12.
[2] For Kemys, see Holmes, *British Politics in the Age of Anne*, p. 332.
[3] P.R.O., C. 234/26, Norfolk: 17 Mar. 1711/12. For Turner, see Plumb, *Sir Robert Walpole, The Making of a Statesman*, p. 182. It is worth observing that

Harcourt had now developed a routine in which the issue of new commissions of the peace was concentrated in the months before the winter and summer assizes. This pattern was followed for his fourth wave of changes in June and July 1712, when eleven commissions were sealed before a lull until December 1712. Several of these are of interest. Wiltshire received its first commission since December 1709, and Harcourt made up for his tardiness with really sweeping alterations. Cowper had dismissed more living justices — twenty-nine — for Wiltshire than for any other county, except, probably, Middlesex. Harcourt now restored nineteen of them, including eight of the fourteen disgraced for 'refusing to act' in March 1708, and he added forty-four new names, making sixty-three inclusions all told. For the most part these were undistinguished squires, but among them were Robert Loggan and John Younger, the Chancellor and Dean of Salisbury respectively, and five M.P.s, all members of the October Club. Harcourt also dismissed twelve of the forty-one justices added by Cowper. Those disgraced included members of traditional 'justice families' in Wiltshire, like Joseph Ashe, Walter Ernle, and Thomas Long, and also some of the county's leading Whigs, most notably Josiah Diston, who had been unseated for Devizes after the 1710 election.[1]

Peterborough received its first commission since as long ago as February 1708. The nine gentlemen put in were unremarkable except for Richard Halford, the Tory M.P. for Rutland, but the nine put out to make room for them included six put in by Cowper in 1708. Edward Wortley, the 'Country Whig' M.P. for Huntingdon, was one of these. Also dismissed were White Kennett, Dean of Peterborough, then a target for High Tory antagonism; the Sub-Dean, Richard Reynolds; and Archdeacon Richard Cumberland. These three clergymen were often divided over diocesan

Walpole himself apparently remained in the Norfolk commission throughout the period 1710-14.

[1] P.R.O., C. 234/40, Wiltshire: 17 June 1712. The five M.P.s put in were John Codrington (Bath), Benjamin Gifford (Dorchester), Thomas Lewis (Winchester), George Pitt (Hampshire), and Thomas 'Diamond' Pitt (Old Sarum).

matters, but in 1712 they were united in their Whig political stance in Church and State.[1]

In four counties receiving their second commissions from Harcourt in the summer of 1712, quite substantial changes were made. In Sussex, the forty-two gentlemen added in February 1711 were joined in July 1712 by nine more, and five justices, every one of whom had been put in by Cowper in 1706 or 1707, were dismissed. Nine were also added in Devonshire to bring the total of Harcourt's additions for that county to thirty-three. Harcourt's first commission for Buckinghamshire had added gentlemen in large numbers, but there had been no purge. Now that county received a commission which left eighteen justices out, of whom nine had been put in by Cowper in 1706. Simon Mayne, who, as M.P. for Aylesbury between 1705 and 1710, had voted consistently Whig, was also among those dismissed. In their places, twelve gentlemen were put in. Seven justices were dismissed in Glamorgan, although here the pattern was less clear-cut. The veteran Whig Sir Rowland Gwynne was among those discarded, along with two justices put in by Somers in 1699 and 1700, but Harcourt also put out two justices whom he had himself included in August 1711, while the wealthy and independent Whig M.P. for Monmouthshire, John Morgan of Tredegar, was one of the three gentlemen put in. Morgan was perhaps being rewarded for his promised support for an attack on Marlborough earlier in the year.[2] The changes in these four counties and in Wiltshire and Peterborough were the only really significant alterations in the summer of 1712, but two more otherwise routine commissions for Shropshire and Worcestershire are worthy of notice. Both were sealed on the same day as that for Glamorgan, which suggests the same guiding hand, possibly that of Lord Treasurer Oxford himself. Lord Herbert, a former Junto supporter in the Lords now compelled by financial necessity to conciliate the Tory administration, was gratified by insertion in both

[1] P.R.O., C. 234/92, Peterborough: 22 July 1712; G. V. Bennett, *White Kennett, 1660–1728, Bishop of Peterborough* (London, 1957), pp. 120–1, 198–9, 208–9.
[2] P.R.O., C. 234/37, Sussex: 5 July 1712; C. 234/9, Devonshire: 5 July 1712; C. 234/3, Buckinghamshire: 15 July 1712; C. 234/85, Glamorgan: 22 July 1712. For Morgan, see Holmes, *British Politics in the Age of Anne*, pp. 142, 480 n. 102.

commissions. Oxford's brother, Edward Harley, was also put in for Shropshire.[1]

III

Harcourt's concern with electoral politics naturally intensified during the election year of 1713, when he departed to some extent from his routine of concentrating the issue of commissions of the peace into the months of February, March, June, and July. Between December 1712 and August 1713, when the elections began, he sealed forty-two commissions for thirty-four counties. Those for some small counties, like Carmarthenshire, Holland, Lindsey, Kesteven, Pembrokeshire, and Peterborough, were routine, although it is perhaps surprising that the new lists for some larger counties, notably Surrey and Somerset where only two and three names were added respectively, were similarly unremarkable.[2] Eight counties received two commissions, so that the number of counties which did not receive a commission at all in the year before the election was as high as twenty-three.

All the same, it was not a coincidence that the greatest changes were made in counties boasting large numbers of seats: for example, in Devonshire (fourteen put in, in two commissions), Kent (nineteen put in, twelve put out), Hampshire (fourteen put in, in two commissions), and the West Riding (fifteen put in, two put out).[3] The most obvious case of regulation in a manner slanted towards the election is naturally Cornwall, with its forty-four seats. Fourteen names were added; seven of these were sitting M.P.s, and two more were successful candidates. One sitting M.P. was put out, along with seven more justices, four of whom had been put in by Cowper in September 1709.[4] Cornwall experienced the

[1] P.R.O., C. 234/32, Shropshire; C. 234/41, Worcestershire: both 22 July 1712. For Herbert, see Holmes, op. cit., p. 393.

[2] P.R.O., C. 234/36, Surrey: 19 Mar. 1712/13; C. 234/33, Somerset: 15 July 1713.

[3] P.R.O., C. 234/9, Devonshire: 20 Mar. 1712/13, 15 July 1713; C. 234/18, Kent: 14 July 1713; C. 234/14, Hampshire: 9 Apr., 27 June 1713; C. 234/44, West Riding: 5 June, 23 July 1713 (the second fiat only left out one of those added in the first).

[4] P.R.O., C. 234/6, Cornwall: 27 Apr. 1713. The M.P.s put in were John Anstis (St. Mawes); Paul Orchard (Camelford); Thomas Pask (Cambridge University); Francis Robartes (Bodmin); John Rolle (Devonshire); Henry Vincent, junior

most striking alteration involving M.P.s, but in eighteen more counties at least one sitting or future M.P. was added to the list of justices. Over the whole country, twenty-six sitting M.P.s were put in, and all but three of these were re-elected in 1713. Seventeen more gentlemen were added to the commissions who were to be elected for the first time in 1713.

However, two points arise which perhaps modify the straightforward conclusion that the commission of the peace was being manipulated to win elections for candidates of whom Harcourt and his ministerial colleagues approved. The first is that less than half of the M.P.s put into commission were put in for counties in which their present or future constituency lay. The intention was thus not necessarily to strengthen the candidate's appeal to, or influence over, the voters by elevating him to the county bench. The second is that, while the majority of M.P.s put in were clearly Tory in sympathy, as measured by 'membership' of the October Club or by voting behaviour, some M.P.s were put in who cannot be described as Tories at all. For example, four of those about to be elected in September 1713 who were added to the commission by Harcourt shortly before the election, were to vote with the Whigs against the expulsion of Richard Steele in 1714.[1] One explanation of both these points might be that Harcourt, or those making the recommendations to Harcourt's office, was not concerned so much with the progress of the elections themselves, as with the goodwill of

(Fowey); and Sir Bourchier Wray (Camelford). The successful candidates were Sir John Coryton (Callington) and Sir Edmund Prideaux (Tregoney). The M.P. put out was John Worth (Tiverton), who had been described as 'Doubtful' in 1710 and who was to vote with the Whigs against the French Commerce Bill in June 1713. He was, however, re-elected in 1713.

[1] *A Collection of White and Black Lists*, pp. 30–2; the four were Edward, Lord Hinchinbrooke (Huntingdon), put in for Huntingdonshire; Sir Samuel Ongley (Maidstone), put in for Kent; James Brudenell (Chichester) put in for Northamptonshire; and Henry Pierce (Northallerton), put in for the North Riding. Lord Hinchinbrooke was a bizarre choice as a justice of the peace on other grounds. He was a member of the notorious London gang of street ruffians, the 'Mohocks'. Jonathan Swift, *Journal to Stella*, ed. H. Williams (Oxford, 1948), ii. 511 n. 19; P.R.O., S.P. 44/113, p. 71: memorandum by the Treasury Solicitor, 24 Apr. 1712; p. 98: Dartmouth to the Attorney General, 27 May 1713.

those elected towards the Court, which distributed local power and local office.[1]

The commissions sealed between December 1712 and August 1713 present few features of interest apart from the Chancellor's preoccupation with the impending election. Apart from Kent and Cornwall, the only county in which justices were put off the bench in significant numbers was Rutland. Six were dismissed, three of whom had been put in by Cowper in 1709, and six more were brought in. Cumberland belatedly received its first commission since Harcourt's appointment, but Harcourt was content to add the youthful Viscount Lonsdale in the hope of winning him away from the influence of Whig friends, and one other. The addition of Lonsdale was the only change made in Westmorland.[2] In most of the commissions sealed at this time, Harcourt's main concern seems to have been to strengthen Tory representation in the magistracy, with moderate rather than swamping additions. Mostly the names were of Tory squires. Some were young men, just come of age, like Sir Thomas Seabright, who was added for Bedfordshire and Hertfordshire, or the Marquess of Carmarthen, heir to the Duke of Leeds, who was put in for all three Ridings of Yorkshire. Others had presumably come into their inheritances, like Thomas Cowslade, Richard Head, Sir Robert Rich, and Richard Stonhouse in Berkshire, who replaced respectively Joseph Cowslade, John Head, Sir William Rich, and James Stonhouse, put out in the same fiat as having died. A secondary consideration was to discomfit with dismissal a very few local Whig leaders, like William Monson in Hertfordshire and Sir Henry Peachey in Sussex.[3] However, the national totals of 213 gentlemen put in and 37 gentlemen put out during the period from December 1712 to August 1713 indicate the emphasis on

[1] George Lockhart hinted at both motives in requesting changes in the Tory interest in the Scottish commissions of the peace in December 1712. H.M.C., Portland MSS. v. 252–3.

[2] P.R.O., C. 234/31, Rutland: 30 June 1713; C. 234/7, Cumberland; C. 234/39, Westmorland: both 15 July 1713. For Lonsdale, who died anyway in December, see H.M.C., Portland MSS. v. 343.

[3] P.R.O., C. 234/1, Bedfordshire: 5 Mar. 1712/13; C. 234/16, Hertfordshire: 24 Feb. 1712/13, 15 July 1713; C. 234/42–4, Yorkshire: three fiats all dated 5 June 1713; C. 234/2, Berkshire: 24 Feb. 1712/13; C. 234/37, Sussex: 3 July 1713.

inclusion rather than exclusion in the regulation before the election.

The 1713 election reflected the continuing dominance of the Tories in the countryside by strengthening Tory representation in the House of Commons.[1] However, during the three years in which Harcourt had held the great seal, the political situation both at Court and in Parliament had changed. In Parliament, issues had emerged which tended to divide the Tories: the Peace, the French Commercial Treaty, and, perhaps most of all, the attitude to be taken by the ministers to the Queen's Protestant successor in Hanover. A substantial group of moderate Tories was acting with the Whigs at Westminster.[2] At Court, a deep-rooted antipathy between Lord Treasurer Oxford, with his deprecating approach towards party faction, and Secretary St. John, created Viscount Bolingbroke in 1712, had become intense by the summer of 1713.[3] The estrangement between the two ministers was a complex development, and one of the elements in it was a difference of opinion over the treatment of office-holders who were not committed Tories. There is some evidence that, as far as the commission of the peace was concerned, Oxford restrained the desire of the more extreme Tories to purge the Whigs.[4] It is surely significant that, by September 1713, every county in England and Wales had received a new commission of the peace from Harcourt's hands except Radnorshire, one in which Oxford himself took an interest. The Radnorshire bench had remained unchanged since Cowper had added four gentlemen in 1707. Oxford had then strenuously objected to one of these, but he had since taken no steps to have him removed. Oxford's other county, Herefordshire, had also been treated very mildly. Since 1710 only eight justices had been put in and two dismissed, in two commissions. This kind of moderation had, in the past,

[1] W. A. Speck, *Tory and Whig, The Struggle in the Constituencies 1701–1715* (London, 1970), pp. 110, 113; Ellis, 'The Whig Junto', pp. 775–88.

[2] Holmes, *British Politics in the Age of Anne*, pp. 280–4.

[3] Holmes, 'Harley, St. John, and the Death of the Tory Party', p. 225; Biddle, *Bolingbroke and Harley*, Chapter VI, *passim*; Bennett, *The Tory Crisis in Church and State, 1688–1730*, p. 172.

[4] J. Macpherson, *Original Papers containing the Secret History of Great Britain . . .* (London, 1775), ii. 420; *Lockhart Papers*, ed. A. Aufrere (London, 1817), i. 411; Trevelyan, *England under Queen Anne*, iii. 259, 262.

appealed to the Queen, but in the winter of 1713/14, Oxford's influence over Anne was weakening, and she was beginning to show signs of surrender to the committed party men among the Tories.[1] Bolingbroke was pressing for a more ruthless purge of office-holders in order to consolidate the divided Tory party before the anticipated crisis of the Queen's death. He openly expressed a desire to eliminate the Whigs from any share in central and local government. As Secretary of State, he embarked on a programme of dismissing Whig army and navy officers in the early spring of 1714.[2]

From Bolingbroke's point of view, Harcourt's changes in the commission of the peace down to the election of September 1713 had not gone far enough. He had been assiduous in putting gentlemen in, for most of the counties; a total of 1,505 justices had been added in England and Wales.[3] It would be impossible to say that all were Tories, but there was clearly a heavy weighting towards gentlemen of Tory sympathies. But there had not, as yet, been anything like a comprehensive purge of Whig justices of the peace. Harcourt had dismissed fifteen or more living justices in four counties: Buckinghamshire, Kent, Surrey, and Wiltshire.[4] But even in Kent, the county for which most dismissals — forty-two — had been ordered, more than half of those included by Cowper between 1705 and 1710 remained in commission by September 1713, while the figure of forty-two put out is swollen by four justices who were subsequently put back again by Harcourt and four more who had originally been put in by Harcourt himself.[5] A block of counties in the North had not, as yet, been purged at all. No living justices had been dismissed since 1710 in Northumberland, the North and East Ridings, Derbyshire, or Nottinghamshire. Moreover, in spite of the large aggregate total of gentlemen put in, the commissions of the peace for some of the smaller counties in Wales

[1] H. T. Dickinson, *Bolingbroke* (London, 1970), pp. 116-17.

[2] A. N. Newman, 'Proceedings in the House of Commons, March–June 1714', *B.I.H.R.* xxxiv (1961), 213, 214; Dickinson, *Bolingbroke*, p. 120.

[3] Excluding Middlesex and Durham.

[4] Middlesex would almost certainly make a fifth; eighteen had been left out by Harcourt's fiats for the liberty of Westminster, the commission for which ran closely parallel to that for Middlesex.

[5] P.R.O., C. 234/18, Kent: comparison of all fiats signed by Cowper and Harcourt to 14 July 1713.

and the North of England had hardly been expanded sufficiently to allow for a preponderance of Tories on the bench
at quarter sessions. In Cumberland, especially, the Tory
squires and clergy were begging Oxford in the summer of
1713 to counterbalance the continuing dominance of Whigs
in positions of local power.[1] Bolingbroke's desire for a more
thorough purge of local office thus had some force.

IV

Harcourt sealed no county commissions of the peace during
September and October 1713, except one for Middlesex for
which the fiat does not survive.[2] Then thirteen commissions
were issued between November 1713 and March 1714, and
twenty-four more between May and July 1714. Seven counties
received two commissions, so that altogether Harcourt had an
opportunity to change the justices in thirty counties between
the election and the Queen's death on 1 August 1714. Twenty-
seven counties were neglected. Among them were Kent and
Wiltshire, where substantial changes had already taken place;
those counties in the North-East and North Midlands which
had not so far been purged by Harcourt and which therefore
remained unpurged until the end of Anne's reign; and the
counties in North Wales. The commissions sealed during this
period for counties in the West of England added justices in
small numbers, and only in Dorset was one inconspicuous
gentleman, John Henley, left out.[3] The remaining counties,
which received commissions making more significant alterations, were concentrated in three areas: the North-West;
Central and South Wales; and the South-East.

    In the North-West, new commissions were sealed for
Cumberland and Westmorland in July 1714. In Cumberland,
two young baronets, Sir Charles Dalston and the sitting M.P.
for Carlisle, Sir Christopher Musgrave,[4] were put in, with

---

[1] H.M.C., *Portland MSS.* v. 304-5, 342-3.

[2] The fiat for a simultaneous commission for Westminster added six and left
out Horatio Walpole, Richard Steele, and two others. P.R.O., C. 234/25, Westminster: 15 Oct. 1713.

[3] Two gentlemen were added in Dorset to replace Henley. Four names apiece
were added in Cornwall, Devonshire, and Somerset, and one in Herefordshire.

[4] The successor to the squire of the same name active in William III's reign,
Sir Christopher was twenty-five years old in 1714.

Thomas Gibbon, the newly appointed Dean of Carlisle, and also Alexander Carleton and Dr Hugh Todd, who had both complained to Oxford about Whig domination of the Cumberland bench the year before. Twelve more second-rank Cumberland squires brought the number of additions for that county to seventeen. Five were dismissed, among them two put in by Cowper in 1707 and one put in by Somers in 1700. Dean Gibbon was also put in for Westmorland with one other clergyman and five squires, and as many as eight Westmorland justices were left out. Admittedly, two of these had been put in by Harcourt himself in 1711, and two more by Wright in 1704. Even so, when the commission reached Westmorland, the Whig gentry of that county were alarmed since those left out were all 'hearty and sincere' for the Protestant Succession.[1] These changes in the North-West are probably to be explained by the appointment in May 1714 of the Tory Earl of Thanet as *custos* of both Cumberland and Westmorland, to replace the Earls of Carlisle and Wharton respectively.

In most of the counties in Wales that received new commissions, the emphasis was on inclusion rather than dismissal. Breconshire and Carmarthenshire were treated with moderation; five and three new justices respectively were put in. The first Radnorshire commission for seven years was sealed in July 1714, but it only added four names and brought the list up to date by leaving out six who had died. The Glamorgan commission added as many as nine. Here the Tories seem to have been rather pressed for suitable candidates among the squires, for three of the nine were clergymen and another had been among those put out by Harcourt two years before. Monmouthshire was more severely treated. Six justices were dismissed in March, and eleven came in, headed by the Tory M.P. for Bramber, Andrews Windsor, who was to attempt to exchange Bramber for Monmouth in the next Parliament. Three more gentlemen, all M.P.s, were put in a little later to bring the total included during this period to fourteen.[2]

---

[1] P.R.O., C. 234/7, Cumberland, C. 234/39, Westmorland: both dated 9 July 1714; B.L., Stowe MSS. 750, f. 55: Edward Wilson to Lord Chief Justice Parker, 5 Aug. 1714.

[2] The three M.P.s were James Bertie (Middlesex), Francis Clarke (Oxfordshire), and Dodington Greville (Warwick); none of them had any obvious connection with Monmouthshire.

Montgomeryshire also received two commissions. The first added only two but dismissed four, two of them Cowper's inclusions from 1707, and the second added three and dismissed one more. A total of five inclusions and five dismissals for a county with fewer than forty justices altogether marks a remodelling which, if inconspicuous, was still more than routine.[1] These alterations in Wales are not readily explained in terms of changes in the lieutenancy or among the *custodes*. One reasonable hypothesis is that those persons in the area who were pressing for more vigorous regulation, notably the Jacobite Duke of Beaufort, were beginning to break through the restraints placed upon them by Oxford and his friends.

The changes in the South-East varied in intensity from county to county. Four counties were purged fairly drastically. The remodelling of the Essex bench was the most spectacular and is almost certainly to be explained by the appointment of Bolingbroke himself as lord-lieutenant and *custos* following the death of Lord Rivers in August 1712.[2] Before the 1713 election, Bolingbroke had made extensive changes in the militia.[3] Now he turned to the commission of the peace. Harcourt had so far only once renewed the Essex commission, in December 1710, when thirty-one had been added and eight dismissed. In March 1714 twenty-three more gentlemen were put in. Three of them were sitting M.P.s and one was a candidate in an impending by-election at Harwich. Thirteen were put out, and Bolingbroke was not afraid to disgrace a baronet and two knights. In July 1714 three more were added, and also Dr Thomas Dent was restored after being among those put out in March. Bolingbroke was presumably satisfied that the Whigs had all been purged, as no more justices were dismissed.[4] Roughly the same pattern was

[1] P.R.O., C. 234/79, Breconshire: 9 July 1714; C. 234/81, Carmarthenshire: 9 July 1714; C. 234/90, Radnorshire: 22 July 1714; C. 234/85, Glamorgan: 12 July 1714; C. 234/87, Monmouthshire: 15 Mar. 1713/14, 4 June 1714; C. 234/88, Montgomeryshire: 18 Nov. 1713, 4 June 1714.

[2] Bolingbroke was explicitly said to have been responsible in a letter written in 1715. Herts. R.O., Cowper (Panshanger) MSS. D/EP F153: Earl of Suffolk to Cowper, 6 Jan. 1714/15.

[3] Dickinson, *Bolingbroke*, p. 115.

[4] P.R.O., C. 234/12, Essex: 2 Mar. 1713/14, 9 July 1714. The M.P.s put in

followed in Surrey. In March seventeen new names were added to the list, of which five were those of sitting M.P.s. Eighteen justices were dismissed. There were no baronets or knights among them, but John Weston, the second esquire in a list of about 150, was disgraced, as was John Dibble, M.P. for Okehampton in the 1710–13 Parliament. Then, in July, four more names were added, among them William Jordan who was one of the eighteen dismissed four months earlier.[1]

Some of Bolingbroke's ruthlessness in Essex spilled over into the neighbouring county of Suffolk. Seven gentlemen, including the Tory M.P. for Cambridge, Sir John Hynde Cotton, were added in two commissions in December 1713 and July 1714. More significantly, ten were left out in the July commission, among them three baronets, one knight (Sir Isaac Rebow, M.P. for Colchester in the 1710–13 Parliament, whose petition on his re-election had failed in May 1714), and one of Walpole's Whig friends from Norfolk, Waller Bacon.[2] The last of the four comparatively heavily purged commissions in the South was Oxfordshire, the county which Harcourt himself knew best. Seven were put out. One of these was Francis Atterbury, whose removal is explained by his translation from Christ Church to the bishopric of Rochester, but three of the remaining six had been put in by Cowper, another by Somers, and a fifth was Sir John Clerke, who had been added in February 1711 as the Tory M.P. for Haslemere but who had defected to the Whigs over the French Commerce Bill. George Smalridge, the new Dean of Christ Church, was put in, with the young M.P. for Banbury, Sir Jonathan Cope, and seven more, two of them

were Thomas Bramston (Maldon), Clement Currance (Oxford), and Richard Goulston (Hertford); the future M.P. for Harwich was Carew Harvey *alias* Mildmay; the baronets and knights put out were Sir Samuel John Tryon, Sir William Cole, and Sir Godfrey Webster.

[1] P.R.O., C. 234/36, Surrey: 20 Mar. 1713/14, 9 July 1714. The five sitting M.P.s put in were Clayton Milborne (Monmouth), Sir William Poole (Bossiney), John Sharp (Ripon), Thomas Vernon (Whitchurch), and Sir John Walter (Oxford); all these names except Milborne's are later insertions in the fiat, suggesting that the decision to add the M.P.s was an afterthought.

[2] P.R.O., C. 234/35, Suffolk: 1 Dec. 1713, 5 July 1714. The three baronets put out were Sir Robert Barnardiston, Sir Cane James, and Sir Edward Ward. Thomas Betts, added in December, was put out again in July.

clergymen.[1] In four more southern and eastern counties, the number of justices added was more than routine: thirteen in Sussex, seventeen in Buckinghamshire, and nine apiece in Hampshire and Huntingdonshire. These four counties were not, however, purged to any significant extent.[2]

The grievance of Bolingbroke and the more extreme Tories in the summer of 1713, that too many Whigs were left in office, had thus been partially met in some areas of the country by July 1714. Bolingbroke expressed a wish in April that ruthless action against the Whigs had been tried a year earlier, implying that he was pleased with the belated results of such tactics.[3] However, although five or more living justices had been disgraced since the election in eight counties, much more remodelling of the commissions of the peace was required, especially in the Midlands and the North, before he could be satisfied. In early July, Bolingbroke was thought to be planning the final overthrow of Oxford, and three weeks later it was unreliably rumoured that he and Harcourt would 'rule the world . . . and not a Whig left in place a month hence'.[4] The Queen's death doubtless forestalled an extension of the campaign against Whig justices.

It is, however, unlikely that Bolingbroke's own efforts in Essex could have been duplicated elsewhere on the same scale. In the commissions sealed in the last nine months of Anne's reign there were some odd anomalies illustrating how difficult it was, even for a Chancellor who was a committed party politician, to control the nominations to the county magistracy. Harcourt restored a number of justices whom he had himself put out, such as Dent in Essex and Jordan in Surrey, and he dismissed some justices whom he had himself put in, such as Clerke in Oxfordshire. Another feature of

[1] P.R.O., C. 234/30, Oxfordshire: 24 Feb. 1713/14, redated to 2 Mar. 1713/14.
[2] P.R.O., C. 234/37, Sussex: 17 Feb. 1713/14; C. 234/3, Buckinghamshire: 1 Mar. 1713/14, 29 June 1714; C. 234/14, Hampshire: 13 May 1714; C. 234/17, Huntingdonshire: 2 Mar. 1713/14. This leaves, in the South-East, Bedfordshire (5 added), Cambridgeshire (4), and Hertfordshire (2). One justice was left out in Bedfordshire. Three counties receiving a commission at this time do not fit into the geographical grouping: Lindsey (6 added), Northamptonshire (2), and Warwickshire (4).
[3] B.L., Add. MSS. 49970: Bolingbroke to Strafford, 23 Apr. 1714.
[4] Bennett, *The Tory Crisis in Church and State, 1688–1730*, p. 179; H.M.C., Fourteenth Report, Appendix IV, *Kenyon MSS.*, p. 456.

these commissions was the quite high number of sitting M.P.s put in, as was usual during the year after an election. Many of these were Tories who were already justices in other counties, but in Huntingdonshire, for instance, two gentlemen were put into the commission of the peace just fifteen days before they joined the Whigs in voting against the expulsion of Richard Steele.[1] Also, Harcourt's apparent concern to put in unusually high numbers of peers and peers' sons produced some odd results. Three added for Bedfordshire in June 1714 were unexceptionable: Oxford's son, Edward Lord Harley; William Lord St. John of Bletsoe, who had succeeded to that title in May; and Thomas Trevor, who had just come of age and was the son of Lord Trevor. A fourth, John Lord Ashburnham, was, however, a very unreliable Tory who had once sworn never to support the Tory ministers, although admittedly by 1714 he seems to have been classed among the supporters of the Court in the Lords.[2] The Earl of Suffolk's son, Lord Walden, who after 1714 proved to be a firm Whig, was included shortly after his twenty-first birthday in July 1714 for Bolingbroke's own county, Essex. Even stranger was the inclusion of the youthful John, second Duke of Montagu, who was of impeccable Whig lineage, for Buckinghamshire, Huntingdonshire, Northamptonshire, and Warwickshire, all in the first six months of 1714. Such appointments suggest that the Court was fishing for supporters. They reflect a rather less violent approach to party in the choice of names for the commission than might have been expected after Bolingbroke's promises to his impatient friends.

The political crisis at the centre of politics came to a climax on 27 July 1714, when Oxford was dismissed. Less than a week later, the Queen died. A Council of Regency assumed control of domestic government until the arrival of George I from Hanover. Harcourt, as Lord Chancellor, was ex officio one of these Regents, but his colleagues included several Whigs appointed by King George.[3] The Whigs were confident of the major share of the King's favour. Cowper

[1] John Fitzwilliam (Peterborough) and Sir John Brownlow (Grantham).
[2] P.R.O., C. 234/1, Bedfordshire: 24 June 1714. For Ashburnham's erratic politics, see Holmes, *British Politics in the Age of Anne*, pp. 227n., 331-2, 425.
[3] Trevelyan, *England under Queen Anne*, iii. 292-307, 311.

was their natural choice as Lord Chancellor. Harcourt could not expect to keep the great seal much longer.

Under the terms of the Regency Act, the commissions of the peace, like other commissions, did not determine until six months after the death of the Queen, and the authority of the justices of the peace was confirmed by proclamation on 5 August. All justices could be resworn, and writs of *dedimus potestatem*, for which no fees were charged, were issued for this purpose a week later.[1] Harcourt was still empowered to seal new commissions, but he resisted the temptation to mark his last weeks as Chancellor with a desperate campaign against Whig justices, and indeed it is unlikely that he even contemplated such action. He signed only one fiat after the Queen's death, for Gloucestershire. This made no additions at all, but it dismissed one justice, James Rooke, whom Harcourt had himself included in February 1711.[2] On 21 September, the King sent for the great seal and bestowed it upon Cowper, who accepted gratefully. The four-year period of Tory control of the commission of the peace was over.[3]

V

Harcourt's handling of the commission of the peace over his whole period of office can be summed up briefly in numerical terms. He had sealed 180 commissions. Four were for Durham and nine were for Middlesex, and for these no fiats remain.[4] Leaving these counties aside, a total of 1,725 justices had been put in, and 405 living justices had been dismissed. Cowper, who had held the great seal a year longer, had added 1,044 justices and left out 195, so Harcourt's alterations had manifestly been more extensive. However, the Tory Harcourt's changes were not simply a reversal of those made by the Whig Cowper. Harcourt dropped 180 of Cowper's justices while they were still alive; admittedly this was

[1] 6 Anne c. 41; P.R.O., P.C. 2/85, pp. 34–5; C. 231/9, p. 312; Lincs. A.O., Monson MSS. 7/11/25: Joshua Blackwell, clerk of the peace for Kesteven, to Sir John Newton, 20 Aug. 1714.

[2] P.R.O., C. 234/13, Gloucestershire: 4 Sept. 1714.

[3] *Private Diary of William, First Earl Cowper*, pp. 57–8; Campbell, *Lives of the Chancellors*, iv. 345–6, 483.

[4] In addition, three fiats for commissions for Welsh counties are missing, and five fiats seem not to have been embodied in commissions.

quite a high proportion of his 405 dismissals. He also removed 62 who had died. More dead men may have been omitted without their names appearing in the fiats, and Cowper had dismissed a few of his own appointees. Of Cowper's 1,044 inclusions, therefore, a reasonable estimate would be that between two-thirds and three-quarters were still justices of the peace when Harcourt surrendered the great seal in September 1714. Equally, Harcourt restored 78 of the 195 gentlemen dismissed by Cowper — exactly 40 per cent, leaving 60 per cent unaccounted for, not all of whom can have died. The element of straightforward transposition between Cowper's justices and Harcourt's justices was thus less strongly marked than might have been expected.

These somewhat colourless statistics obscure the fact that a number of counties undoubtedly underwent a drastic revision of their commissions of the peace in the Tory interest, while others remained more stable. The heaviest additions to the lists of justices were in the southern counties. Harcourt promoted 102 gentlemen to the bench in Kent, and the magistracy in eleven other counties was augmented by fifty or more.[1] Eight Welsh counties were among the thirteen at the other end of the scale which received fewer than fifteen inclusions, though it is perhaps surprising to find Derbyshire and Nottinghamshire also in this category.[2] It was again the counties in the South which were most extensively purged. Surrey and Kent lost forty-three and forty-two living justices respectively, and in five more southern and eastern counties, fifteen or more living justices were dismissed.[3] Of the twenty counties which were not purged at all heavily — that is, which lost two or less living justices — only two, Berkshire and Huntingdonshire, were within fifty miles of London.[4] The southern counties thus tended to receive

[1] Gloucestershire (78), Sussex (71), Buckinghamshire (66), Wiltshire (63), Hampshire (62), Essex, Shropshire, Surrey (58), Cornwall (56), Berkshire (51), and Devonshire (50).

[2] Denbighshire (15), Anglesey (13), Nottinghamshire, Montgomeryshire (12), Breconshire, Derbyshire (11), Peterborough (10), Herefordshire, Cardiganshire (9), Holland (8), Radnorshire (4), Flintshire (2), and Merionethshire (1).

[3] Essex (21), Buckinghamshire (19), Oxfordshire, Suffolk (17), and Wiltshire (16).

[4] Anglesey, Berkshire, Breconshire, Cardiganshire, Carmarthenshire, Denbighshire, Derbyshire, Flintshire, Herefordshire, Holland, Huntingdonshire, Kesteven,

commissions making alterations which were more extensive than those in the more remote northern and western counties, and this remains true even if allowance is made for the relative difference in size of the commissions involved.

Some general points remain to be made about Harcourt's manipulation of the commissions of the peace. The first is that Harcourt and his Secretary of Commissions seems to have supervised all nominations themselves. There was no example, during the period, of either the Privy Council or the Secretaries of State forwarding instructions to put specified gentlemen into or out of the commission for a particular county. The absence of any centrally authorized changes, involving, however formally, the Queen's pleasure, is a small break with previous practice. A very few communications from other ministers directing alterations in the commissions of the peace occur after 1714, but on the whole it is fair to say that the Harcourt era marks a development in the independence of the Chancellor's control over this area of his patronage.

A second point of interest concerns the extent to which Harcourt's reshaping of the magistracy actually affected local government. In those counties which did not receive a commission until late in Harcourt's period of office, such as Cumberland and Radnorshire, and in those where the changes were comparatively moderate, such as Herefordshire, Nottinghamshire, and the East Riding, the bench may well have retained throughout the last years of the Queen's reign the complexion which Cowper had given it. Also, even in counties where substantial alterations, including purges, had taken place, it is not necessarily true that the character of the active magistracy changed very markedly during Harcourt's Chancellorship. The Crown Office, as usual, obstructed the process by which magistrates were appointed by demanding individual fees from each justice for his *dedimus potestatem*. Baron Price wrote in August 1711 from Cornwall, where thirty-eight gentlemen had been added the previous February, that there was an acute shortage of justices who would act in that county, and indeed all over England, simply because the

Lindsey, Merionethshire, Northumberland, Nottinghamshire, Radnorshire, Staffordshire, and the East and North Ridings.

gentlemen put in would not pay the fees. In the same year, the judges recommended, apparently collectively, that justices who neglected to act should automatically be removed from the commission of the peace.[1] It is thus possible that, in some counties, Harcourt's alterations had little practical effect. For instance, the magistrates of Hampshire found some difficulty in persuading four of Harcourt's additions to act even in the emergency of severe corn riots in December 1712.[2]

On the other hand, the Tory justices in other counties seem to have been more active. Although only seven gentlemen out of twenty-seven put in for Buckinghamshire in January 1711 acted as justices out of sessions in the course of the following year, and although only four out of eighteen put out in July 1712 had been active magistrates, yet the Tories dominated the bench at Buckinghamshire quarter sessions in October 1712, when only two Whigs were present among sixteen or eighteen justices.[3] The Crown Office *dedimus* book is admittedly unreliable as a guide to the willingness of justices to act since it only records the names of justices who took out their *dedimus* through the office of the Secretary of Commissions, but even so, it affords some suggestive evidence. In Kent and Essex, for example, over half of the gentlemen added in 1711 had acquired a *dedimus* by the beginning of 1714, and several more presumably qualified themselves at assizes, so the reluctance of Cornish justices to pay for a *dedimus* was not universal.[4] Also, Cowper's correspondence in 1715 indicates that, in several counties, men described as violent Tories put in 'to serve a turn', had been active as justices at quarter sessions in the last years of the Queen's reign.[5]

[1] H.M.C., *Portland MSS.* v. 72; H.M.C., *House of Lords MSS.*, N.S. ix. 157.

[2] P.R.O., S.P. 34/37, No. 171: Attorney General's report on Hampshire riots, 18 Dec. 1712, with several enclosures.

[3] P.R.O., C. 234/3, Buckinghamshire: 16 Jan. 1710/11, 15 July 1712; *Buckinghamshire Sessions Records*, ed. W. Le Hardy and G. L. Reckitt (Aylesbury, 1933–51), ii. 454–6, iii. 306–8; Verney, *Verney Letters of the Eighteenth Century*, i. 243.

[4] P.R.O., C. 193/43.

[5] Herts. R.O., Cowper (Panshanger) MSS. D/EP F153, F154, *passim*. Some more detailed evidence, relating to Wiltshire and bearing on the effect of political change on the active magistracy, is reserved for Chapter 9.

Finally, some discussion is required of the question of whether Harcourt was prepared to favour committed Jacobites who were willing to use their local power to facilitate the succession of the Pretender on the Queen's death. There is no doubt that prominent Jacobites were put into the commission of the peace by Harcourt. Some notable examples are Sir William Wyndham in Somerset, Lord North and Grey in Essex, Charles Caesar in Hertfordshire, John Anstis in Cornwall, Francis Atterbury in Oxfordshire and later in Kent, and Sir John Hynde Cotton in Cambridgeshire and Suffolk. 'General' Thomas Forster, who rose for the Pretender in 1715 in the North-East, and John Hall, who retained the nickname 'Justice' Hall when executed for treason in 1716, were both justices of the peace for Northumberland who had been put in by Harcourt in 1711.[1] Harcourt had put in for Cheshire three of the gentlemen of that county who met to consider whether or not to join the Pretender in 1715, subsequently commemorating their decision to refrain by commissioning their portraits.[2] In some counties, Harcourt was later to be accused of an attempt to swamp the bench with Jacobites immediately before the Queen's death. This rather unconvincing 'conspiracy theory' prevailed, for instance, in Glamorgan, where seven of the nine gentlemen added in July 1714 were said to have been Jacobites.[3]

However, in cases like that of Bishop Atterbury in Kent, the inclusion of a Jacobite in the commission of the peace amounted to routine recognition of a position of authority within the county. In other examples, Harcourt was simply putting in young men of high social position who had recently attained their majority or inherited their estates. Gentlemen such as Sir Coplestone Warwick Bampfield in Devonshire and Somerset, Sir William Carew in Cornwall, Corbet Kynaston in Shropshire, and Sir Thomas Seabright in Bedfordshire, Hertfordshire, and Oxfordshire, all Jacobites, were aged 25 or less in 1710. Sir John Hynde Cotton was

---

[1] For Hall, see *Diary of Mary Countess Cowper, 1714–1720*, ed. S. Cowper (London, 1864), p. 113.

[2] G. Ormerod, *History of the County Palatine and City of Chester* (2nd edn., London, 1882), i. 557 n. 'b'.

[3] Herts. R.O., Cowper (Panshanger) MSS. D/EP F155: anonymous list of Jacobites put into the Glamorgan commission 'a week before the death of the Queen'.

only 22 when added for Cambridgeshire. Jacobites of this type could be set against those young men of high rank, and subsequently of Whig principles, whom Harcourt presumably included because it would have been unusual to have kept them out: for example, Lord Hinchinbrooke in Huntingdonshire, or Lord Walden in Essex. It would almost certainly be wrong to assume that the insertion of some notorious Jacobites in the commissions of the peace was part of a conscious system of preparation for a Stuart counter-revolution. There is no evidence that the bench in any county was dominated at any time by Jacobites. The succession of King George passed off peacefully in London and the localities. Harcourt's Whig successor had already held the great seal for some months before Jacobite riots took place on a large scale in the spring and summer of 1715. As far as the isolated disturbances before then are concerned, there was no shortage of active magistrates ready to take affidavits and forward them to the Secretaries of State, to be thanked for their zeal in the King's service.[1] Although there are a few cases of gentlemen using their powers as justices to demonstrate distaste for the Hanoverian Succession, these were not especially serious.[2] It seems fair to conclude that Jacobitism was not obviously made more of a threat to the Hanoverian regime than it already was because a number of Jacobites were in the commissions of the peace.

After Harcourt had been dismissed, he retired, though only temporarily, into private life. He devoted much time after 1714 to the patronage of literature.[3] His later career in active

[1] P.R.O., S.P. 44/115, pp. 280-1: Bromley to two Hampshire justices, relating to a case of drinking damnation to King George, 2 Sept. 1714; S.P. 44/116: Townshend to Joseph Earle, relating (probably) to riots at Bristol, 26 Oct. 1714; series of letters from Townshend to the Attorney General and the Solicitor General, relating to riots at Salisbury, Taunton, Birmingham, Tewkesbury, Canterbury, and Shrewsbury, beginning 8 Nov. 1714; S.P. 44/117, pp. 52, 56, 58: three more letters from Townshend to the Attorney General, relating to riots at Shrewsbury, Worcester, and Hertford, 26 Nov., 13 Dec., 16 Dec. 1714.

[2] Herts. R.O., Cowper (Panshanger) MSS. D/EP F152: affidavit of Richard Scholfield that two Worcestershire justices had allowed the oaths to be taken in an improper manner, [1714]; affidavits of Stephen Newton and John Oldham that three Warwickshire or Staffordshire justices, including the two M.P.s for Tamworth (Samuel Bracebridge and William Inge), had prosecuted as rioters persons celebrating King George's coronation, 27 Nov. 1714.

[3] Campbell, *Lives of the Chancellors*, iv. 484-500.

politics is not relevant to the present study, but it is worth
noticing that he took no part in Jacobite conspiracy, that he
concerted with Townshend in the defeat of the impeachment
of Oxford in 1717, and that in 1721 he accepted an earldom
and a place on the Privy Council from Walpole.[1] He died in
1727, having weathered the transition from the Bolingbroke
era to the Walpole era with adroit discretion.

---

[1] Plumb, *Sir Robert Walpole, The Making of a Statesman*, p. 255; A. S. Foord,
His Majesty's Opposition (Oxford, 1964), p. 68.

8

THE COMMISSION OF THE PEACE AND THE HANOVERIAN SUCCESSION, 1714-20

I

In the months after the Hanoverian Succession, the preconditions for massive changes in the commissions of the peace were all assembled. Cowper's second term as Lord Chancellor began in an atmosphere of Whig euphoria at the centre of politics. Halifax, Orford, Sunderland, Townshend, and Stanhope filled the principal 'offices of business'. Wharton and Somers were also in the Cabinet. Their single Tory colleague was Nottingham, who was Lord President, and he had been acting with the Whigs anyway since 1711. Among the younger politicians, Walpole became Paymaster General and Pulteney Secretary at War.[1] The Privy Council was overwhelmingly Whig.[2] During the autumn of 1714, Tory placemen of all kinds were dismissed, partly to ensure the return of a Whig majority in the House of Commons to be elected in late January and early February 1715, partly to guard against the possibility that Tories in positions of responsibility might prove to be unreliable supporters of the new dynasty.[3] In particular, living lords-lieutenant and *custodes rotulorum* were replaced between October 1714 and January 1715 in more than half the counties, and the new leaders of county society were almost without exception Whigs. Also, the character of the justices of the peace themselves was a topic of concern among politicians at the centre. Even before the arrival of George I from Hanover, the appointments made by Harcourt

[1] W. Michael, *England under George I: The Beginnings of the Hanoverian Dynasty* (London, 1936), pp. 92-102.

[2] P.R.O., P.C. 2/85, p. 86.

[3] *The Wentworth Papers, 1705-1739*, ed. J. J. Cartwright (London, 1883), pp. 419-20; Verney, *Verney Letters of the Eighteenth Century*, i. 316; R. Sedgwick, *The History of Parliament: The House of Commons, 1715-1754* (London, 1970), i. 62; W. R. Ward, *The English Land Tax in the Eighteenth Century* (Oxford, 1953), p. 64; Roberts, *Growth of Responsible Government*, p. 382; Foord, *His Majesty's Opposition*, p. 49.

had attracted attention among the Regents, who seemed especially anxious to investigate the dismissals of Whigs.[1]

Moreover, the dislocations caused by a change of Chancellor were less apparent than usual in 1714. Cowper was of course already familiar with the intricacies of Crown Office procedure, and his Secretary of Commissions, Richard Woollaston, was an experienced member of the Chancery secretariat who had been Cowper's purse-bearer from 1705 to 1710.[2] Woollaston's book of the peace was prepared during the week following Cowper's appointment on 21 September, and before the month was out Cowper had already signed three fiats. Ten followed in October, nine in November, nineteen in December, and thirteen in January.[3] The only English counties not dealt with before the elections were Berkshire and Rutland. On 3 March 1715 Cowper noted that every county except Breconshire, Carmarthenshire, Denbighshire, and Flintshire had received a new commission since the Queen's death.[4] By May 1715 the tally was complete.

This combination of a drastic change at the centre of politics, a reshuffle of office-holders in numerous spheres of government, and the comprehensive issue of new commissions of the peace in the space of eight months, seems to support the hypothesis that the county magistracy underwent a considerable upheaval. However, there are grounds for thinking that it would be incautious to assume that Tories were displaced on the county benches by Whigs in a series of wholesale purges, even before the evidence provided by the fiats is examined in detail. In the first place, the Tory party was not irretrievably ruined by the Queen's death. George I was reluctant to establish a one-party government, and places were offered to Sir Thomas Hanmer and William Bromley in the autumn of 1714. Although, unlike Nottingham, they declined to serve, the fact that the offers were made suggests that the new King was not enthusiastic about the prospect of a Whig monopoly. Meanwhile, Atterbury was urging the Tories to rely on their parliamentary strength and to unite as

[1] *Letters of Joseph Addison*, p. 418.
[2] Luttrell, *Brief Relation*, v. 601.   [3] P.R.O., C. 231/9, pp. 314 ff.
[4] Herts. R.O., Cowper (Panshanger) MSS. D/EP F152: paper endorsed 'An account of what Commissions of the Peace have been renewed & what not to the 3rd of March 1714/15'.

a formidable, yet respectable, opposition party.[1] The Tories had scored an overwhelming victory in an election as recently as 1713, and the strength of the party lay in the allegiance of many of the country gentry. It seems a reasonable conjecture that Cowper was aware that, by dismissing the Tories from the county magistracy in large numbers, he would be fulfilling Atterbury's purpose by driving the Tory squires into a disgruntled opposition united by a common grievance. In the second place, neither Cowper, nor a number of other Whigs, thought that he did, in fact, conduct a purge in the Whig interest in the twelve months after the Queen's death. The memorandum to George I on the commissions of the peace, which has so frequently been quoted, was written in July 1715, and in it Cowper was concerned as much as anything to defend himself to the King against Whig colleagues who complained that he had not left enough Tories out.[2] Cowper's arguments in the memorandum will be discussed at greater length in due course; the commissions sealed in 1714-15 themselves must now be considered.

II

Cowper's experience enabled him to organize an efficient system of local recommendation fairly rapidly in the autumn of 1714. He sent a Crown Office list of the justices in commission at the Queen's death for each county separately to a Whig magnate of influence within that county, usually the peer who was shortly to be appointed *custos*. He may have sent such lists to more than one magnate in some counties, but the regular pattern seems to have been that Cowper relied in the first instance on one influential Whig. When the list reached the county, the Whig grandee would consider it, probably in conjunction with the locally prominent Whig squires. He would then either return the list to Cowper, annotated with his comments about the justices and recommending gentlemen as fit to be added, or he would keep the list and send Cowper a set of suggested changes. Examples of both types of recommendation survive among Cowper's

---

[1] Bennett, *The Tory Crisis in Church and State, 1688-1730*, pp. 185-6; Holmes, 'Harley, St. John, and the Death of the Tory Party', pp. 233-5.

[2] Herts. R.O., Cowper (Panshanger) MSS. D/EP F152.

papers.[1] Woollaston sometimes simply recopied a corrected list received from a county, so that the fiat is in the form of a complete list of all the justices who were to be in the new commission. Alternatively, the fiats were in the more usual form of an instruction to put some gentlemen in and to leave other gentlemen out.[2] Cowper also received some apparently unsolicited recommendations, and he probably invited verbal suggestions from peers who happened to be in London.

In the course of his first revision of the commissions of the peace, extending to the election of 1715 or shortly after, Cowper did not conduct a fully comprehensive campaign against the Tories in any one county. Indeed, in only two counties, Sussex and Leicestershire, did a really substantial purge take place at all. As many as forty-two Sussex justices who had been put in by Harcourt between 1710 and the Queen's death were put out, while six of the thirteen dismissed by Harcourt were restored. But even in Sussex, twenty-seven justices included by Harcourt remained in commission, and among those left in were Tories such as Sir William Wyndham, Leonard Gale, Charles Eversfield, Thomas Chowne, Henry Campion, Robert Leeves, and William Elson.[3] Similarly, in Leicestershire eighteen out of the thirty-three gentlemen put in by Harcourt were excluded in January 1715, apparently on the recommendation of the Duke of Rutland. Most of these were of 'small estates' or were not sworn, and one was Samuel Bracebridge, a Tory shortly to be elected at Tamworth. Even so, Sir Nathan Wright, Sir Thomas Cave, Sir John Chester, and Sir Justinian Isham, along with other Tory squires, remained on the bench.[4]

A few counties where Harcourt's changes had been relatively

---

[1] Herts. R.O., Cowper (Panshanger) MSS. D/EP F153, F154, F155, *passim*.

[2] The presence of complete lists serving as fiats makes it impossible to compile aggregate totals of justices put in and put out, as can be done for the period 1705–14. Even so, the changes made since the last commission sealed by Harcourt can often be deduced from the order of the names in the lists.

[3] P.R.O., C. 234/37, Sussex: 21 Dec. 1714. The gentlemen named had been M.P.s in one or both of the last two Parliaments of the Queen's reign, when they had displayed Tory proclivities.

[4] P.R.O., C. 234/19, Leicestershire: 4 Jan. 1714/15; Herts. R.O., Cowper (Panshanger) MSS. D/EP F153: annotated list of Leicestershire justices in 1714; list of gentlemen 'turned out by Lord Denbigh'; Duke of Rutland's recommendations, none dated but all clearly *c.* December 1714.

mild were now remodelled in such a way as to give a clear Whig superiority of numbers. Harcourt had added twelve justices in Nottinghamshire; Cowper left out three of these, including George Nevill, described by the Earl of Clare as a 'flaming Tory, almost a madman', and three more, and added eleven completely new names.[1] The commissions for Ely, Holland, Peterborough (where the clergymen left out by Harcourt in 1712 were restored as early as September 1714), and Westmorland were also revised in such a way as to outnumber the justices added by Harcourt and suffered to remain, by justices now restored or put in for the first time.

Taken together, these seven counties do not amount to a very vigorous remodelling of the bench in the Whig interest. Cowper was more often content to add names in just sufficient numbers to 'balance' the gentlemen added by Harcourt who remained in the commission. Among counties treated in this way were some where what looks superficially like a considerable regulation took place. One such case was Gloucestershire. In October 1714 sixty-three gentlemen were added (including every one of the five left out by Harcourt) and fifteen gentlemen put in by Harcourt were left out, only one of whom was dead. But Harcourt had added seventy-eight gentlemen altogether, so that sixty-three of his justices remained in; his inclusions and those made by Cowper exactly equalled each other. Gloucestershire apparently had an inexhaustible pool of gentry of justice status, and it is surprising that the opportunity was not taken in 1714 to dismiss from an overloaded bench such prominent Tories as Sir Robert Jenkinson, Thomas Masters, Thomas Rowney, and John Snell, all of whom were elected to Parliament in 1715, and other gentlemen of Tory sentiments such as John Essington, formerly M.P. for Aylesbury, and Thomas Webb, formerly M.P. for Gloucestershire.[2] The same thing happened in Essex, where thirty-nine names were added to balance (inadequately) the fifty retained from the period from 1710 to 1714. Harcourt's list was kept almost intact, as only five of his inclusions

---

[1] P.R.O., C. 234/29, Nottinghamshire: 13 Jan. 1714/15; Herts. R.O., Cowper (Panshanger) MSS. D/EP F154: paper endorsed 'My Lord Clare's list for Nottinghamshire given in the 13 Jan. 1714/15'.

[2] P.R.O., C. 234/13, Gloucestershire: 27 Oct. 1714.

were certainly left out in 1714. Cowper was clearly trying to bring Whig numbers on the bench up to the level of the Tories. Among those retained were Tories of the calibre of Clement Currance, John Comyns, William Gore, Richard Goulston, and Thomas Bramston, all of whom were past or future M.P.s who recorded Tory votes. Three months later the Earl of Suffolk was agitating for the removal of more of the gentlemen added by Bolingbroke in 1714.[1] In two commissions in Bedfordshire, twenty-four new justices weighed against twenty-two of Harcourt's justices still left in, notwithstanding a quite severe purge of nineteen justices recommended by the Duke of Kent, whose reasons for their exclusion were sometimes political ('put in by the late ministry to serve a turn'), sometimes routine ('gone out of the country', or 'his father in commission'), and sometimes ambiguous ('a violent irregular man in his office', or 'oppressive to his neighbours').[2] In Shropshire, too, the net effect of what appears on the surface to have been a major revision in the Whig interest was, in fact, to 'balance' the bench. Every one of the six dismissed by Harcourt was put back in December 1714, on representations from the Earl of Bradford that 'the worst justice in England', one Eldred Lancelot Lee, had secured their dismissal. Thirty-nine gentlemen were added, and of the fifteen put out, fourteen had been added by Harcourt. Despite these apparently severe changes, forty-two of Harcourt's inclusions remained in commission as against the thirty-nine added by Cowper.[3] On a smaller scale, a number of Welsh counties illustrate a similar approach. In Cardiganshire, for instance, seven were added and six left out; in Carmarthenshire, eleven inclusions exactly replaced eleven omissions. In both these cases, the respective *custodes*, Viscount Lisburne and the Marquess of Winchester, took the

[1] P.R.O., C. 234/12, Essex: 2 Oct. 1714; Herts. R.O., Cowper (Panshanger) MSS. D/EP F153: Suffolk to Cowper, 6 Jan. 1714/15.

[2] P.R.O., C. 234/1, Bedfordshire: 4 Oct. 1714, 10 Jan. 1714/15; Herts. R.O., Cowper (Panshanger) MSS. D/EP F153: paper endorsed 'The Duke of Kent's list for Bedfordshire for a second commission', no date.

[3] P.R.O., C. 234/32, Shropshire: 17 Dec. 1714; Herts. R.O., Cowper (Panshanger) MSS. D/EP F154: Bradford to Cowper, 27 Dec. 1714, ten days later than the date of the fiat but recommending changes which were incorporated in the new commission, which survives at Shrops. R.O., Quarter Sessions Records, Box 292.

view that evidence of the unfitness of the justices whose disgrace they desired would prod Cowper into action. The Chancellor could hardly ignore such comments on individual justices as 'has been in gaol', 'of weak understanding', 'half mad', 'very troublesome to the country', and 'a wild sotting young fellow'. Winchester added revealingly that some of the Carmarthenshire justices were 'mean men not thought of for the commission until Sir Thomas Powell had them put in to support his interest', but Cowper failed to take the hint, and Powell, the defeated candidate in the county election, remained in the commission.[1] In general, the pattern of a moderate purge and inclusions which roughly equalled the survivors from the Harcourt regime was a common one. It was followed in large counties like Devonshire and small counties like Rutland. Even the electorally important county of Cornwall, where if anything the Cornish Tories retained a slight majority on the bench, was treated in this way.

In some counties, Cowper tried to secure a balanced bench by mass inclusions rather than by a purge. Only two of Harcourt's justices were dropped in Surrey (one of them, however, was Sir Thomas Hanmer) and fifty-three were retained. The order of names in the list serving as a fiat suggests that fifty-five gentlemen were brought in.[2] Similarly, only two justices were put out in Lindsey, both 'practising Sollicitors and Attorneys' according to the *custos*, but twenty were added, and these nearly, but not quite, balanced the twenty-four included between 1710 and 1714 and still retained.[3] Cowper was more successful in outnumbering the Tories in Dorset where thirty-seven new names came in to swamp the nineteen gentlemen appointed by Harcourt who survived.[4]

The bench in several counties was still packed with Harcourt's appointments at the time of the 1715 election. Even after two commissions, sealed in September 1714 and

[1] P.R.O., C. 234/80, Cardiganshire: 15 Jan. 1714/15; C. 234/81, Carmarthenshire: 15 Mar. 1714/15; Herts. R.O., Cowper (Panshanger) MSS. D/EP F155, annotated lists and recommendations from Lisburne and Winchester.

[2] P.R.O., C. 234/36, Surrey: 12 Oct. 1714.

[3] P.R.O., C. 234/22, Lindsey: 13 Jan. 1714/15; Herts. R.O., Cowper (Panshanger) MSS. D/EP F153: Castleton to Woollaston, 12 Nov. 1714; paper endorsed 'Lincoln, Lord Finch', no date; recommendations of the Earl of Lindsey, the *custos*, 'given in' 12 Jan. 1715.

[4] P.R.O., C. 234/11, Dorset: 16 Dec. 1714.

February 1715, fifty-eight gentlemen included by Harcourt were still justices in Buckinghamshire, and only twenty-two new justices had been appointed.[1] Ten new names were included for Hampshire, but fifty-three gentlemen put in between 1710 and 1714 made up about one-third of the total commission.[2] A surprising feature of the Hertfordshire commission sealed in December is the small number of restorations. Only two of the twenty-eight put out by Harcourt were put back; thirty-three gentlemen added by Harcourt remained. Moreover, Cowper, who knew Hertfordshire well, inexplicably left in crypto-Jacobites and Tories, such as Charles Caesar, John Gape, Richard Goulston, Samuel Robinson, Sir Thomas Seabright, and Sir George Warburton.[3] Another county in which the Tories retained at any rate a theoretical numerical superiority was, predictably, Oxfordshire, where Cowper left out two of Harcourt's forty-two inclusions and three more, restored six of Harcourt's omissions, and appointed eight new names. The *custos* had sent a formidable list of justices who had not qualified themselves to act, but this was ignored. Cowper evidently felt that he had to be sure of his ground before disgracing the Oxfordshire Tories. Of the five put out, John Clarke, in spite of lucid intervals, was 'distracted once again', Harry Cole was guilty of administrative rather than political misdemeanours, and Thomas Napier had not only read the seditious *English Advice to the Freeholders of England* at Woodstock market, but also lived in a 'scandalous manner'.[4] The addition of twenty-eight names (nine of them restorations) for Wiltshire hardly balanced the forty-nine who had been added in 1712 and were still in commission. Cowper had put fourteen gentlemen out between 1705 and 1710, mostly for 'refusing to act', and Harcourt had restored them; Cowper might have been expected to have left them

---

[1] P.R.O., C. 234/3, Buckinghamshire: 29 Sept. 1714, 16 Feb. 1714/15; Herts. R.O., Cowper (Panshanger) MSS. D/EP F153: paper endorsed 'Bucks. From Lord Bridgwater', no date.

[2] P.R.O., C. 234/14, Hampshire: 5 Oct. 1714.

[3] P.R.O., C. 234/16, Hertfordshire: 21 Dec. 1714.

[4] P.R.O., C. 234/30, Oxfordshire: 13 Jan. 1714/15; Herts. R.O., Cowper (Panshanger) MSS. D/EP F154: paper endorsed 'List of Alterations in the Commission of the Peace for the County of Oxford'; separate paper endorsed 'Oxford. E[arl of] G[odolphin]'.

out again in 1714, but he did not.[1] All fourteen of those to be left out for Kent had originally been added by Harcourt, but eighty-five gentlemen in the first Hanoverian commission, between one-third and one-half of the total list, had been added during the last four years of the Queen's reign. Cowper added thirty-four gentlemen for the first time and restored twenty-four more who had been left out by Harcourt, but these fifty-eight additions fell short of balancing Harcourt's inclusions.[2] Cumberland, Northumberland, and Glamorgan were three more counties regulated so as still to leave a majority of gentlemen put in by Harcourt over gentlemen put in by Cowper. Perhaps the strangest case of remodelling occurs in Worcestershire. Two commissions were sealed. The first, in September 1714, left out eight of Harcourt's twenty-eight inclusions, restored all eight gentlemen whom Harcourt had dismissed, and added at least five, and probably more, new justices. This was clearly a prompt, if not quite complete, 'balancing' operation. But the second commission, a month later, displaced well known Whigs such as Sir Joseph Jekyll, and Charles and Richard Dowdeswell; restored the Jacobites John Parsons, Sir John Packington, and Sir William Keyt, who had been left out in September; and retained Sir Thomas Seabright and other Tories.[3]

The over-all impression left by Cowper's first set of commissions is that, while he was making what were undeniably quite substantial changes in the Whig interest, he was not as yet prepared to conduct a comprehensive reversal of the Tory changes made by his predecessor. It may be that the picture of changes in individual counties here presented is a little misleading, because it is likely to be an unwarrantable assumption that every justice put in by Harcourt between 1710 and 1714 was Tory in sympathy. Even so, an unexpectedly high number of identifiably Tory and even Jacobite gentlemen remained in the commission of the peace for most of the

[1] The fiat was dated 2 Dec. 1714, the commission itself 27 Dec., but even so, some later suggestions made by the *custos*, the Marquess of Dorchester, seem to have been incorporated. P.R.O., C. 234/40, Wiltshire: 2 Dec. 1714; Wilts. R.O., A 1/1/2; Herts. R.O., Cowper (Panshanger) MSS. D/EP F154, Dorchester to Cowper, 1 Jan., 6 Jan. 1715.

[2] P.R.O., C. 234/18, Kent: 19 Oct. 1714.

[3] P.R.O., C. 234/41, Worcestershire: 28 Sept., 1 Nov. 1714.

counties during and after the 1715 election. The effect of the changes that Cowper did make on the progress of the elections is not very clear. The Tories did rather worse than they had expected in the county seats,[1] but it is difficult to relate any Whig capture of a single county to recent changes in its list of magistrates. A very few Tory candidates were dismissed, but were elected nonetheless, like George Bruere, elected for Great Marlow although displaced in Buckinghamshire. Many Tory candidates, however, remained on the bench. Even in Sussex, where a substantial purge had taken place, the Jacobite Sir Harry Goring was not removed, and he came top of the poll at Horsham, although he was subsequently unseated on petition.

Some of the recommendations which Cowper received specifically referred to the elections. George Lucy wrote from Warwickshire 'I take this occasion to observe to you that in case there is not some Regulations here in the Commission of the Peace as well as in other Places, the Tory Interest will always inevitably prevail, for the Bench of Justices have such an Influence over the Freeholders in this County that they insult those poor wretches to such a degree that out of fear they seem to loose all sense of liberty. . . .' Of those put in by the late Tory ministry, Lucy singled out five for disgrace who had small estates, and suggested seven in their places. He added that, since the Tory gentry did not act, the Whigs would, after this relatively modest regulation, be the greater party on the bench.[2] Adolphus Oughton, the Whig candidate for Coventry, suggested at least three more names, plus himself, to help the 'poor depress'd Whiggs' in the Warwickshire elections.[3] In the event, only one justice, William Inge, who had originally been included by Wright, was dismissed; but he was returned unopposed for Tamworth. Sir William Keyt, who according to Lucy had a very small estate, and had been put in only as a check on the Whigs in Barlichway Hundred, was kept in. Oughton's self-nomination was disregarded, possibly because Cowper remembered dismissing him in 1707 for 'refusing to

[1] W. A. Speck, 'The General Election of 1715', *Eng. Hist. Rev.* xc (1975), 514.
[2] Herts. R.O., Cowper (Panshanger) MSS. D/EP F154: Lucy to [Woollaston?], 21 Nov. 1714.
[3] Ibid.: Oughton to [Woollaston?], 30 Nov. 1714.

act', but, as in Inge's case, it does not seem to have mattered much whether or not he was a justice of the peace, since he was elected for Coventry. However, all twenty-five of Harcourt's justices remained in the commission and only eleven were added, and it is therefore not surprising that the 'poor depress'd Whiggs' were unable to oppose the election of two Tories for the county.[1] Changes to assist the elections were also suggested in neighbouring Staffordshire. An anonymous source recommended William Chetwynd to help the Chetwynd interest at Stafford, and also suggested the omission of an 'enemy to the Protestant Succession', Henry Vernon. The *custos*, Lord Uxbridge, returned an annotated list which recommended Walter and William Chetwynd, and he also suggested that several be disgraced: some were of small estates, Henry Vernon and John Congreve abused the office of justice of the peace for Tory electoral purposes, while Richard Dyott was a flagrant Jacobite.[2] In January 1715 the two Chetwynds duly joined another Walter Chetwynd already in the commission, and all three of them were elected at Stafford and Lichfield. The gentlemen of small estates, plus Congreve, were dismissed. Richard Dyott, however, was one of the Tory candidates at Lichfield, yet he remained in the commission of the peace, as did his Tory partner, John Cotes. Neither was elected. Henry Vernon also remained in commission and was returned for Newcastle-under-Lyme after a stiff fight with two Whigs. Cowper sealed another commission in February, after the election. Vernon, Cotes, and Dyott all reappear, although Cowper introduced a touch of delicate, if puzzling, finesse by leaving William Inge, the M.P. for Tamworth recently dismissed for Warwickshire, out of the Staffordshire quorum.[3] Vernon's continued status as a magistrate perhaps assisted his election, although he was unseated on petition in June.[4]

These cases of what almost amounts to neglect of Whig

[1] P.R.O., C. 234/38, Warwickshire: 1 Jan. 1714/15.

[2] Herts. R.O., Cowper (Panshanger) MSS. D/EP F154: unsigned paper, no date, recommending William Chetwynd; list annotated by Uxbridge, no date; separate paper endorsed 'Received the 5 Jan. 1715 of My Lord Uxbridge'.

[3] P.R.O., C. 234/34, Staffordshire: 7 Jan., 22 Feb. 1714/15.

[4] For details of the elections and the political outlook of the candidates, see Sedgwick, *The House of Commons, 1715-1754*, i. 319-21, 339.

electoral interests may not be typical. Even so, in both Warwickshire and Staffordshire Cowper had received explicit suggestions for desirable changes but had not acted upon them. Probably in many counties the publication of the new commission at quarter sessions in January confirmed in a general way an impression that Whig influence was dominant in the control of patronage, but specific cases of manipulation in the Whig interest seem to have been unusual, and it is possible that Cowper took the view that an unduly vigorous regulation among justices of the peace would have done more harm than good.

III

In the course of 1715 the Whigs consolidated their hold on the ministry and on patronage. Bolingbroke fled to France in March and became, shortly afterwards, the Pretender's Secretary of State. The Jacobite rising in Scotland and the North of England in the autumn of 1715 confirmed in Whig eyes the identification of Toryism with treason. The younger Whigs in the ministry, notably Walpole and Townshend, were as much in favour of proscription in local office as a weapon in central politics as their Junto predecessors or Bolingbroke had been. There is a widely accepted hypothesis that in the months after the election, and especially during and after the Jacobite rising, the Whigs completed a wholesale regulation of the commissions of the peace.[1] Between March 1715 and January 1716, when he was compelled by illness to suspend business temporarily,[2] Cowper sealed commissions for twenty-six counties which had already received at least one commission since September 1714. Townshend wrote in the autumn that 'the Commissions of the Peace will . . . be put into such hands as the Government can depend on', although perhaps Townshend's reference to 'commissions' in the plural disguises the fact that he was referring specifically to Lancashire.[3]

At the end of 1715, however, it does seem that the number

[1] Plumb, *The Growth of Political Stability*, p. 165; *Sir Robert Walpole, The Making of a Statesman*, pp. 213–14.

[2] *Diary of Mary Countess Cowper*, p. 75.

[3] P.R.O., S.P. 44/118: Townshend to Maxwell, 27 Oct. 1715.

of counties where a significant purge of Tory justices had taken place was still very small: a dozen at most. The changes in Peterborough, already remodelled in September 1714, were completed in July 1715 in a commission which contained thirty-eight names, of which two had been added by Harcourt and sixteen by Cowper since the death of the Queen. Cowper was following the recommendations of the Fitzwilliam family. John Fitzwilliam had stigmatized several Peterborough justices as violent Tories put in by the Earl of Exeter during Oxford's ministry; they had no estates in Peterborough (and two of them had no estates anywhere). Accordingly, they were put out.[1] Dorset, where Cowper had already swamped the Tories with inclusions, lost twenty-three living justices, among them Sir William Poole, who had been M.P. for a number of West Country constituencies in Anne's reign, but who did not stand in 1715. Only ten gentlemen added by Harcourt remained on the bench. Among these, admittedly, were the Tory knights of the shire, Thomas Strangeways and George Chafin, but the Whigs dominated the Dorset bench.[2] In Kent, too, the number of gentlemen in the commission who had been included by Harcourt (eighty or more at the time of the election) was whittled down to forty-three in July 1715, while over seventy names, some new, some restorations of those dismissed by Harcourt, had been added since the death of the Queen. The Earls of Dorset and Rockingham advised the purge, describing several of those disgraced as violent Tories, Jacobites, or men of small estates. It was not complete, since not all of Rockingham's suggestions were implemented, and Sir Edward Knatchbull and Percival Hart, the Tory candidates defeated in the 1715 county election, and John Hardres, the Tory M.P. for Canterbury, remained in commission; even so, more than fifty Kent justices had been dropped.[3] Shropshire

[1] P.R.O., C. 234/92, Peterborough: 18 July 1715; Herts. R.O., Cowper (Panshanger) MSS. D/EP F154: list of gentlemen to be in the Peterborough commission, sent by Lord Fitzwilliam; paper signed by John Fitzwilliam, the son of Lord Fitzwilliam and M.P. for Peterborough.

[2] P.R.O., C. 234/10, Dorset: 24 Sept. 1715.

[3] P.R.O., C. 234/18, Kent: 28 July 1715; Herts. R.O., Cowper (Panshanger) MSS. D/EP F153: paper endorsed 'Kent. Received from the E. of Dorset', 27 July 1715; paper headed 'Kent. Justices to be left out' and endorsed 'From E. of Rockingham's hand, July 1715'. There were a little over two hundred names in the Kent commission all told.

had lost thirty-three of Harcourt's fifty-eight inclusions by December 1715, and the survivors — among whom, admittedly, were one or two recognizable Tories like Whitmore Acton and Acton Baldwyn — were swamped by the forty-seven gentlemen brought in since 1714. In Radnorshire, where, admittedly, Harcourt's changes had been minimal, Edward and Thomas Harley were dismissed, and only two justices survived who had been appointed in the years of Tory dominance.[1] At the other end of the scale, large alterations seem to have taken place for Middlesex. The fiats do not survive, but the Earl of Clare had certainly recommended changes that were accepted before the end of 1714, and forty-four were added and sixty-eight dismissed in July 1715.[2] It is, however, worth remembering that the Middlesex list was the longest in the country, and that even sixty-eight put out does not necessarily mean that a comprehensive purge of Tory justices took place.

One interesting but ambiguous case is that of Anglesey, where a fiat for September 1715 embodied a savage campaign of dismissals. It was proposed to drop more than half of the forty or so justices, and not one of the thirteen gentlemen added by Harcourt would have been left in the commission. However the docquet book does not record the sealing of a commission of the peace for Anglesey at this time, and some of those to be dismissed were again ordered to be left out in later fiats.[3] Possibly Cowper did not approve of the violence of the proposals, especially as Viscount Bulkeley, a Jacobite and the leader of the Anglesey Tories, was counter-attacking by complaining of riots at Beaumaris quarter sessions committed by several of the justices who were to have been retained.[4]

These counties, plus those like Sussex in which justices had

[1] P.R.O., C. 234/32, Shropshire: 24 Aug., 26 Dec. 1715; C. 234/90, Radnorshire: 5 Dec. 1715.
[2] Herts. R.O., Cowper (Panshanger) MSS. D/EP F153: Clare to Cowper, 7 Dec. 1714; B.L., Stowe MSS. 228, f. 205: list of persons left out of and put into the commission of the peace for Middlesex, attributed to July 1715 by internal evidence.
[3] P.R.O., C. 234/82, Caernarvonshire: strayed fiat for Anglesey, 17 Feb. 1714/15; C. 234/78, Anglesey: 24 Sept. 1715.
[4] Herts. R.O., Cowper (Panshanger) MSS. D/EP F155: information against several justices in North Wales, 1, 2 Aug. 1715.

been left out in relatively large numbers before the election, were the only ones in which, by the end of 1715, anything in the nature of a severe purge had taken place. Even then, the Sussex *custos* admitted in the summer of 1715 that more justices might have to be left out in the future, which suggests that the policy of keeping some possibly disaffected gentlemen on the bench, as it were on probation, was deliberate.[1] It seems inappropriate, therefore, to describe the alterations of 1714–15 collectively as 'ruthless' or 'comprehensive'. Perhaps the only real example of 'ruthless' changes directed by the central government was that of Lancashire, the one county that was not within the field of Cowper's patronage.[2]

Elsewhere Cowper had continued in 1715 to 'balance' the county benches, by inclusions and by moderate rather than sweeping removals. A good illustration of his methods is provided by the case of Pembrokeshire. In November 1714 Cowper had dismissed eight gentlemen put in by Harcourt and added sixteen to outnumber the nine survivors from the period of Tory supremacy.[3] This was quite a substantial remodelling in a commission containing just over fifty local names altogether, but Sir Arthur Owen, the *custos*, later complained to Cowper about the scandalous practices and unabashed Toryism of some of those left in. He enclosed an annotated list of gentlemen in commission, which was then annotated again, probably by Woollaston, in such a way that the commission for Pembrokeshire sealed in August 1715 can be reconstructed with a reasonable degree of certainty although the fiat for that commission does not survive.[4] It appears that Cowper left out those of low social status whom Owen described as Tories, those who never acted, and those who refused the oaths to King George. However, Sir George

[1] Herts. R.O., Cowper (Panshanger) MSS. D/EP F154: Earl of Hertford to Cowper, 18 Aug. 1715.
[2] See below, pp. 291–4.
[3] P.R.O., C. 234/89, Pembrokeshire: 24 Nov. 1714.
[4] Herts. R.O., Cowper (Panshanger) MSS. D/EP F155: paper headed 'A List of the Justices of the Peace of the County of Pembrock as it was November the 27th 1714'. Owen recommended several men 'well-affected to the present government', signed the list, and dated it 9 August 1715. His animosity to one of those added by Harcourt was such that he advanced two reasons for his dismissal: one, that he did not act, and two, that he was dead.

Barlow, 'The Head of the Tory Party on all Occasions', John Barlow, his brother, 'as violent', William Allen, who 'joyns in all violent measures with the Tories', and Thomas Knowles, 'A Violent man in acting with the Tories in all matters', were left in. Thus, while the Pembrokeshire bench was predominantly Whig by the end of 1715, some Tories remained in commission although Cowper had been informed about their character. Sir George Barlow was a notorious Jacobite who had stood at Pembroke and Haverfordwest in the 1715 election, but he remained a justice of the peace for Pembrokeshire until his death in 1721.

Cowper was thus not prepared to disgrace socially prominent justices of Tory principles, and although he conducted modest purges of the socially inferior squires in a number of counties, he left Tory grandees on the bench. Buckinghamshire, Cheshire, Cornwall, Hampshire, Hertfordshire, Northamptonshire, and several Welsh counties besides Pembrokeshire are all examples of a similar pattern.[1] In Staffordshire, William Inge was belatedly dismissed in December 1715, but Richard Dyott and Henry Vernon remained. Sir John Hynde Cotton was still in the Suffolk commission with Tories such as Clement Currance and Dudley North. Moreover, Waller Bacon and Sir Isaac Rebow, two consistent government supporters in the House of Commons who had been left out by Harcourt in July 1714, were not gratified by restoration to the Suffolk commission. Somerset was another county where socially prominent Tories were not dismissed. Sir Coplestone Warwick Bampfield, Francis Gwyn, John Rolle, the Colstons of Bristol, Thomas Strangeways, Sir William Wyndham, and Francis Popham were still on the Somerset bench at the end of 1715, although Cowper had probably included enough new names to outnumber the Tories. Essex was not significantly purged, although twenty justices of the peace drank the health of their late lord-lieutenant, Bolingbroke, after Easter quarter sessions at Chelmsford in 1715. By the end of the year, all but three of the twenty-seven added early in 1714 were still in commission.[2]

---

[1] For Buckinghamshire, see Verney, *Verney Letters of the Eighteenth Century*, ii. 38.

[2] P.R.O., C.234/34, Staffordshire: 26 Aug., 31 Dec. 1715; C. 234/35, Suffolk:

Cowper thus cannot be said to have established a Whig monopoly over the commissions of the peace by the end of 1715. The reason for this was probably that he recognized the danger of antagonizing the gentry in Parliament. In July 1715 a group of Tories in the House of Commons, led by that Samuel Bracebridge whom Cowper had dismissed in Leicestershire six months earlier, mounted an indirect attack on the Chancellor by drawing attention to the neglect of some disaffected justices in failing to suppress riots at Wolverhampton. Bracebridge converted this unpromising episode into an ironical piece of Tory propaganda. Clearly the justices had been at fault; therefore the lists of justices in all the commissions should be investigated and compared with the lists at the time of the death of Anne.[1] Cowper's friends defeated this proposal, and Cowper avenged himself on Bracebridge by leaving him out of the Warwickshire commission in October.[2] However, Cowper knew that, limited as his changes had been, they were still extensive enough to leave him exposed to Tory malice in the Commons. His memorandum to George I was a lucid explanation of this point. Cowper began by referring to criticisms of his moderation in 'adjusting' the commissions of the peace. Then, after a brief excursion into the recent history of the appointment of justices,[3] he mentioned Harcourt's inclusion of Tories and Jacobites, and continued

. . . accordingly all the Commissions of the Peace being to be renewed on your Majesty's accession to the Crown, I did as much as the hurry of doing such a work all at once . . . would permit, turn out according to the best accounts I could get, great numbers of persons disaffected & otherwise not well qualifyd, & put in all I could have well recommended as to Estate & affection to your Government: and as to those who were of Estate & quality Sufficient in their Country, but wer represented by your Majesty's friends as of suspected inclinations; I thought it for your Majesty's interest not to displace them on bare general Suspicion; unless they who sollicited their Removal would give in writing some particular instance or objection to their Conduct. . . . This I requird not that [it]

12 Mar. 1714/15, 2 Nov. 1715; C. 234/33, Somerset: 22 Dec. 1714, 25 June 1715; C. 234/12, Essex: 2 Oct. 1714, 11 Apr. 1715; Herts. R.O., Cowper (Panshanger) MSS. D/EP F153: certificate signed John Wroth and F. Gardiner, 19 May 1715.

[1] *C.J.* xviii. 227–8.   [2] P.R.O., C. 234/38, Warwickshire: 3 Oct. 1715.
[3] See above, pp. 6–7, 172.

would have been any defence to me in case the contrary party had provd strong enough to call my Conduct in Question; but that at least I might by having recourse to my papers, be able to alledge a reason for my proceeding to any that should come to expostulat with me. . . .

Cowper said that few such written reasons for disgracing justices were forthcoming, and that it was therefore unreasonable to expect him to displace any more than he had done without credible reasons that he could cite in his defence. The gentlemen recommended for dismissal, he wrote, were in most cases 'perfect strangers' to him. It would have been 'partial and unjust' to have gone any further on the basis of 'private whispers', and it would have done more harm than good. However, Cowper said that a revision of the commissions was in hand which was designed to remove those who displayed their disaffection by neglecting to act as justices. He added a postscript which referred to Bracebridge's proposal; this, he said, showed 'That at the same time the Whigs complain the alterations have been too few, the Torys are of opinion that so many have been removd as could not well be justifyd, if they might appear before the House at one view.'[1] Cowper was thus evidently concerned to avoid the mistakes of his predecessor, Sir Nathan Wright. Chancellors were vulnerable. Cowper was not prepared to gratify the more extreme Whigs with draconian purges, without adequate safeguards for himself.

IV

In 1716, after his illness, Cowper sealed a number of commissions which met Whig grievances in about half a dozen counties. The bloated Gloucestershire commission was purged of forty of the more obscure Tory squires. Bedfordshire lost thirteen justices, among them Sir John Chester, Sir George Warburton, Sir George Downing, and William Levinz, and also the Whig lawyer Nicholas Lechmere, temporarily in disgrace with his party for eccentric voting in Parliament following his forced resignation as Solicitor General in December 1715. The M.P.s Richard Goulston and Clement Currance were put out in Essex along with sixteen less noteworthy

[1] Herts. R.O., Cowper (Panshanger) MSS. D/EP F152: Memorandum for George I. It is this postscript that dates the manuscript to mid-July 1715.

figures. Twenty-one gentlemen were dropped in Surrey, among them William Newland, the Tory M.P. for Gatton; Arthur Moore, the former associate of Bolingbroke; John Ward, M.P. for Reigate from 1710 to 1713; and Thomas Scawen, a future knight of the shire. In Anglesey, a slightly more moderate version of the comprehensive purge planned in September 1715 was implemented in March 1716 with the omission of thirteen justices. Eight Cambridgeshire justices, including Sir William Wyndham who had recently been released on bail from the Tower, disappeared from a list of fewer than seventy names. Ten gentlemen were put out for Cornwall, headed by the knight of the shire, Sir William Carew, who like Wyndham had been imprisoned on suspicion during the Jacobite rising the year before.[1] These relatively severe assaults on the Tory gentry were accompanied by dismissals on a less striking scale in almost all of the commissions sealed in the spring and early summer of 1716. Seven or fewer justices, most of them inconspicuous, were dismissed in each of twelve counties.[2]

These alterations in the spring and summer of 1716, which of course incorporated the recruitment of well-affected gentlemen in greater or lesser numbers as well as the removals, reflect the aftermath of the Jacobite rising.[3] Possibly the minor gentry now dismissed had attracted unfavourable notice for their neglect of government orders for the seizure of the arms and horses of Catholics, or for their lack of enthusiasm for the 'Voluntary Associations' promoted in some counties by zealous Whigs on the model of 1696.[4] The disgrace of some justices was of course wholly predictable. It was hardly to be expected, for instance, that Thomas Forster

---

[1] P.R.O., C. 234/13, Gloucestershire: 28 Mar. 1716; C. 234/1, Bedfordshire: 7 Mar. 1715/16; C. 234/12, Essex: 8 Mar. 1715/16; C. 234/36, Surrey: 24 Mar. 1716 (*sic*, but to be understood as 1715/16); C. 234/78, Anglesey: 24 Mar. 1715/16; C. 234/4, Cambridgeshire: 7 Aug. 1716; C. 234/6, Cornwall: 27 June 1716.

[2] Glamorgan, Hampshire, Hertfordshire, Holland, Kent, Kesteven, Lindsey, Norfolk, Northumberland, Somerset (where Sir William Wyndham was one of four disgraced), Westmorland, and Wiltshire.

[3] Although a number of M.P.s were left out at this time, there seems to have been no obvious connection with the debates on the Septennial Bill in April.

[4] P.R.O., S.P. 44/118: Townshend to Dodington and others, 25 Oct. 1715; same to Lord Sondes, 15 Nov. 1715.

should remain a justice of the peace. He was technically entitled to sit on the Northumberland bench while commanding the Jacobite army at Preston, but he lost this distinction in May 1716.[1]

During the period from the summer of 1716 to Cowper's resignation in April 1718, the great majority of the commissions of the peace were of a routine character. New names were added, sometimes in quite large numbers, but it was unusual for living justices to be removed. When they were, the reason was often simply misdemeanour. For example, John Dineley *alias* Goodeve was left out for Worcestershire after Cowper learned of his brutality and inexpertise as a magistrate, and of his undignified tendency towards what would nowadays be called indecent exposure.[2] Only two counties received commissions which left justices out in significant numbers. The eighteen Essex gentlemen purged in March 1716 were followed into retirement in November by seven more, among them Anthony Bramston of Skreens, whose son Thomas was M.P. for Maldon. In March 1717 twenty-one justices were omitted from the Oxfordshire commission; eighteen of these had been added by Harcourt. Elsewhere, Charles Caesar was displaced for Huntingdonshire, and Robert Leeves was put out for Sussex in the week following the loss of his seat in the Commons.[3] On the whole, however, the commissions sealed in 1717 and early 1718 were remarkable only for the absence of severe regulation.

The changes in central politics in 1717 were not reflected in local government at all. Townshend was dismissed from the ministry in April, and he was followed out of office by Walpole, the Duke of Devonshire, George Dodington, and a group of M.P.s who thereafter embarrassed the ministers by voting with the Tories against the government. From November 1717 this group of Opposition Whigs was associated with the Prince of Wales, who had quarrelled with the

[1] P.R.O., C. 234/28, Northumberland: 16 May 1716.
[2] Herts. R.O., Cowper (Panshanger) MSS. D/EP F154: informations of Edward Corner, 5 Oct. 1716, and Samuel Jackson, 26 Oct. 1716; P.R.O., C. 234/41, Worcestershire: 12 Dec. 1716.
[3] P.R.O., C. 234/12, Essex: 19 Nov. 1716; C. 234/30, Oxfordshire: 8 Mar. 1716/17; C. 234/17, Huntingdonshire: 2 Mar. 1716/17; C. 234/37, Sussex: 18 Apr. 1717.

King.[1] However, Townshend retained the lord-lieutenancy of Norfolk; Dodington, that of Somerset; and Devonshire, that of Derbyshire. It is possible that some of the recalcitrant M.P.s lost their standing as Privy Councillors in all the commissions of the peace and were not reinstated in their native counties, but this is unlikely since none of them seem to have complained. One plausible reason for Cowper's relative inactivity in 1717 as far as the commissions of the peace were concerned was that Woollaston, his Secretary, had made frivolous and untrue accusations against certain Middlesex justices, who had refused to lend him money, to secure their dismissal from the bench. Cowper sacked him and appointed John Hughes, the poet. There was a marked lapse in the frequency with which commissions were sealed in the autumn of 1717 during these upheavals in the Chancellor's secretariat.[2]

Cowper had contemplated resignation during his illness in early 1716, and in fact his health was poor until his death in 1723. The real reason for his resignation in April 1718, however, was probably the tension in the ministry, since Cowper was also a confidant of the Prince of Wales. When out of office, he provided a focus for opposition in the House of Lords, reconciled himself to the retired Earl of Oxford, and found himself almost in the position of an unofficial crypto-Jacobite leader. At the end of their lives, therefore, Cowper and Harcourt had exchanged their political roles more or less completely.[3]

v

The career of Cowper's successor, Thomas Parker, Lord Chief Justice since 1710, Lord Parker from 1716, and subsequently Earl of Macclesfield, was overshadowed by his dismissal in 1725 for conniving at fraudulent irregularities practised by

[1] Sedgwick, *The House of Commons, 1715–1754*, i. 26, 82; Foord, *His Majesty's Opposition*, pp. 61-2; Plumb, *Sir Robert Walpole, The Making of a Statesman*, pp. 241 ff.; Hill, *The Growth of Parliamentary Parties 1689–1742*, pp. 164 ff.

[2] Herts. R.O., Cowper (Panshanger) MSS. D/EP F157: Ashurst to [Cowper], 23 Oct. 1717; Woollaston to Cowper, no date, defending himself.

[3] Campbell, *Lives of the Chancellors*, iv. 380–91; Foord, *His Majesty's Opposition*, pp. 61, 64, 74; Bennett, *The Tory Crisis in Church and State, 1688–1730*, pp. 231–2; Hill, *The Growth of Parliamentary Parties 1689–1742*, p. 181.

the Masters in Chancery. He was impeached, found guilty, and briefly imprisoned in the Tower, living thereafter in retirement until his death in 1732. Notwithstanding this disgrace, his forensic skills were considerable, and he was a distinguished judge.[1] Among other improvements in the administrative work of Chancery, he initiated the practice of adding names to the commissions of the peace without the need for the lengthy preparation of a new commission, and he revived the process of disgracing justices guilty of misdemeanour by writs of *supersedeas*.[2] On his appointment in May 1718, he was a firm supporter of the Stanhope–Sunderland ministry, and he retained his connections with these ministers after the reconciliation of the Opposition Whigs in 1720, later acting with Carteret rather than with Walpole after Stanhope and Sunderland had died.[3]

Parker had held the great seal for two months before he ordered a *liber pacis* for his own use.[4] He sealed six commissions of the peace in the summer of 1718, in one of which, for Buckinghamshire, eleven gentlemen were left out, among them seven put in by Harcourt. Some justices were also left out for Oxfordshire, although the fiat is missing.[5] Parker sealed no commissions of the peace at all in the autumn of 1718, possibly because of the indisposition of John Hughes, whom he had inherited from Cowper.[6] Parker may have conceived his role in the ministry to be to improve on the somewhat languid performance of Cowper in exercising the patronage of the great seal.[7] If so, he started slowly.

However, in the winter of 1718/19, a number of commis-

---

[1] Holmes, *The Trial of Doctor Sacheverell*, pp. 149–50; Campbell, *Lives of the Chancellors*, iv. 522 (misprinted 552)–560.

[2] See above, pp. 19–20.

[3] C. B. Realey, *The Early Opposition to Sir Robert Walpole, 1720–1727* (Kansas, 1931), pp. 98, 137–9; J. M. Beattie, *The English Court in the Reign of George I* (Cambridge, 1967), p. 150.

[4] P.R.O., C. 231/9, p. 454: *c.* 23 July 1718.

[5] P.R.O., C. 234/3, Buckinghamshire: 15 July 1718; H.M.C., *Portland MSS.* vii. 239. The rumour there reported that clergymen were being displaced 'all over England' was without foundation.

[6] Bodl. MS. Montagu d. 13, ff. 295–6: Hughes to Cowper, 25 Oct. 1718; *Letters by several eminent persons deceased*, i. 141; iii. 65–6.

[7] H.M.C., *Portland MSS.* v. 559; for a suggestion that Parker was hostile to Cowper, see E. Hughes, 'Some Clavering Correspondence', *Archaeologia Aeliana*, 4th Ser. xxxiv (1956), 25.

sions making substantial changes were sealed. The most serious purge was in Kent, where thirty-one justices were put out, headed by Sir Edward Knatchbull, the parliamentary diarist, who was a moderate Tory, Sir Thomas Twisden, whose Toryism was rather more extreme, Archdeacon Sprat of Rochester, and several more justices appointed by Harcourt. Parker added twenty-four new names, so by 1719 the survivors of the gentlemen included by Harcourt were heavily outweighed on the Kent bench. Also, fourteen justices were dismissed in Surrey.[1] Justices were left out in small numbers for Bedfordshire, Berkshire, Cambridgeshire, Holland, Kesteven, Lindsey, Staffordshire, and Wiltshire. In the spring and summer of 1719 several more counties received commissions of the peace which left a few living justices out. Parker was not afraid to disgrace some prominent and influential Tories. Edward Harley, Thomas Foley, and Walwyn Shepherd were dismissed in Herefordshire with four more who 'never acted'. Samuel Robinson, who had been put out of the Hertfordshire commission in 1709 and restored by Harcourt in 1710, and who as M.P. for Cricklade had been a 'member' of the October Club in the last years of the Queen's reign, was left out again for Hertfordshire. Clement Currance was dropped for Suffolk with his brother-in-law Robert Davers.[2] Two Tory justices of the peace in Somerset, Sir John Smith and John Codrington, the M.P. for Bath, had discouraged zeal against sedition; they were dismissed by order of the Lords Justices who were responsible for domestic government while the King was in Hanover, and they were subsequently convicted at Taunton assizes for abusing their powers as magistrates in a factious spirit.[3] Also put out in this commission was another Tory, Giles Strangeways, represented to the government by John Speke of Whitelackington as inactive and disaffected to the government.[4]

[1] P.R.O., C. 234/18, Kent: 10 Jan. 1718/19; C. 234/36, Surrey: 21 Mar. 1719 (*sic*, but to be understood as 1718/19).

[2] P.R.O., C. 234/15, Herefordshire: 6 May 1719; C. 234/16, Hertfordshire: 29 June 1719; C. 234/35, Suffolk: 3 July 1719.

[3] P.R.O., C. 234/33, Somerset: 17 Sept. 1719; S.P. 44/279: Lords Justices' minutes, 30 July 1719; S.P. 44/278, p. 18: Delafaye to Parker, 1 Aug. 1719; S.P. 35/21 f. 43: Adderley to Delafaye, 7 Apr. 1720; Oldmixon, *History of England*, p. 669.

[4] P.R.O., S.P. 35/12: John Speke to Stanhope, 10 May 1718.

These exertions in 1719 probably reflect the ministers' uneasiness at Jacobite activity abroad, which culminated in an abortive invasion in March and April. Parker's manipulation of the commissions thereafter became more moderate. The reasons for dismissals are noted in the fiats with increasing frequency and few of these are exceptionable. 'At his own request' is common, one East Riding justice was 'infirm', and some justices in Berkshire had left the county. Henry Whitehead was left out in Hampshire for conniving at smuggling.[1] One commission of the peace, that for Radnorshire, did, however, prove difficult to settle. The trouble had started in May 1719, when Parker had signed a fiat which embodied some suggestions made by the lord-lieutenant, the Earl of Coningsby, who desired, among other changes, the omission of the father of Thomas Lewis, M.P. for Radnor — Thomas Lewis senior, of Harpton. Thomas Lewis junior was a steady government supporter by 1719, and Parker sensibly revised his fiat by revoking the order to leave the father out, although he ignored some of Lewis's other recommendations of 'Whigs who would be answered for'.[2] The following year, Coningsby proposed the omission of both Lewises and of several more of his enemies in Radnorshire local politics. This time, after the matter had been discussed by the Lords Justices, Parker accepted the recommendations of Lewis and ignored those of Coningsby.[3] Coningsby retaliated with a stream of paranoid letters directed against the Chancellor. In 1721 he lost the lieutenancy and found himself in the Tower, his sanity in some question.[4] These difficulties in Radnorshire were unusual, however. Otherwise, the routine commissions sealed in 1720 suggested that the

[1] P.R.O., S.P. 44/280: Lords Justices' minutes, 15 Oct. 1719: C. 234/14, Hampshire: 29 Feb. 1719/20.

[2] P.R.O., C. 234/90, Radnorshire: 6 May 1719, re-dated to 27 July 1719; S.P. 35/17, ff. 93-8: paper book endorsed 'Mr Lewis. Radnor', 16 July 1719.

[3] P.R.O., S.P. 44/283, pp. 9 ff.: Lords Justices' minutes, 23 June, 14 July, 19 July 1720; S.P. 44/285, pp. 15-16: Delafaye to Lewis, 24 June 1720; S.P. 35/22, ff. 64-5: Lewis to Delafaye, 19 July 1720; ff. 133-47, Coningsby to Lords Justices, 3 Aug. 1720, with copies of several earlier letters; C. 234/90, Radnorshire: 22 Aug. 1720.

[4] P.R.O., S.P. 35/23, f. 466: Coningsby to Parker, 29 Nov. 1720 (copy); S.P. 35/24, f. 7, same to Delafaye, 3 Dec. 1720; ff. 52-5: same to [Stanhope?], 9 Dec. 1720; ff. 158-63: same to [same?], 31 Dec. 1720; Sedgwick, *The House of Commons, 1715-1754*, i. 570-1.

transitional period of the Hanoverian Succession was over, and that the county magistracy was settling into a stable form.

VI

The case that the Whigs ruthlessly eliminated the Tories from the county magistracy after the Hanoverian Succession to establish a cast-iron monopoly of local power clearly cannot be taken to an extreme. Sir John Hynde Cotton survived as a Cambridgeshire justice of the peace until 1726.[1] The Duke of Somerset successfully protected the status as a Sussex magistrate of the Jacobite Sir Harry Goring.[2] Sir Thomas Cave, Tory knight of the shire for Leicestershire, grumbled in 1715 that, having been cashiered from the militia, he was only a 'Puny Justice of Quorum' — which he remained until he died.[3] Later, Sir William Wyndham recovered in 1727 the place on the Somerset bench which he had lost in 1716.[4] The fortunes of these prominent Tories help to illustrate the fact that some gentlemen of identifiably similar principles remained in the commissions of the peace in the majority of counties. Moreover, in a few not insignificant counties, notably Derbyshire (Parker's home ground) and Monmouthshire, there was very little alteration in the magistracy between the death of Queen Anne and the early 1720s.[5] Finally, it is plausible that a number of rank and file Tory families were discreetly following the example of the Foxes, Legges, Winningtons, Harcourts, and others by transforming themselves into Whigs,[6] and it would have been absurd to have discouraged this process.

The view that the Tories were gratified with local power to compensate them for proscription in central politics is, similarly, less than satisfactory though not wholly wrong.[7]

---

[1] Cotton was restored on taking office in the 'Broad Bottom' coalition of 1744. P.R.O., C. 234/4, Cambridgeshire: 26 July 1726, 28 Oct. 1745.

[2] B.L., Add. MSS. 32686, f. 53: Newcastle to an unknown correspondent, 29 Sept. 1719.

[3] Verney, *Verney Letters of the Eighteenth Century*, i. 341.

[4] P.R.O., C. 234/33, Somerset: 11 Nov. 1727.

[5] P.R.O., C. 234/8, Derbyshire: 31 Dec. 1714, 30 June 1720; C. 234/87, Monmouthshire: 4 Nov. 1714, 22 July 1720.

[6] Hill, *The Growth of Parliamentary Parties 1689–1742*, pp. 159–60.

[7] G. M. Trevelyan advanced this argument on the grounds that the fictional Squire Western was a justice of the peace. *England under Queen Anne*, iii. 319.

A great many Tory justices were put out, although the
timing of the purges should include the spring of 1716 and
the spring and summer of 1719 as well as 1715. The cumu-
lative effect of a series of commissions in counties such as
Kent or Essex was to eliminate a high proportion of the
squires added between 1710 and 1714 and to outnumber
with reliable men the few who remained. In the 1720s and
1730s, the Tories were aware of a grievance at being excluded
from the bench. The renewed proposal to raise the property
qualification for justices, which eventually bore fruit in 1732,
implied Tory resentment at a Whig usurpation of local power.
The Tories were anxious to be reinstated on the county
benches when some of their leaders were taken into the
ministry in 1744, and when, in 1747, the Prince of Wales
made advances to the Tories, one of the baits he offered was
a bill empowering all who paid the land tax for £300 a year
to act *ipso facto* as justices of the peace.[1]

One county of obvious interest in the early Hanoverian
period has so far been mentioned only in passing: namely
Norfolk, the home of the allegedly intransigent Whig zealots.
The reconstruction of the Norfolk commission after 1714, so
far from demonstrating an uncompromising 'party' approach,
actually provides a good case study of Cowper's ideal, a
'balanced' commission from which Whig dominance might
gradually emerge. By the end of 1715, sixteen of Harcourt's
forty-nine inclusions had been dismissed or had died, leaving
thirty-three on the bench. Cowper had added thirty-nine
names, of which eight were restorations of gentlemen left
out by his predecessor. There followed a further mild purge
in March 1716, when Walpole's enemy Richard Ferrier was
disgraced with Sir Robert Kemp and four more. Henry
Heron, the Tory M.P. for Boston, also lost his place in 1720.
The Tories still in commission were by now outnumbered
quite heavily — fifty-seven appointments had been made
altogether between 1714 and 1720 — but George England, a
debt-ridden Tory M.P. who sat for Great Yarmouth, and Sir
John Wodehouse, a crypto-Jacobite, with one or two more
of similar type, remained justices in Norfolk. The Norfolk

[1] Sedgwick, *The House of Commons, 1715–1754*, ii. 431; J. B. Owen, *The
Rise of the Pelhams* (London, 1957), pp. 260–4, 313.

bench had certainly been remodelled, but there had not been a comprehensive revision occurring all at once.[1]

Norfolk, in short, illustrates what was a common pattern. Cowper, and also Parker (perhaps with less conviction), followed the principle that Whigs should enjoy a preponderance, but not a monopoly, of local power at quarter sessions. This was both more practicable and more judicious than the alternative, a vigorous exercise of the power of patronage in the interests of party. The relatively moderate approach of Cowper and his successors was acceptable to George I, and also to George II.[2] The cautious memorandum of July 1715 was thus the theoretical foundation on which the majority of the English and Welsh commissions of the peace were constructed after the Hanoverian Succession.

[1] P.R.O., C. 234/26, Norfolk: 2 Oct. 1714, 9 Apr. 1715, 12 Mar. 1715/16, 18 Feb. 1716/17, 27 July 1720, 25 June 1722; Herts. R.O., Cowper (Panshanger) MSS. D/EP F154: paper endorsed 'Norfolk from Lord Townshend and Sir Charles Turner', recommending the not especially remarkable changes implemented in April 1715. For Ferrier, see Plumb, *Sir Robert Walpole, The Making of a Statesman*, pp. 210-12.

[2] Lord King, *Notes of Domestic and Foreign Affairs during the last years of the Reign of George I and the early part of the Reign of George II*, appended to, and paginated separately from, his *Life of Locke* (London, 1830), ii. 48-50.

9

THE COMMISSION OF THE PEACE IN
POLITICS, 1675-1720

I

The names of the gentlemen in the commissions of the peace for most or all of the English and Welsh counties were re-shuffled in an organized and, roughly speaking, simultaneous regulation on twelve occasions between 1675 and 1720: in 1680, 1681, 1687, 1688, 1689, 1696-8, 1700, 1702, 1704, 1705-6, 1710-11, and 1714-15. On two of these occasions, in 1702 and 1714-15, the government was taking advantage of its obligation to renew the commissions on the demise of the Crown to introduce some changes which reflected a different political situation in the new reign. In 1689, also, a revolutionary regime was reversing the alterations made by the government it had overthrown in an analagous situation. The magistracy was also revised, less comprehensively but still on a relatively large scale, in 1694, 1698-9, 1701, early in 1714, 1716, and 1719. Of course, at any time the commission of the peace for a single county was liable to be remodelled, usually in response to local pressures. Norfolk in 1676 at the beginning of the period under examination, and Radnorshire in 1720 at the end of it, are examples of such cases.

Of the twelve comprehensive or near comprehensive regulations, six were markedly more successful in political terms than the others. Those of 1680 and 1681 were conducted by the same government for similar purposes. In 1680 the ministers prepared to meet the second Exclusion Parliament by changes designed to consolidate the King's loyal friends into a party confident enough to meet the challenge of Shaftesbury's Whigs. In 1681 they followed up their success in central politics by demonstrating the reward of loyalty and the penalty of faction to adherents and opponents in the countryside. These operations contributed substantially to the quiet succession of a Roman Catholic to the throne, and to the election of what looked like a loyal Parliament, in 1685. At the beginning of Anne's reign, the Tories, secure in the Queen's favour, conducted a regulation which helped to produce a majority in the 1702 Parliament. In what was perhaps an unexpectedly restrained remodelling in 1705-6, the Whigs nevertheless conducted a discreet revision of the magistracy in their interests. In 1710-11 the Tories celebrated their return to favour at Court and their success in the election of 1710 by alterations designed to establish a preponderance of Tory justices of the peace. In 1714-15 these changes were subtly reversed, and the commissions were manipulated in such a way as to leave no doubt that local patronage was controlled by the Whigs, although considered as a purge this regulation was rather less ruthless than has generally been supposed.

Three of the regulations were relatively neutral operations. That of 1689 was designed to restart the machinery of local government after it had ground almost to a standstill in the winter of 1688/9. It did not reflect any uniform party bias, not necessarily because the first ministry of William III's reign had any special commitments to non-party principles, but because, in the confusion of the period immediately after the Revolution, the central government was obliged to abdicate its over-all supervision of the personnel of local government to the magnates entrusted with the great county offices. The revision of 1700 was conducted by a conscientious Privy Council anxious to investigate and remedy complaints that the magistracy was not in a satisfactory condition. The Council recommended the appointment of large numbers of new justices in an apparently deliberate desire to establish a 'broad bottomed' bench. In response to similar complaints in 1704 the well-intentioned but possibly bewildered Wright renewed the commissions of the peace for every county in a regulation of which the underlying purpose was probably as obscure to contemporaries as it is today.

Two of the regulations were complete failures. In 1687 Jeffreys, acting on instructions from the Privy Council, implemented the King's desire that Roman Catholic gentlemen who were suitably qualified by ancestry and estates should share with Protestants the honour and responsibility of acting as justices of the peace. In 1688, in purges of remarkable vigour, the Protestant squires were dismissed and the Catholics were joined on the bench by other persons alleged to be unqualified because of their dissenting views on religion, their shady political past, or their inferior estates and birth. The result of two such political revolutions in the localities in two consecutive years was a counter-revolution, in which the majority of the disgraced squires demonstrated their resentment at indiscriminate interference with their local status by their acquiescence in the substitution of King William for King James.

The last of the twelve regulations, that of 1696–8, was also a failure, though it was less disastrous in its consequences. Neither the changes ordered by the Privy Council following the Association movement nor the alterations ordered on his own initiative by Somers at about the same time qualify as a regulation that was comprehensive, in the sense that not all the English and Welsh counties were covered. None the less, the two operations taken together add up to an extensive, politically motivated revision, designed to give the Whig ministry established in 1693–4 a solid base of support in the countryside by eliminating from the magistracy those whose opposition could be interpreted as treason. However, the implementation of the alterations was clumsily conducted, and the changes that did take place seem to have done little to assist the Whigs in the election which followed in 1698.

The 1696–8 regulation illustrates a number of qualifications to the view that the commission of the peace was an instrument of patronage which the ministry of the day could easily turn to profitable account. Some persons in high places disapproved of making the commission of the peace into a weapon of party advantage. William III himself, and also probably Godolphin, took this view in the mid-1690s. Later, Robert Harley in 1710–13 and Lord Chancellor Cowper himself in 1714–15 resisted demands for excessive change made by zealous colleagues. Also, the Chancellor was always obliged to depend on advice from the counties. It was difficult for him at any time to discover which gentlemen to retain and which to leave out, and this was never more true than in 1696–8, when Somers was required by the Privy

Council to rely on tardy *custodes rotulorum*. Finally, the process by which commissions were written and sealed was complex, and Somers discovered between 1696 and 1698 that he could not work the machinery smoothly. The Clerk of the Crown was disgruntled because he was not receiving all his fees, and his office experienced some difficulty in remembering what changes were to be made.

The successful regulations were those which complemented, or contributed to, a redirection of ministerial politics at the centre. This suggests that the power to appoint and dismiss justices of the peace was most valuable to politicians as part of a 'spoils' system. A ministry which enjoyed the favour of the Crown and a majority in Parliament might enhance its position in the localities by using the patronage of the great seal to gratify already euphoric friends and to discourage already disconsolate opponents. But ministries past their heyday, or struggling against difficulties, like the Junto Whigs in 1698-9, the Tories in 1704, and the Whigs in 1708-9, discovered that control of the commissions of the peace could not be employed to turn weakness into strength. Even for ministries enjoying success at the centre, extensive remodelling was dangerous. Purges that were too severe were counterproductive because they created a group of discontented men united in their resentment at a common disgrace. Inclusions on too large a scale led to suggestions that the newcomers were men of mean estates, low social position, or moral or intellectual inferiority. Such claims were a regular tactic of opposition, and they could usually be relied upon to arouse the indignation of the country squires in the House of Commons. Nottingham, Somers, Wright, and Cowper were all subjected to sharp criticism for their handling of appointments to the county magistracy. Harcourt seems to have evaded specific attack, but the promotion of a bill for the qualification of justices in 1711 may well have been accompanied by complaints about the extensive changes he had made, and the Regents initiated an investigation into his purges in August 1714. Jeffreys seems to be a curious exception to the rule that Chancellors tended to be called to account for their manipulation of the patronage of the great seal, but there can be little doubt that, had Parliament sat in 1687 and 1688, it would have scrutinized the enormous upheaval of local government in those years. In any case, Jeffreys was bitterly hated for other reasons by December 1688, when, disguised as a coal-heaver, he had to be rescued from a hostile mob in Wapping, and after the Revolution his alterations in the commissions of the peace seemed among the least noteworthy of his crimes.

The connection between changes in the commissions and success in elections is difficult to measure. There were sixteen general elections within the period from 1675 to 1720. Recent manipulation of the commission of the peace contributed discernibly to the over-all success of the ministry only in those of 1685, 1702, and 1713. Even then, the precise nature of this contribution is obscure. To dismiss a rival candidate or his friends from the magistracy was to give him an opportunity to pose as a victim of Court malice. A place in the county commission of the peace was possibly a somewhat irrelevant reward for supporters in borough elections. It would have been absurd to have attempted to win county seats, with their large electorates, by distributing places on the bench to even a small proportion of the forty-shilling freeholders. The advantage conferred by the supervision of the commissions of the peace was of an indeterminate kind. The arrival of a new, revised commission might produce a vague impression in the minds of uncommitted voters that a particular group of men possessed the kind of influence that controlled admission to the world of county authority. Admittedly, judicious regulation of a county bench for a specific electoral purpose might, in some circumstances, produce the right result. Charles Cox seems to have had a clear grasp of the possibilities of the exercise when he secured the dismissal of John Lade for Surrey just before his own election for Southwark in 1708. Examples such as this are infrequent, however, and such manœuvres might rebound on those that employed them, as Sir Christopher Musgrave discovered in 1701 when he found himself at the bottom of the poll in Westmorland after ejecting opponents from the list of justices for that county. It was usually more profitable to include newly elected M.P.s in the commissions for their counties. For instance, a man like Josiah Diston at Devizes might well have found a place on the Wiltshire bench a useful extension of his local power. On the other hand, Sir Brian Stapylton does not seem to have been overcome with gratitude towards the Whigs for making him a West Riding magistrate as a newly elected M.P. in 1698, since he remained a firm Tory to the end of Queen Anne's reign.[1] The power to appoint and dismiss justices of the peace did count for something in electoral politics, therefore, but it was a weapon to be used with judgement and caution.

II

A point that is in danger of being overlooked in any description of the value of the commission of the peace in central politics, is that the magistracy in each county was an organic body, in spite of variations in membership and size. Except possibly for the brief period of violent remodelling in 1688, the bench of justices reflected the county community in a continuous existence. This consideration raises the problem of whether the changes in the lists of those empowered to serve involved the active or the inactive magistracy. The evidence provided by one case study, for Wiltshire, indicates that local administration may have been less affected by the alterations in the commissions than the scale of those alterations might suggest. In 1712 Wiltshire had received a commission which added sixty-three names and left out sixteen.[2] Of the sixteen disgraced justices, nine had attended quarter sessions or had been active out of sessions or both, so the regulation was reasonably effective in so far as it was a purge.[3] However, if it was intended to swamp the Wiltshire bench with new justices, the results were disappointing. Fifty-one out of the sixty-three included never acted as Wiltshire justices. If the names of those attending quarter sessions in the year of hypothetical 'Whig predominance' from April 1709 to January 1710 are compared with the names of those attending during the year of hypothetical 'Tory predominance' from April 1713 to January 1714, it appears that at least two-thirds of those who had attended in 1709–10 were

[1] See above, pp. 184–5, 149, 181, 128.   [2] See above, p. 215.
[3] The information about the activity of Wiltshire justices is taken from Wilts. R.O., Q.S. Great Rolls; Minute Book; Order Book.

still in commission in 1713-14, and that at all but one of the four towns at which quarter sessions were held in Wiltshire, at least 40 per cent of the magistrates who had attended in 1709-10 chose to attend again in 1713-14.[1]

After the Hanoverian Succession, the new commission for Wiltshire, sealed in December 1714, added twenty-eight justices and dismissed eighteen.[2] Again, the impact of this remodelling on local affairs was less than dramatic. A nucleus of active justices survived from the period from April 1713 to January 1714 to the corresponding period of April 1716 to January 1717, although the Whigs might have been expected to have reasserted themselves. For instance, out of the thirteen gentlemen on the bench at Salisbury in January 1717, seven had attended in January 1714; and of the four who had attended in 1714 but did not reappear in 1717, two were still in commission and could presumably have attended if they had chosen to do so, while a third had died.[3]

It thus seems that there was in Wiltshire no block transference of local power from Whigs to Tories in 1712, or from Tories back to Whigs after the Hanoverian Succession, in spite of striking alterations in the commission of the peace. In Wiltshire, and perhaps in other counties as well, it is arguable that the active magistrates were a minority who bore the burden of county government regardless of the changes made in the list of their nominal but inactive colleagues. The livelihood of a justice of the peace did not depend on his place. Many found the duties of magistracy tedious, and chose not to act. Admittedly, even the inactive justice normally regarded his place on the bench as a valued concomitant of his social position, and he would resent the implied disgrace of losing it. Even so, it might be the case that the importance of the changes in the commissions of the peace can be overestimated in the context of local administration. Perhaps the regulations of the lists of county justices, especially those

[1] The exception was Marlborough, where Michaelmas sessions were usually held. In 1709 nine justices attended, of whom six were still in commission in 1713 and one more had died; but only two of the six were present in 1713 out of a total attendance of seven.

[2] See above, pp. 242-3.

[3] The fourth was Robert Loggan, Chancellor of Salisbury, who had been included by Harcourt in 1712 and dismissed by Cowper in 1714.

that took place late in the period, were to some extent notional operations, without much relevance to the real exercise of local power in the countryside.

III

Notwithstanding this reservation, there can be little doubt that the manipulation of the county commissions of the peace was a factor in politics during the period from the Exclusion Crisis to the Hanoverian Succession. The alterations in the lists of justices of the peace played a significant part in conditioning the gentry to accept the Revolution of 1688. In somewhat less spectacular fashion, the judicious revision of the county magistracy was an element in the temporary re-establishment of the stability of the Stuart monarchy in the early 1680s, in the suppression of disaffection to the regime of William III, and in the consolidation at the local level of the success at the centre of the Tories in 1702 and 1710 and of the Whigs in 1705–6 and 1714–15. When Cowper modestly admitted in his memorandum for George I that, on his resignation in 1710, the commissions of the peace had been 'in a very good state with a sufficient balance in favour of the honest interest', it was apparent that even this avowedly moderate Lord Chancellor was unable to contemplate the county magistracy without thinking simultaneously of the nationwide politics of party.

10

POSTSCRIPT – THE SPECIAL CASE OF LANCASHIRE

I

The commission of the peace for Lancashire was the responsibility of the Chancellor of the Duchy of Lancaster, who signed his own fiats and sealed the parchments with his own seal, quite independently of the commissions issued for other counties by the Lord Chancellor. The sequence of fiats for Lancashire does not begin until 1727,[1] but the names of the Lancashire justices of the peace are contained in the original commissions preserved in the Lancashire Record Office. Apart from two breaks, from August 1679 to September 1682 and again in the first six months of 1689 when the first post-Revolution commission is missing, the series appears to be complete for the years from 1675 to 1720.[2] Lancashire also possesses full quarter sessions records, and, in the Kenyon collections, a voluminous body of papers relating to the office of the clerk of the peace.[3] The materials for the study of the Lancashire magistracy are therefore unusually extensive.

The Chancellorship of the Duchy had generally been held in Elizabeth's reign by a politician who was expected to manipulate the electoral influence attached to the office in the interests of the Court, and to represent the Court himself in the House of Commons.[4] This tradition was continued after the Restoration with the appointments of Sir Thomas Ingram, M.P. for Thirsk, in 1664; Sir Robert Carr, M.P. successively for Lincolnshire and Preston, in 1672; and Sir Thomas Chicheley, who had a safe seat at Cambridge, in

[1] P.R.O., Duchy of Lancaster Papers, D.L. 20/9.
[2] Lancs. R.O., QSC 77–166. Two more commissions outside this sequence are at P.R.O., County Palatine of Lancaster Papers, P.L. 28/38: 24 Mar. 1679; and Lancs. R.O., Kenyon MSS. DDKe 2/12(7): 7 Mar. 1715.
[3] Lancs. R.O., Kenyon MSS. DDKe; and H.M.C., Fourteenth Report, Appendix IV, *Kenyon MSS.*
[4] J. E. Neale, *The Elizabethan House of Commons* (London, 1949), pp. 221-32.

1682. Chicheley was dismissed in March 1687, and for a time it seemed that James II was resolved to abolish the Duchy and County Palatine altogether, though he relented with the appointment of Robert Phelipps as Chancellor in May.[1] In response to a similar proposal to extinguish the Duchy in the 1690s, a Duchy official argued that its existence enabled the king to reward and enrich deserving subjects and that the Chancellorship was held as a 'recompense or bounty'.[2] In short, the Duchy was a source of royal patronage too valuable lightly to be sacrificed. This observation reflected a change in the character of the office after the Revolution. The Chancellor of the Duchy tended to be, not a Court party politician in the Commons, but a peer concerned more with the profits of the place. Lord Willoughby d'Eresby, the eldest son of a peer, was M.P. for Boston when he was appointed in 1689, but he was called to the Lords in his own right early in 1690. He was succeeded in 1697 by the Earl of Stamford, an ally of the Junto Whigs. Sir John Leveson Gower, M.P. for Newcastle-under-Lyme, replaced Stamford shortly after Queen Anne's accession, but he became Lord Gower in 1703. In 1706 Gower was replaced in turn by the Earl of Derby, an appointment which aroused some alarm. Whereas earlier Chancellors of the Duchy had little or no connection with Lancashire, the Earls of Derby were by far the most prominent and influential landowners in the county. Derby was also lord-lieutenant and *custos rotulorum*, and his predecessor Stamford was alert to the danger of uniting all civil and military power in his hands.[3] Stamford's protests had little effect and Derby remained Chancellor until 1710 when, in the ministerial reshuffle of the early autumn, Lord Berkeley of Stratton was appointed. After the Hanoverian Succession, the Earl of Aylesford, a Hanoverian Tory, held the office for eighteen months, but the Earl of Scarborough took over in

[1] *Cal. Treas. Books*, viii. 626, 863, 1236; P.R.O., D.L. 13/40: draft patent for putting the Duchy into commission, 14 Mar. 1687.

[2] P.R.O., D.L. 41/19/10: 'Reasons against the Bill for takeing away the Dutchy and County Pallatine of Lancaster', no date, ascribed by Sir Robert Somerville in a manuscript note to Benjamin Ayloffe.

[3] Herts. R.O., Cowper (Panshanger) MSS. D/EP F149: paper endorsed 'Lord Stamford's Memorial of the Chancellor of the Duchy & L.L. of Lancaster being inconsistant', no date.

1716. Only in 1717 was there a reversion to the earlier practice of allowing a commoner to hold the Chancellorship for
any length of time with the choice of Nicholas Lechmere,
who became Attorney General as well in 1718 and was
promoted to the peerage only in 1721.

The commissions of the peace for Lancashire were similar
in most important respects to those for other counties. The
Privy Councillors were not named as *ex officio* justices until
1687, but thereafter they appeared at the head of the list as
was usual elsewhere. Some County Palatine and Duchy
officials were normally included although they rarely if ever
acted as justices. As was the case in other counties, the
number of local names increased in the late seventeenth and
early eighteenth centuries. There were 71 justices in 1675,
of whom 48 were in the quorum, and 117 in the last commission before Queen Anne's death in 1714, although there was
then a temporary shrinkage to 95 justices in 1720 of whom
91 were in the quorum. In one respect, however, the Lancashire commission was different from those for other counties;
the frequency with which commissions were sealed did not
decline after 1689. Lancashire regularly received two commissions a year in George I's reign, although it was becoming
common for other counties to have to wait for twelve
months or longer for a renewal of their commissions.

II

The Lancashire magistracy was fairly stable in the mid-1670s.
Sir Robert Carr made few changes in the Lancashire commission of the peace beyond the routine removal of dead justices
and the admission of new men of appropriate status. Very
occasionally, a trouble-maker might be dismissed. For
example, Alexander Nowell, a notorious persecutor of Dissenters, was left out for a few months during the period when
Charles II's Declaration of Indulgence was in force.[1] Such
cases were rare, and Carr seems to have ignored complaints,
like those levelled against John Hartley of Strangeways in
1674, that justices were contentious and corrupt.[2]

[1] Lancs. R.O., QSC 74-5: 11 Oct. 1672, 12 Mar. 1673; *Note-Book of the Rev.
Thomas Jolly*, ed. H. Fishwick (Chetham Soc., N.S. xxx, 1894-5), 16-18, 26.
[2] *Palatine Note-book*, iii. 37-40; iv. 87-90.

Carr, who was a political ally of Arlington rather than of Danby, was himself out of favour towards the end of the decade. He was dropped from the Privy Council from 1678 to 1680 for supporting the wrong candidate in a by-election at Grantham.[1] However, he resisted the temptation to join forces with the Country opposition, and during the Exclusion Crisis he defended the Lancashire bench successfully against Whig encroachment. Lancashire was overlooked completely in the attempt to remodel the magistracy in the Whig interest in 1679, and the two commissions sealed in that year showed little serious alteration.[2] Early in 1680 an attempt was made to discredit four Lancashire justices who were remiss in executing the laws against the Catholics, but Carr changed his fiat for displacing them at the last moment, and in the event the new commission, which does not survive, seems only to have left out two Exclusionist M.P.s, Henry Booth and Edward Rigby, plus the Scottish peer, Lord Ancram, who as M.P. for Wigan had voted against Exclusion.[3] Admittedly, Rigby was restored six months later, in October 1680, and the Whigs recovered more ground after the investigations of the House of Lords committee in November, when Booth and his protege Sir Thomas Mainwaring were reinstated.[4] This Whig revival was short-lived, however, and the Court strengthened its control over the Lancashire magistracy following Monmouth's turbulent visit to Cheshire in the autumn of 1682.[5] Sir Thomas Chicheley's first commission, in March 1683, brought in ten reliable Anglicans and left out the leading Whigs who had entertained Monmouth, notably the Earl of Macclesfield, Henry Booth and his veteran father Lord Delamer, and Sir Thomas Mainwaring, along with some lesser men.[6] It would not be precisely true to say that the Lancashire bench was solidly Tory thereafter; three justices, William Knipe, Curwen Rawlinson, and Thomas Cole, were

[1] P.R.O., P.C. 2/66, p. 352: 12 June 1678; P.C. 2/69, p. 124: 15 Oct. 1680; H.M.C., *Ormonde MSS.*, N.S. iv. 433–4.
[2] P.R.O., P.C. 2/68, pp. 42, 47–8; P.L. 28/38: 24 Mar. 1679; Lancs. R.O., QSC 83: 13 Aug. 1679.
[3] P.R.O., P.C. 2/68, p. 344: 8 Jan. 1680; H.L.R.O., Main Papers, H.L., 9 Nov. 1680, ff. 28–30; committee minute book, p. 24.
[4] P.R.O., P.C. 2/69, p. 97: 15 Sept. 1680; p. 207: 4 Feb. 1681; see above, pp. 48–9, 52.
[5] See above, p. 56.   [6] Lancs. R.O., QSC 85: 9 Mar. 1683.

accused of reluctance to act with their colleagues in the suppression of conventicles, yet they remained in the commission, and so too did two more, Thomas Braddyll and Ralph Livesay, who genially overlooked some seditious words implying disbelief in the Rye House Plot spoken by Livesay's son.[1] Even so, the Lancashire bench was dominated, if not quite monopolized, by Tories in the last years of Charles's reign.

This Tory ascendancy continued during the election of 1685 and the eighteen months which followed. Seven commissions sealed during this short period made only minor changes individually, but Cole and another Anglican, John Entwisle, were disgraced and a handful of gentlemen with Catholic wives or family connections were admitted, like Christopher Carus of Halton and Edward Ogle of Whiston.[2] However, the real influx of Catholics came in 1687 and 1688. The Privy Council regulation early in 1687 brought in ten Catholics headed by Viscount Molyneux and his son William, plus two others, and another commission in July, the first sealed by Phelipps, added thirteen local names of which ten were certainly those of Catholics. These two commissions together left out twenty-one justices, most of whom were still alive.[3] After putting the Three Questions to the Lancashire gentry and receiving an unfavourable response from the majority of the Protestant survivors, Molyneux, lord-lieutenant since August 1687, recommended through the Board of Regulators a list which contained only three out of the sixty-five local names in the last commission of Charles's reign only a little over three years before.[4] The implementation of this drastic regulation was delayed by the accidental loss of Molyneux's list in London,[5] but when the new commission eventually appeared in April 1688 it was found to contain forty-six

[1] H.M.C., Fourteenth Report, Appendix IV, *Kenyon MSS.*, pp. 167, 169, 172; H.M.C., *Ormonde MSS.*, N.S. vii. 288-9; *Cal. S.P. Dom., July-Sept. 1683*, p. 377; *Cal. S.P. Dom., 1683-4*, p. 46; *Cal. S.P. Dom., 1684-5*, pp. 180-1; P.R.O., P.C. 2/70, p. 255: 19 Nov. 1684; p. 279: 17 Dec. 1684.

[2] Lancs. R.O., QSC 88-94: seven commissions of the peace sealed in 1685 and 1686.

[3] P.R.O., P.C. 2/71, p. 379; Lancs. R.O., QSC 95-6: 12 Jan., 30 July 1687.

[4] H.M.C., Twelfth Report, Appendix VII, *Le Fleming MSS.*, pp. 205-7; Duckett, *Penal Laws and Test Act*, ii. 276-9.

[5] *Cal. S.P. Dom., 1687-9*, pp. 174, 181.

local names, of which between twenty-five and thirty were those of Catholic squires. The remainder were Protestant 'Whig collaborators' like Lord Brandon, who had recently been pardoned for his complicity in the Monmouth rising, and whose father, the Earl of Macclesfield, spent much of James's reign in Holland; or Protestant Dissenters, most notably the Presbyterian Lord Willoughby of Parham, who was very old and very poor, with his son Hugh. The three survivors from Charles's reign, Roger Kirkby, John Warren, and Nicholas Townley, plus a fourth, Viscount Fauconberg, who was presumably retained as a local peer although he was not in Molyneux's list, were undeniably swamped. In August, three more gentlemen, among them a former Cromwellian soldier, Roger Sawrey, were added by the peripatetic election agents.[1]

Virtually the whole of the traditional political establishment in Lancashire was now excluded from local office. Derby, the leader of that establishment, had been sacked as lord-lieutenant and *custos*, and he was no longer in the commission of the peace. Catholics, accompanied by Dissenters and distrusted opportunists like Brandon, staffed the militia, the commission of *oyer and terminer*, and the bench. Roger Kenyon was dismissed as clerk of the peace.[2] The Catholic justices were active in Lancashire affairs from quarter sessions at Easter in 1687, when eight of the ten appointed in January appeared on the bench. The Catholic gentry of Lancashire were, in many cases, men of distinguished ancestry and considerable wealth, but the attitude of all levels of Protestant society to the new regime was succinctly, if coarsely, summed up by the overseer of the poor at Leyland, who, on being shown an order from the justices at Ormskirk quarter sessions, was alleged to have observed 'I can make you as good an order for a fart of my arse . . . for they were Catholick Justices that made it.'[3]

James's attempt to reverse his programme in the autumn of 1688 was mismanaged in Lancashire, as it was elsewhere.

[1] Lancs. R.O., QSC 99–100: 11 Apr., 21 Aug. 1688; Duckett, *Penal Laws and Test Act*, ii. 301.

[2] P.R.O., P.L. 28/38: commission of *oyer and terminer*, 30 July 1687; *Cal. S.P. Dom., 1687–9*, pp. 122, 123.

[3] Lancs. R.O., QSO 2/56: Order Books, 1687–8.

A commission of the peace sealed on 20 October restored fourteen Anglican justices, presumably in the hope of persuading them to act as deputy-lieutenants as well. William Molyneux's attempts to mobilize the militia on behalf of his father were unavailing, as the elder Molyneux was replaced as lord-lieutenant by Derby on 17 October, while the newly restored justices proved reluctant to act as long as they were required to serve with Catholics.[1] Phelipps produced another commission some weeks after Jeffreys's office had ceased to function; this finally removed the Catholics and restored Derby and Macclesfield, but otherwise it named a curious jumble of Dissenters and the Anglicans reinstated in October.[2] This last commission, sealed when James was already in France, served little useful purpose and was probably ignored.

Lancashire was, perhaps, unusual in that many of the Catholic gentlemen appointed to the bench were, in social and economic terms, the equals of the Anglicans they replaced. Men like Viscount Molyneux, Sir Charles Anderton of Lostock, Richard Townley, Thomas Tildesley, Edmund Trafford, and William Standish were disqualified only by the law relating to their religion from serving as justices of the peace. Their inclusion in the commission led to something like a breakdown in local government, not because they were socially inferior, incompetent, or even inexperienced, but because of the antagonism that their presence on the bench aroused. An absurdly optimistic address from the 'Protestant justices of Lancashire' to the King, to thank him for recruiting Catholic gentlemen of discretion and interest to the magistracy, attracted precisely two signatures.[3] At some point shortly after the Revolution, a meticulous analysis of the recent history of the Lancashire commission of the peace was conducted, possibly by the clerk of the peace and his staff, to demonstrate how sixty justices had been dismissed in the space of two years, and how the vacancies had been supplied by recusants.[4] The Lancashire gentry were well

---

[1] Lancs. R.O., QSC 101; *Cal. S.P. Dom., 1687-9*, pp. 289, 299, 311, 320, 323, 324; H.M.C., Fourteenth Report, Appendix IV, *Kenyon MSS.*, pp. 203-4; H.M.C., Twelfth Report, Appendix VII, *Le Fleming MSS.*, p. 213.

[2] Lancs. R.O., QSC 102: 29 Dec. 1688.

[3] H.M.C., Fourteenth Report, Appendix IV, *Kenyon MSS.*, p. 187.

[4] Lancs. R.O., QSC 221: 'An account of the justices when and how they were

aware that their exclusive community had been shattered. What, perhaps, they did not foresee, early in 1689, was that it was to prove impossible to reconstruct it in its former shape.

III

The main development in Lancashire local politics as the Revolution took its course was a sudden and unexpected decline in the influence wielded by the Earl of Derby, the incumbent lord-lieutenant at the time of James's flight. Derby, a somewhat colourless personality in his mid-thirties, had drifted inconspicuously into the position of leader of the Anglican Tories in Lancashire and Cheshire to which his wealth and status entitled him. After William's invasion he was outwitted by two relative upstarts: Henry Booth, who had succeeded his father as Earl of Delamer in 1684, and Brandon. Derby and Delamer had agreed early in November 1688 that Delamer would rise for William, and that Derby would follow his example after he had mobilized the militia, but Delamer later alleged that Derby's promised support was not forthcoming at the critical time. Derby may have returned to his allegiance to James at exactly the wrong moment, early in December, in the hope of securing a grant of the Lancashire estates of the deceased Duke of Albemarle; at any rate, by Christmas his stock had fallen, while that of Delamer was rising fast.[1] The eventual outcome was that William, after some hesitation, rewarded Delamer with the lord-lieutenancy of Cheshire. Derby felt that it was inconsistent with his honour to accept the lieutenancy of only one of the two counties after occupying both, and he refused to continue in Lancashire. Meanwhile, Brandon had jettisoned his career as a collaborator in James's policies in time to be elected one of Lancashire's knights of the shire in the Convention, where

put in and out', no date; QSC 222: 'The names in the commission of the peace when Col. Philips was Chancellor of the Duchy', with a list of Catholic justices, no date.

[1] H.M.C., Fourteenth Report, Appendix IV, *Kenyon MSS.*, pp. 198-202, 205-7, 210, 214; *Autobiography of Henry Newcome*, ed. R. Parkinson (Chetham Soc. xxvi-xxvii, 1852), ii. 269; D. H. Hosford, *Nottingham, Nobles, and the North* (Hamden, Connecticut, 1976), pp. 37-8, 85-95, 105-7.

he turned out to be a firm Whig. It was Brandon who stepped into the vacant Lancashire lieutenancy, and he added the office of *custos* in November. Thus Derby, to the dismay of his numerous supporters among the gentry, was left with nothing, and, although his wife was a close friend of the new Queen, his influence within the counties which his family had dominated for generations was much reduced.[1]

The new Chancellor of the Duchy, Lord Willoughby d'Eresby, probably sealed a commission of the peace for Lancashire in the early summer of 1689 which does not survive. He received lists of suggestions from various sources in the spring; Derby provided one, but, as the M.P. for Wigan observed, 'there might be some other papers delivered in besides, by others that pretend to as great interest there'. The commission was in the county by early June, when the deputy clerk of the peace was attempting, not altogether successfully, to persuade the gentlemen named in it to qualify themselves by taking the new oaths.[2] The first extant commission sealed after the Revolution is dated 9 August 1689, and this probably does not differ markedly from the missing commission since those who refused the oaths in June were not purged.[3] Ninety-two justices were named. Of these, forty-five were former justices who had been dismissed in the course of James's reign, mostly in 1687 and 1688. Three, possibly four, were restored after disgrace in 1682 or 1683.[4] Three had survived all the way through James's reign,[5] and three more had been added during James's reign and were continued.[6] Perhaps the most interesting feature of the commission, though, was the fact that as many as thirty-seven names were completely new. Admittedly, many of these were young members of old families who were taking their natural place on the bench, but it is difficult to escape the impression that the Revolution, in Lancashire as in

[1] H.M.C., Fourteenth Report, Appendix IV, *Kenyon MSS.*, pp. 212-13, 218, 219, 222-3, 233, 234-5; P.R.O., C. 231/8, p. 215: Delamer's commission as lord-lieutenant of Cheshire, 12 Apr. 1689; p. 222: Brandon's commission as lord-lieutenant of Lancashire, 13 May 1689.
[2] H.M.C., Fourteenth Report, Appendix IV, *Kenyon MSS.*, pp. 219, 221, 223-4.
[3] Lancs. R.O., QSC 104 (numbered out of sequence in the series).
[4] Delamer, Macclesfield, Thomas Ashurst, and possibly William Hulme.
[5] Fauconberg, John Warren, and Roger Kirkby.
[6] Brandon, Hugh Willoughby, and Stephen Alcock.

other counties, led to a dilution of the traditional elite of ruling families.

Brandon, who presided over this inexperienced magistracy, was now the most prominent figure in Lancashire affairs. He threw himself into the suppression of disaffection, and also into a turbulent by-election at Lancaster in November 1689, with such energy that although many of the long-established Lancashire gentry regarded him with disapproval he was thought to be high in the King's favour.[1] His management of recommendations to the commission of the peace was one of his more controversial activities. Willoughby d'Eresby, a member of the Bertie family and an ally of Carmarthen in central politics, was not a cipher in the choice of justices, and Brandon found it necessary to mount an attempt to acquire complete control over nominations in November 1690. He complained to the Privy Council that the Chancellor of the Duchy, having included names on his own initiative in 1689, still presumed to put gentlemen in and out 'at his pleasure' although Brandon had since become *custos rotulorum*. Brandon's case was technically unsound — there was, of course, nothing to compel the Chancellor of the Duchy to accept suggestions even from the *custos* — but in general terms there was something in his accusation, since it must have been Willoughby who had decided to leave out the Presbyterian Sir Charles Hoghton and one or two others in the most recent commission. However, although Brandon produced a list of proposed changes, the matter does not seem to have been pursued by the Council, and the adjustments in the next commission were unspectacular.[2]

Brandon's next move was to secure a letter to Willoughby d'Eresby from the Secretary of State to 'signify the King's pleasure' that ten of his names be added to the Lancashire magistracy.[3] This apparently unanswerable exercise of Court

---

[1] *Cal. S.P. Dom., 1689–90*, pp. 150–1, 163, 166–7, 268; Bodl. MS. Rawl. D. 863, f. 42: Gilbert Wallis to Sir Thomas Rawlinson, 19 Nov. 1689; H.M.C., Twelfth Report, Appendix VII, *Le Fleming MSS.*, p. 266.

[2] P.R.O., P.C. 2/74, pp. 60, 66: 20 Nov., 27 Nov. 1690 (the details of Brandon's proposed purge do not survive); Lancs. R.O., QSC 106: 24 Aug. 1690; QSC 107: 6 Jan. 1691.

[3] P.R.O., S.P. 44/99, pp. 57, 59: Sidney to the Chancellor of the Duchy, 18/28 May 1691 (copied twice).

influence was met by a firm declaration from 'the best gentlemen and Parliament men' of the county that they would not
sit on the same bench with Thomas Patten and Seth Clayton,
two of Brandon's nominees. The matter was again referred to
the King, who returned the gnomic reply from the Low
Countries that the lord-lieutenant was accountable if he
recommended unfit men.[1] Brandon moderated his suggestions and procured another letter to Willoughby d'Eresby
from the Secretary of State, but the next commission of the
peace, dated the following day, ignored Brandon's names
completely. Another six months passed before Willoughby
d'Eresby unbent sufficiently to include five of Brandon's
suggestions; neither Patten nor Clayton was included.[2] It is
hardly surprising that it was at about this time that Brandon
complained to the King that, though his zeal in supporting
the government had perhaps been mistaken in its methods, it
had been sincere and deserved a better reward.[3] In the following year, Roger Kenyon, who had recovered the clerkship
of the peace and was now a Tory follower of the semi-retired
Derby, observed in ironical bewilderment that the commission of the peace was filled with 'justices of so many minds,
that those whose office it is to preserve the peace are too
often divided upon the Bench'.[4]

The Lancashire commission of the peace was thus one
minor arena in which the conflict between the Court Tories,
represented by Willoughby d'Eresby, and the Whigs, represented by Brandon, was fought out in the early 1690s. In
1693 it was Brandon's fortunes that improved, as he attached
himself to Sunderland. He was gratified with a regiment, and,
having inherited the Macclesfield title in January 1694, he
succeeded in partially remodelling the Lancashire magistracy
in March.[5] At least a dozen living justices were left out,

[1] Browning, *Danby*, ii. 205–6.
[2] P.R.O., S.P. 44/99, p. 106: Sidney to the Chancellor of the Duchy, 29 Feb.
1692; Lancs. R.O., QSC 110: 1 Mar. 1692; QSC 111: 9 Aug. 1692.
[3] Dalrymple, *Memoirs of Great Britain and Ireland*, ii, Appendix, Part II,
182–3.
[4] H.M.C., Fourteenth Report, Appendix IV, *Kenyon MSS.*, p. 273.
[5] N.U.L., PwA 1222: Sunderland to Portland, 10 July [1693]; Horwitz, *Parliament, Policy and Politics in the reign of William III*, p. 117. The Gerard earldom
of Macclesfield became extinct in Queen Anne's reign, and the title borne by Lord
Chancellor Parker in the 1720s was a new creation.

among them such prominent local Tories as Sir Geoffrey Shakerley and Peter Legh of Lyme. One of them, John Hartley, used the classic phrase that he was glad to have been put off the bench at a time when so many other worthy gentlemen were similarly displaced. Twenty-five names were added. Some of them were respectable enough, and one surprise was the inclusion of Ambrose Pudsey, who was an opponent of Macclesfield's interest in the local politics of Clitheroe, but Roger Kenyon and others were dismayed by the appearance of some notorious Dissenters as magistrates.[1]

The bench had therefore already been altered in the Whig interest when the 'Lancashire Plot', a murky and ultimately unsuccessful attempt by unscrupulous informers to accuse some leading members of the Lancashire Catholic community of active Jacobite conspiracy, became a matter of national interest in the summer of 1694.[2] Thomas Norris, M.P. for Liverpool, thought that some Lancashire justices had been less than zealous in acting against the suspected men.[3] A severe regulation of the magistracy seemed likely, and in the winter of 1694/5 there were reports 'to make honest gentlemen's hearts very heavy' that an extensive remodelling would remove those 'not brisk enough against the prisoners' and add others of low social status.[4] The Catholic suspects had been acquitted in October 1694, however, and the trial was enough of a fiasco to deter the Lancashire Whigs from using the episode as an excuse to purge the commission, the rumours notwithstanding. The only significant alteration in the next commission of the peace was the exclusion of one prominent Tory, Sir Edward Chisenhall.[5]

Macclesfield, evidently disappointed with the outcome of the trial, made yet another attempt to secure the support of

[1] Lancs. R.O., QSC 114: 15 Mar. 1694; H.M.C., Fourteenth Report, Appendix IV, Kenyon MSS., pp. 287-8, 290-1.

[2] Ibid., pp. 292 ff.; The Jacobite Trials in Manchester in 1694, ed. W. Beaumont (Chetham Soc. xxviii, 1853); The Trials at Manchester in 1694, ed. A. Goss (Chetham Soc. lxi, 1864); H.M.C., House of Lords MSS., N.S. i. 435-55; E. L. Lonsdale, 'John Lunt and the Lancashire Plot', Transactions of the Historic Society of Lancashire and Cheshire, cxv (1964), 91-106.

[3] Cal. S.P. Dom., 1694-5, p. 255.

[4] H.M.C., Fourteenth Report, Appendix IV, Kenyon MSS., pp. 373, 374, 377, 378.

[5] Lancs. R.O., QSC 116: 8 Mar. 1695.

the central government for a purge of the Lancashire bench the following summer. He wrote to the Lords Justices entrusted with domestic affairs during William's absence to complain of the composition of the Lancashire bench and, presumably, to recommend new names. Baron Turton, the assize judge, was called in to report on his suggestions, but the Lords Justices contented themselves with a promise to lay the matter before the King, and with instructions to Turton to be particularly careful to encourage 'backward' justices on his next circuit.[1] A commission of the peace was sealed a month later, but this merely added the name of another assize judge to accompany Turton and weeded out five justices who had died.[2]

After these frustrations, the Assassination Plot did lead to a reshuffle in the Whig interest in 1696 and 1697. During these years of Whig ascendancy, four commissions were sealed for Lancashire. One made virtually no change, but the other three, dated March 1696 and March and August 1697, together added a net total of thirty-eight justices and left out twenty-four, of whom probably fewer than half were dead.[3] Among those added were Jasper Mauditt, William Norris, and Thomas Molyneux, all sitting M.P.s; Sir Charles Hoghton, the Presbyterian left out in 1690; and Thomas Patten, to whom the Lancashire gentry had objected so strongly in 1691. Roger Kenyon bitterly described six of the new justices as, variously, the son of a collier, an apothecary, a shopkeeper, a trader, a former preacher at conventicles, and the younger of a pair of trading brothers. All six were Dissenters, and others among those added were occasional conformers.[4] Those dismissed included Willoughby d'Eresby, replaced by Stamford as Chancellor of the Duchy in May 1697; two M.P.s who had refused the Association, Peter Shakerley and Thomas Brotherton; one of the counsel for the prisoners in

[1] *Cal. S.P. Dom., 1694–5*, pp. 493, 497, 510.
[2] Lancs. R.O., QSC 117: 29 July 1695.
[3] Lancs. R.O., QSC 118: 20 Mar. 1696; QSC 119: 11 Mar. 1697; QSC 120: 20 Aug. 1697.
[4] H.M.C., Fourteenth Report, Appendix IV, *Kenyon MSS.*, pp. 411-12. Kenyon's social strictures were clearly partisan; his 'shopkeeper', for instance, was Thomas Johnson, a great tobacco merchant at Liverpool and a future M.P. in eight Parliaments.

the Jacobite trials, Sir Christopher Greenfield; and several of those whose disgrace had been rumoured but not implemented in 1695. Some gentlemen now dropped from the commission had actually signed the Association — one such, for instance, was the exceptionally active justice Jonathan Blackburne, who had not once failed to attend quarter sessions since his inclusion in 1692 — so it is unlikely that Macclesfield made any serious use of the Association oath rolls, which he presented to the King from Lancashire, as a formal test of those to be retained or dismissed.[1] Moreover, Macclesfield's return of Lancashire non-subscribers to the Privy Council was dilatory and Lancashire was not among the counties regulated by the Council at this time.[2] It seems likely, therefore, that the revision was undertaken privately on the initiative of Macclesfield, who prodded Willoughby d'Eresby and Stamford into action.

Unexpectedly, the next Lancashire commission of the peace, in March 1698, reversed many of Macclesfield's changes. Macclesfield had been unsuccessful in a bitter, protracted struggle to secure the appointment of a Whig Recorder at Wigan, but it is unlikely that he had come to believe that party spirit was running too high for safety in view of the impending elections; in May he was to send a choleric letter to Somers, denouncing his antagonists at Wigan, which shows no sign of slackening party fervour.[3] It is more probable that Stamford had been intimidated, in his first year as Chancellor of the Duchy, by vehement protests from the Lancashire Tories that the new men were unfit. At all events, more than twenty local men were put out, among them Thomas Patten and twelve more who had been added during the previous two years. Nearly all those described by Roger Kenyon as socially inferior were dropped. Jonathan Blackburne was restored, and five gentlemen of reputable antecedents, if also

[1] *Cal. S.P. Dom., 1696*, p. 175; P.R.O., C. 213/138/1-6, C. 213/139-144; W. Gandy, *Lancashire Association Oath Rolls* (privately printed, 1921).

[2] P.R.O., P.C. 2/76, p. 546: 26 Nov. 1696.

[3] J.R.L., Crawford MSS. 47/2: papers relating to the Recordership of Wigan, Oct. 1697–May 1698; *Cal. S.P. Dom., 1697*, p. 448; *Cal. S.P. Dom., 1698*, p. 264; H.M.C., Fourteenth Report, Appendix IV, *Kenyon MSS.*, pp. 423-4; P.R.O., P.C. 2/77, pp. 142, 146, 176: 23 Dec. 1697, 13 Jan., 12 May 1698; Surrey R.O., Somers MSS. L. 22: Macclesfield to Somers, 21 May 1698.

of Whig sympathies, were put in for the first time.[1] This commission was in force during the general election in August, when Macclesfield's campaign proved less successful than he would have liked,[2] and the bench remained stable during the next two and a half years, since only routine adjustments were made down to the summer of 1700.

The Privy Council's regulation in 1700 did not extend to Lancashire.[3] However, Stamford, probably rather reluctantly, entered into the spirit of that operation with a contemporaneous commission adding twelve names. Three sitting M.P.s were included and the 'broad bottom' nature of the exercise was illustrated by the fact that two of them, Sir Roger Bradshaigh and Thomas Brotherton, had refused the Association in 1696, while the third, Thomas Stringer, was a supporter of the Court. Tory representation was also strengthened in this commission by the inclusion of Richard Bold, who was to be elected knight of the shire in February 1701.[4]

This commission, which was to remain virtually unchanged except for the removal of dead justices until the accession of Anne, was presumably that scrutinized by the House of Commons in 1701.[5] It contains two features worthy of notice. One, a detail, is that as many as thirty-three of the eighty-seven justices were not in the quorum, and some quite distinguished men were not accorded this extra distinction, among them, astonishingly, the Earl of Derby, who seems deliberately to have been left out of the list in 1699.[6] The other point is that only thirty-one justices out of the eighty-seven had also been named in the first post-Revolution commission in 1689. Of these, nineteen — less than a quarter of the total — had survived without interruption.[7] Thus nearly

---

[1] Lancs. R.O., QSC 121: 10 Mar. 1698.

[2] *Vernon Correspondence*, ii. 145, 152, 153; *Cal. S.P. Dom., 1698*, pp. 376–7.

[3] Lancashire is not mentioned in the changes ordered at P.R.O., P.C. 2/78, pp. 63–83.

[4] Lancs. R.O., QSC 127: 15 Aug. 1700.   [5] *C.J.* xiii. 378, 384.

[6] Lancs. R.O., QSC 124: 10 Apr. 1699.

[7] The nineteen continuously in commission were: the three peers, Derby, Macclesfield, and Rivers; two Duchy or County Palatine officials, Sir Gervase Elwes and Edward Northey; and Sir Ralph Assheton, John Entwisle, John Fenwick, Sir Daniel Fleming, John Hodgson, John Hopwood, Joshua Horton, William Hulme, Roger Kirkby, Thomas Rigby, Miles Sandys, John Warren, Edward Wilson, and Joseph Yates. To these can be added James Stanley, Fitton Gerard,

two-thirds of the justices of the peace in Lancashire in 1700 had been recruited since the Revolution eleven years before; a remarkably high proportion, which reflects, not only the party conflicts of the 1690s in local affairs, but also the extent to which the Revolution completed the work begun by James II of the destruction of the stable regime of Charles II's last years.

IV

The hierarchy of Lancashire society experienced an upheaval in 1702 caused partly by accident and partly by the changed political situation at the centre. Macclesfield died in November 1701. His Lancashire offices were briefly taken over by his former rival for the affections of his wife, Earl Rivers, but in June 1702 the Earl of Derby at last recovered the lord-lieutenancy and the position of *custos*.[1] Meanwhile Queen Anne had bestowed the seals of the Duchy on Sir John Leveson Gower, an ally of Rochester and a firm Tory who had refused the Association in 1696. Gower immediately set about the task of purging the administration of the Duchy and the County Palatine in readiness for the elections to be held in late July and August. He did not co-operate particularly closely with Derby in this, and there is a little evidence to suggest that the relationship between the two was cool.[2]

Gower's first commission of the peace for Lancashire was sealed about a fortnight before the elections, and it made alterations comparable with those for other counties at the same time. Fifty-one gentlemen were added. Of these, sixteen had formerly been justices but had been dismissed in the Whig purges of the 1690s. Sir Edward Chisenhall, Peter Legh, John Hartley, Sir Christopher Greenfield, and Peter Shakerley were notable figures in this category. The new men were also in many cases recognizable Tories, like Robert Heysham, M.P. for Lancaster, and the two Thomas Leghs, of

and Hugh Willoughby, left out evidently by mistake in 1690 and restored shortly afterwards. Elwes, Entwisle, Fleming, and Warren were the last survivors of the first extant Restoration commission, which is dated 1664.

[1] P.R.O., C. 231/9, pp. 35, 53.
[2] B.L., Add. MSS. 29588, f. 86: Henry Finch to [Nottingham], 11 July 1702; f. 91: Derby to [Henry Finch?], 12 July 1702.

Lyme and Ridge respectively, who shared the representation of the Legh family's constituency at Newton, while rank and file Tories like William Buckley and John Wright appeared at the end of the list. To make room for these new justices, thirty-seven gentlemen were dropped. Some had died, but at least twenty and probably more were still alive. The most startling omissions were those of Fitton Gerard, the Whig M.P. for the county from 1698 to 1700, who had succeeded his brother as Earl of Macclesfield; Lord Willoughby of Parham, the Dissenter; John Entwisle, a justice since the Restoration (except in James II's reign), with Bertie Entwisle, the Whig candidate for the Recordership of Wigan in 1697-8, and Richard Entwisle; John Fenwick, the Recorder of Lancaster; and Jasper Mauditt, formerly M.P. for Liverpool. Willoughby, Fenwick, Mauditt, and all three Entwisles were active justices, and a number of equally conscientious men, like Joseph Yates and John Andrews, the only two justices on the bench at quarter sessions at Manchester the previous April, were also discarded.[1]

The transformation in Lancashire county society in 1702 was completed by the deaths at the end of the year of the third Earl of Macclesfield, whose title became extinct, and Derby. Derby's successor, his brother James, was an active soldier who had been knight of the shire for Lancashire since 1690. He had been a Court Whig in William's reign and in the political climate of 1702-3 his appointment as lord-lieutenant and *custos* of Lancashire directly after inheriting his title can only be explained by the absence of suitable alternatives, since Delamer, who had been created Earl of Warrington in 1690, had died in 1694 and his son had not replaced him as lord-lieutenant even of Cheshire. The new Earl of Derby was undoubtedly a more formidable character than his ineffectual brother, with whom he had quarrelled on personal and political grounds in the 1690s.[2] He counterbalanced the Tory Gower in Lancashire politics, and the two grandees struggled

[1] L.R.O., QSC 130: 11 July 1702; QSO 2/69-71, for details of activity and attendance.
[2] One fraternal disagreement had ended in a defamation case at Lancaster assizes, and the two had been on opposite sides in the 1702 election. P.R.O., P.L. 28/1, p. 101: 7 Sept. 1698; B.L., Add. MSS. 29588, ff. 121-2: Peter Shakerley to Nottingham, 8 Aug. 1702.

to strengthen their interest with the gentry and the corporations over such matters as the disposal of the ruins of Liverpool Castle.[1]

The commission of the peace was fairly stable during the remainder of Gower's period in office, perhaps because Derby was unable to force his candidates on an unwilling Chancellor of the Duchy, while Gower found it impracticable to follow up his already sweeping changes against the wishes of a hostile *custos rotulorum*. It was presumably Derby who recommended the restoration of Richard Entwisle with two more active ex-justices in 1703, and also the inclusion of Jonathan Case, about whom Gower had doubts, in the same year. In 1705 Derby seems to have interceded successfully on behalf of the Whig Richard Norris of Speke, whom Gower had planned to dismiss. Gower for his part was able to add Richard Shuttleworth at the age of twenty-one in 1704 before he was elected M.P. for the county against the Derby interest the following year, while William Heysham was included in a commission sealed shortly before his election as a Tory at Lancaster in 1705. Lancashire was involved in the parliamentary investigations of the commission of the peace in 1704-5, but Gower's activities did not attract special attention, and the addition of Heysham was the only change of any significance made before the 1705 elections.[2]

Gower remained in office a little longer than Sir Nathan Wright, but he was dismissed in late May 1706. Derby himself became Chancellor of the Duchy, and his first commission of the peace, sealed in July, made alterations which bear comparison with those conducted by Cowper in other counties at the same time. A modest but by no means fully comprehensive swing back to Whig representation on the bench seems to have been Derby's aim. Ten obvious Tories were dismissed; the most prominent was Sir John Bland, M.P. for Pontefract, who had inherited the extensive estates of a branch of the Mosley family near Manchester. Nineteen gentlemen were

[1] *The Norris Papers*, ed. T. Hayward (Chetham Soc. ix, 1846), 104, 108-9.

[2] Lancs. R.O., QSC 131-5: commissions sealed between 2 Mar. 1703 and 14 Mar. 1705; *Norris Papers*, pp. 51, 78, 111, 143; *L.J.* xvii. 489, 659, 665; H.L.R.O., Committee Book, H.L., 17 Feb. 1705, p. 76; H.M.C., Fifteenth Report, Appendix IV, *Portland MSS.* iv. 183.

added, of whom eight had been put out in 1702. Among
these restored justices were Lord Willoughby of Parham,
Bertie Entwisle, and John Fenwick.[1] However, more than
thirty of those brought in by Gower in 1702 remained in the
list, while one of the more obscure men recruited by Derby
in 1706, Thomas Smith, turned out to be a vehement Tory.

It is odd that Derby did not do more for the Lancashire
Whigs. For instance, his choice as Vice-Chancellor of the
County Palatine was George Kenyon, who had been the successful Tory candidate in the Wigan Recordership contest.
Although Kenyon was later to be accused of having deserted
the Church party, his appointment to an influential office
remains a curious one.[2] Moreover, after the changes in 1706,
Derby did little more than tinker with the Lancashire commission of the peace, adding names in small numbers (nineteen altogether, spread over seven commissions in four years)
and leaving out for the most part only justices who were
dead.[3] Two of those inserted at this time, William Bamford
and Richard Valentine, proved, like Thomas Smith, to be
Tories. There can be no doubt that Derby was a firm Whig —
his voting record in both Houses of Parliament demonstrates
as much[4] — but his approach to local politics seems to have
been ambivalent, for reasons that can only be conjectured. It
may be that Derby was unwilling to abandon those, like the
Kenyons, who had backed his family's interest in the 1690s
against the usurper Macclesfield, in order to take over
Macclesfield's party. It is likely that he disapproved of the
socially inferior candidates for a place on the bench that
Macclesfield had patronized. In 1710, for instance, there was
a suggestion that one Sawrey Rigby be added to the commission, for reasons that deserve to be quoted at length: '. . . His
wife (who is a discret woman) wishes him in, for no other
reason than it may estrange him from some very mean asso-
ciates of his, and ashame him out of an idle habit of profane
swearing. It can have no ill to the government, and will be

[1] Lancs. R.O., QSC 136: 30 July 1706.
[2] H.M.C., Fourteenth Report, Appendix IV, *Kenyon MSS.*, pp. 438-9, 445.
[3] Lancs. R.O., QSC 137–43: commissions sealed between 17 Sept. 1706 and
19 Aug. 1710.
[4] Horwitz, *Parliament, Policy and Politics in the reign of William III*, p. 355;
Holmes, *British Politics in the Age of Anne*, p. 427.

a lasting tie upon him to my Lord [Derby]'s interest.'[1] Derby ignored this singular application, even though it was endorsed by his brother Charles, who was M.P. for the county. It is also possible that Derby's lack of vigour in manipulating the commission of the peace stemmed from his general inadequacy as Chancellor of the Duchy. His lawyer tried to blackmail him as a means of acquiring Duchy office by threatening to expose his secrets, and Derby was accused of employing his judicial powers to further his family interests in Lancashire. An admittedly hostile observer remarked that he was not personally popular in the county and that he wielded less influence there than might have been expected. A Whig, Thomas Johnson, regretted that Derby was 'not active as some men are' in Lancashire affairs.[2] He may thus have been discouraged, or distracted, from any serious attempt to remodel the magistracy in the interests of the Whigs after his first efforts in 1706.

Derby's dismissal was rumoured to be imminent in August 1710, and it duly took place in September. Lord Berkeley of Stratton, his successor, confessed to his dependence on local advice, being a 'great stranger' to Lancashire, though this did not prevent him from exploiting the influence of the Duchy in the elections in October.[3] Derby was also sacked as lord-lieutenant and *custos* in favour of the Duke of Hamilton, who had acquired large estates in Lancashire through his second marriage in 1698.[4] The Derby interest was thus quite suddenly eclipsed, and the first commission of the peace under the new regime again reflected changes at the top of the county hierarchy. Sixteen justices were dropped and twenty came in. Many familiar names were involved. The Tories Sir John Bland, William Buckley, and three more were restored, having been added by Gower and dismissed by

[1] H.M.C., Fourteenth Report, Appendix IV, *Kenyon MSS.*, p. 444.

[2] Surrey R.O., Somers MSS. L. 28: Derby to Somers, 16 May 1707; P.R.O., P.C. 2/81, pp. 378, 398–9, 406–7; Leics. R.O., Finch MSS. Box VI, Bundle 22: Anglesey to Nottingham, [1707]; H.M.C., *Portland MSS.* viii. 280; *Norris Papers*, p. 166.

[3] J.R.L., Crawford MSS. 47/2: Berkeley to Sir Roger Bradshaigh, 30 Sept., 10 Oct., 31 Oct. 1710; H.M.C., Fourteenth Report, Appendix IV, *Kenyon MSS.*, p. 445; H.M.C., Fifteenth Report, Appendix IV, *Portland MSS.* iv. 570, 576, 578.

[4] P.R.O., C. 231/9, p. 220; H.M.C., Fifteenth Report, Appendix IV, *Portland MSS.* iv. 608, 615–16.

Derby. Richard Entwisle, John Fenwick, and a number of others dismissed in 1702 and restored in 1706 were now again left out.[1] Fourteen of Berkeley's justices were completely new, and thereafter he pursued a policy of unspectacular but steady recruitment without significant purges, so that by 1714 the list of justices had expanded in size. More than one-third of the 116 names in the last commission sealed in the Queen's reign had been added by Berkeley.[2] These gentlemen joined those included by Gower and not subsequently removed, and also with Tories like Smith, Bamford, and Valentine who had inadvertently been added by Derby, to form a confident numerical superiority on the bench. Nineteen justices attended Lancashire quarter sessions just before the Queen's death; only two of these, Charles Stanley and Jonathan Case, were Whigs, and the rest can all be classified as Tories. Six of them had been added by Berkeley since 1710.[3]

Derby recovered the lord-lieutenancy of Lancashire, which had been vacant since Hamilton's death in a famous duel in 1712, in the first month of George I's reign. He was not, however, reinstated as Chancellor of the Duchy. This post was reserved for a Hanoverian Tory, Nottingham's brother Lord Guernsey, who had just been created Earl of Aylesford.[4] From the point of view of the Lancashire Whigs, the choice could not have been worse. Nottingham and Aylesford advocated the reconciliation of at least the 'honest' Tories to the Hanoverian regime by keeping them in local office.[5] Also, Aylesford's contacts in Lancashire were Tory; his brothers Edward and Henry Finch were clergymen in Lancashire and close friends of the Leghs of Lyme. Predictably, Aylesford's first two commissions of the peace did not materially alter the balance of parties on the bench. He restored three Whigs (John Braddyll, William Knipe, and

[1] Lancs. R.O., QSC 144: 26 Dec. 1710.

[2] Lancs. R.O., QSC 151: 27 Feb. 1714.

[3] Lancs. R.O., QSO 2/83: attendance at quarter sessions, July 1714.

[4] P.R.O., C. 231/9, p. 312; *The Wentworth Papers, 1705–1739*, ed. J. J. Cartwright (London, 1883), pp. 435–6.

[5] Horwitz, *Revolution Politicks*, pp. 246–9, 260–1; but see H.M.C., *Egmont Diary*, ii. 67, for a later reminiscence by Aylesford's son that Nottingham had been 'as violent as any to turn out the Tories' in 1714.

Thomas Bateman), but he also added three more Tories, besides promoting two Duchy and County Palatine officials who were alleged to be Nonjurors, and the Tories still dominated the magistracy at the time of the elections in February 1715.[1]

The apprehension of the Whigs at Aylesford's inactivity turned to anger and alarm when anti-Dissent and Jacobite riots broke out in and near Manchester in June. Townshend was obliged to ask Whig justices from as far away as Liverpool and Clitheroe to enforce the law, since the county justices living locally encouraged rather than suppressed the disorders.[2] In a series of letters from the county which were translated into French for George I's perusal, Aylesford's neglect in failing to remodel the magistracy was specifically blamed for what had evidently developed into an ugly situation.[3] Aylesford responded by sealing a commission which restored Richard Entwisle and Samuel Hallowes and added Oswald Mosley and George and James Chetham, all of whom lived near Manchester, but he still took no steps to purge the magistracy of its strong Tory element.[4] Lancashire's disaffected state was a matter of concern in view of the impending Jacobite insurrection, and in the autumn of 1715 Townshend, Derby, and apparently also Cowper took action. Among Cowper's papers are a list of disaffected Duchy officials, a list of thirty-three Lancashire justices of the peace marked to describe political affiliations, and also a detailed proposal for a new commission containing fifty-nine names. The first of these is endorsed 'From Lord W.', and probably all three emanated from the same source. The identity of 'Lord W.' is a mystery, but he was possibly the second Earl of Warrington, a Whig in the somewhat eccentric family

---

[1] Lancs. R.O., QSC 153: 11 Dec. 1714; Kenyon MSS. DDKe 2/12(7): 7 Mar. 1715.

[2] P.R.O., S.P. 44/116: Townshend to Sir Ralph Assheton, Robert Maudesley, Bertie Entwisle, Jonathan Case, Edward Norris, Ambrose Pudsey, and Mr Wyvill, various dates between 19 June and 23 July 1715; *Palatine Note-book*, ii. 240–4; *Lancashire during the Rebellion of 1715*, ed. S. Hibbert Ware (Chetham Soc. v, 1845), 16.

[3] B.L., Stowe MSS. 228, ff. 61, 68–9, 72, 75: 3 July, 22 July, 26 July, 29 July 1715. The second of these contains the phrase '. . . aucun Tory ne sera changé tant que M[ylor]d Aylesford sera Chancellier. . . .'

[4] Lancs. R.O., QSC 154: 29 June 1715.

tradition.[1] Meanwhile, Townshend acquired a list of changes made by Aylesford, possibly to find out just how little the Chancellor of the Duchy had already done, and a suggestion for a complete new commission similar to that in Cowper's possession, though different in detail and containing ten more names.[2] Derby was summoned to London in September. He was sworn as a Privy Councillor in late October, and on 3 November a list of gentlemen to be named in the commission of the peace for Lancashire was approved by the Privy Council. The King gave the appropriate instructions to Aylesford and the new commission was duly sealed.[3]

The alterations embodied in this commission, baldly stated, were remarkable. Sixty-seven gentlemen were left out, that is, more than half the total number in the previous commission. The majority of these were, of course, Tories, ranging from veterans like Sir Edward Chisenhall, whose name had first appeared in a Lancashire commission of the peace in 1672, to youthful Jacobites like Sir John Bland, who had just succeeded to his father's baronetcy. Eighteen of the sixty-seven had been included for the first time by Gower in 1702 and 1703. Twenty-three had been introduced by Berkeley between December 1710 and 1714. At least six, and possibly one or two more, had previously experienced dismissal by the Whigs in the mid-1690s; four had been left out in Derby's milder purge in 1706 and then reinstated under Berkeley. Peter and Thomas Legh of Lyme, William Buckley, John Wright, William Bamford, and Thomas Smith were all displaced, and some relatively moderate Tories were sacked as well, like George Kenyon and even Sir Roger Bradshaigh, whose progress from semi-Jacobite in the mid-1690s to impoverished Court Whig by 1715 had passed unnoticed by 'Lord W.', who classed him as a 'violent Tory'.[4] Twenty-nine

[1] Herts. R.O., Cowper (Panshanger) MSS. D/EP F153. The annotated list describes seventeen 'violent Tories', four 'Tories', six who 'dos the Country's business well, tho calld Tories', and six Whigs. 'Lord W.' is unlikely to have been Charles, Lord Willoughby of Parham, who died in June 1715.

[2] P.R.O., S.P. 35/2, f. 127; S.P. 35/3, f. 212.

[3] P.R.O., S.P. 44/118: Townshend to Derby, 14 Sept. 1715; P.C. 2/85, pp. 300, 303–4; Lancs. R.O., QSC 156: 3 Nov. 1715; see also Townshend's letter to Maxwell in late October referred to above, p. 246.

[4] M. Cox, 'Sir Roger Bradshaigh, 3rd Baronet, and the Electoral Management of Wigan, 1695–1747', *Bulletin of the John Rylands Library*, xxxvii (1954),

gentlemen were added, of whom nineteen became justices
for the first time while the remainder had been excluded at
some point by Berkeley. Miles Sandys, John Fenwick,
Samuel Crooke, and John Walmesley were actually experienc-
ing their second restoration after dismissal at the hands of,
successively, Gower and then Berkeley. Only one justice in
the commission, Sir Ralph Assheton, had been a Lancashire
magistrate continuously since the Revolution.

The new commission contained ninety names all told, and
a few gentlemen of high social or political status whose background had been Tory or Hanoverian Tory were retained
although they had been overlooked in the shorter lists submitted to Cowper and Townshend. Lord Barrymore, Richard
Shuttleworth, John Cleveland, and Robert and William
Heysham, all M.P.s or ex-M.P.s, and Edward Vaudrey and
Edward Blundell, two County Palatine officials described by
'Lord W.' as Nonjurors, were included. Peter Shakerley was
another Tory whose name continued to appear. It should,
perhaps, be added that with the possible exception of Barrymore, who had attended quarter sessions on his first inclusion in the commission of the peace in 1713, these politicians
and officials were rarely if ever active as justices.

The regulation of 1715 in Lancashire was undoubtedly a
very severe one, conducted in a most unusual way. The Privy
Council had often ordered that individuals be added to or
subtracted from the commissions of the peace, but not since
the days of the Board of Regulators in James II's reign had
the central government nominated a complete county bench.
Moreover, the commission in November 1715 ignored the
conventional gradations of the county hierarchy, and the
names appeared in a jumbled order. Such solecisms as the
insertion of Langham Booth, brother to the Earl of Warrington, in the ruck of squires instead of before the knights, or
the placing of respected names like Roger Nowell, Bertie
Entwisle, and Thomas Ashurst at the end of the commission
after the newly appointed men, were again reminiscent of the
cavalier methods of the Board of Regulators. The Privy
Council had forgotten to mention the quorum, and Aylesford

121–4; Herts. R.O., Cowper (Panshanger) MSS. D/EP F153; B.L., Stowe MSS.
228, f. 75: letter from Preston translated into French for George I, 29 July 1715.

met the difficulty by putting every one of the ninety names into the quorum list. However, although the remodelling was clumsy and botched, the government could plead urgent necessity, and this was unanswerable in view of the fact that it was on 7 November, four days after the date of the Council meeting and the new commission, that Forster's Jacobite army entered Lancashire from the north.[1] The commission itself probably did not reach Lancashire until after Forster surrendered at Preston on 14 November, but its eventual arrival no doubt facilitated the process of restoring order to the county in the winter of 1715/16. The bench at quarter sessions in January 1716 was as Whig as that in July 1714 had been Tory.[2] Townshend wrote to one of the justices named in the new commission, '. . . since we have at last got the Commissions for the Peace setled, I hope it may be a means of putting things on a better Foot for the future.'[3]

The Earl of Scarborough, Aylesford's successor, unscrambled the order in which the names appeared in his first commission in March 1716. He also restored Sir Roger Bradshaigh, and he flushed out two Tories, Robert and Edward Parker, who had been overlooked in 1715. Thereafter the Lancashire magistracy settled quickly into stability. Apart from the addition of seven Commissioners for Forfeited Estates in 1716 and a curious purge of the quorum in 1719, which may have been either an attempt to rectify the absurdity that every justice was named in it or a clerical oversight, there was little further change. By 1720 about twenty of the ninety installed in 1715 had died, and they had been replaced in ones and twos.[4] The creation of a stable 'Whig oligarchy' among the Lancashire magistrates after the Hanoverian Succession was thus unusually dramatic, rapid, and complete.

---

[1] *Lancashire during the Rebellion of 1715*, p. 85.

[2] Lancs. R.O., QSO 2/84. Lancashire's experience was thus different from that of Wiltshire; see above, p. 268.

[3] P.R.O., S.P. 44/118: Townshend to Daniel Wilson, 8 Nov. 1716. Wilson lived in Westmorland, but he had been a Lancashire justice since 1706, and there can be little doubt that, in spite of his reference to 'commissions', Townshend specifically meant the regulation of Lancashire's bench by the Privy Council.

[4] Lancs. R.O., QSC 157–166: commissions sealed between 17 Mar. 1716 and 22 Aug. 1720.

V

The changes in the Lancashire magistracy more or less correspond to the pattern established for other counties over the
whole period. The first commission of the peace sealed by
every newly appointed Chancellor of the Duchy before Aylesford made elaborate changes in the list of names; thus the
justices of the peace were reshuffled by Chicheley in 1683,
by Phelipps in 1687, by Willoughby d'Eresby in 1689, by
Stamford in 1697, by Gower in 1702, by Derby in 1706, and
by Berkeley in 1710. These dates coincide roughly with
periods when counties under the supervision of the Lord
Chancellor could expect changes. Also, Lancashire's magistracy was remodelled in 1688, 1694, 1700, and 1715, at
times when similar changes were taking place elsewhere.
Admittedly, Lancashire escaped lightly at the time of the
Exclusion Crisis; there was, perhaps, an unusually numerous
sequence of commissions embodying significant alterations
through the 1690s as Macclesfield strove to fulfil his ambition to dominate the county; Lancashire avoided the adjustments made elsewhere in the North-West in 1701; and clearly
the circumstances surrounding the purge of the Tories in
1715 were exceptional, and that purge was both untypically
delayed and remarkably comprehensive. On the whole,
though, Lancashire was as much influenced by considerations
relating to the state of central politics and parties as other
counties, and the timing and also the character of the regulations of the bench were not so far out of step from those
elsewhere as to arouse contemporary comment.

Nevertheless, there has always been a flavour of 'difference'
about Lancashire. In the sixteenth century it was argued that
among the qualities required by the Chancellor of the Duchy
were those suitable for choosing justices of the peace of
'good religion and sufficient living' and for dealing with
people who were 'troublesome, clamourous, and impatient of
delay'.[1] As late as 1946 the du Parcq Report recommended
that the Chancellor of the Duchy should retain his powers
with respect to the appointment of Lancashire justices, since

[1] R. Somerville, *History of the Duchy of Lancaster, 1265–1603* (London,
1953), pp. 325–6.

the system worked well and any change would be resented in the county.[1] This Lancashire postscript has not, therefore, been appended as a 'case study' to demonstrate the continuous history of a single county bench between 1675 and 1720. It is, rather, an attempt to fill one of the gaps — the others being Middlesex, Durham, and the smaller liberties — in the coverage over the whole country of the political background to the choice of justices of the peace. Lancashire is to be regarded, not as a representative county, but as a separate case, where nevertheless the considerations that applied in the selection of magistrates proved, revealingly, to be broadly similar to those in other counties which can more legitimately be thought of as typical.

---

[1] *Royal Commission on Justices of the Peace*, 1946–8, Cmd. 7463, p. 12.

BIBLIOGRAPHY

A. MANUSCRIPT SOURCES

Blenheim Palace, Oxfordshire

These papers have been transferred to the British Library, but they have not yet (1978) been allotted call numbers. In consequence they are here identified by the classification in use at Blenheim Palace.

A I, A II, B I, B II	Correspondence of John Churchill, first Duke of Marlborough.
C I–6	Minutes of Cabinet, 1706–10.
C I–35 to 37, 39 to 40	Papers of Charles Spencer, third Earl of Sunderland, Secretary of State 1706–10.
D II–6 to 10	Miscellaneous and undated papers.
F I–39	Trevor papers.
Box VII Bundle 18	Affidavits relating to riots, 1710.
Box VIII Bundle 22	Appointment of deputy-lieutenants and magistrates.
Box IX Bundle 29	Petitions for patronage.

Bodleian Library, Oxford

MS. Arch. f. c. 6 (formerly MS. Rawl. A. 139B)	Lists of deputy-lieutenants and J.P.s, 1688.
MS. Carte 79, 109, 233	Wharton papers.
— 130	Beaufort papers.
MS. Clarendon 128	Letters relating to Oxfordshire, 1683–5.
MS. English History B.204	Papers of Sir Edmund Warcup, J.P.
— B.209–210	Diary of Richard Cox, J.P.
MS. North a.3, b.2	Papers of William, Lord North and Grey.
— b.1, b.8, b.24, c.5	Papers of Lord Keeper North.
MS. Rawlinson A.139A	Answers to the Three Questions, 1687–8.
— A.245	Autobiographical notes of Anthony Hammond, J.P.
— C.42	Commonplace book of an anonymous J.P.
— C.719	Commonplace book of 'Judge Twysden'.
— D.372	Inquiry into moneys levied on Dissenters, 1688.
— D.383	Informations, affidavits, and other legal papers.
— D.666	Papers relating to Hampshire.
— D.851	Papers of Dean Grenville of Durham.

— D.862–863	Papers of Sir Thomas Rawlinson.
— D.918, 924	Miscellaneous political papers.
— D.1041	Collections of a Surrey J.P., *temp.* William III.
— D.1135–1137	Collections of Sir Thomas Sclater, J.P.
— Letters 45–48	Letters of Sir Edmund Warcup, J.P.
MS. Tanner 25–42	Papers and correspondence of Archbishop Sancroft.
— 144	Papers relating to Cheshire.
— 259	Letter book of Sir John Holland, J.P.
— 290	Miscellaneous letters, seventeenth century.

British Library (formerly British Museum), London

Additional MSS. 15643	Minute book of Committee of Intelligence, 1679–81.
— 15895	Hyde papers and correspondence, 1688–1709.
— 17748	Papers of the Crown Office in Chancery, 1679–89.
— 25125	Secretary Coventry's letter book, 1676–80.
— 28070	Letters from Queen Anne.
— 29548–29596	Correspondence and papers of the families of Finch and Hatton, 1676–1725.
— 29674	Lists of Yorkshire J.P.s collected by William Paver, antiquary.
— 30000A–30000E	Transcripts of the dispatches of Frederick Bonet, Prussian Resident in London, 1696–1701.
— 32686	Papers of Thomas Pelham-Holles, first Duke of Newcastle; the first of over three hundred volumes, this extends to 1723.
— 33053	Papers of Thomas Pelham-Holles, first Duke of Newcastle; contains memorandum on the Middlesex commission of the peace, 1758.
— 33058	Papers relating to Sussex.
— 33060	Papers relating to Nottinghamshire.
— 33084	Pelham correspondence, 1543–1722.
— 33923	Diary of Sir John Knatchbull, J.P.
— 34515	Newsletters, 1687–8.
— 34730	Papers of the Marriot family.
— 35600–35604	Lord Chancellor Hardwicke's papers relating to the commission of the peace, mid-eighteenth century.

— 36901–36927   Correspondence and papers of the families of Aston and Norris, sixteenth and seventeenth centuries.

— 40771–40790   Papers of James Vernon, Secretary of State 1697–1702.

— 49970–49971   Letter books of Viscount Bolingbroke, Secretary of State 1710–14.

Egerton MSS. 921–922   Sir Robert Walpole's commonplace book.

— 2557   *Liber pacis*, 1661.

Harleian MSS. 286   Miscellaneous papers on state affairs, sixteenth and seventeenth centuries.

— 5137   Simon Harcourt's commonplace book as a J.P., *temp.* Queen Anne.

— 6822   Miscellaneous legal papers, sixteenth to eighteenth centuries.

— 6850   Miscellaneous papers on state affairs, sixteenth to eighteenth centuries.

— 7020   Lists of officers, including J.P.s for some counties, seventeenth century.

— 7512   *Liber pacis*, April 1702.

Lansdowne MSS. 232   Henry Powle's commonplace book, *temp.* Charles II.

— 569   Law student's notebook, seventeenth century.

Portland Loan 29/29   Miscellaneous papers.

— Loan 29/50   Papers relating to Herefordshire.

— Loan 29/125–166   Letters to Robert Harley.

— Loan 29/183–205   Letters to Robert Harley; calendared in H.M.C., *Portland MSS.* iii–v.

— Loan 29/236–238   Papers of Henry Cavendish, second Duke of Newcastle, and John Holles, first Duke of Newcastle by a new creation; calendared in H.M.C., *Portland MSS.* ii.

— Loan 29/263–264   Letter books of Robert Harley, Secretary of State 1704–8.

— Loan 29/312   Miscellaneous letters.

Stowe MSS. 222–229   Hanover State Papers, 1692–1716.

— 416   Lord Chancellor Macclesfield's papers, 1718–25.

— 750   Letters received by Lord Chancellor Macclesfield, 1704–32.

Cambridge University Library

Additional MSS. 435   *Liber pacis*, 1653.

Baker MSS. 29   Commonplace book of Thomas Baker, antiquary.

Devon Record Office, Exeter
Q/JC   Commissions of the peace from 1675.
Q.S. Order Books   Records of quarter sessions.

Hertfordshire Record Office, Hertford
Cowper (Panshanger) MSS.   Papers of Lord Chancellor Cowper.
   D/EP F149, F151–F157

House of Lords Record Office
Committee Book, 1704–10
Main Papers, H.L., 9 Nov. 1680 *Liber pacis* and committee book.
— 19 Nov. 1680   Investigation of Catholics in the army,
                                          the navy, and the militia.
— 3 Dec. 1680   Returns of Catholics sent from the coun-
                                          ties.
— 20 March 1704   Justices of the peace put out since 'Mid-
                                          summer 1700'.
— 16 Feb. 1705   Justices of the peace put in and out
                                          since 'the last session'.

John Rylands Library, Manchester
Crawford MSS. 47/2   Papers of Sir Roger Bradshaigh, J.P.,
                                          mostly relating to Wigan.
English MSS. 213   Collections of papers relating to the
                                          activities of J.P.s in the North-West
                                          against Catholics, sixteenth to eight-
                                          eenth centuries.
— 914   Commonplace book touching on the
                                          activities of Lancashire J.P.s, seven-
                                          teenth century.
Mainwaring MSS., MS. Books Diary of Sir Thomas Mainwaring, J.P.
   20A, 20B

Lancashire Record Office, Preston
QSC 77–166   Commissions of the peace from 1675.
QSC 221–225   Miscellaneous papers relating to Lanca-
                                          shire commissions of the peace.
QSO 2/45–89   Quarter sessions order books from 1675.
QSV 11/1–2   Proceedings of Lancashire J.P.s at the
                                          'sheriff's table' (at assizes), 1628–9,
                                          1661–94.
DDKe   Papers of Roger and George Kenyon,
                                          clerks of the peace.

Leicestershire Record Office, Leicester
QS 1/1–15   Commissions of the peace from 1675.
Finch MSS. General Series   Correspondence of Daniel Finch, second
                                          Earl of Nottingham.

—— Law MSS. 15   Papers relating to J.P.s in Wales, 1688–9.

Lincolnshire Archives Office, Lincoln
Commissions of the peace,   From 1687.
    Kesteven
Commissions of the peace,   The first is dated 1718.
    Lindsey
Monson MSS. 7/11–13   Papers of Sir John Newton, J.P.
—— 27/3   Lists of Lincolnshire J.P.s collected by
                                  the sixth Lord Monson.

Longleat House, Wiltshire
Coventry MSS. iv–vi, xvi,   Papers of Henry Coventry, Secretary of
    lxxxiii, xcii   State 1672–80.
Thynne Papers xii–xix, xxiv   Correspondence of Thomas Thynne, first
                                  Viscount Weymouth.

Manchester Central Library
Farrer MSS. 73   Lancashire lieutenancy book, 1660–86.

National Library of Wales
MS. 11020E   Miscellaneous papers relating to Welsh
                                  counties, seventeenth century.
MS. 17071E   *Liber pacis*, March 1701.

Northern Ireland Public Record Office, Belfast
De Ros MSS. 13   Letters of John Pulteney, Under-Secre-
                                  tary of State *temp*. William III.

Nottingham University Library
PwA   Correspondence and papers of William
                                  Bentinck, first Earl of Portland.
Pw2   Correspondence and papers of John
                                  Holles, first Duke of Newcastle.
Pw2 Hy   Miscellaneous papers of Robert Harley.

Public Record Office
  Records of Assizes
Assizes 5   Oxford Circuit.
Assizes 16   Norfolk Circuit.
Assizes 35   Home Circuit.
  Records of Chancery
C.191   Fiats for commissions of sewers.
C.192   Fiats for various commissions for the
                                  County Palatine of Durham (none
                                  for commissions of the peace).
C.193/12   Entry books of commissions of the
                                  peace and *libri pacis*.

C.193/43	*Dedimus Potestatem* book, 1701–13.
C.213	Association Oath Rolls, 1696.
C.231/7–9 (formerly Index 4214–6)	Crown Office docquet books, 1660–1721.
C.234	Fiats for commissions of the peace.

Records of the Duchy of Lancaster

D.L. 20/1–5	Draft commissions for judges.
D.L. 20/9	Fiats for commissions of *oyer and terminer* and for commissions of the peace for Lancashire.
D.L. 41/19/10	Arguments against abolishing the Duchy.

Records of the County Palatine of Lancaster

P.L. 25	Assize rolls (mostly presentments of the grand jury).
P.L. 28/1	Minute book of assizes, 1686–1742.
P.L. 28/38	Commissions of *oyer and terminer*, with one commission of the peace for Lancashire.

Records of the Privy Council

P.C. 1	Privy Council miscellaneous papers.
P.C. 2	Privy Council registers.

Deposits of non-archival MSS. in the Public Record Office

P.R.O. 30	Papers of the Earls of Shaftesbury.

State Papers Domestic

S.P.8	King William's Chest.
S.P.29	State Papers Domestic, Charles II.
S.P.31	State Papers Domestic, James II.
S.P.32	State Papers Domestic, William and Mary.
S.P.34	State Papers Domestic, Anne.
S.P.35	State Papers Domestic, George I.
S.P.38	Miscellaneous docquets.
S.P.43	Hanover correspondence during Regencies.
S.P.44	Entry Books originating in the office of the Secretaries of State (correspondence, warrants, caveats, King's letters, minutes of Lords Justices, military letters, petitions, and miscellaneous entry books).
S.P.45	Precedent books and miscellanea.
Adm. 77	Newsletters.

Shropshire Record Office, Shrewsbury

Quarter Sessions Records Box 292	Commissions of the peace from 1700.
Attingham MSS. 112/3	One letter from the Marquess of Carmarthen, 1690.

Somerset Record Office, Taunton

Q/JC 81–104   Commissions of the peace from 1676
                                     (the sequence ends in 1691 and is
                                     not resumed until 1724).
CQ 2 2/3 (2)–(3)   Quarter sessions minute books.
Sanford MSS. DD/SF   Papers of the families of Clarke and San-
                                     ford.

Surrey Record Office, Kingston-upon-Thames

Somers MSS. A., B., E., J.   Correspondence of Lord Chancellor
                                     Somers.
— L.   Applications and petitions.

Wiltshire Record Office, Trowbridge

A 1/1/1–6   Commissions of the peace from 1688
                                     (one for 1688 and a series beginning
                                     in 1714).
Q.S. Great Rolls, Minute   Records of quarter sessions.
Books, Order Books

B. PRIMARY SOURCES IN PRINT

The place of publication is London, unless otherwise stated.

1. *Official and semi-official publications, Calendars, and Parliamentary
   Papers*
Calendar of State Papers Domestic, 1673–1704.
Calendar of Treasury Books, 1672–1718.
Calendar of Treasury Papers, 1557–1728.
Journals of the House of Commons, ix–xix.
Journals of the House of Lords, xi–xxi.
The London Gazette.
Parliamentary Papers, 1814–15, xi, Copy of the Report of the Lords
   Commissioners appointed to make a survey of the different Courts
   . . . as to the Court of Chancery . . . Dated 8 November 1740 (1815).
Parliamentary Papers, 1844, xiv, Report from a Select Committee on
   the Clerk of the Crown in Chancery (1844).
Royal Commission on Justices of the Peace, 1946–8, Report, Cmd.
   7463 (1948); Minutes of Evidence issued in daily supplements
   (1946–7).
Royal Commission on the Selection of Justices of the Peace, Report,
   Cd. 5250 (1910); Minutes of Evidence, Cd. 5358 (1910).
The Statutes of the Realm (11 vols., 1810–22).

2. *Contemporary Materials*
BLACKERBY, S., *The Justice of the Peace his Companion* (1711).
BOHUN, E., *The Justice of the Peace, His Calling and Qualifications*
   (1693).

—, *Three Charges Delivered at the Quarter Sessions Holden at Ipswich for the County of Suffolk in the Years 1691, 1692* (1693).

BOND, J., *A Compleat Guide for Justices of the Peace* (3rd edn., 1707).

The Speech of Henry Booth, Esq., Spoken in Chester, 2 March 1680/1, At his being elected one of the Knights of the Shire for the County (1681). See also 'Warrington'.

BOYER, A., *History of the Reign of Queen Anne, digested into Annals* (11 vols., 1703–13).

—, *The History of King William III* (3 vols., 1702).

CHAMBERLAYNE, R., *The Complete Justice* (1681).

A Collection of White and Black Lists (4th, corrected edn., 1715).

DALTON, M., *The Countrey Justice* (1618, and several subsequent editions).

The Great Case of the Justices Stated and Determined, Touching their Duty of putting the Laws in Execution, whether Dissenters were Indulged, or not (1688).

Memoirs of the Life of Charles Montagu, late Earl of Halifax, appended to the 2nd edn. of his *Poetical Works* (1716).

J., W., *Officium Clerici Pacis, A Book of Indictments, Informations, Appeals and Inquisitions, also the Manner of Holding Sessions of the Peace* (1675).

KEBLE, J., *An Assistance to Justices* (1683).

KILBURNE, R., *Choice Presidents upon all acts of Parliament relating to the office and duty of a Justice of the Peace* (3rd edn., 1685).

LAMBARDE, W., *Eirenarcha, or the Offices of the Justices of Peace* (1581, and several subsequent editions).

L'ESTRANGE, H., *Justices' Law* (1720).

A List of the Commissioners of Lieutenancy of the City of London, as Constituted in the Year 1690 [1693?].

N., S., *A Catalogue of the Names of all His Majesty's Justices of the Peace in Commission in the Several Counties Throughout England and Wales . . .* (1680).

NELSON, W., *The Office and Authority of a Justice of the Peace* (2nd edn., 1707).

The Obligations of a Justice of the Peace, to be Diligent in the Execution of the Penal Laws against Prophaneness and Debauchery (1702).

OLDMIXON, J., *History of England During the Reigns of King William and Queen Mary, Queen Anne, King George I . . .* (1735).

Practick Part of the Office of a Justice of the Peace (1682).

Memoirs of the Life of John Lord Somers (1716).

The Works of Henry [Booth], Late Lord Delamer and Earl of Warrington, ed. J. Delaheuze (1694). See also 'Booth'.

3. *Editions of Quarter Sessions Records*

County of Buckingham: Calendar to the Sessions Records, 1678–1718, ed. W. Le Hardy and G. L. Reckitt (4 vols., Aylesbury, 1933–51).

Quarter Sessions Records, with other Records of the Justices of the Peace, for the County Palatine of Chester, 1559–1760, ed. J. H. E.

Bennett and J. C. Dewhirst, Lancashire and Cheshire Record Society, xciv (1940).

Hertford County Records: Notes and Extracts from the Sessions Rolls, ed. W. J. Hardy (9 vols., Hertford, 1905–39).

Minutes of Proceedings in Quarter Sessions held for . . . Kesteven, 1674–1695, ed. S. A. Peyton, Lincoln Record Society, xxv, xxvi (2 vols., 1931).

The Minutes of the Justices of the Peace for Lanarkshire, ed. C. A. Malcolm, Scottish History Society, Third Series, xvii (1931).

Lancashire Quarter Sessions Rolls, 1590–1606, ed. J. Tait, Chetham Society, New Series, lxxvii (1917).

Middlesex County Records, ed. J. C. Jeaffreson and W. Le Hardy, Middlesex County Records Society (7 vols., 1886–1937).

Nottinghamshire County Records: Notes and Extracts, Seventeenth Century, ed. H. H. Copnall (Nottingham, 1915).

Oxfordshire Justices of the Peace in the Seventeenth Century, ed. M. S. Gretton, Oxfordshire Record Society Series, xvi (1934).

Shropshire County Records, 1638–1726, ed. Sir Offley Wakeman and R. L. Kenyon (2 vols., 1901–4; several subsequent volumes).

Quarter Sessions Records for the County of Somerset, ed. E. H. Bates-Harbin and M. C. B. Dawes, Somerset Record Society, xxiii, xxiv, xxviii, xxxiv (4 vols., 1907–19).

Collections for a History of Staffordshire: Staffordshire Quarter Sessions Rolls, 1581–1690, ed. S. A. H. Burne and D. H. G. Salt, Staffordshire Record Society (6 vols., 1929–49).

Surrey Quarter Sessions Records, ed. D. L. Powell and H. Jenkinson, Surrey Record Society, xxxv, xxxvi, xxxix (3 vols., 1934–8).

Warwick County Records, ed. S. C. Ratcliffe, H. C. Johnson, and N. J. Williams (9 vols., Warwick, 1935–64).

Records of the County of Wilts., being extracts from the Quarter Sessions Great Rolls of the Seventeenth Century, ed. B. H. Cunnington (Devizes, 1932).

North Riding Quarter Sessions Records, ed. J. C. Atkinson, North Riding Record Society (9 vols., 1884–92).

For monographs based largely on, and quoting extensively from, quarter sessions records, see also Section C of this Bibliography, *sub* J. C. Cox (Derbyshire), E. G. Dowdell (Middlesex), J. S. Furley (Hampshire), and A. H. A. Hamilton (Devonshire).

4. *Publications of the Historical Manuscripts Commission*

Early (foolscap) series
Third Report, Appendix.
Fourth Report, Appendix.
Fifth Report, Appendix.
Sixth Report, Appendix.
Seventh Report, Appendix, i.
Ninth Report, Appendix, i.

Later (octavo) series

Series 13 *Westmorland (Apethorpe) MSS. and others.*
Series 17 *House of Lords MSS., 1678–1714.*
Series 20 *Dartmouth MSS., i, iii.*
Series 22 *Leeds MSS. and others.*
Series 23 *Cowper MSS., ii, iii.*
Series 24 *Rutland MSS., ii.*
Series 25 *Le Fleming MSS.*
Series 27 *Beaufort MSS. and others.*
Series 29 *Portland MSS., ii, iii, iv, v, vii, viii, ix, x.*
Series 32 *Fitzherbert MSS. and others.*
Series 35 *Kenyon MSS.*
Series 36 *Ormonde MSS.*
Series 41 *Foljambe MSS.*
Series 45 *Buccleuch MSS. (Montagu House), i, ii.*
Series 51 *Leyborne-Popham MSS.*
Series 52 *Frankland-Russell-Astley MSS.*
Series 55 *MSS. in Various Collections, i, viii.*
Series 58 *Bath MSS., i, iii.*
Series 62 *Lothian MSS.*
Series 71 *Finch MSS., i, ii, iii, iv, v.*
Series 75 *Downshire MSS., i.*
Series 78 *Hastings MSS., ii, iv.*

5. *Other Printed Sources*

The Letters of Joseph Addison, ed. W. Graham (Oxford, 1941).
Memoirs of Thomas, Earl of Ailesbury, ed. W. E. Buckley, Roxburghe Club (2 vols., 1890).
The Epistolary Correspondence, Visitation Charges, Speeches, and Miscellanies of the Right Reverend Francis Atterbury, D.D., Lord Bishop of Rochester, ed. J. Nichols (4 vols., 1783–7).
Diary and Autobiography of Edmund Bohun, Esq., ed. S. Wilton Rix (Beccles, 1853).
BOLINGBROKE, Henry, Viscount, *A Letter to Sir William Wyndham* (1753).
Letters and Correspondence of Henry St. John, Viscount Bolingbroke, ed. G. Parke (4 vols., 1798).
The Autobiography of Sir John Bramston, ed. Lord Braybrooke, Camden Society, First Series, xxxii (1845).
The Diary of John Hervey, First Earl of Bristol (Wells, 1894).
Letter Books of John Hervey, First Earl of Bristol (Wells, 1894).
BURNET, G., *History of His Own Time* (6 vols., Oxford, 1833).
Supplement to Burnet's History of My Own Time, ed. H. C. Foxcroft (Oxford, 1902).
Letters of Philip, Second Earl of Chesterfield, to several celebrated individuals of the time of Charles II, James II, William III, and Queen Anne, with some of their replies (1829).

The Correspondence of Henry Hyde, Earl of Clarendon . . . with the Diary of Lord Clarendon, ed. S. W. Singer (2 vols., 1828).

CLARKE, J. S., *The Life of James II* (2 vols., 1816).

The Correspondence of Sir James Clavering, ed. H. T. Dickinson, Surtees Society, clxxviii for 1963 (1967).

'Some Clavering Correspondence', ed. E. Hughes, *Archaeologia Aeliana*, Fourth Series, xxxiv (1956).

Collectanea Curiosa, ed. J. Gutch (2 vols., 1781).

The Diary of Mary Countess Cowper, ed. S. Cowper (1864).

The Private Diary of William, First Earl Cowper, ed. E. C. Hawtrey (Roxburghe Club, Eton, 1833).

COXE, W., *Memoirs of John, Duke of Marlborough* (new edn. revised by John Wade, 3 vols., 1847-8).

DALRYMPLE, Sir John, *Memoirs of Great Britain and Ireland* (3 vols., 1771-88).

The Letters of Daniel Defoe, ed. G. H. Healey (Oxford, 1955).

The Diaries and Papers of Sir Edward Dering, Second Baronet, 1644 to 1684, ed. M. F. Bond (1976).

DUCKETT, Sir George F., *Penal Laws and Test Act* (2 vols., 1882-3).

Recusant Documents from the Ellesmere Manuscripts, ed. A. G. Petti, Catholic Record Society, lx (1968).

The Ellis Correspondence, ed. Hon. G. A. Ellis (2 vols., 1829).

The Diary of John Evelyn, ed. E. S. de Beer (6 vols., Oxford, 1955).

FOXCROFT, H. C., *Life and Letters of Sir George Savile, Bart., first Marquis of Halifax* (2 vols., 1898).

GREY, A., *Debates of the House of Commons, 1667-1694* (10 vols., 1769).

The Diary of Sir David Hamilton 1709-1714, ed. P. Roberts (Oxford, 1975).

The Correspondence of Sir Thomas Hanmer, Bt., ed. Sir H. Bunbury (1838).

The Harcourt Papers, ed. E. W. Harcourt (13 vols., privately printed, no date).

Miscellaneous State Papers from 1501 to 1726 from the collection of the Earl of Hardwicke, ed. Philip, second Earl of Hardwicke (2 vols., 1778).

Correspondence of the family of Hatton, ed. E. M. Thompson, Camden Society, New Series, xxiii (1878).

Herbert Correspondence, ed. W. J. Smith, Board of Celtic Studies, University of Wales, History and Law Series, xxi (1963).

HOSFORD, D. H., 'The Peerage and the Test Act: a List, c. November 1687', *Bulletin of the Institute of Historical Research*, xlii (1969).

Letters by several eminent persons deceased, including the correspondence of John Hughes, Esq., and several of his Friends (3 vols., 1772).

KING, Lord, *Notes of Domestic and Foreign Affairs during the Last Years of the Reign of George I and the Early Part of the Reign of George II*, appended to volume ii of his *Life of Locke* (1830).

Charges to the Grand Jury at Quarter Sessions, 1660–1677, by Sir Peter Leicester, ed. E. M. Halcrow, Chetham Society, Third Series, v (1953).
The Lexington Papers, ed. Hon. H. Manners Sutton (1851).
The Lockhart Papers, ed. A. Aufrere (2 vols., 1817).
LONSDALE, John, Lord, *Memoirs of the Reign of James II* (York, 1808).
LUTTRELL, N., *A Brief Historical Relation of State Affairs* (6 vols., Oxford, 1857).
The Parliamentary Diary of Narcissus Luttrell, 1691–3, ed. H. Horwitz (Oxford, 1972).
MACPHERSON, J., *Original Papers Containing the Secret History of Great Britain* (2 vols., 1775).
MANCHESTER, William, Duke of, *Court and Society from Elizabeth to Anne* (2 vols., 1864).
The Marlborough–Godolphin Correspondence, ed. H. L. Snyder (3 vols., Oxford, 1975).
An Account of the Conduct of the Dowager Duchess of Marlborough (1752).
Private Correspondence of Sarah, Duchess of Marlborough, ed. [Lord John Russell] (2 vols., 1838).
Poems and Letters of Andrew Marvell, ed. H. M. Margoliouth (second edn., 2 vols., Oxford, 1952).
NORTH, Hon. Roger, *Examen, or an Inquiry into the Credit and Veracity of a Pretended Complete History . . .* (1740).
——, *Lives of the Norths* (3 vols., 1826).
Original Letters Illustrative of English History, ed. H. Ellis (First Series, 3 vols., 1825; Second Series, 4 vols., 1827; Third Series, 3 vols., 1846).
Parliamentary History, ed. W. Cobbett and others (36 vols., 1806–20).
Letters of Humphrey Prideaux to John Ellis, ed. E. M. Thompson, Camden Society, New Series, xv (1875).
Memoirs of Sir John Reresby, ed. A. Browning (Glasgow, 1936).
The Diary of Mr Justice Rokeby (privately printed, 1887).
SANDERS, G. W., *Orders of the High Court of Chancery and Statutes of the Realm relating to Chancery, from the Earliest Period to the Present Time* (1845).
Private and Original Correspondence of Charles Talbot, Duke of Shrewsbury, ed. W. Coxe (1821).
The Spectator, ed. D. F. Bond (5 vols., Oxford, 1965).
The Somers Collection of Tracts, ed. Sir W. Scott (13 vols., 1809–15).
The Prose Writings of Jonathan Swift, ed. H. Davis (14 vols., Oxford, 1939–65).
The Works of Sir William Temple (4 vols., Edinburgh, 1754).
Diary and Correspondence of Ralph Thoresby, ed. J. Hunter (4 vols., 1830–2).
VERNEY, Frances P. and Margaret M., *Memoirs of the Verney Family during the Civil War and from the Restoration to the Revolution* (4 vols., 1892–9).

VERNEY, Margaret, Lady, *Verney Letters of the Eighteenth Century* (2 vols., 1930).

Letters illustrative of the Reign of William III . . . Addressed to the Duke of Shrewsbury by James Vernon, ed. G. P. R. James (3 vols., 1841). Cited as *Vernon Correspondence*.

'The Journals of Edmund Warcup, 1676-84', ed. K. Feiling and F. R. D. Needham, *English Historical Review*, xl (1925).

'The Journal of Rev. Francis Welles, J.P. for Gloucestershire 1715-56', *Law Magazine and Law Review*, New Series, xxii, vol. xi (1861).

The Wentworth Papers, 1705-1739, ed. J. J. Cartwright (1883).

The Life and Times of Anthony Wood, 1632-1695, ed. A. Clark, Oxford Historical Society, xix, xxi, xxvi, xxx, xl (5 vols., 1891-1900).

C. SECONDARY WORKS

The volumes of the *Victoria County History*, the productions of eighteenth and nineteenth century genealogists, antiquaries, and county historians, and the biographical compilations of G. E. Cokayne (for peers and baronets) and W. R. Williams and others (for M.P.s) proved of much value in accumulating information about individual justices of the peace, but are here omitted to avoid the prolongation of this section of the Bibliography to an unreasonable length. Modern studies of the social and political history of single counties for periods before 1675 and after 1720, and many of the monographs, biographies, and articles from which detailed information about the background of national politics was drawn, are not included for the same reason. As in Section B, the place of publication is London unless otherwise stated.

1. *Books*

BEARD, C. A., *The Office of a Justice of the Peace in England, in its Origin and Development* (New York, 1904).

BELOFF, M., *Public Order and Popular Disturbances, 1660-1714* (reprinted edn., 1963).

BENNETT, G. V., *The Tory Crisis in Church and State, 1688-1730: The Career of Francis Atterbury, Bishop of Rochester* (Oxford, 1975).

BLACKSTONE, W., *Commentaries on the Laws of England* (4 vols., Oxford, 1765-9).

BROWNING, A., *Thomas Osborne, Earl of Danby and Duke of Leeds, 1632-1712* (3 vols., Glasgow, 1944-51).

CAMPBELL, John, Lord, *The Lives of the Chancellors and Keepers of the Great Seal of England, from the Earliest Times till the Reign of George IV* (second edn., 10 vols., 1846).

CHALKLIN, C. W., *Seventeenth Century Kent* (1965).

CHAMBERS, J. D., *Nottinghamshire in the Eighteenth Century* (second edn., 1966).

COCKBURN, J. S., *A History of English Assizes, 1558-1714* (Cambridge, 1972).

COX, J. C., *Three Centuries of Derbyshire Annals, as illustrated by the Records of the Quarter Sessions* (2 vols., 1890).

DAWSON, J.P., *A History of Lay Judges* (Cambridge, Mass., 1960).

DICKINSON, H. T., *Bolingbroke* (1970).

DODD, A. H., *Studies in Stuart Wales* (Cardiff, 1952).

DOWDELL, E. G., *A Hundred Years of Quarter Sessions: the Government of Middlesex from 1660 to 1760* (Cambridge, 1932).

EVERITT, A. M., *Change in the Provinces: the Seventeenth Century* (Leicester, 1969).

FEILING, K., *A History of the Tory Party, 1640-1714* (reprinted edn., Oxford, 1965).

FOORD, A. S., *His Majesty's Opposition, 1714-1830* (Oxford, 1964).

FORSTER, G. C. F., *The East Riding Justices of the Peace in the Seventeenth Century*, East Yorkshire Local History Publications, xxx (1973).

FOSS, E., *The Judges of England, with Sketches of their Lives . . .* (9 vols., 1848-64).

FURLEY, J. S., *Quarter Sessions Government in Hampshire in the Seventeenth Century* (Winchester, 1937).

GANDY, W., *A Guide to some Original Manuscript Sources of British and Colonial Family and Political History: the Association Rolls of 1696* (privately printed, 1921).

GLEASON, J. H., *The Justices of the Peace in England, 1558 to 1640* (Oxford, 1969).

HALEY, K. H. D., *The First Earl of Shaftesbury* (Oxford, 1968).

HAMILTON, A. H. A., *Quarter Sessions from Queen Elizabeth to Queen Anne: Illustrations of Local History and Government drawn from Original Records, chiefly of Devon* (1878).

HILL, B. W., *The Growth of Parliamentary Parties 1689-1742* (1976).

HOLDSWORTH, Sir William S., *A History of English Law* (reprinted edn., 16 vols., 1956-66).

HOLMES, G. S. (ed.), *Britain after the Glorious Revolution* (1969).
—, *British Politics in the Age of Anne* (1967).
—, *The Trial of Doctor Sacheverell* (1973).

HORWITZ, H., *Parliament, Policy and Politics in the reign of William III* (Manchester, 1977).
—, *Revolution Politicks: The Career of Daniel Finch, Second Earl of Nottingham, 1647-1730* (Cambridge, 1968).

HOSFORD, D. H., *Nottingham, Nobles, and the North* (Hamden, Connecticut, 1976).

HUGHES, E., *North Country Life in the Eighteenth Century*, i, *The North East, 1700-1750* (1952).
—, *North Country Life in the Eighteenth Century*, ii, *Cumberland and Westmorland, 1700-1830* (1965).

JONES, J. R., *The First Whigs* (1961).
—, *The Revolution of 1688 in England* (1972).

Justices of the Peace through Six Hundred Years, 1361-1961 (published by the journal *Justice of the Peace*, Chichester, 1961).

KEETON, G. W., *Lord Chancellor Jeffreys and the Stuart Cause* (1965).

KENYON, J. P., *The Nobility in the Revolution of 1688* (Hull, 1963).

—, *Robert Spencer, Earl of Sunderland, 1641-1702* (1958).

LACEY, D. R., *Dissent and Parliamentary Politics in England, 1661-1689* (New Brunswick, 1969).

LANDON, M., *The Triumph of the Lawyers: their Role in English Politics, 1678-1689* (Alabama, 1970).

LEVIN, J., *The Charter Controversy in the City of London, 1660-1688, and its Consequences*, University of London Legal Series, ix (1969).

MAITLAND, F. W., *Justice and Police* (1885).

MAXWELL-LYTE, Sir Henry C., *Historical Notes on the Use of the Great Seal* (1926).

MILLER, J., *Popery and Politics in England, 1660-1688* (Cambridge, 1973).

MINGAY, G. E., *English Landed Society in the Eighteenth Century* (1963).

—, *The Gentry: The Rise and Fall of a Ruling Class* (1976).

MOIR, E., *The Justice of the Peace* (1969).

OGG, D., *England in the Reign of Charles II* (second edn., 2 vols., Oxford, 1955).

—, *England in the Reigns of James II and William III* (Oxford, 1955).

OSBORNE, B., *Justices of the Peace, 1361-1848* (Shaftesbury, 1960).

PLUMB, J. H., *The Growth of Political Stability in England, 1675-1725* (1967).

—, *Sir Robert Walpole*, i, *The Making of a Statesman* (1956).

REDLICH, J. and HIRST, F. W., *Local Government in England* (2 vols., 1903).

ROBERTS, C., *The Growth of Responsible Government in Stuart England* (Cambridge, 1966).

RONALDS, F. S., *The Attempted Whig Revolution of 1678-1681* (Urbana, Illinois, 1937).

RUBINI, D., *Court and Country, 1688-1702* (1967).

SACHSE, W. L., *Lord Somers, A Political Portrait* (Manchester, 1975).

SEDGWICK, R. R. (ed.), *The House of Commons, 1715-1754* (History of Parliament, 2 vols., 1970).

SPECK, W. A., *Tory and Whig: the Struggle in the Constituencies, 1701-1715* (1970).

STEPHENS, E., *The Clerks of the Counties* (1961).

TREVELYAN, G. M., *England under Queen Anne* (new impression, 3 vols., 1948).

TROTTER, E., *Seventeenth Century Life in the Country Parish, with Special Reference to Local Government* (Cambridge, 1919).

WEBB, Sidney and Beatrice, *English Local Government* (reprinted edn., 11 vols., 1963).

WESTERN, J. R., *Monarchy and Revolution: The English State in the 1680s* (1972).

——, *The English Militia in the Eighteenth Century: The Story of a Political Issue, 1660–1802* (1965).

2. *Articles and essays*

BARNES, T. G. and SMITH, A. H., 'Justices of the Peace from 1558 to 1688 — A Revised List of Sources', *Bulletin of the Institute of Historical Research*, xxxii (1959).

BOWEN, I., 'Grand Juries, Justices of the Peace, and Quarter Sessions in Wales', *Transactions of the Honourable Society of Cymmrodorion* (1933–5).

BROWNING, A., 'Parties and Party Organisation in the Reign of Charles II', *Transactions of the Royal Historical Society*, Fourth Series, xxx (1948).

BURTON, I. F., RILEY, P. W. J., and ROWLANDS, E., 'Political Parties in the Reigns of William III and Anne: the Evidence of the Division Lists', *Bulletin of the Institute of Historical Research*, Special Supplement No. 7 (1968).

COCKBURN, J. S., 'The North Riding Justices, 1690–1750', *Yorkshire Archaeological Journal*, xli (1965).

DICKINSON, H. T., 'The October Club', *Huntington Library Quarterly*, xxxiii (1970).

DODD, A. H., 'Tuning the Welsh Bench', *National Library of Wales Journal*, vi (1950).

GLASSEY, L. and LANDAU, N., 'The Commission of the Peace in the Eighteenth Century: A New Source', *Bulletin of the Institute of Historical Research*, xlv (1972).

HABAKKUK, H. J., 'English Landownership, 1680–1740', *Economic History Review*, Second Series, x (1939–40).

HORWITZ, H., 'Parties, Connections, and Parliamentary Politics, 1689–1714: Review and Revision', *Journal of British Studies*, vi (1966–7).

JONES, J. R., 'The First Whig Party in Norfolk', *Durham University Journal*, New Series, xv (1953).

——, 'James II's Whig Collaborators', *Historical Journal*, iii (1960).

LEWIS, T. H., 'Attendances of Justices and Grand Juries at the Courts of Quarter Sessions in Wales', *Transactions of the Honourable Society of Cymmrodorion* (Session 1942; published 1944).

——, 'The Justice of the Peace in Wales', *Transactions of the Honourable Society of Cymmrodorion* (Session 1943–4; published 1946).

MAITLAND, F. W., 'The Shallows and Silences of Real Life', in *Collected Papers of Frederic William Maitland*, ed. H. A. L. Fisher (3 vols., Cambridge, 1911).

MUNBY, L. M., 'Politics and Religion in Hertfordshire, 1660–1740', in *East Anglian Studies*, ed. L. M. Munby (Cambridge, 1968).

PLUMB, J. H., 'The Organisation of the Cabinet in the Reign of Queen Anne', *Transactions of the Royal Historical Society*, Fifth Series, vii (1957).

PUTNAM, B. H., 'Justices of the Peace from 1558 to 1688', *Bulletin of the Institute of Historical Research*, iv (1927).

RICHARDS, T., 'Declarasiwm 1687: Tipyn o'i Hanes a Barn Cymru am Dano', *Cymdeithas Hanes Bedyddwyr Cymru* (Trafodion, 1924).

WILLMAN, R., 'The Origins of "Whig" and "Tory" in English Political Language', *Historical Journal*, xvii (1974).

3. *Unpublished Dissertations*

CARMICHAEL, E. K., 'The Scottish Commission of the Peace, 1707–60', University of Glasgow Ph.D. thesis (1977).

CARTER, J. J., 'The Administrative Work of the English Privy Council, 1679–1714', University of London Ph.D. thesis (1958).

ELLIS, E. L., 'The Whig Junto in relation to the development of Party Politics and Party Organisation, from its inception to 1714', University of Oxford D.Phil. thesis (1961).

WILSON, J. S., 'The Administrative Work of the Lord Chancellor in the Early Seventeenth Century', University of London Ph.D. thesis (1927).

Additional Note

The names of the Welsh justices of the peace to 1689 are printed in J. R. S. Phillips, *The Justices of the Peace in Wales and Monmouthshire, 1541 to 1689* (Cardiff, 1975). I regret that this important compilation came into my hands too late to be utilized in Chapters 2, 3, and 4.

INDEX

NOTE: The following abbreviations are used in the Index:

d.   died
CDL   Chancellor of the Duchy of Lancaster

LC Lord Chancellor
LK Lord Keeper